A GUIDE TO HEIDEGGER'S
BEING AND TIME

SUNY series in Contemporary Continental Philosophy
Dennis J. Schmidt, editor

A Guide to Heidegger's *Being and Time*

Magda King

Edited by
John Llewelyn

STATE UNIVERSITY OF NEW YORK PRESS

Published by
State University of New York Press, Albany

© 2001 State University of New York

All rights reserved

Printed in the United States of America

No part of this book may be used or reproduced in any manner whatsoever without written permission. No part of this book may be stored in a retrieval system or transmitted in any form or by any means including electronic, electrostatic, magnetic tape, mechanical, photocopying, recording, or otherwise without the prior permission in writing of the publisher.

For information, address State University of New York Press,
90 State Street, Suite 700, Albany, NY 12207

Production by Marilyn P. Semerad
Marketing by Dana E. Yanulavich
Composition by Baker Typesetting

Library of Congress Cataloging-in-Publication Data

King, Magda.
 A guide to Heidegger's Being and time / by Magda King ; edited by John Llewelyn.
  p. cm. — (SUNY series in contemporary continental philosophy)
 Includes bibliographical references and index.
 ISBN 0-7914-4799-5 (hc : alk. paper) — ISBN 0-7914-4800-2 (pbk. : alk. paper)
  1. Heidegger, Martin, 1889–1976. Sein und Zeit. 2. Ontology. 3. Space and time. I. Llewelyn, John, 1928– II. Title. III. Series.

B3279.H48 S46632
111—dc21

00-027620

10 9 8 7 6 5 4 3 2 1

To
A. K.

Contents

Editor's Foreword	xiii
Author's Foreword	xvii
Acknowledgments	xxi
Bibliography and Key to Abbreviations	xxiii

PART ONE
What Is the Question?

Introductory	1
Exposition	5
1. A Formal Statement of the Question	5
2. A Provisional Explanation of "Meaning" (*Sinn*): The Theme of *Being and Time* Restated	6
3. Why Has Traditional Ontology Failed to Get to the Root of the Problem of Being?	11
4. The Uniqueness of the Concept of Being: The Problem of Its Unity. Aristotle's "Unity of Analogy"–A Lead into Heidegger's Question	15
5. How Is the New Inquiry into Being to Be Concretely Worked Out? Difficulties Arising from the Nature of the Problem Itself	19

PART TWO
Basic Features and Problems of *Being and Time*

Introductory	25
I. *The Being of Da-sein*	29
1. Existence, Everydayness and Da-sein	29
(a) Existence and Care, in Contrast with Reality	29
(b) The Two Basic Ways of Existing: Owned or Authentic and Disowned or Inauthentic Existence. The Undifferentiated Modality of Everydayness	40
(c) The Ontological-Existential Terminology of *Being and Time*	42
2. A Discussion of the Meaning of *Da-sein*	47
II. *The Worldishness of World*	51
1. The Fundamental Existential Constitution of Da-sein: Being-in-the-World. Heidegger's Conception of World	51
2. The Theoretical and Practical Ways of Taking Care of Things	65
3. The Ontic Basis of the Ontological Inquiry into World: The *Umwelt* of Everyday Existence. The Meaning of *Umwelt*	68
III. *The Reality of Beings within the World*	71
IV. *Being-with-Others and Being-One's-Self*	75
1. The Basic Concept of Being-with	75
2. The Everyday Self and the "They"	80
3. The Publicity of Everydayness	83
(a) Discourse and Language: Everyday Discourse as Idle Talk	83
(b) The Everyday Way of Seeing: Curiosity	86
(c) Ambiguity	87
4. Falling and Thrownness	88
V. *The Basic Mood of Dread* (Angst) *and the Being of Da-sein as Care*	91
1. The Disclosure of Being through Dread	91
2. The Structure of Da-sein's Being as Care	97

VI. *Truth, Being, and Existence: Heidegger's Existential Interpretation of Truth*   101

VII. *The Concept of Phenomenology*   109

VIII. *A Preview of the Tasks and Problems of Division Two*   119

PART THREE
Division Two of *Being and Time*: Da-sein and Temporality

Introductory   127

IX. *The Articulation, Language, and Method of Division Two*   131

   1. The Articulation of Division Two   131
   2. The Language of Division Two   132
     (a) Timeishness   134
     (b) The Tenses of "To Be"   135
     (c) Heidegger's Tautologies   136
     (d) Primordial Time (*Ursprüngliche Zeit*)   141
     (e) The "Originality" of an Ontological Interpretation   142
   3. The Method of Division Two   142

X. *Da-sein's Possibility of Being-a-Whole and Being-toward-Death*   145

   1. Can Da-sein be Experienced as a Whole?   145
   2. Experiencing the Death of Others   146
   3. Incompleteness, End, and Wholeness   147
   4. The Existential Analysis of Death in Contrast with all Other Kinds of Interpretation   150
   5. A Preliminary Sketch of the Existential Structure of Death   151
   6. Being-Toward-Death and Everydayness   153
   7. Everyday Being Toward an End and the Full Existential Concept of Death   155
   8. The Existential Structure of an Owned, Authentic Way of Being-Toward-Death   158

XI. *Witness to an Owned Existence and Authentic Resolution*   163

   1. Conscience as the Call of Care   163
   2. Understanding the Call and Owing   167

3. Interpolation: Ground-Being and Nothing ... 175
4. Owing, Guilt, and Morality: The Authentic Hearing of the Call of Conscience and the Existential Structure of Owned or Authentic Existence ... 187

XII. *Authentic Ability-to-Be-a-Whole and Temporality as the Meaning of Care* ... 201

   1. Anticipatory Forward-Running Resoluteness as the Authentic Way of Being-a-Whole ... 201
   2. Justification of the Methodical Basis of the Existential Analysis ... 207
   3. Care and Selfhood ... 212
   4. Temporality as the Ontological Meaning of Care ... 217
   5. A Primordial Repetition of the Existential Analysis Arising from the Temporality of Here-Being [Da-sein] ... 225

XIII. *Temporality and Everydayness* ... 229

   1. The Temporality of Disclosedness in General ... 230
      (a) The Temporality of Understanding ... 230
      (b) The Temporality of Attunement ... 236
      (c) The Temporality of Falling ... 243
      (d) The Temporality of Discourse ... 252
   2. The Temporality of Being-in-the-World and the Problem of the Transcendence of the World ... 256
      (a) The Temporality of Circumspect Taking Care ... 257
      (b) The Temporal Meaning of the Way in Which Circumspect Taking Care Becomes Modified into the Theoretical Discovery of Things Objectively Present in the World ... 261
      (c) The Temporal Problem of the Transcendence of the World ... 276
   3. The Temporality of the Roominess Characteristic of Here-Being ... 284
   4. The Temporal Meaning of the Everydayness of Here-Being ... 290

XIV. *Temporality and Historicity* ... 295

   1. The Vulgar Understanding of History and the Occurrence of Here-Being ... 300
   2. The Essential Constitution of Historicity ... 302
   3. The Historicity of Here-Being and World History ... 315

XV. *Temporality and Within-Timeness as the Origin of the Vulgar Concept of Time*   327

    1. The Incompleteness of the Foregoing Analysis of the Temporality of Here-Being   327
    2. The Temporality of Here-Being and the Taking Care of Time   329
    3. Time Taken Care of and Within-Timeness   336
    4. Within-Timeness and the Genesis of the Vulgar Concept of Time   343
    5. The Contrast of the Existential and Ontological Connection of Temporality, Here-Being, and World-Time with Hegel's Interpretation of the Relation between Time and Spirit   349
        (a) Hegel's Concept of Time   351
        (b) Hegel's Interpretation of the Connection between Time and Spirit   356

XVI. *Conclusion: An Attempt to Outline Heidegger's Answer to the Question Asked at the Beginning of* Being and Time   363

Notes   369

Glossary of German Expressions   383

Index   387

Editor's Foreword

Born in Budapest in 1910, Magda King was educated there, in Vienna and at Edinburgh where she conducted seminars on the work of Martin Heidegger and contributed papers to philosophical journals. This book is the most comprehensive and detailed commentary on both divisions of his *Being and Time*. The chapters on Division One reproduced with certain changes here were published originally in 1964 by the Macmillan Company, New York, and by Basil Blackwell, Oxford, under the title *Heidegger's Philosophy: A Guide to His Basic Thought*. I found that guide very helpful and have been told by many others that they did too. What they and I liked especially was the directness with which it indicates the nature and radicality of the change in our thinking that Heidegger was seeking to bring about. Magda King writes with the precision that is possible only for the commentator who has reread a text to the point of being able both to inhabit it and to see it from the outside.

The papers that came to my attention after her death included typescript studies of each of the chapters of Division Two of *Being and Time*. Discovering that they were as refreshingly direct, as ingenious in their renderings into English of Heidegger's key words, and as communicative of surprise as were her earlier studies, I requested permission to edit a single volume in which her considerations of both divisions would be contained. I thank Simon & Schuster, successors in this regard to the Macmillan Company, New York, for generously granting my request, and Blackwell for giving the project their blessing.

Although Magda King's original guide was not the only one to omit close examination of Division Two of *Being and Time*, this division receives such attention in the new book. After the "basics" of Division

One are presented in a manner suited to students who have not yet made an extensive or intensive study of philosophy, the much longer chapters in which she treats Division Two, while still untechnical, are models of how to read and analyze paragraph by paragraph with the slowness a great text deserves.

Heidegger's Philosophy was one of the earliest commentaries on *Being and Time* to appear in English. Its composition was virtually complete before the translation of Heidegger's masterpiece by John Macquarrie and Edward Robinson appeared. Since then the long-awaited translation by Joan Stambaugh has come out. This is the translation I reproduce in citations, but, where there is a difference, I elsewhere use both it and the no less insightful renderings of key terms for which Magda King argues and upon which her comments sometimes turn. Her alternatives are recorded in the new glossary and index.

Perhaps the most controversial departure in the original guide compared with the Macquarrie-Robinson and the Stambaugh translations was her willingness to countenance "man" as a rendering of *Da-sein* provided it "be remembered that *man* is a purely ontic term and is incapable of bringing into play the ontological meaning of *Da-sein*." That is what she says in the second part of the first chapter of Part Two in defense of her willingness to use the word in this way and in spite of her acknowledgment of the reason Heidegger gives in *Sein und Zeit* for using the word *Da-sein* rather than *Mensch*—though it should be noted that in some works composed after this one he seems ready to use *Mensch* in places where he would formerly have written *Da-sein*. Magda King notes further that the expression "human being" has the drawback that "it defines 'being' by the humanity of man, whereas *Da-sein* asks us to do exactly the opposite." In favor of using "man" she cites its simplicity. In my judgment the disadvantages of its use, which she herself stresses, outweigh this virtue of simplicity. She appears to have come around to this view herself by the time she undertook her commentary on Division Two, for there she frequently uses the term *Da-sein*. Her original objection to that solution was that "although in many ways the best," it is exposed to "the danger that *Da-sein* might become merely a technical term in a Heideggerian terminology, instead of being rethought and genuinely understood." I believe that her own exegeses forearm the reader so effectively against this danger that to choose *Da-sein* is indeed the best solution. I have therefore opted for the now standard practice she herself appears to have come to favor and have as a consequence made substitutions where called for in her treatment of Division One. It seems to me that the risk incurred by using the word *Da-sein* is less serious than that run by frequent recourse to "man." This does not mean that this familiar word has to be eschewed altogether, so long as we keep her warning in mind. As for her phrases "man's being-there" and "man's here-being," they express admirably the ontic-ontological ambiguity on which Heidegger's work turns, the original ambiguity or "ontological difference" implicit in the Greek word *on*.

Magda King welcomed and adopted many suggestions from the first full English translation of *Being and Time*, for instance "ownmost" for Heidegger's *eigenst*, which is kept too in Joan Stambaugh's translation. The present editor is in the fortunate position of being able to draw on all three of these sources and others. He is of the opinion that it is by ringing the changes judiciously through a range of available offerings that the reader may be conducted between the extremes of oversimplification and excessive artificiality toward a horizon where the matter itself, the *Sache selbst*, is "rethought and genuinely understood." An approach to this objective can be facilitated, or rather made less difficult, if a neologism or paleonym can be hit upon that is unfamiliar without being too far-out. For example, Magda King's "spaceish" substitutes for "spatial" a word that sounds strange enough to the English ear to make us think harder about what Heidegger might mean by *räumlich*. It and "timeish" and "worldish" and "published" (for *öffentlich*) are to my mind and ear strokes of genius. She exploits the same suffix in "stand-offishness," her graphically concrete translation of *Abständigkeit*, for which Stambaugh and Macquarrie and Robinson give the more Latinate "distantiality."

In his endeavor to refresh philosophy, Heidegger, like Hegel, draws on the earthy roots of his language and dialect. So a promising way of achieving this refreshment would be the exercise of translating *Being and Time* into Anglo-Saxon. Or Welsh. Or Hebrew. For it is at the Janus edge of the going over, the unstable instant of transition from one linguistic field to another, that takes place the paradoxical happening of simultaneously being and not being at home that is registered in the word *Unheimlichkeit*, one of the keys to Heidegger's book. This frontier can also be historical. On or near it perhaps teeters the word *dread*. Although and because this was revived in certain Existentialist applications of Heidegger, it has tended to get eclipsed in translations and discussions of his work by *anxiety* or by *Angst* left untranslated. Alluding to A. E. Housman's list of the physical symptoms that accompanied his remembering a line of poetry, she remarks that "it might equally well be said that the first time one truly understands Heidegger's questions one knows it by a cold shiver running down one's spine." That cold shiver—the *Schaudern* that Goethe's Faust declares to be humankind's best part, Shakespeare's "dread bolted thunder"—can be felt in the word *dread*. I have therefore respected Magda King's preference for it, but without excluding the others. This is not the only transcription by her that may provoke the disagreement she would have seen as a manifestation of the alertness she wanted to encourage. Whether or not her own lexical and philosophical alertness owes something to her having learned German and English as second and third languages, I fancy no one will disagree that it is abundantly manifested in this guide.

With a couple of exceptions for which she excuses herself, the author deliberately abstains from discussing the secondary literature already available to her. Her aim is the same as Heidegger's: to bring readers to experience a raw contact with the topic. Anyway, without that accessibility how could readers be confident that they had reached a position from which to judge the book, as of course it must and will be judged, in light of other Heideggeriana? Texts additional to *Being and Time* to which she does refer are listed in the bibliography, which I have expanded by including information about recent editions, translations, and secondary literature. I have also expanded her notes and the references given in her text by adding indications to this material in them.

But it is above all in the sensitive intelligence with which its author listens and responds to Heidegger's own words that lies what I consider to be the strength of this book. We can all think of philosophical or other commentaries composed decades ago that retain their power of illumination today, whatever scholarship has come up with in the interim. I believe that *A Guide to Heidegger's "Being and Time"* has that classic quality and that generations of students of Heidegger will join with me in thanking State University of New York Press, in particular Jane Bunker and Marilyn Semerad, and their philosophy series editor Dennis Schmidt, for the professional manner in which they have shown that my belief is shared.

JOHN LLEWELYN

Author's Foreword

The studies contained in this volume are intended to help the reader toward an understanding of Heidegger's philosophy as it is expressed in *Being and Time*. Even the best translations cannot avoid a certain distortion of the original text, imposing additional difficulties on their readers. The main purpose of this book is to help such readers over the greatest initial difficulties presented by *Being and Time*. Heidegger claims to have made a new departure in Greek-Western thinking by raising a radically new problem. What this problem is, and how it differs from the central problem of traditional philosophy, is hard to grasp and harder to explain; but it must be at least roughly explained and understood before any detail of Heidegger's thought can fall into place.

Accordingly, the first theme of this book is simply the question Heidegger asks. The discussion of this question will at the same time introduce readers to *Being and Time* in a general way and prepare them for the second and main theme of this book: an exposition of those features and problems of *Being and Time* which are both basic to its understanding and are usually found hardest to grasp, such as, to mention only one example, Heidegger's conception of world. The first seven studies will deal with problems basic to *Being and Time* as a whole, and the eighth will give a preview of the special problems raised in Division Two in preparation for the close investigation of that division which follows. A concluding study will attempt to indicate Heidegger's answer to the question raised at the beginning of his inquiry.

The difficulty of Heidegger's thought was for many years held to be almost insuperable in the medium of a foreign language, especially English. That this opinion is no longer so widely held can be seen both from the rapidly increasing number of translations of Heidegger's works and from the interest of a growing readership. There are signs, moreover, that as a thinker of our own age, Heidegger may be of interest to many who do not claim to have a wide knowledge of traditional metaphysics or whose concern with him may not be primarily philosophical at all. Such readers have a certain advantage in bringing an open mind to a new problem, but they also have special difficulties in grappling with Heidegger. Every effort has been made to carry these readers along in this work. Wherever possible, difficult ideas are approached through concrete examples and illustrations. Care has been taken to explain frequently used metaphysical terms, which are elementary to the expert in philosophy, but may be unfamiliar to the less well-prepared reader. Any unnecessary use of technical language has been avoided and a simple, straightforward English aimed at.

Heidegger's own key words present a special problem to translator and expositor alike, a problem that can never be entirely satisfactorily or finally solved. As Heidegger rightly insists, every translation is in itself an interpretation. The English renderings of key concepts which this work gives have grown entirely from its own understanding of Heidegger's thought, and may differ considerably from other translations. The first English version of *Sein und Zeit* appeared only after the body of the present book had been completed, but as even a hasty comparison shows, there are many similarities and many more divergencies in the rendering of Heidegger's key words. This is all to the good. Since in most cases the English expression can only be an approximation to the German, it unavoidably weights the original in one way or another. Something like a standard English terminology of Heidegger's concepts is not only an impracticable aim, but would in advance rob his thought of its rich possibilities and drive it into the narrow channel of only one possible interpretation. For this reason, no effort was made to adapt the terminology of this book to that of the translation of *Being and Time* made by John Macquarrie and Edward Robinson, except where the translators have found an especially felicitous way of expressing what seems to me the primary meaning of a word, as for instance, in their inspired translation of *eigenst* by "ownmost." This and several other excellent renderings have been gratefully taken over, and the term "division" for *Abschnitt* has also been adopted.

An exposition has the advantage of far greater freedom than is permissible to a translation; it can not only paraphrase and expound a concept at length, where necessary, but it is one of its positive tasks to unfold all the implications enclosed in a key concept. Even so, when all this has been done, the inadequacy of the English rendering is often still so painfully felt that there is a constant temptation to go on using the German original. With exception made for *Da-sein*, this temptation will be resisted in this work, on the principle that an inadequate English word is preferable to an unfamiliar foreign word, always provided that it has been carefully explained how and where the English fails to harmonize with the original. [German expressions are retained where they occur in citations from Joan Stambaugh's translation. They have also been added occasionally in brackets elsewhere. Ed.]

Heidegger's practice of putting into quotation marks, for no apparent reason, such familiar words as *subject, know, world,* and the like, although a minor difficulty, cannot be entirely disregarded. The quotation marks indicate that these words are not to be taken at their face value, either because they are used in a new sense or because they are a loose way of speaking, not strictly appropriate to the matter under discussion but unavoidable because they have grown from a long habit of thought and are easily understandable to the reader.

Heidegger's practice will be applied in this book only within strict limits. On the other hand, quotation marks will occasionally be used for purely linguistic reasons. The word *being*, when it stands for the substantive *das Sein*, may sometimes have to be distinguished from a gerund or a present participle that belongs to the sentence construction. English is exceptional in that it does not have a noun form of the infinitive *to be*, a peculiarity that can lead to confusion and obscurity when the *to be* is the main theme of the inquiry. Many philosophical works try to overcome this difficulty by spelling the gerund with a capital letter: Being. This practice, unfortunately, can lead to another confusion: the mere sight of the word *Being* suggests the divine Being, when what is meant is simply the humble *to be*. The verbal noun *being* will therefore be spelled with the small initial letter, but it will stand in quotation marks when any doubt could arise about its meaning.

Finally, two closely connected points must be briefly mentioned. The first concerns the bibliography. Among Husserl's works only those have been mentioned there to which either direct reference is made or which were found to be especially helpful as a preparation for *Sein und Zeit*. I have not discussed commentaries and critical works on Heidegger, since to have done so would almost inevitably have raised controversy and interfered with the main purpose of taking the reader directly to Heidegger's thought as that is presented in his own works.

For similar reasons, no attempt has been made at a critical appraisal of Heidegger's philosophy. Where criticisms and comparisons with other thinkers occur, these are incidental and subordinate to the positive task of helping the reader to a clear and firm grasp of Heidegger's fundamental ideas. This is by no means easy, but once it is done, it will put the reader in a position both to explore more deeply Heidegger's thought for himself and to form a fair judgment of its power and original contribution to philosophy.

ACKNOWLEDGMENTS

I wish to thank the Niemeyer Verlag for kind permission to quote and translate passages from the original edition of *Sein und Zeit*, copyright by Max Niemeyer Verlag, Halle/Saale (now Tübingen), 1927.

The manuscript has greatly benefited from my husband's advice and fruitful criticism; to him I owe deepest gratitude. I gladly take this opportunity also to thank George Kay for his most generous and constructive help through many years; and Thorir Thordarson and Martin Gray for their encouragement and support.

BIBLIOGRAPHY AND KEY TO ABBREVIATIONS

(Abbreviations of titles as indicated are used in references made in the text and notes.)

HEIDEGGER

BPP   *The Basic Problems of Phenomenology*, trans. Albert Hofstadter (Bloomington: Indiana University Press, 1982).

BW   *Martin Heidegger: Basic Writings*, ed., David Farrell Krell (New York: Harper & Row, 1977).

BZ   *Der Begriff der Zeit* (Tübingen: Niemeyer, 1989).

CT   *The Concept of Time*, trans. William McNeill (Oxford: Blackwell, 1992).

DT   *Discourse on Thinking*, trans. John M. Anderson and E. Hans Freund (New York: Harper & Row, 1966).

EB   *Existence and Being*, ed., Werner Brock (London: Vision, 1949).

EGT   *Early Greek Thinking*, trans. David Farrell Krell and Frank A. Capuzzi (New York: Harper & Row, 1975).

EHD   *Erläuterungen zu Hölderlins Dichtung* (Frankfurt: Klostermann,1951). G4.

EM   *Einführung in die Metaphysik* (Tübingen: Niemeyer,1953). G40.

ER   *The Essence of Reasons*, trans. Terrence Malick (Evanston, Northwestern University Press, 1969).

FCM The Fundamental Concepts of Metaphysics: World, Finitude, Solitude, trans. William McNeill and Nicholas Walker (Bloomington: Indiana University Press, 1995).

FD Die Frage nach dem Ding (Niemeyer: Tübingen, 1962). G41.

G Martin Heidegger, Gesamtausgabe (Frankfurt am Main, Klostermann, 1975-).

GE Gelassenheit (Pfullingen: Neske, 1959).

GM Die Grundbegriffe der Metaphysik: Welt–Endlichkeit–Einsamkeit (Frankfurt: Klostermann, 1983). G29/30.

GP Die Grundprobleme der Phänomenologie (Frankfurt: Klostermann, 1975). G24.

HCT History of the Concept of Time: Prolegomena, trans. Theodore Kisiel (Bloomington: Indiana University Press, 1985).

HO Holzwege (Frankfurt: Klostermann, 1950). G5.

HU Platons Lehre von der Wahrheit, mit einem Brief über den "Humanismus" (Bern: Francke, 1947).

ID Identität und Differenz (Pfullingen: Neske, 1957).

ID(E) Identity and Difference, trans. Joan Stambaugh (New York: Harper & Row, 1969).

IM An Introduction to Metaphysics, trans. Ralph Manheim (New York: Doubleday, 1961).

KPM Kant und das Problem der Metaphysik (Frankfurt: Klostermann, 1951). G3.

KPM(E) Kant and the Problem of Metaphysics, trans. Richard Taft (Bloomington: Indiana University Press, 1990).

OWL On the Way to Language, trans. Peter D. Hertz (New York: Harper & Row, 1971).

P Pathmarks, ed., William McNeill (Cambridge: Cambridge University Press, 1998).

PGZ Prolegomena zur Geschichte des Zeitbegriffs (Frankfurt: Klostermann, 1979). G20.

PLT Poetry, Language, Thought, trans. Albert Hofstadter (New York: Harper & Row, 1971).

PR The Principle of Reason, trans. Reginald Lilly (Bloomington: Indiana University Press, 1991).

QCT	*The Question Concerning Technology and Other Essays*, trans. William Lovitt (New York: Harper & Row, 1977).
SG	*Der Satz vom Grund* (Pfullingen: Neske, 1958). G10.
SZ	*Sein und Zeit, Jahrbuch für Philosophie und phänomenologische Forschung*, VIII. (Halle: Niemeyer, 1927). G2. *Being and Time*, trans. John Macquarrie and Edward Robinson (New York: Harper & Row, Oxford: Blackwell, 1962). Trans. Joan Stambaugh (Albany: State University of New York Press, 1997).
US	*Unterwegs zur Sprache* (Pfullingen: Neske, 1960). G12.
VA	*Vorträge und Aufsätze* (Pfullingen: Neske, 1954).
W	*Wegmarken* (Frankfurt: Klostermann, 1967). G9.
WCT	*What Is Called Thinking?* trans. Fred D. Wieck and John Glenn Gray (New York: Harper & Row, 1968).
WG	*Vom Wesen des Grundes* (Frankfurt: Klostermann, 1955).
WHD	*Was heisst Denken?* (Tübingen: Niemeyer, 1954). G8.
WM	*Was ist Metaphysik?* Mit Einleitung und Nachwort (Frankfurt: Klostermann, 1955).
WP	*Was ist das–die Philosophie?* (Pfullingen: Neske, 1956).
WP(E)	*What Is Philosophy?* trans. Jean T. Wilde and William Kluback (Schenectady: New College and University Press,1956).
WT	*What Is a Thing?* trans. W. B. Barton, Jr. and Vera Deutsch (Chicago: Henry Regnery, 1967).
WW	*Vom Wesen der Wahrheit* (Frankfurt: Klostermann, 1954).
ZS	*Zur Seinsfrage* (Frankfurt: Klostermann, 1956).

For details of the context and composition of *Being and Time*, see especially John van Buren, *The Young Heidegger: Rumor of the Hidden King* (Bloomington: Indiana University Press, 1994), and Theodore Kisiel, *The Genesis of Heidegger's "Being and Time"* (Berkeley: University of California Press, 1993).

HUSSERL

Cartesianische Meditationen und Pariser Vorträge. Husserliana 1, ed. S. Strasser (The Hague: Nijhoff, 1950).

Cartesian Meditations: An Introduction to Phenomenology, trans. Dorion Cairns (The Hague: Nijhoff, 1960).

Ideen zu einer reinen Phänomenologie und phänomenologischen Philosophie, I, ed. K. Schuhmann, II, ed. M. Biemel, III, ed. M. Biemel. Husserliana 3, 4, 5 (The Hague: Nijhoff, 1950 Bd. 3, 1952 Bd. 4 & Bd. 5).

Ideas Pertaining to a Pure Phenomenology and to a Phenomenological Philosophy, First Book: General Introduction to a Pure Phenomenology, trans. Fred Kersten (The Hague: Nijhoff, 1982).

Ideas Pertaining to a Pure Phenomenology and to a Phenomenological Philosophy, Second Book: Studies in the Phenomenology of Constitution, trans. Richard Roycewicz and André Schuwer (Dordrecht: Kluwer, 1989).

Logische Untersuchungen I and II, ed. Elmar Holenstein, Husserliana 18 (The Hague: Nijhoff, 1975). *Logical Investigations*, trans. J. N. Findlay (New York: Humanities, 1970).

Vorlesungen zur Phänomenologie des inneren Zeitbewusstseins, ed. Rudolf Boehm, Husserliana 10 (The Hague: Nijhoff, 1966).

The Phenomenology of Internal Time Consciousness, trans. James S. Churchill (The Hague: Nijhoff, 1964).

PART ONE

What Is the Question?

INTRODUCTORY

The main body of *Being and Time* is preceded by two expository chapters in which Heidegger explains the question of being as it is to be raised and worked out in this fundamental inquiry. Everything that belongs to Heidegger's question—its motive and aim, the method of the investigation, and the conclusions at which it will arrive—is set out in these two chapters with meticulous care and a masterliness that can only be appreciated after much study. And yet, twenty and thirty years after the publication of *Being and Time*, Heidegger still finds himself obliged to correct misinterpretations of his fundamental work and to point out confusions between his question of being and that raised by traditional ontology.[1]

The difficulty of grasping a radically new problem is, of course, well known to students of philosophy. In addition, Heidegger presents his readers with unusual difficulties, the greatest of which is the fragmentary state of *Being and Time* itself. Divisions One and Two of Part I were published in 1927 as the beginning of a much larger work, consisting of two parts or halves, each containing three divisions. Heidegger intended to conclude his own investigations of the problem of being in Division Three, Part I, while the whole of Part II was to have been a radical critique of traditional ontology. Of this monumental work, the originally published two divisions are all we have. Perhaps nothing can show the stature of *Being and Time* more impressively than the fact that, in spite of its unfinished state, it is one of those rare works whose importance can in no way be measured or foreseen.

Between 1927 and 1960 Heidegger published numerous other works, some of which clearly belonged to Part II of *Being and Time* (see especially *Kant and the Problem of Metaphysics*). On the whole, it may be said that, except for a treatise on Aristotle's interpretation of time, the ground assigned to Part II has been fully covered by Heidegger, although not in the way in which it had been originally planned. In the preface to the seventh German edition of *Sein und Zeit* (1953), Heidegger announced that the second half would definitely not be added to the work.

This announcement still left open the question of the crucially important Division Three of Part I, which was to have borne the suggestive subtitle of "Zeit und Sein" ("Time and Being"). The absence of this division contributed more than any other single factor to the difficulty of the whole treatise. As far as one can judge, it was to have brought not only the solution of Heidegger's final problem, but also the explicit and detailed answer to what might be called his penultimate question. The absence of two sets of answers from *Sein und Zeit* makes its central problem extremely difficult to grasp and even leaves it open to doubt which of the questions raised by Heidegger is the more fundamental.

In 1961, however, Heidegger delivered a lecture on "Zeit und Sein" at the University of Kiel, which was subsequently broadcast in Germany. Despite this, great efforts are demanded from the reader to grasp the central theme of *Being and Time*. Among its many difficulties, the following call for mention here.

First, there is the special use of the word *Sinn* (sense, or meaning), which enters importantly into Heidegger's problem as it is formulated in *Sein und Zeit*. This word is confusing and even positively misleading to readers who are unfamiliar with phenomenology. This difficulty, however, is comparatively easy to overcome.

Second, there is the confusion between Heidegger's and the metaphysical question of being. This difficulty is recurrent and not at all easy to overcome.

Third, the failure to see that there is any difficulty at all. Our familiarity with, and constant use of, the *is* and *am* and *to be*, make it incomprehensible that anyone should find our ability to understand these words astonishing and problematic. This difficulty is chronic and hardest to overcome, because it is not primarily a matter of intellect and thinking. A. E. Housman is reported to have said that the only way in which he could recognize great poetry was by a certain feeling in his stomach. It might equally well be said that the first time one truly understands Heidegger's questions one knows it by a cold shiver running down one's spine.

These difficulties will be specially kept in view in the exposition of Heidegger's central theme, which will be developed as follows.

In sections 1 and 2 the precise meaning of Heidegger's question is explained and illuminated by a discussion of the aims set in Part I of *Being and Time*.

Section 3. A brief summary is given of Heidegger's interpretation of the question of being as it has been asked and worked out in traditional philosophy, in contrast to his own question.

Section 4. The unique nature of the concept of being, and the attempted solutions of the problem of its unity, most notably by Aristotle, are discussed. This leads to a consideration of Heidegger's own attempt to solve the same problem.

Section 5. The concrete working out of Heidegger's problem in *Being and Time* is the main subject. The difficulties inherent in the problem itself are discussed, concluding with a brief indication of the place of *Being and Time* in Heidegger's thought as a whole.

EXPOSITION

1. A FORMAL STATEMENT OF THE QUESTION

Being and Time is an inquiry into the *meaning of being* (*Sinn von Sein*). To this short formulation of his theme Heidegger frequently adds the word *überhaupt*, which is difficult to translate precisely: *the meaning of being as such or in general* is only an approximate statement of the full theme (*Sinn von Sein überhaupt*). Fortunately, this difficulty need not worry us unduly, since Heidegger does not insist on a single formula. In an effort to make his problem concretely understandable he often reduces it to a simple, informal question, as, for example: "was heisst 'Sein'?" (SZ, 26; also KPM, 202, G3, 224, KPM(E), 153; ID, 21, ID(E), 30). Almost literally translated, the phrase means *What is called "being"*? Freely paraphrased, it might be rendered as *What do we mean by "to be"*?

From these various formulations, the core of Heidegger's question emerges with an apparent, not to say misleading, clarity and simplicity. At first sight, we must confess, it is frankly disappointing. Heidegger claims to give philosophy a new start, but it is not at all evident where the newness of his question lies. It strikes us rather as the revival of an old question that has gone out of fashion. Even less does its fundamental character show itself on the surface. It reminds us of the kind of problems that are usually dealt with by logic, but most of all it sounds like a linguistic or a merely verbal problem. Among all the doubts and misgivings aroused by a formal statement of Heidegger's theme, the suspicion that he might be concerned merely with the meaning of a word must evidently be the first to be allayed.

2. A Provisional Explanation of "Meaning" (*Sinn*): The Theme of *Being and Time* Restated

Heidegger's special use of the term "meaning" (*Sinn*) was pointed out already in our introductory remarks. Our present difficulty thus seems to be purely terminological and should be capable of an easy solution: we must simply find out how Heidegger defines the word "meaning." The matter, however, is not quite so simple, as can be readily seen when the definition is actually given. Meaning, in Heidegger's sense, is that from which something is understandable as the thing it is. This definition, while perfectly correct, is for our purpose quite insufficient. Heidegger's terminology grows from a way of phenomenological thinking, which cannot be explained merely by defining words. Phenomenology will be made the subject of one of our later studies, but in the meantime we must find a rough-and-ready way to understand Heidegger's use of "meaning." This can be done by a concrete illustration.

Supposing in a strange town we ask what a certain building is, we may be told that it is a theater. With this explanation the building has explicitly come to our understanding as a theater—that is, as the thing it is. Supposing, however, that we are not familiar with theaters, we must take a further step and have explained to us what a theater is. We shall be told that it is a building intended for the production of plays. Provided that we know at all what a play is, this particular building has now become manifest in what it essentially is. When we understand something as the thing it is, we have understood it in its essential being.

But where in all this is the meaning? Is it in our understanding of the word "theater?" No. Is it in this concrete thing, the theater itself? No. Is it perhaps in the explanation "for the production of plays"? The "for" shows that this thing, the theater, is in advance understood by reference to a purpose. Is that where we find the meaning? This comes much nearer to Heidegger, but is not quite there yet. Meaning, according to Heidegger, is that from which something is understandable as the thing it is. From where can a thing like a theater be understood at all? Only from a world of human existence.

Writing, producing, and appreciating plays is one of our distinctively human possibilities, for the sake of which we have things like theaters. Only from a human world can a thing be understood as a theater. That which makes such understanding possible, Heidegger says, is the meaning. The meaning of the theater is the world to which it belongs.

The world of our own existence is the horizon in which our everyday understanding moves, so that from it and in reference to it the things we come across are intelligible to us as theaters, as buses, as knives and forks; that is, as things that can be useful for some purpose. The horizon of our world is primarily "meaning-giving"; it is a meaning in which we constantly move as a matter of course, so that it usually remains implicit.

One way to make this implied meaning explicit is to turn away from our everyday world and enter into the realm of one of the sciences, say, theoretical physics. At one stroke, things like theaters, buses, knives and forks, become "meaningless." The horizon from which things are now understood is the substantiality of matter. Why has such a startling change taken place? Because the horizon, in which the physicist's understanding moves, has undergone a profound modification. The world of human existence has become modified into a theoretical conception of material nature, articulated into such categories or basic concepts as mass, motion, or energy. Since this horizon alone is "meaning-giving" for the physicist, anything whatever that falls under his observation must show itself and can only show itself as a complex motion of material bodies. This horizon gives nothing from which things could even be questioned as to their possible relevance to a purpose; their only possibility now is to show themselves in their material properties as moving bodies in a space-time continuum.

Let us sum up the results we have reached so far. Meaning is that which enables us to understand things as the things they are—that is, in their essential being. The meaning does not originally lie in words, or in things, but in the remarkable structure of our understanding itself. We move in advance in a horizon of understanding, from which and in reference to which the things we meet are intelligible to us as so and so and as such and such. The world of our own existence is the horizon from which we primarily understand things as relevant to a purpose. This is capable of modifications, for example, into something like "nature." From this horizon, things become understandable purely as substantial bodies. The modifications in the horizon of our understanding enable us to understand things in different ways, but in each case only in one or another of their possibilities.

What light does this throw on Heidegger's theme? What is Heidegger aiming at when he asks: How is it at all possible for man [Dasein] to understand being? From what horizon does he understand being? What does being mean? These questions, as our discussion has shown, are not three different questions, but are one and the same. The horizon which makes it possible for us to understand being *as* being is itself the meaning of being. What is this horizon? It is, as *Being and Time* sets out to show, time. Already on the first page, Heidegger tells us that the provisional aim of his treatise is the interpretation of *time* as the possible horizon of any understanding of being.

Why does Heidegger call this interpretation his *provisional* aim? Presumably to indicate that, with its achievement, the tasks set to *Being and Time* as a whole are by no means finished. Heidegger's interpretation of time is completed in Division Two, except for the last crucial steps, and these were to have been taken at the beginning of Division Three. This was to have led to the final phase of Heidegger's original investigations: the temporal interpretation of the idea of being as such.

In the absence of Division Three, this final aim of Part I of *Being and Time* would have remained impenetrably obscure had Heidegger not given some illuminating hints in his work entitled *Vom Wesen des Grundes* (*The Essence of Reasons*), published in 1929. Here Heidegger clearly indicates that the idea of being as such is to be articulated into what- and how-being, something, nothing, and notness (*Was-* and *Wiesein, Etwas, Nichts,* and *Nichtigkeit.* WG, 52, W, 69, G9, 173, ER, 125, P, 133).

This formula, bare as it is, and uncertain as its interpretation must be, yet helps to define Heidegger's central theme and deserves to be carefully considered. It contains, in fact, the basic design of the new ontology that is to be founded—that is, brought back to its source and ground—in *Being and Time*. The strangeness of Heidegger's philosophical approach makes itself felt already in the concepts into which the idea of being is articulated, among which the "nothing" and the "not" occupy the most important place. This seems paradoxical indeed, for, to our usual way of thinking, "nothing" and "notness" are the very opposite of being. Our later studies will show, however, that these concepts receive an entirely new interpretation in Heidegger's thought, in the light of which their central philosophical importance will become fully understandable. In the meantime, we shall turn to those articulations of the idea of being that seem familiar and more within our immediate grasp.

The two closely connected articulations of what- and how-being become much easier to comprehend when they are rephrased into what-(a thing)-is and how-(it)-is. The being of things is manifest to us in what they are, traditionally called the "essence," and in how they are—that is, whether they exist actually, or possibly, or necessarily. It should be noted, however, that these traditional conceptions should never be taken over unexamined and mechanically applied to Heidegger's philosophy. The reason for this will gradually emerge in the course of our studies. Meanwhile, a more urgent point to decide is what we are to understand by the "thing" whose being is articulated into what and how.

In the primary and narrow sense, things are the concrete things that are accessible to us through the senses and are capable of an independent existence, such as mountains, stars, plants, and animals. These things stand there, so to speak, on their own feet, and in so standing, they are, they exist. Things in a very wide sense, however, can mean anything at all: beings as such and as a whole, and things in this wide sense constitute the sphere of philosophical inquiry. Within the realm of beings as a whole, however, the concrete, sensible things have played an eminently important part, so that nonsensible phenomena, like mind, knowledge, and number, have tended to be understood in comparison with and in contrast to them. In other words, the reality (*Wirklichkeit*) of one kind of thing has tended to be measured by the reality of another kind of thing.

But if the fundamental problem of philosophy is to be raised in a new way, not only the idea of being but also the idea of beings must be reconsidered and defined. The third articulation of the idea of being gives us the widest possible concept of beings as such: they are something and not nothing. A delusion, the meaning of a poem, God, hope, thinking, seeming, becoming, and so on, are evidently something and not nothing, although they are not concrete sensible things in the primary sense of the word. Starting from the idea of something, a "real thing" is no longer played off against an "ideal thing" and the one measured by the other; both are set off against the nothing as the totally other to all things, and understood in their most fundamental character as "not nothing." Heidegger's idea of being formulates the demand that ontology must start from the widest and deepest of all distinctions: the difference between something and nothing. With this start, the problem of the nothing would be drawn into the very center of philosophy; and this, Heidegger maintains, would be the first fruitful step toward "overcoming nihilism" (EM, 155, IM, 170, G40, 212).

All this sounds intolerably paradoxical at present, because we do not in the least know as yet what Heidegger means by the nothing. For the same reason, it is hard to imagine that the nothing and the not can have anything to do with time, and yet they must have, if Heidegger is serious in announcing that the final aim of *Being and Time* is to unfold the temporal meaning enclosed in the idea of being as such.

This culminating point of Heidegger's investigations will unfortunately remain obscure even at the end of our studies, since the whole temporal analysis of the idea of being was to have been carried out in Division Three. But, it will be asked, what of all the works Heidegger has written since *Being and Time*? Is it possible that none of them brings at least a partial solution to Heidegger's final problem? One of them does: the *Einführung in die Metaphysik* (*Introduction to Metaphysics*). The lecture, delivered in 1935, on which this book is based, has rightly been felt to be unique among all Heidegger's works. Its true theme, however, has often been only imperfectly understood. It brings, it is true, the temporal interpretation of an idea of being, but not of Heidegger's own idea. The interpretation given is of a restricted conception of being which has been central to metaphysical thinking: the idea of substantial being.

What is the temporal meaning hidden in the idea of substantiality? Heidegger formulates it as "standing presentness" or "persistent presentness" (*ständige Anwesenheit*) (EM, 154, IM, 169, G40, 211). This is the horizon into which traditional philosophy, unknown to itself, looks out in advance, and with a view to which it determines, differently in different ages, what kind of things have "true being" and which are in comparison mere shadows. It is not an accident, for instance, that Greek-Western thinking has ascribed an extraordinary dignity to the formal sciences like logic and mathematics. The purely formal concepts and their relations studied by these sciences preeminently satisfy the idea of permanence and unchanging presence, which is the temporal meaning of substantiality (SZ, 89ff., esp. 95–96). The fact that the modern mathematical-theoretical sciences have grown from the soil of Greek-Western philosophy, and from no other soil, testifies to the hidden power of an idea of being which has carried and shaped the course of our history. But the possibilities of this idea have now been worked out. If the question of being has to be asked anew, this cannot be a mere whim or even a "stroke of genius" on the part of an individual; it can only arise from historical necessity.

How is this question to be worked out in *Being and Time*? The main stages can now be roughly delimited. The ultimate goal, as was shown above, is the temporal interpretation of the idea of being as such—that is, of what- and how-being, something, nothing, and notness. (Projected for Division Three.) This aim requires for its indispensable basis the solution of a provisional or penultimate problem: How is it at all possible for man to understand being? How is it that time is the horizon from which being is understandable? How is time itself to be interpreted? (Completed in Division Two, except for the last crucial steps, which were to have been taken at the beginning of Division Three.) This problem, in turn, requires for its indispensable basis a preliminary inquiry into the being of man as Da-sein. The task of this investigation is to discover all the essential structures of man's existence, thereby illuminating the way in which man understands both his own being and the being of other beings (completed in Division One).

Having brought the broad outline of Heidegger's treatise into focus, we can now summarize his question as follows. It is the question of the inner possibility of our understanding of being and of the temporal meaning enclosed in the idea of being as such. This is what Heidegger often calls the question of being as being, but the phrase is misleading, because the central problem of traditional ontology is usually defined in the same way. In view of the radical difference between the two, would it be justified to change the definition of traditional ontology to the one proposed by Heidegger? Is Heidegger's claim that he is providing a fundamental ontology—that is, the foundation for all ontology—to be upheld? The problem of our understanding of being, Heidegger maintains, lies already in all the questions philosophy can ask, and lies in them in such a way that it cannot even be raised as a problem, let alone be solved, on the traditional soil. On what grounds does Heidegger put forward such a thesis? Is there sufficient evidence to make the thesis tenable, or should it be rejected as a dogmatic assertion? These matters demand an examination of traditional philosophy, whose nature and limits have so far been only briefly indicated.

3. Why Has Traditional Ontology Failed to Get to the Root of the Problem of Being?

The character and limits of Western philosophy are decisively determined by its Greek origins. The early Greek thinkers asked: What are beings as beings? What are beings as a whole? In spite of many profound changes in the course of Greek-Western thinking, the questions it asks are still fundamentally the same as they were at the beginning, or are derivations from them. Traditional ontology, Heidegger maintains, was and remains an inquiry into beings as beings, and not into being as such.

Beings[2] is a rendering of the German word *das Seiende*. This is Heidegger's translation of the essentially ambiguous Greek expression *to on*, which can mean both being and beings (*ta onta*). Since in Heidegger's translation the weight falls on the latter, it will usually be rendered by "beings," and sometimes also by "things." There are other ways, in themselves better and clearer, of translating *das Seiende*—for example, "the existent," "the entity," or "entities." These translations are avoided here just because they are clearer. They cover over an ambiguity which Heidegger holds to be the very essence of metaphysical thinking. Phrases like "the being of the existent," or "the being of entities," have a first-blush understandability that is entirely spurious. They hide the problem that the phrase "the being of beings" wears, so to speak, on its sleeve.

Ta onta means: that which is, the things that are. Formally, the word *beings* approximates quite well to *ta onta*, but in English it is applied mainly to living beings, and primarily to human beings. We must now try to think this word in exactly the opposite way, because the beings par excellence that traditional ontology has in view are not the beings we ourselves are, but primarily things, in the sense of concrete sensible things. When Greek-Western philosophy speaks of *to be*, it thinks of the *is* of a thing; in other words, *to be* has come to mean predominantly the infinitive of *is* (EM, 70, IM, 77, G40, 98).

What do we mean when we say that a thing *is* (exists)? We mean that it is really there among the all of things, that it occurs, that it can be found somewhere in the natural universe. When we talk of reality, we mean primarily the actual presence of something among the totality of beings. The reality of the *res* (thing) in a very wide sense may be called the central conception of being in traditional ontology. The basic character of reality is substantiality. The seemingly irreconcilable trends in our philosophical tradition spring mainly from varying interpretations of what is meant by substance or what manner or class of beings may properly be called substances.[3] In ancient philosophy alone, substance has been as variously defined as matter, as material bodies, as essence, as number, as idea or form, as the indissoluble unity of matter and form, not to speak of modern variations on the same theme. Yet all these differences can be differentiated and all these opposites opposed only on the ground of an underlying sameness: an idea of being as substantial reality.

No matter how variously traditional ontology may define the substance, it always does so with a view to self-subsistence, self-maintenance without recourse to other beings, unchanging presence as an independent self. And just because independence and self-subsistence are the basic characters of substantial being, its perfect embodiment must be self-produced, or unproduced, uncaused, uncreated. Anything that is brought into being is necessarily dependent, needs maintenance, and is liable to pass away—that is why perishable, finite beings cannot satisfy the idea of the perfect substance.

Any problem that arises in traditional ontology is in advance understood in the horizon of substantiality. But this idea of being, Heidegger maintains, is too narrow and restricted to be able to explain all the ways and senses in which we can understand being. Above all, it is incapable of explaining the distinctively and uniquely human way of being. Man exists such that his being is manifest to him, and it is *man-*

ifest to him as his own. That is why each of us must say of himself: I am. *Being and Time* will show that the whole meaning and structure of the being we express by the *am* is totally different from the real existence of a thing.

Once we begin to think about it, it must strike us as curious that the infinitive *to be* should have drawn its meaning primarily from the *is* of things, when the *am* would seem to be much nearer and more easily comprehensible to us. Does Heidegger ascribe this strange feature of our tradition to a lack of insight or deep thought on the part of metaphysical thinkers? Far from it. He holds that the greatness of their thought has been the distinction of Europe. Was, then, the question, What are beings as beings? simply a wrong start, accidentally made and perpetuated through two and a half thousand years? Historical decisions, Heidegger maintains, do not come about by accident, but spring from the basic possibilities of man's existence, possibilities that are neither made by man, nor, on the other hand, are merely blindly and passively endured by him, as a thing may be thought to "endure" the contingencies that happen to it.

The tendency to interpret human being from the being of things may be roughly and provisionally explained by one of the basic ways in which man can and usually does exist: he loses himself to the things he meets in his world. Owing to his fundamental tendency to give himself away, to scatter himself among his makings and doings, man literally finds himself "there," among the things with which he is busy. Hence the impression arises that *to be* means *I am* in exactly the same way as it does when *to be* is applied to a thing. Thus the *to be* remains undifferentiated and is applied in the vague, average sense of presentness and occurrence to any beings that are accessible at all, including man himself.

It is from this average understanding of being that metaphysics grows. The horizon from which being is understood does not become explicit and its possible differentiations cannot become even a problem. What is differentiated is not being, but beings. Traditional philosophical distinctions start from beings, defining and dividing them into regions and classes according to their essence, their whatness. Man himself is enrolled into the region of living beings, of animals, among which, ontologically speaking, he subsequently remains (HU, 65ff., W, 154ff., G9, 323ff., P, 246-47, BW, 203ff.). Man is the animal who speaks, who has a soul, reason, mind, spirit, self-consciousness, who can think. The interpretation of man's essence undergoes many changes in Greek-Western ontology; what does not change is that man's existence is in advance understood as the real occurrence of a peculiar species among the all of beings.

It may be objected that Heidegger's interpretation of the history of Greek-Western philosophy is too extreme and one-sided. It may apply to ancient ontology, but it seems to leave out of account the influence of Christian theology on a considerable period of Western thought. There is a fundamental difference between the medieval and the Greek interpretation of man. And when we come to the modern era, has Descartes not radically reversed the Greek start with his "I think therefore I am"?

Heidegger's answer to these objections may be briefly indicated as follows:

(a) The idea of the transcendence of man, that man reaches out beyond sheer rationality, that he is more than merely an intelligent animal, undoubtedly has its roots in Christian anthropology (SZ, 49). But what is decisive for the question of being is that man's *existence* never becomes an ontological problem. In Christian theology, man has a preeminent place among all other beings by virtue of a soul to be saved, but his existence is sufficiently explained by his being an *ens creatum*, a creature in a created world. For purely ontological problematics, the situation is not radically altered from the antique period: "to be created" is a Christian reinterpretation of "to be brought forth," which is a basic character of being already in Greek ontology.

(b) In spite of the far-reaching change introduced into philosophy by Descartes, Heidegger repudiates the claim that a fundamentally new start is made with the "I think therefore I am" (SZ, 89ff.). Descartes uncritically takes over the medieval conception of being as the substantiality of substance. He follows the Scholastic division of substances into the infinite and finite substance, the *ens increatum* and the *ens creatum*. Far from raising the question of being in a radically new way, Descartes does not even attempt to get to the root of the meaning enfolded in the idea of substantiality, nor does it occur to him to ask whether the being of God or of man can be appropriately determined by this idea.

The philosopher's God, as Heidegger frequently points out, is totally different from the God revealed in religious experience (ID, 70, ID(E), 71–72; WM, *Einleitung*, 20, W, 208, G9, 379, P, 287–88). God as the uncreated being is a purely ontological concept. It is the perfect embodiment of what is explicitly or implicitly meant by subtantiality: an uncaused, self-subsistent being that needs nothing apart from itself to remain constantly present as an unchanging self.

As against the most perfect, uncreated substance, created beings can only be called substances in a relative sense. Even among them, however, two regions can be distinguished that are relatively independent of production and maintenance: the *res cogitans* and the *res extensa*, the thinking thing and the extended thing. Descartes thus defines the essence of the created thing as extension on the one hand and as "I think" on the other hand. The "I am" is not only left unexamined, but is understood as a matter of course as the produced (created) presence of the thinking thing. Broadly and roughly speaking, "I think therefore I am" means: as the subject of the "I think," I am indubitably, necessarily present (as the absolutely unshakable ground of truth) in my representations.[4]

Far from making a new beginning with the problem of being, the modern age of science and technology brings to an unparalleled and extreme unfolding the implications that lie already in the Greek start. The extraordinary levelling down of everything to a uniform sameness witnessed by modern man in every sphere of experience is explained by Heidegger in the following way. In the latest stage of the modern era, even the object, with its last specific what-character of extension, disappears. A thing no longer manifests its being by standing face to face with man as an object (*Gegenstand*) present for a subject, but by standing up to a thoroughgoing calculation, whereby its persistent availability and producibility (*Bestand*) is in advance made certain. It is by no means an accident that logic and the mathematical-theoretical sciences, with their formal-symbolic, nonvisual representation of nature, now come to an unheard-of predominance. They are the executors of the idea of being as substantiality and objective presence, which now reaches its apotheosis in reducing the what and how of things to the persistence of a characterless product, whose being lies solely in its calculable availability and disposability anywhere, at any time ("Die Frage nach der Technik," VA, 13, "The Question Concerning Technology," QCT, 3-4, BW, 284; WM, *Nachwort*, 48, W, 104-105, G308-309, EB, 387-88).[5]

4. The Uniqueness of the Concept of Being: The Problem of Its Unity. Aristotle's "Unity of Analogy"— A Lead into Heidegger's Question

The preceding discussions already indicate that logical methods of analysis and definition cannot be appropriate to the new inquiry into being. Logic has grown from the soil of traditional ontology; its methods, justifiable within certain limits, are applicable only to defining beings (SZ, 3-4). But being is nothing like beings; it cannot be brought to definiteness and clarity by having beings ascribed to it. As Aristotle clearly saw, being is not the highest genus. The universality of the concept of being is of a totally different order from the generality of those concepts that gather beings into one class. While Aristotle's deep and subtle reasoning cannot be entered upon here, its point can be graphically illustrated as follows.

A genus, which through its subordinate species contains individual beings, can always be exemplified and thus brought to definiteness and clarity. The genus animal, for instance, can always be explained by pointing to a sheep or a horse. But to explain the concept of being, we should vainly point to a horse or the sun, saying "Look, that is what I mean by *is*." The very absurdity of this attempt shows the baffling character of our most universal concept. While everything that we can know, feel, experience in any way is understandable to us in terms of its being, being itself can in no way be explained from or by beings. Its universality transcends, goes out beyond any possible beings or classes of beings.

The uniqueness of being gives rise to the important philosophical problem: What constitutes the unity of this universal concept? The unity of a genus, like *animal*, may be explained by the common character of the beings that fall under it, but this cannot be done with being. And yet, all the ways and senses in which we use the term *to be* have a recognizable and definite unity, and the philosophical task is to explain how this unity is possible.

This is the problem Aristotle tried to solve with his teaching of the analogous meanings of being. With this discovery, Heidegger remarks on page 3 of *Being and Time*, "Aristotle placed the problem of being on a fundamentally new basis." But even Aristotle, Heidegger goes on to point out, failed to solve the problem of those "categorial connections" which he himself had raised; nor could the medieval Schoolmen, who took over the doctrine of the unity of analogy, arrive at any solution in principle.

Why does Heidegger draw attention so pointedly to this doctrine in the opening pages of *Being and Time*? What is it that Aristotle and the Schoolmen failed to solve? Why must the whole problem remain in principle insoluble within metaphysics itself? The answer to these questions must obviously throw a great deal of light not only on traditional attempts, but on Heidegger's own attempt to grapple with the fundamental problems of philosophy. The whole matter, therefore, is well worth considering, even though we can do so only briefly and by way of illustrations.

The specific problem the Schoolmen tried to solve was how it was possible to say "God is" and "the world is," when there is an infinite difference between the being of the Creator and of the created world (SZ, 93). Following Aristotle's teaching, the Schoolmen explained that the word *is* does not mean exactly the same in every instance. God *is* (exists) in the primary and full sense of the word *to be*. The world *is* only in a derivative sense, which is understood by analogy; that is, by reference to the first and unqualified meaning of the term.

According to Aristotle, only "substance" *is* (exists) in the primary and independent sense of *to be*. Anything that belongs to a category other than substance—for example, the category of quality, quantity, state, or relation—is said to be only in a qualified sense, being the quality, quantity, state, or relation of a substance. For example, the "concrete and unique substance," the moon, which Aristotle holds to be eternal and divine, *is* (exists) in the primary and full sense of the word *be*. But when we say "The moon is white," or "The moon is eclipsed," the meaning of the *is* has been qualified. The difference between the subtance moon and its quality of whiteness or its state of being eclipsed is evident: the whiteness could not exist by itself, whereas the moon could very well change its color and yet remain substantially the moon. Similarly, the eclipse has no separate existence apart from the moon, whereas the moon remains identically the same without being eclipsed. And yet, we do not speak ambiguously or improperly when we ascribe being of a kind to quality, or state, or quantity, because in these instances we do not mean by the word *is* the same as when we speak of substance. We are using the term analogously, that is, by reference to its first and unqualified meaning.

Why does Heidegger draw attention to the importance of the "unity of analogy" at the beginning of *Being and Time*? Because here is the nearest approach that can be made from metaphysics toward a new inquiry into being. Aristotle sees clearly that the problem cannot be solved by dividing beings into genera and species, but that the "to be" itself must be articulable and modifiable. He sees further that the modifications can be explained by *reference* to a primary meaning. But even Aristotle's genius cannot leap out of an idea of being as being-a-substance, which determines traditional ontology from its start.

What is it, among other things, that the unity of analogy fails to illuminate? It fails to illuminate the primary meaning of being. How is it, Heidegger would ask, that "to be" must primarily mean "to-be-substance"? And why must substantiality mean self-subsistence, self-maintenance in unchanging identity? Are these basic characters of being the arbitrary invention of philosophers? Or have they, on the contrary, been wrung from the phenomena themselves in the highest efforts of thinking? If the latter is the case, as Heidegger holds it is, then the question must at last be asked, How is it possible for us to understand something like substantial-being at all? From where and in reference to what is this primary meaning of being understood? Self-subsistence, unchanging presence, persistence as an identical self—in all this there lies a distinct reference to time. Time is the horizon in which not only the traditional but any understanding whatever of being in advance moves.

Until time is explicitly laid bare as that which makes our understanding of being as being possible, and until the original phenomenon of time itself is properly explained, the problem of the unity of being remains in principle insoluble. When, on the other hand, it has been shown that all possible differentiations, not merely of beings but of the *to be* itself, have indeed been drawn from time and can be explained as modifications of and derivations from time, then this ancient and troubling philosophical problem will have found a radical solution.

Traditional ontology draws its central idea of being from only one mode of time—the present, the now. The more persistently something is present, the more truly it *is*. "The philosopher's God," it can now be seen, most perfectly satisfies this idea of being: to be ever-present in unchanging self-sameness in an infinite succession of nows. By a curious reflex action, this idea of being is turned back upon the time from which it had been drawn. Time itself is conceived as something that is, and its being is characterized as an infinite succession of now-points of which only each present now is "real." The past is conceived as a now that no longer is, the future as a now that is not yet. This interpretation of time has maintained itself from the Greek period down to our own day. It will be the task of *Being and Time* to show that the *infinite* now-time, in which things come into being and pass away, while it is a genuine time phenomenon, is not the *original* phenomenon of time.

Where and how does the now-time of our philosophical tradition become accessible? It is accessible in a preeminent presentation, which has of old been called *noein*, the pure, nonsensuous apprehending of the being of beings. This philosophical "seeing" presents to itself beings in respect of their pure presence. According to Heidegger, however, time is originally manifest to us not in what and how things are, but in our own being, the *I am*, and this time is *finite*. The finite time of our own existence, however, is too inexorable to disclose itself to a mere harmless "looking at it." It is elementally and originally disclosed in dread (*Angst*). The extraordinary importance of dread in *Being and Time* does not make this work into an existentialistic *Angst-Philosophie*. The importance of dread lies in its ontological function of disclosure. The pure, nonsensuous apprehending, the *noein*, which has traditionally been regarded as the one proper approach to the being of beings, proves to be inadequate to the inquiry into being as being.

5. How Is the New Inquiry into Being to Be Concretely Worked Out? Difficulties Arising from the Nature of the Problem Itself

Our discussions so far have had the aim of bringing the central problem of *Being and Time* into focus. The solution proposed by Heidegger has to some extent been indicated, not in the hope of making it understandable at this stage, but in order to illuminate the fundamental nature of the problem itself and its departure from tradition. On the other hand, the way in which Heidegger works out his theme has so far been only briefly mentioned, and needs a somewhat fuller discussion.

The subtitles of the two divisions we have of *Being and Time* seem to suggest that this work is an ontological inquiry of the usual style into the being of man. Division One is entitled "The Preparatory Fundamental Analysis of Da-sein"; Division Two, "Da-sein and Temporality."[6] To all appearances, *Being and Time* sets out to repair the omission of traditional ontology to inquire into man's existence and not only into his essence. If we follow the customary division of the all of beings into great ontological regions—the modern practice is to separate the region "nature" from the region "mind"—it seems perfectly appropriate to call *Being and Time* a "regional ontology of man," or, to use an equivalent expression, to call it a "philosophical anthropology."

The only obstacle to such a reasonable interpretation is Heidegger's own, almost obstinate insistence that his treatise is not a regional but a fundamental ontology (KPM, 188ff., G3, 208ff., KPM(E), 142ff.). Its sole aim is to show how an understanding of being is at all possible, and why the being understood in it must have a temporal character. The inquiry into man's existence, Heidegger insists, is only the concrete way toward this aim. Why is this plain and unambiguous statement yet so puzzling? Because it is by no means self-evident why Heidegger's sole aim should make an analysis of all the essential structures of man's being necessary. Why cast the net so widely to catch a single fish? To understand being, we are inclined to think, must surely belong to man's reason, or self-consciousness, or to whatever faculty of understanding he may be shown to possess. Why does Heidegger take such an apparently circuitous way for working out his problem?

Because, according to Heidegger, man's understanding of being is not an isolated faculty, nor merely a part of himself, but determines through and through his whole way of being: man's way to be is to understand. Man is so that in his concrete, factical existence his being is manifest to him as *I am*. This unique character of man, that he exists understandingly, is not confined merely to his thinking or cognitive activities, but a priori determines all the ways in which he can be; for instance, he cannot be even a body in the same way as a merely living organism (HU, 67, W, 155-56, G9, 324, P, 247, BW, 204-205).

It is man's unique way of existing that metaphysical thinkers tried to explain by ascribing his understanding of being to his soul, or reason, or self-consciousness, or to whatever other interpretation of man's essence they may have given. With such interpretation, however, man is broken into two, if not three, layers—body, soul, and spirit—so that an explanation of his being becomes well-nigh impossible. What should be the ontological character of this pieced-together man? Does he exist really, or ideally, or partly one way and partly another way? Man, Heidegger insists, cannot exist ideally, as a disembodied spirit, as a pure I, as an absolute consciousness, because, as we shall see later, his "thrownness" into a world a priori belongs to and helps to constitute his "spirituality." Nor, on the other hand, can man exist merely really like a stone, which is essentially hidden to itself in its being. Man's way to be is unique: it is as far removed from an ideal-being as it is from the real-being of a thing. Even the living-being of the highest animals is separated by an abyss from man's way of existing (HU, 69, W, 159, G9, 327, P, 249, BW, 207). Beings like plants and animals are not merely real like stones: their way to be is to live. But they are wholly absorbed in living, whereas man transcends, goes out beyond living; that is, to him the finiteness of living is wholly disclosed, and this alone, as *Being and Time* sets out to show, is what enables him to understand both himself and others in their being.

No animal as such, not even the highest, can treat a thing as the thing it is. This way of understanding things, as far as we know, is the unique distinction of man. But just because it is native to him, it usually remains unnoticed. In his ordinary, everyday existence, man lives in a "preontological," that is, implicit understanding of being as a matter of course. It seems the greatest commonplace to him that to the merest glance a thing like a tree, for instance, should present itself as something that is. He is usually too absorbed in his business with the tree itself to notice the remarkable fact that if the *is* were missing from the tree, not merely the word "is" would disappear, but also the tree *as* tree. He might, it is true, be still aware of it in some other way which is difficult for us even to imagine, but the tree could no longer present itself as the thing it is, in its specific tree-being. Consequently, there could be no such word as "tree." If the *is* were missing from our language, there would be not a single other word and no language at all (EM, 62, IM, 68, G40, 87).

Since in his usual absorption in things, man constantly overlooks that which enables him to exist as man, his unique understanding of being, philosophy is needed to take being for its explicit and, according to Heidegger, its only proper theme. At the same time, philosophy can be nothing other than a radicalization of the vague, average understanding of being in which man always and already exists. "The covert judgments of common reason," and they alone, as Kant said, are "the business of philosophers" (quoted by Heidegger on page 4 of *Being and Time* and frequently elsewhere). Accordingly, Heidegger chooses just the ordinary, everyday manner of existence for the concrete basis of his "Preparatory Fundamental Analysis of Da-sein" (Division One). Its task is not only to show what is essentially, a priori constitutive of man's average manner of being, but at the same time to explain the elemental trend toward the world that characterizes everyday existence. Only when the self-disguise that lies in man's lostness to his world has been explicitly laid bare, can a more original and radical understanding of being be made accessible for investigation (Division Two). Man's way to be is to understand being. This way of being is unique to man. Consequently, all possible articulations in the idea of being must come to light in the essential structures of man's existence, and it is only there that they can come to light. Once this is clearly seen, it becomes evident that in examining how the whole man is, and how he wholly is, Heidegger is far from taking a circuitous route to a distant goal. He is, in a sense, at the goal already with the first step; that is, he is already examining the possibilities enclosed in the idea of being as such. On the other hand, it is true that in each of its phases the inquiry moves into a deeper ontological level, so that while the whole of *Being and Time* makes up the fundamental ontology, it is only in Division Three that the fundamental ontology can come fully to itself.

Some of the most basic and most puzzling features of the detailed working out of Heidegger's problem will be the theme of the series of studies contained in this book. Formidable difficulties of thought and language will be encountered by us there, but they are, in the last resort, only the visible outcrop of far simpler, much more basic difficulties that arise from the nature of the problem itself. To consider these briefly is the immediate and final task of the present exposition of Heidegger's question.

The first difficulty is not peculiar to Heidegger, but characterizes all ontological inquiry. It is a curious feature of *Being and Time* that while it evidently addresses itself first and foremost to the philosophical world, Heidegger by no means takes a genuine understanding of ontology for granted. On the contrary, he constantly stresses the unique character of ontology: that its proper theme is being; that being is nothing like beings or their real properties and qualities and cannot be derived from our experience of them and, above all, that to realize all this is the first indispensable step toward any philosophical understanding.

Heidegger's frequent recurrence to this theme is so marked that one would be inclined to ascribe it to some special circumstances connected with *Being and Time*, were it not that the same tendency becomes even more pronounced in Heidegger's later works. In these, the reader is constantly invited not to accept on hearsay, or be content with a merely verbal comprehension of the statement that being only "is" in the understanding and not in things, but to take his first step into philosophy genuinely by experiencing for himself the impossibility of finding the *is* in any of the things that are concretely accessible to him (e.g., WHD, 107, WCT, 173–74).

Why is this step into philosophy so difficult to take? Partly because being is much less easy to grasp than beings, but partly also because experiencing things in terms of their being seems so natural to us that it is as if it could not be otherwise. The tree, for instance, presents itself to the merest idle glance as something that *is*; it seems to bring its *is* along with itself. The impression is hard to eliminate that the *is* somehow belongs to the tree just as much as its shape, its color, the texture of its bark, the glossiness of its leaves. A little thought, however, will show that all these things are something; they belong to the real of beings, so that we already understand them in terms of the *are*. We may examine the tree further, we may even think of the things we cannot directly experience, such as the processes of life going on in the tree, growth, nutrition, chemical changes, and so on. But again, all these things are something, they belong to beings, and not one of them can give us the slightest hint or clue as to how we have come by the *is* and the *are*. Only one thing is certain: being is not something in addition to beings, but is the way in which these beings come to our understanding. They themselves can therefore never explain how we have come to understand them the way we do.

If the *is* can be found anywhere, it can evidently be found only in ourselves. But when we turn to ourselves, what do we find? Sensations, thoughts, feelings, desires—and these also are something, although not in the same way as the tree. Strictly speaking, we should not talk of our thoughts and feelings as though they were objects, but should say: I am feeling so and so; I am thinking this or that; I am experiencing such and such a sensation, and so forth. It turns out, then, that the *am* is already understood in all that we can concretely grasp in ourselves, just as much as the *is* is understood in the tree. The *am*, far from being more easily cornered than the *is*, seems to be even more elusive. We never seem to be able, as it were, to get "behind" it, but, on the contrary, it is there before us in every concrete experience of ourselves.

Our constant familiarity with the *is* and the *am* brings about a difficulty that has a special bearing on Heidegger's problem—the difficulty of genuinely experiencing how strange and even uncanny it is that we should understand ourselves and other beings in terms of the *am* and the *is*. Without some such experience, Heidegger's thought can indeed be comprehended as an intellectual construction, but the philosophic passion and excitement which are almost palpable in *Being and Time*, and which alone could sustain the stupendous effort of thought embodied in this work, remain strange and baffling.

The commonplace familiarity of our understanding of being not only makes it hard to appreciate what Heidegger is "worrying about," but even raises a doubt whether his undertaking is not doomed to failure. Is it not hopeless to try to find out how our understanding of being is possible, when it is so near us that we can never get away from it? There is, according to Heidegger, one possibility: although being is always manifest to us, we can experience it in a new way, when it suddenly loses its matter-of-course familiarity. It is dread that reveals the commonplace in its utter strangeness and uncanniness. Dread singles each man out and brings him elementally face to face with the *that I am*. Hence the incomparable revelatory power of this basic mood and its methodological importance to an inquiry that seeks to penetrate through man's being to the meaning of being as such.

But the *that I am*, as Heidegger insists, can only be understood by a man in his own unique, factical existence. The remarkable ontological "circle-structure" of man's being, to which Heidegger repeatedly draws attention, leads us to the inmost meaning of the problem of being. On the one hand, the manifestness of being a priori determines man's whole way to be, enabling him first of all to exist as man, but, on the other hand, being requires and needs the unique, factical existence of a man for its manifestness. The "circularity" of the problem of being, however, is totally different from the "vicious circle" which may lie in a deductive proof. Nor must it be thought of as a geometrical circle. It is a circling whereby being and man circle round each other. The circularity of its problem is not a secret weakness at the heart of philosophy, but rather is its distinction. The task is not to avoid or suppress the circle, but to find the right way to get into it. The way found by Heidegger in *Being and Time* has been briefly indicated: the approach to being is made through the analysis of the being of man. If we now ask whether there are other ways of "getting into the circle," the question aims at taking *Being and Time* out of the isolation in which we have hitherto discussed it and showing its place in Heidegger's thought as a whole.

The extraordinary difference between the two divisions we have of *Being and Time* and Heidegger's later works has been the subject of much comment. The change is indeed startling enough to have given rise to the opinion that there is a complete break between *Being and Time* and other early works, and those that come after. The manifest untenability of this view, however, soon led to the opposite extreme. The tendency in recent years has been to minimize the difference and ascribe it mainly to a change of theme, of style and language. While this view is not unsound, it still fails to go to the heart of the matter. What changes in Heidegger's later works is his way of "getting into the circle." Being is no longer approached through man's understanding, but rather it is man's understanding that is approached through the manifestness of being. Only some such change could explain why so fundamental a concept as the "horizon of understanding" completely disappears from Heidegger's later thought (GE, 38ff., DT, 64ff.). Through a lifetime of philosophical activity, embodied in a wide range of works, Heidegger asks the same question, but he illuminates it by different ways of circling the same circle.

PART TWO

Basic Features and Problems of Being and Time

INTRODUCTORY

The first question usually addressed to a work of such universal scope as Heidegger's is how its theme has been divided and articulated. This question is of special importance in approaching *Being and Time*, because, unless it is properly answered at the start, the whole treatise remains incomprehensible. As a fundamental ontology, *Being and Time* differs radically from other ontologies that divide the realm of beings into regions and subregions. What is articulated in *Being and Time* is not the all of beings, but man's [Da-sein's] way to be, and that means at the same time his way to understand being. Its articulation gives the following threefold unity.

1. Da-sein understands itself first and foremost in its own being. This being is called by Heidegger existence (*Existenz*). The full structure of Da-sein's being, whose difference from existence will be discussed presently, receives the name of care (*Sorge*).
2. Da-sein understands itself as being in a world. An understanding of world is an essential, irreducible constituent of Da-sein's way of

existing. The inquiry into the being of world goes hand in hand with the analysis of Da-sein's existence. The ontological structure of world is called by Heidegger the worldishness or worldliness of world (*die Weltlichkeit der Welt*).[1]

3. An understanding of its own being in a world enables Da-sein to meet other beings within the world and disclose them in their being. Some of these beings are like himself; they are fellow men, whose being has the same character of existence as his own. Some are unlike himself; they are things in the strict sense of the word, and their being has the character of reality (*Vorhandenheit, Realität*). The inquiry into the being of other beings goes hand in hand with the analysis of Da-sein's own existence (self) and of world.

As this short sketch already indicates, Heidegger unfolds his theme, in its threefold articulation, as a single unity. It is true that he may turn his attention specially now to Da-sein's self, now to world, and so on, but since these are in advance seen as articulations of a single understanding of being, the highlighting of one does not plunge the other two into darkness but brings them simultaneously to greater clarity. Heidegger conducts his inquiry as the driver of a three-in-hand handles his team, flicking now one horse, now another, but urging them forward all the time as one single team.

Heidegger is well aware that his approach may lay him open to the charge of being purely "subjective." Hence it is his constant concern to correct such misapprehensions, by stressing that Da-sein's understanding of his own being in a world is precisely what gives him access to other beings and gives them the chance to show themselves in what and how they are. It is important that the approach to things should be appropriate to their way of being, so that they can show themselves genuinely as they are. The most difficult among all beings to approach, however, is Da-sein himself, owing to his tendency to cover over his understanding of his own being by giving himself away to things.

Finding proper access both to Da-sein and to other beings, and securing original evidence for every conclusion reached, is Heidegger's constant preoccupation throughout *Being and Time*. The method he employs is one founded and developed by Husserl. Heidegger's method, in fact, is an application and adaptation of Husserl's phenomenology to his own problems. But it should be pointed out straightaway that this method is one of the grave difficulties of *Being and Time* for those readers who are unfamiliar with Husserl's work, even the basic principles of which are hard to grasp. And just because they are, a discussion of phenomenology has been deferred to the seventh chapter of this part, though the logical order would require it to be placed at the beginning.

One of the characteristics of *Being and Time*, owing largely to its method, is the marked difference between Divisions One and Two, and there is no doubt that if Division Three had been added to the work, it would have proved different again from what has gone before. The peculiar "phasing" of the investigation poses a problem for anyone writing a general introduction to *Being and Time*. At this stage, therefore, the present writer has deemed it best to set out Heidegger's principal themes in separate studies. The series of studies contained in this part are grouped as follows.

I. The Being of Da-sein

The unique character of man's or Da-sein's being is discussed in contrast to the being (reality) of things. The meaning of existence and care is provisionally explained, and the conclusion is reached that Da-sein's being must be characterized as a finitely free being. The basic ways in which Da-sein is "free" to exist are then examined. This is followed by an explanation of the most important technical terminology of *Being and Time*, concluding with a separate discussion of the meaning of *Da-sein* and of its possible renderings in English.

II. The Worldishness of World

The fundamental structure of Da-sein's being as being-in-the-world is the subject. Because of its exceptional difficulty, Heidegger's idea of world is here treated at considerable length. Then follows a discussion of theory and practice, and of the meaning of *Umwelt*.

III. The Reality of Beings within the World

The reality of the beings Da-sein meets within his world will prove to be understandable in two main ways: as substantial reality or objective presence and as handy reality (*Vorhandenheit* and *Zuhandenheit*). These are distinguished and explained.

IV. Being-with-Others and Being-One's-Self

The self in relation to other selves, and the repercussions on one's own self of being together with others in the world, are the themes unfolded in this chapter. The inquiry leads to the exposition of the fundamentally "falling" ("falling prey," "entangled," disowned) way in which Da-sein is himself mostly in his everyday existence.

V. The Basic Mood of Dread (Angst) and the Being of Da-sein as Care

The culmination of Division One in the analysis of dread and in the exposition of the structure of care is presented in a summarized form and elucidated as far as possible.

VI. Truth, Being, and Existence

Heidegger's existential interpretation of truth, and the way in which existence and being essentially belong together with the phenomenon of truth, are the subjects of this study.

VII. The Concept of Phenomenology

Heidegger's explanation of the concept of phenomenology is summarized and the importance of the phenomenological method for *Being and Time* discussed. A few steps into Husserl's phenomenology are taken, and the point at which Heidegger diverges from Husserl is indicated.

VIII. A Preview of the Tasks and Problems of Division Two

A short outline is given of the theme and development of Division Two, serving the twofold purpose of a preliminary introduction to more detailed study to be made in Part III of this Guide, and of indicating the perspective in which Division One must be seen to be fully understood.

I

The Being of Da-sein

1. EXISTENCE, EVERYDAYNESS AND DA-SEIN

(a) Existence and Care, in Contrast with Reality

"Da-sein exists." This frequently repeated sentence is the hardest to understand in the whole of *Being and Time*. Its difficulty has to be specially stressed at this point, not only because the sentence itself looks simple, but because it might be thought that it should be understandable already on the basis of our preceding discussions. In fact, we are still only slightly prepared for it. There is only one thing that is already certain: the sentence cannot be a statement of fact. Different as a fundamental ontology may be from other ontologies, it must share with them the general character of ontological statements. Their distinction is that they do not tell us about facts, but about the way in which something must a priori, necessarily, be by virtue of its own essence. Heidegger's sentence must conform to a general type, which may be formulated as follows. Insofar as there is an *X* at all (e.g., a material thing, nature, space, number, language, etc.), it must a priori, by essential necessity, be in such and such a way, otherwise it could not be *X*. Accordingly, "Da-sein exists" tells us that insofar as there is Da-sein at all, it must by essential necessity be in the way of "existence," otherwise it could not be Da-sein.

The character of Heidegger's sentence makes it clear that, in its context, the term *exist* cannot have the usual meaning of *real existence*.

If it had, Heidegger would be saying nothing about the distinctively human way of being, but would be giving us a pure tautology. Granted, however, that Heidegger is really saying something essential about man as Da-sein, the term *exist* can only mean the unique way in which man is: he *is* so that he understands himself in his being. To be in this way, that is, to exist, is according to Heidegger the "essence" of man.

The expressions *to exist* and *existence* are in *Being and Time* exclusively reserved for man.[2] The "real existence" of beings other than man is called by Heidegger "real being" or "objective presence" (*Vorhandensein*), and the structure of this mode of being is called "reality" (*Realität*). The living-being of plants and animals is only occasionally differentiated from the real-being of things, although Heidegger often stresses the difference between them and urges the need for an ontology of life. This task, however, cannot be taken in hand in *Being and Time*, because it requires for its basis an already completed fundamental analysis of Da-sein. The full structure of Da-sein's being would have to be reduced and deprived of its uniquely "existential" features to arrive at what must necessarily be, in order that merely-living-being should be possible (SZ, 50).

The basic distinction drawn in *Being and Time* is thus between the existence of Da-sein and the reality of beings that are not Da-sein. "To exist" and "to be real" are the two main ways in which beings can be. A real thing like a stone *is* in such a way that it is essentially hidden to itself in its being. Its reality is characterized by a certain passivity, in the sense that it is manifest only to us, but not to the stone itself. Hence the stone is necessarily indifferent to its own being, or, more precisely, it *is* in such a way that it is incapable even of indifference.

At the other end of the scale, Da-sein exists in an actively disclosing way. The disclosure concerns first and foremost Da-sein himself: it is its own being that Da-sein most originally understands. This understanding, moreover, does not belong to Da-sein in general, but belongs to each Da-sein singly and uniquely. It is only in his own factical existence that a man can understand "I myself am this man; this being is *mine*." The extreme individuation of Da-sein, that to each one his being is manifest as *my* being, is an essential and therefore "universal" character of existence. Da-sein is thrown into and delivered over to the being which is his and which he *has* to be. His ability to be this being is for him at stake (*es geht um*).

In the three words, *es geht um*, Heidegger gives us a first hint of the peculiarly "out-going" and "fore-going" structure of existence, but, as often happens, the hint is unavoidably lost in translation. The general meaning of *es geht um*, "it is at stake" or "it is the issue," is certainly intended by Heidegger. For Da-sein, it is his own being that is at stake. But it is a distinction of Heidegger's language that many of his key words and phrases directly exhibit the thought to be conveyed and carry the attention forward to other important ideas with which they are closely connected. In the phrase we are considering, for instance, the key word *um*, "for," in advance refers us to the basic character of existence as the original and primary *Umwillen*, "for the sake of." Since for Da-sein his own being is at stake, his existence has the basic character of *for the sake of*. The connection, which Heidegger shows simply and directly by the language itself, can only be established in translation by long and roundabout explanations. On the other hand, such explanations can often be very helpful in introducing a new theme and leading into the detailed analyses in which Heidegger painstakingly works out his theme and brings the requisite evidence. Needless to say, without a thorough study of the latter even the most correct comprehension of Heidegger's key concepts hangs rootlessly in the air.

Our present discussion can conveniently take its start from the *for the sake of* as the fundamental character of existence. What does *for the sake of* imply? It undoubtedly suggests something like a purpose, an aim, an end; and not merely a partial end, which may in turn be used as means to some further end, but what is usually called an "end in itself." Heidegger, however, does not have a specific end in view, which may be either chosen by us or given to us, but seeks to explain, among other things, how man must a priori be in order to be capable of conceiving something like an end or aim at all. To understand this more concretely, let us start from the familiar experience of pursuing some definite aim and consider what is necessarily required to make this experience possible.

The most obvious characteristic of an aim is that it cannot be a fact, something that a man already is or has: according to common experience, an aim is something that a man has "before him," "ahead of him." When a man sets himself a specific aim, for instance, of climbing Mount Everest, he conceives it as a possibility that he may or may not achieve sometime in the future. Until then, he lets this possibility in advance determine all the steps he takes here and now: he undergoes most rigorous training, exposes himself to hardship and danger, bends his energies toward organizing his expedition, collecting the equipment, and so forth—and all this for the sake of a possibility that may never be realized, and on whose outcome he stakes his life.

Remarkable as the pursuit and achievement of such an aim is, for Heidegger it is even more remarkable how man must be to be capable of conceiving something like an aim at all. For this, he must be able to throw himself forward into a future, to discover as yet completely "nonexistent" things and events and take his direction from them for what should be done "here and now." Above all, he must be able to understand himself not only in that I am, but in the possibility that I can be (e.g., I can be the Mount Everest climber), and thus come toward himself, so to speak, clad in his possibilities. In other words, man must be able to transcend, to go out beyond himself as he already is to the possibilities of his being, and it is this unique way of being that Heidegger calls existing.

If man were merely real in every here and now, and his existence were made up from a series of hops from now to now, he would be incapable of disclosing possibilities, of understanding himself in his own ability-to-be (or potentiality-of-being, *Seinkönnen*), and so of conceiving any aim or end at all. But more than that, the remarkable way in which man exists in and from his possibilities is not merely incidentally tacked onto his *I am*, but is the way in which man most essentially is and understands himself. To be constantly ahead of, in advance of, itself is the basic character of existence, and is made possible by the "fore-throw" structure of understanding, which will be more fully discussed in the next chapter. The *I am* is primarily understood from the fore-throw of an *I can be* (I am able to be); man as Da-sein exists primarily from the future.

In the phrases "it is at stake" and "for the sake of" Heidegger gives us a first hint of how Da-sein is disclosed to itself in its possible-being (I can be), and so brings us to the heart of the concept of existence, because it is in the disclosure of possibilities that the utmost illumination of man's own self is gathered. To exist as himself, moreover, is not merely one of man's possibilities among many others; it is his *truest* or *ownmost possibility*. What Heidegger means by "ownmost possibility" (*eigenste Möglichkeit*) is, of course, still obscure, and it is in the nature of such concepts that they can never be wrenched open all at once or be fully penetrated in any single approach. All that is clear at the moment is that the difficulty and problem of existence gathers itself in the concept of possibility, and to clarify this must be our immediate aim.

As soon as we begin to consider what is meant by possibility, we are dismayed by the diffuseness and elusiveness of this concept. The diffuseness shows itself in the many different ways and senses in which the concept can be legitimately applied. First and most frequently, we talk of possibilities in an empirical sense, meaning that this or that can happen to a thing, or that such and such occurrences may or may not take place. These possibilities are contingencies applicable, in Heidegger's sense, only to real beings (things). It is true that this and that can also happen to Da-sein, but, just because for Da-sein its own being is at stake, even the accidents that can befall it have quite a different meaning from the contingencies that can happen to a thing. Further, we talk of possibilities in the sense of potentialities—for example, the potentiality of a seed to grow into a tree, or the possibilities of Da-sein to develop its inborn faculties and dispositions.

These factical possibilities, however, are obviously not what Heidegger has primarily in view in his inquiry. Let us turn, therefore, to the philosophical meaning of *possibility*. Here again we find that the term has a wide range. First, there is the empty, logical concept of possibility as the sheer thinkability of something—that is, something can be thought without contradiction or absurdity. Further, possibility is one of the modalities or modal categories of being, in contrast to actuality and necessity. Here possibility means what is only possible, but need not be actual and is never necessary. Traditionally, possibility is held to be "lower" than actuality and necessity, whereas Heidegger emphasizes that, as the ontological character of existence, possible-being is "higher" than any actuality (SZ, 143f.). Further, the essence, the whatness of a thing, is traditionally also called possibility. The essence is that which makes it possible for a thing to be as it is.

Possibility in the last-named sense is relevant also to Heidegger, who calls it *Ermöglichung*. It is the constitutive "power" that "empowers," "enables," "makes capable of. . . ." When Heidegger speaks of the "essence" (*Wesen*) of Da-sein, he usually means possibility in the sense just defined. Accordingly, the well-known statement that the "essence" of Da-sein lies in its existence (SZ, 42) does not mean, as some interpretations would have it, that Da-sein first of all "really exists" (really occurs) and then proceeds to produce its own essence; that is, to make itself into who it is by exercizing its freedom of choice. It means that understanding itself in its own ability-to-be enables Da-sein to be Da-sein in the most essential respect, namely in respect of its self.

Confusing as the many meanings of possibility already are, an even greater difficulty arises from the elusiveness of this concept. There is something quite ungraspable about a possibility, even when we think of it in the most concrete sense as the possibility of some real happening. The question is whether this ungraspability is due to some failure in our thinking, or whether it lies in the very being of possibility itself. In what way can a possibility *be* at all?

To answer this question, let us consider an empirical possibility in contrast to an empirical fact. Supposing on a journey we approach a certain district and come on a scene of devastation caused by an earthquake the day before, the disaster comes to our understanding as a fact which, having occurred, is and cannot be altered or undone. Now let us suppose that we approach another district and find people fleeing from it, because an earthquake had been predicted for the following day. This earthquake obviously comes to our understanding in quite a different way from the one we experienced as a fact. What and how is this earthquake which is not yet, but is coming? It is not a fact; it is not real; it does not "exist" at all; and yet it is—as a possibility. The whole being of this earthquake lies in our understanding it as a possibility, as something that can be. The disaster that has already happened is a real event, regardless of whether any man discovers it and understands it in its reality. But an earthquake that has not yet happened, *only* is insofar as there is man to discover it in its possible-being. Had the earthquake tomorrow not been predicted, and it really happened, it would always be discoverable as a fact, but never again as it is now, as a possibility that bears down on us in its uncertainty and threat, not the less threatening because it may not really happen after all.

Events that come toward us from the future evidently only *are* as possibilities, as events that *can be*. The remarkable thing about them is that their being is in advance determined by a *not*. The *can be* in itself implies that it can also *not* be. It would be impossible for us to understand the "can" unless we understood it as "possibly not." Even when we are so certain of something that we say it *must* be, we are implying that it cannot be otherwise, because the conditions are such that all possibilities except one are *impossible*. It does not matter, therefore, how some future event is disclosed—for example, whether the earthquake is predicted by the strictest scientific calculation, or on empirical evidence, or by casting a horoscope. This determines only the ground and degree of its certainty, or likelihood, but does not in the least take away the *not* that in advance belongs to our understanding of possibilities as such.

It is clear, therefore, that the disquieting elusiveness of possibilities lies in their very being, and does not primarily arise from the imperfection of our thinking or the uncertainty of our knowledge. But if already an empirical possibility, such as we have discussed, is hard to grasp, how much more so Heidegger's interpretation of existence as "possible-being," (potentiality-of-being, ability-to-be). The manifold implications of this concept are for the most part still obscure, but one meaning at least is beginning to emerge: existence is that way of being which is capable of going out beyond what is to what is not, and so discloses not actual things or beings, but the *possibility* of beings, the being of beings in the mode of possibility.

But how is such a remarkable thing possible that Da-sein can understand the being of something that is not? Presumably only so that the *not* in advance reveals itself in and with Da-sein's own being. The key phrase, *es geht um*—it is at stake—gives us a first hint of how the *not* is originally manifest to Da-sein. How could his own being be at stake for Da-sein, unless it were in advance disclosed as a being he stands to lose? Da-sein exists, that is, understands himself in his being from the constant possibility that he can also *not* be. This harsh and forbidding *not* is far from being a mere negativity, an "empty nothing." It is in the highest sense positive. It enables Da-sein to understand the possibilities of his own being and those of other beings. It is the source of possibility as such.

Understanding himself in the jeopardy of his being reveals to Da-sein that the being he stands to lose is solely and singly his, and not another's. The *not* that can end his being threatens him alone in his own ability *to be*, and so brings him into the uniqueness of a finite self. To exist as himself is Da-sein's *ownmost* possibility. It is most his own as against his other possibilities of being with other beings. His ability to be himself is disclosed from the utmost end of Da-sein's being, and cannot therefore be referred to any further "end." The possibility of his own end, moreover, does not reveal itself to Da-sein as some indifferent "fact," but strikes at him in the heart of his being. Hence Da-sein's ability to be can never be the means to some end beyond itself, but is for its own sake.

Accordingly, when Heidegger says that Da-sein exists for the sake of himself, he is not advocating, as might easily be thought, a ruthless selfishness, but is stating the ontological problem of who is and how there can be a finite self. If in his concrete existence Da-sein is able to understand something like a "for your sake," "for his sake," "for this and that" at all, and so set himself specific aims and ends, it is only because his own self is in advance disclosed to him in its finite possibilities as the primary and original "for the sake of" (WG, 37, W, 53–54, G9, 157, ER, 85, P, 121–22).

Da-sein's existence is thus at the opposite extreme from the reality of a thing, which is such that it can neither care nor not care for its own being. Da-sein not only cares, but, as Heidegger's interpretation will show, Da-sein's being *is* care.

The concept of care, which is elucidated only at the end of Division One (chap. 6), is apt to lead to confusion and bewilderment. Why, the reader may not unreasonably ask, does Heidegger first define Da-sein's being as existence, only to show in the end that it really is care? To make matters even more difficult, the elaborate care-structure worked out by Heidegger at the end of Division One refuses to show the slightest resemblance to any care we may have concretely experienced. It is, as Heidegger himself stresses, a purely ontological-temporal concept, whose meaning (*Sinn*) will be shown in Division Two to be time.

The reason why the concept of care cannot be elucidated earlier in the inquiry lies in the extraordinary complexity of Da-sein's being, which can be brought to light only gradually in the course of a long and difficult analysis. Heidegger, it is true, announces already at the beginning (SZ, 57) that the being of Da-sein is to be interpreted as care. The trouble is that this preliminary announcement, as well as all further references to care in the course of Division One, remain ultimately incomprehensible without a much fuller explanation than Heidegger stops to give. To alleviate the reader's difficulties, we shall now attempt a provisional sketch of what is meant by care, and especially of the relation in which it stands to existence.

Care is Heidegger's name for how the whole Da-sein is, and how he wholly is. But Da-sein is in an extremely complex way, which can be articulated into three main structures: existence (self), thrownness (facticity), and fallenness (or falling prey or entanglement). The first of these three articulations of care we have already discussed: in existing, Da-sein is constantly out beyond himself, throwing himself forward into what is not, disclosing it as a possibility. This original disclosure is not a conscious discovery or a thinking out of what might come, but lies in the fore-throw or pro-jective structure of care, which Heidegger calls *understanding*. The temporal meaning of this "forwardness" or "ahead-of-itself-ness" of care is evidently the future. In Heidegger's interpretation, the future will turn out to be the primary mode or ecstasis (standing-out-of-itself) of time.

But Da-sein can only be ahead of, beyond himself, insofar as he already *is*. Bringing his possibilities toward himself, he necessarily comes back to himself as he already, in fact, *is*. The "fact" of his being, which Heidegger calls facticity, is revealed to Da-sein as his being already here, thrown into a world, left to himself to be as he can in the midst of beings upon which he is dependent. The whence and whither of his being are hidden, but the fact "that I am and have to be" stares him in the face in inexorable mysteriousness (SZ, 136). The curious phenomenal character of the *I am* is that it can never be grasped except as *I already am*—that is, *I am as having been*. The time-character of Da-sein's thrownness is the past, the has-been or having-been.

Fallenness, or as it might be more fully paraphrased, "falling prey or captive to the world" (*Verfallen*), is a trend toward the world which is basic to Da-sein's being, and which has already been mentioned as Da-sein's tendency to give himself away to things, to scatter himself in his occupations in company with other people, literally to disown himself. The ecstatic character of fallenness is the present.

A genuine understanding of this short sketch is not possible at this stage. Its purpose is to show how the three main structures of Da-sein's being—existence (self), thrownness (facticity), and fallenness, falling prey or entanglement—are articulations of the original whole of care, and not parts or components of which the whole is made up. And care itself, it should be observed, is the unity of time—future, past, and present. Even so, this might be misleading were Heidegger's interpretation of time not kept in view, an interpretation designed to show that Da-sein does not merely exist "in time" like a thing, but "originates," or "brings himself to ripeness" as time (*sich zeitigt*). Man himself exists as time: when there is no man, there is no time.

But now, to return to the question of existence, just because it is as care that Da-sein exists in such a complex and excentric way—ahead of himself, thrown back on to himself, losing himself—we can legitimately say that "Da-sein exists," meaning the whole of his being and not merely a part of it. In the articulated whole of care, it is true, existence names only one strucure, but it is a structure in a whole which is so originally one that any one of its articulations necessarily implies the others. When we say "Da-sein exists," we are already saying, though not explicitly expressing it, that he exists factically (facticity, thrownness), and that thus factically existing, he is already falling away from himself to the things he meets within his world. Similarly, when we speak of thrownness, we already imply that this thrown Da-sein is in the way of existence, because only in coming back to himself in the possibilities of his being can Da-sein find himself already thrown into a world, and not merely occur in it like a thing. Similarly, when we speak of falling or fallenness, we are already implying existence and thrownness, for only a being who understands his being in a world can lose himself to the things he meets within it. For a stone, it is impossible to lose itself.

Nevertheless, it is not without reason that Heidegger says emphatically "Da-sein exists," rather than "Da-sein is thrown" or "Da-sein is falling away from himself." In the articulated whole of care, existence has a certain precedence, it plays a "leading" role. In it is gathered the most unique character of Da-sein's being and the possibility of its utmost illumination. As the "fore-going" way of care, existence may be called in a preeminent sense the "light" of Da-sein's being. At the same time, as Heidegger always emphasizes, Da-sein has an ontological circle-structure: the "light" of existence is only possible to a thrown and fallen being. The same thought is implied in one of the formal announcements (*formale Anzeige*) that Heidegger gives of existence: each Da-sein "*is* always essentially" his possibility. He "does not merely 'have' that possibility only as a mere attribute of something objectively present" (SZ, 42).

How is this cryptic sentence to be understood? A thing, according to Heidegger, cannot be its possibility, but may in an imprecise way be said to "have" it. We say, for instance, that a meteorite "has" the possibility of falling in space, of entering the earth's atmosphere, becoming overheated, exploding, and so on. As we have seen earlier, the whole being of a possibility lies in its being disclosed as a possibility. From where are the possibilities of the meteorite disclosable at all? From its essence, its whatness, that is, its being a material thing. The possibility of its motion, heat, divisibility, and so on, is manifest from the properties of matter and not from its own unique being. The meteorite is only a sample of the possibilities of material things in general, which do not in the least require the "existence" of this particular meteorite for their disclosure.

With Da-sein, on the contrary, the factical existence of a unique self is required to be its own possibility. The essence of Da-sein is to understand his being as the possibility that is singly and uniquely his own. This possibility cannot be disclosed by some "Da-sein in general," but only by a single Da-sein, to whom it is his own being that is at stake. Each Da-sein, therefore, is his possibility—only his own factical existence can manifest itself as the possibility that is uniquely his. The circle-structure of Da-sein's being comes to evidence, and must do so, whenever he is regarded in the light of his own essence—and his essence is centered in that "forward-going" way of care that Heidegger calls existence.

It is clear, therefore, that if Da-sein is to be explained fundamentally, from the way of being distinctive of him, and not merely empirically, from some specific point of view, for instance, for medical or sociological purposes, within the strict limits that such purposes prescribe, the inquiry must in advance have the whole Da-sein in view in his own unique existence. It cannot reduce Da-sein to something less than he is in himself, and explain him from what he is, from his genus and species, his environment and his society. On the contrary, the inquiry will have to show, among other things, what are the ontological conditions of the possibility that Da-sein can be social, and why it is that a world not only essentially belongs to him, but that he tends to lose himself to it.

But, it may be asked, is it not strange that Heidegger should consider Da-sein's tendency to lose himself so fundamental to him, when at the same time he holds that to exist as himself is the very essence of Da-sein? This strange inconsistency, however, will prove to be only apparent when we turn to a topic that has not yet been touched upon, namely the various possibilities that lie in existence itself. In developing this theme, we shall also come to understand more fully the statements discussed above, that each Da-sein "*is* always essentially" his possibility. He "does not merely 'have' that possibility only as a mere attribute of something objectively present." The theme to be considered now may be briefly summed up in the thesis that existence is in itself a *free* way of being.

How is freedom to be understood in an ontological sense? It obviously cannot be what we usually mean by freedom—for example, the ability to choose this course of action rather than that, or to pursue this end in preference to another one. All these "freedoms," all acts of will aiming at achieving this end rather than that, already presuppose that we understand the possible being of what is aimed at and that we can direct ourselves to it as a "for its sake." For Heidegger, freedom means the original disclosure of being, and in a preeminent sense our understanding of our own being as the primary *for the sake of* (*Umwillen*; literally, for the will of). This freedom is the original "will" that brings before itself its own possibilities as "for the will of." The disclosure of the possibilities of his being sets Da-sein free for different ways of being himself. It is, therefore, not a priori determined by the structure of existence how a Da-sein's being is to be his. On the contrary, it enables Da-sein to relate himself to his own ability-to-be in profoundly different ways, and so leaves it open how each factical existence is a self. Existence is thus a *free* way of being, because the possibility of various modifications lies in its own structure.

But, as we have seen, all possibility, all *can be*, is in advance determined by a *not*. In transcending to his possibilities, Da-sein *is* free, but always and only in the way in which he can be free, namely finitely. It lies in the nature of finite freedom that, in giving possibilities, it at the same time withdraws them. Each Da-sein is his possibility, but always and only in one of the ways which are open to him. Da-sein cannot exist in a vague generality, but only in one or another of its definite possibilities. Each Da-sein is one of his possibilities, the others he is not. It now begins to be faintly visible why notness and nothing enter so importantly into Heidegger's idea of being. This *not* which reveals itself so inexorably to each Da-sein, makes possible and articulates through and through his existence as a *finitely free being*.

For a proper approach to *Being and Time*, nothing could be more helpful than to grasp, however roughly and provisionally, the idea of a finitely free being. It is this idea that, in advance, guides and articulates Heidegger's whole inquiry and determines the way in which he gets to grips with his subject. The essence of Da-sein cannot be defined by *what* he is, by the attributes and qualities of a rational animal, because Da-sein is finitely free: his fundamental possibilities do not lie somewhere outside himself but in his own being as care, which is "free" to modify itself in certain basic ways. The essence of this being lies in existence (self). *How* Da-sein is can therefore be defined only by the basic modes or manners (*Seinsarten*) in which it is possible for him to exist, that is, to be a self. It is from Da-sein's basic possibilities that the inquiry must take its lead. Hence each division of *Being and Time* is an analysis of Da-sein's being in a different mode of existence. What the basic possibilities of existence are will be the task of the next section to consider.

(b) The Two Basic Ways of Existing:
Owned or Authentic and Disowned or Inauthentic Existence.
The Undifferentiated Modality of Everydayness

Heidegger calls the two basic possibilities of existence *Eigentlichkeit* and *Uneigentlichkeit*, the usual translation of these terms being "authenticity" and "inauthenticity." This translation, while it is perfectly correct, shifts the weight of the German words from the center to the circumference. Their weight, as Heidegger explicitly says, lies in *eigen*, which simply means *own*. Therefore, while not abandoning the usual translation altogether, we shall speak of owned and disowned existence, or of being one's own self and of being a disowned self. Since, however, *owned* and *disowned* are very clumsy to use adverbially, we shall occasionally resort to such phrases as "to be a self properly" or "not-properly," where "properly" must be understood in the strictly literal sense of *proprius*, one's own.

The terminology adopted here, especially the word *disowned*, could easily be misleading if it were understood in the sense of an attitude deliberately taken up or a course of action willfully pursued by Da-sein toward himself. This would imply an interpretation of the self that is completely alien to Heidegger. What does Heidegger mean when he speaks of the self? Does he mean that Da-sein first of all exists, and then in addition he is or acquires something called a self? No. Heidegger means that Da-sein is a self in existing, that is, in understanding that "I myself am this Da-sein; this being is *mine*." *How* a Da-sein is himself is determined by the way in which he lets his being be his. No Da-sein has freely chosen his being; he may not have wished it if he had had any say in the matter; nonetheless, he can freely take over his being as his own responsibility, he can turn to it face to face, letting it fully disclose itself as singly and uniquely his. Existing in this way, Da-sein is wholly his own self, according to the fullest possibility of his finite being. Or he can turn away from himself, not letting his being fully disclose itself as his own, covering over its finiteness by throwing himself into those "endless" possibilities that come to him from his world. Existing in this way, Da-sein disowns the possibility of the utmost illumination of which his being is capable and falls into the disguise that characterizes his lostness to the world.

While these basic ways of existing are neither subconscious "mechanisms" nor conscious and deliberate "attitudes," they definitely imply something like a "relation" of Da-sein to himself. Heidegger, in fact, frequently and explicitly speaks of the ways in which Da-sein can "relate himself" (*sich verhalten*) to himself, and means: Da-sein bears himself toward, holds himself in, stands fast in, the possibilities of his being in one way or another, not primarily by thinking about them, but by throwing himself into them as best he can. This "relation" is very near to what we have in mind when we speak of the way in which a Da-sein lives. It is in his "way of living" that a Da-sein stabilizes himself as the factical self he is, that he stands fast in the being he bears in his thrownness as care.

But if each Da-sein's being, regardless of how it is his, is yet essentially his own, it might be reasonable to suppose that he would tend to "own" his being, while a disowned existence would seem to be an exceptional falling away from the average, the norm. Heidegger's thesis, however, is that the opposite is the truth: Da-sein's fundamental tendency is to turn away from himself to a self-forgetful absorption in his occupations in company with other people. Before his existence can be properly his own, Da-sein has usually to wrest it back from its lostness to the world.

In the first place and for the most part (*zunächst und zumeist*), Da-sein understands himself not from his own being, but from what other people think. Instead of the utmost illumination of which he is capable, Da-sein exists in a sort of "public disclosedness," whose very publicity is a way of covering over that each Da-sein's being is singly his own. In the first place and for the most part, this is the way in which Da-sein is himself from day to day, his average day, his every day. Everydayness (*Alltäglichkeit*) is Heidegger's name for the average, undifferentiated way in which Da-sein exists over most of his lifetime, living unto the day, taking for variety what the day brings, what chances and events, what successes and failures come to him from his world. In his everydayness, Da-sein is so decisively orientated toward the world that the possibility of understanding himself from his own being remains obscured. When Heidegger speaks of an "indifferent" everydayness, he does not mean that this mode of existence ceases to be care, or that Da-sein no longer exists for the sake of himself, let alone that he exists neither in one definite way nor in another, but means that the difference between an owned and disowned self does not come to light, it remains undifferentiated.

For Heidegger's "Preparatory Fundamental Analysis of Da-sein" it is precisely this undifferentiated everydayness that is of utmost importance, because it constitutes the average manner of Da-sein's being. But even in this levelled-down uniformity, Da-sein still exists, he still understands himself in his being. Da-sein can only be average in the way of existence and not as an egg or an income is said to be average. Even in the extremity of disownment, Da-sein can never become merely real like a thing, or like an only-living-organism. His way of existing can be modified but can never become a different order of being.

The everyday mode of existence, just because it is nearest and most familiar to us, has been consistently overlooked in philosophy, and its ontological importance has not been realized. As Heidegger's inquiry will show, traditional ontology draws its idea of reality not from the way it is originally manifest in Da-sein's everydayness, but from a secondary and derivative modification of it. A remarkable feature of Heidegger's analysis of everyday existence is its aim to show the complex and mysterious character of this most familiar way of Da-sein's being. It remains the leading theme throughout Division One, while the owned way of existing becomes the main theme at the beginning of Division Two, preparing the way for the interpretation of the fundamental temporality or "timeishness" (*Zeitlichkeit*) of Da-sein's being.

(c) The Ontological-Existential Terminology of Being and Time

Apart from Heidegger's special key words, such as *care, thrownness*, and *worldishness*, there is the purely technical terminology of *Being and Time* to be considered. The new theme of this work requires new terms, some of which are parallel to those of traditional ontology, and some of which are taken over from Husserl's phenomenology, often with a shift of meaning or emphasis. Among the latter, we have already come across *meaning (Sinn)* and *ontological structure (Seinsstruktur)*. We shall now consider the following terms:

Ontological–existential (Ontologisch-existenzial). These two terms are parallel. Understood in the strict sense, ontology should mean in *Being and Time* only those inquiries that have for their theme the being of beings other than man. This restricted meaning of ontology, however, is not consistently adhered to by Heidegger, who often refers to his own analyses as "ontological," when they should be called "existential." The latter term applies only to man's being and to the inquiry that has man's being for its theme. This inquiry calls itself "existential," because it takes its lead from the essence of man, which lies in his existence. Its detailed analyses will show that each of the main structures of care—namely existence, facticity, and fallenness—can be further analyzed into essential constituents (*konstitutive Momente*). These are details in the whole that cannot be detached from the whole, but can be discerned and defined within it as essential to it and helping to make the whole as it is. All the a priori constituents and characters of man's being are given the general name of "existentials" by Heidegger. These require further discussion.

Categories, Existentials (Kategorien, Existenzialien). These two terms are parallel. Categories are those most general characters of being that can be a priori predicated of things—for example, things are of such and such *quality*, *quantity*, so and so *related*, and so on. Categories are hence often called "ontological predicates." This is the general philosophical meaning of *category*, although the term has been variously interpreted in the course of history, and the "tables of categories" set up by different thinkers have varied accordingly. It may be remembered, for instance, that Aristotle includes time and place in his ten categories, whereas in Kant's transcendental philosophy time and space are taken out of the class of categories altogether and receive a new meaning as the a priori forms of intuition. For Heidegger, the decisive distinction is that categories are the a priori characters of the being of things, whereas existentials are the a priori characters of the being of Da-sein. These two, categories and existentials, are called by Heidegger the two main *characters of being* (*Seinscharaktere*).

The new terminology introduced by Heidegger, however, is not merely a convenient way of making fine distinctions; it is demanded by the nature of Heidegger's theme. This can be especially well demonstrated by the difference between a category and an existential. A close study of *Being and Time* shows that the existential characters of Da-sein have an "active" form, and the categorial characters of things a "passive" form. This is not an accident but expresses the difference between Da-sein and things. Da-sein in an active and transitive sense "constitutes" ("forms") being, while the being of things is necessarily a "constituted" being. Let us, for example, consider space. Da-sein is "spaceish"—that is, he in an active way discloses space. The existential constituents of Da-sein's spaceishness are called by Heidegger "de-distancing" or "un-distancing" (*ent-fernen, Ent-fernung*), that is, bringing near, removing or diminishing distance; and "directing" (*ausrichten*), that is, directing himself or something else toward . . . , taking a direction to or from. Undistancing and directing are existentials, which show themselves as the categories of distantness (nearness) and directedness (e.g., to the left, above, below, etc.) in the spatial characters of a thing.

It is, however, not only spatially but also in many other ways that Da-sein can relate himself or refer himself to things. The existential character of self-relating or self-referring (*Verweisung*) appears as the category of relatedness or referredness, which defines the being of things.

Only when the difference between an existential and a category has been grasped, does it become understandable what Heidegger means by saying that the characters of Da-sein's being are not "properties" but ways in which it is possible for him to be (SZ, 42).[3] All existentials, such as undistancing, directing, self-referring, and the like, are ways in which Da-sein is, whereas the corresponding categories show themselves as properties and attributes—that is, the spatial properties, the attribute of relatedness, and so on—whereby the being of things can be determined.

Fundamental ontological-existential constitution (Ontologische-existenziale Grundverfassung or Seinsverfassung). The basic meaning of *constitution* (*Konstitution*) was indicated in the preceding section. The active and transitive verb *to constitute, to make up, to form,* must be primarily heard in the noun *constitution*. In Husserl's phenomenology the term refers to those activities of transcendental consciousness that constitute the essence, the whatness of beings in their familiar types. In other words, these activities originally form the categorial structure of the great ontological regions, which are divided by Husserl into nature and spirit, and subdivided into subregions such as material nature, animality, personal world, and intersubjectivity.

The original meaning of constitution necessarily implies a second meaning—namely an organized categorial whole that defines the essence of a region of beings—and it is in this sense that Heidegger uses the term *Seinsverfassung*. When the term is applied to Da-sein's being, Heidegger usually speaks of *existenziale Verfassung*, existential constitution. A similar meaning can be assigned to the term *Grundverfassung,* basic or fundamental constitution, but it should be noted that a fundamental constitution need not necessarily be sufficient fully to define the being under consideration.

This point will prove to be of some importance for understanding the role that the fundamental constitution of Da-sein, "being-in-the-world," plays in *Being and Time*. Since we are not yet in a position to discuss this difficult structure and show how and where it is deficient, let us try to understand the point in question by considering a more familiar example. If we think, for instance, of nature, it is immediately evident that space must belong to its fundamental constitution, since material phenomena cannot show themselves at all except as being "in space." Descartes, indeed, holds *extension* to be the fundamental ontological character of material nature. The question relevant to our discussion is this: Does the spatial constitution of nature, fundamental as it is, sufficiently and fully define its being? Evidently not, since it alone cannot explain the essential "materiality" of nature. As Husserl, for instance, points out, the merely extended thing of Descartes could never be distinguished from a phantom, a ghost of a thing (*Ideen* II, 36–37, 40, *Ideas* II, 39–41). Materiality (substantiality) could never show itself if a thing appeared solely in and by itself, unrelated to other things. Only in its external relations can its materiality be constituted. The thing must show itself as identifiably the same under changing conditions. Something like interrelation (causality), which in turn already implies time, must therefore belong to the categorial structure of material nature as such.

The categorial whole constitutive of the being of things characterizes their mode of being as *reality*. The whole of existentials into which the being of Da-sein can be articulated constitutes the *existentiality* of existence.

A priori, earlier. Even in our simplest awareness of a thing there lies already the disclosure of something like time, space, relation, and so on. What already lies there in every experience as the condition of its possibility is said to be a priori, "earlier." It is generally agreed that the business of philosophy—that is, philosophy in the strict and not the popular sense—is to inquire into the a priori, but different thinkers have given varying interpretations of how this concept is to be understood. Heidegger understands it as "fore-going and going-hand-in-hand-with" experience (*vorgängig und mitgängig*). Roughly speaking, this means that what is already there in experience as the condition of its possibility does not lie somewhere apart from and in a time before experience. On the other hand, it cannot be derived from or learned by experience: it goes before experience, taking it by the hand and leading it. Fore-going to any experience is the existentiality of Da-sein's existence, on the ground of which he is able to understand his own being, and let other beings show themselves in their being.

Ontic-existentiell (Ontisch-existenziell). The adjective *ontic* is the counterpart to *ontological*. It characterizes beings, not their being. Anything that in any way "exists" is ontic. The synonym for ontic is *existent*, the word to be understood in the traditional sense of real existence, and not in Heidegger's special sense. Approximations to *ontic* are *real, concrete, empirical, given in experience*. While these terms can be used for *ontic* in certain contexts, they do not have nearly so wide a meaning. Heidegger uses the word "ontic" constantly, applying it to Da-sein as well as to things.

Existentiell is only approximately parallel to *ontic* and has a much more restricted meaning, applying only to Da-sein. Heidegger uses the word *existentiell* primarily to characterize the understanding we each have of our concrete existence and of all that belongs to it. For this, a theoretical insight into the a priori existential structure of our existence is not in the least necessary. Da-sein may have no explicit philosophical understanding of himself, or may interpret his own being as reality. This does not prevent him from having a genuine and profound *existentiell* understanding of himself. Conversely, a philosophical insight does not guarantee that Da-sein is existentielly transparent to himself in his concrete existence.

Summary. It may be found helpful to summarize Heidegger's technical terminology in the following schematic contrast:

existentiell	is parallel to	ontic
existential (adj.)	"	ontological
existential (noun)	"	category
existential structure	"	categorial structure
existential constitution	"	ontological constitution
existentiality	"	reality

It should be noted that Heidegger usually couples the terms as existential-ontological and sometimes also existentiell-ontic. The addition of "ontological" and "ontic" does not alter the meaning of *existential* and *existentiell*, but serves to remind the reader that the inquiry is not one of the traditional style: it is an existential ontology, which is simply another name for fundamental ontology. It must also be stressed once more that Heidegger frequently applies the simple terms *ontological* and *ontic* to Da-sein. This practice will be followed in this book when the long compound expressions would be too clumsy to use.

2. A Discussion of the Meaning of *Da-sein*

The question to be considered first is why Heidegger rejects the word *man* (*Mensch*) and adopts the term *Da-sein*. His reasons have already been touched upon in previous discussions, so that it is sufficient at this stage to recapitulate the relevant points.

(a) *Man is never a "what."* The word *man*, considered from a logical grammatical point of view, is a collective noun like *house, table, tree,* and so on. Nouns of this type gather concrete individuals into a class, and the class indicates the whatness of its members. But man is never a what. His essence (self) lies in his existence. His existential constitution sets him free for different modes of being himself. How a man exists can therefore never be determined by any whatness, and the word *man* is inappropriate to the kind of being man is.

(b) *The being in which each man understands himself is his own.* The class name "man," more precisely defined, is the name of a species of living beings, on a par with horse, sheep, and sparrow. The concrete individuals that belong to a species are regarded as cases or samples representing their species. But a man can never be merely a case or a sample of the species *man*, because what makes it possible for him to exist as man is not his species, but his understanding of himself in his being. For this reason, also, the word *man* has to be rejected as inadequate.

The *positive reason* that led Heidegger to choose the term *Da-sein* can be briefly indicated as follows: The fundamental characters of man's being are not properties and qualities, but ways in which it is possible for him to be. *Da-sein* expresses being, and nothing else. It is a translation into German of the word *existentia*, and its usual meaning is simply *real existence*. Unfortunately, there is no expressive way in which *Da-sein* can be translated into English, as an explanation of its meaning and form will clearly show.

Purely linguistically considered, *Da-sein* is a compound of two words, whose second component, *sein*, means simply *to be* or *being*. This *to be*, since it expresses the being of a man, must be understood as the infinitive of the *am*, and not of the *is* of a thing. The first component, the *Da*, indicates a place, a here and there, and this is why in some translations *Da-sein* is rendered by "being-here" and in others by "being-there." In fact, *Da* is neither here nor there, but somewhere between the two, for which we have no exact equivalent in English; it is a much more open word than either "here" or "there," and does not have a definitely localized meaning.

Is there any way in which *Da* and *Da-sein* can be at least approximately expressed in English? Perhaps the best approach to it can be made by taking the phrases "there is . . ." and "there are . . ." for a starting point. In these phrases, the "there" evidently does not mean a definite place in which something occurs, but the whole phrase means the "thereness" of something. If we take "there-being" ("there to be") as the infinitive of "there is . . . ," we arrive at the traditional meaning of *Dasein*: real existence, the real "thereness" of something.

But as for man, his there-being cannot mean merely the real occurrence of man among the all of beings. On the other hand, Heidegger does not twist the original meaning of *Dasein* out of all recognition: it does mean primarily the factical existence, the thereness of man in a world. Only, this thereness has to be thought in Heidegger's sense as an event which brings the illumination of being into the world-all, and does so because it is a disclosing way of being. The implications suggested by Heidegger with the word *Da-sein* may be unfolded in the following way. When there is man, the "there is . . ." happens; man's factical existence (his being-there) discloses thereness, as the thereness of himself, the thereness of world, and the thereness of beings within the world, some like himself and some unlike himself.

This interpretation of *Dasein* follows Heidegger's own (SZ, 132ff.), and far from saying too much, it does not nearly exhaust all that Heidegger suggests with this simple and eloquent word. As far as its English translation goes, the nearest approach that can be made is probably "there-being" or "being-there." But the shortcomings of this expression are unhappily many. First and most importantly, it refuses to be eloquent. Secondly, it cannot suggest all the meanings required. And thirdly, it is a purely ontological term. While in *Being and Time* the ontological meaning of *Da-sein*, as the illuminated-disclosing thereness of being, on the ground of which man exists as man, is undoubtedly by far the most important, the word carries at the same time an ontic meaning: it names the concrete beings we ourselves are. This, in fact, is how Heidegger defines *Da-sein* when he first introduces the concept (SZ, 7). It is essentially a two-dimensional term, with an ontic-ontological meaning.

It is not surprising that this key word presents a problem to every translator and expositor of *Being and Time*. There seem to be three alternatives open, the first of which is to construct an expression like being-here or being-there. This solution has been rejected in this book, for reasons already stated in the preceding paragraph. Secondly, the German word *Dasein* or *Da-sein* could be used in the English text. This solution is in many ways the best, although it presents the danger that *Da-sein* might become merely a technical term in a Heideggerian terminology, instead of being rethought and genuinely understood. Thirdly, a familiar English expression, like *human being* or *man* could be used, in spite of Heidegger's objections to it. Of these two, human being has the advantage of lending itself to the same ontic-ontological use as *Da-sein*: it could mean both a concrete human being and the human way of being. This, however, is offset by several disadvantages, first among them the weakness and lack of character of the expression itself. Further, it defines "being" by the humanity of man, whereas *Da-sein* asks us to do exactly the opposite, namely to understand man's humanity from his being.

But the decisive consideration is that "human being" presents the almost insoluble linguistic problem whether it should be referred to as it or he or she. Human being, in an ontological sense, could only be called it, whereas it goes against the grain in English to refer to a concrete human being in any other way but as he or she. The same difficulty arises in English with any other two-dimensional expression, which names both man and his being in the same breath.

After weighing up all these alternatives, the following solution was adopted in this book. Where the ontological meaning of *Da-sein* is of exclusive or predominant importance, it will be expressed in a way most suitable to the context—for example, as factical existence, as man's being or being-there or occasionally even as being-here. Mostly, however, preference will be given to the word *Da-sein*. Very infrequently the word *man* will be employed on account of its simplicity, although Heidegger's objections to it must always be borne in mind. Above all, it must be remembered that *man* is a purely ontic term and is incapable of bringing into play the ontological meaning of *Da-sein* expressed, for example, in the statement that Da-sein exists for the sake of himself.

II

The Worldishness of World

1. THE FUNDAMENTAL EXISTENTIAL CONSTITUTION OF DA-SEIN: BEING-IN-THE-WORLD. HEIDEGGER'S CONCEPTION OF WORLD

To exist as a self is Da-sein's ownmost possibility, but not by any means the only one fundamental to him. The possibility of relating himself to other beings inseparably belongs to Da-sein's existence. Da-sein is indeed so essentially self-relating that his understanding of himself as the primary *for the sake of* already gives him his bearings in a world. It directs him in advance to the things he may meet as the *means by which* something can be done *in order to* accomplish this or that. This, in turn, may do service for some purpose, which may be directly or indirectly *for the sake of* a possibility of his own existence. The whole complex of "by means of . . . in order to . . . for . . ." springs from and leads back to Da-sein's own being, with which it is disclosed in an original unity. This relational complex forms the coherence-structure of the world, or more precisely, as will be explained presently, of the specific kind of world that Heidegger takes to exemplify the idea of world as such. The way in which Da-sein foregoingly refers himself to . . . , directs himself toward . . . , is the condition of the possibility that in his factical existence he never finds himself in a vacuum as an isolated self, but in the midst of other beings in the coherent whole of a world. The original disclosure of Da-sein's own being in a relational-whole constitutes the fundamental structure of his being as being-in-the-world.

The original, indivisible unity of being-in-the-world is taken by Heidegger as the *minimal* basis on which Da-sein's being can be explained. In this fundamental constitution ". . . the-world" does not mean a real connection of real things, but characterizes the unique way in which Da-sein understands himself: ". . . the-world" is an existential-ontological concept, which gives no information about any ontic world, but formulates the problem of the possibility of world as such.

At the same time, as Heidegger constantly emphasizes, all ontological concepts must have an ontic basis. If we, in our concrete existence, did not always and, as if it were by necessity, understand ourselves "in a world," the ontological inquiry would remain groundless. The *ontic* concept of world from which Heidegger's analysis starts is that of a world in which a factually existent Da-sein "lives" (SZ, 65). Why Heidegger puts the word *lives* into quotation marks will become clear later. For the moment, it is more important to note that Heidegger takes for the basis of his inquiry the ordinary, workaday world of everyday existence (*Umwelt*). This eminently practical world, in which things hang together as ends and means, is obviously very different from any theoretical conception of "world" as a causally connected natural universe, as well as from the vaguer concept of a totality of beings, which leaves the nature of the "totality" completely undefined. All these ontic concepts of "world"—namely, nature, the natural universe, the all of beings—are decisively rejected by Heidegger, so much so that when he uses the term *world* in any of these senses, he always writes it in quotation marks.

Three different meanings of the term *world* have now been indicated, and, since they must be clearly distinguished in *Being and Time*, the following summary may be found helpful:

1. In the existential constitution of Da-sein as being-in-the-world, ". . . the-world" characterizes the way in which Da-sein exists. It is an existential-ontological concept.

2. The ontic-existentiell concept of a world in which Da-sein "lives," and more specifically, the nearest workaday world of everyday existence (*Umwelt*), forms the basis and starting point of Heidegger's analysis. It is from this world that his concrete illustrations and examples are drawn.

3. The "world," always written in quotation marks in *Being and Time*, means a real connection of real beings, usually understood as nature, or the totality of beings, but sometimes also denoting a more indeterminate whole of things, facts, people, etc., of which we

usually imagine the world to be "made up." It must be judged from the context in which of these senses the "world" is to be understood, but in every case the quotation marks should be noted with care, because they draw attention to concepts that not only diverge from Heidegger's, but no longer mean a world at all. According to Heidegger, the phenomenon of world can never be explained from concepts like nature, the universe, the all of beings, etc., because they themselves already presuppose an understanding of world.

On what grounds does Heidegger put forward such an unusual thesis? Let us consider the concept of nature. Difficult as this may be to define, it is evident that nature in the ontic sense is something that is: it belongs to the realm of real beings. And even when nature is used as an ontological-categorial concept, it can only mean the being, the reality of actual or possible real beings as a whole. Whichever the case may be, certain preconditions must be fulfilled before these real beings can make themselves manifest as the beings they are. The first condition is obviously that they must in some way be accessible to Da-sein, that Da-sein must be able to meet them in the same world in which he already finds himself. To be able to do so, a world must already be disclosed, and can never be retrospectively "made up" from the things met within it.

The same consideration applies to the concept of a totality of beings. In whatever way the "totality" may be explained, one thing at least is certain: the totality must have a radically different character from a sum total, not only because no conceivable addition could ever arrive at the "total," but because every single thing added together would already have met us in the predisclosed whole of a world. It is evident, therefore, that the world cannot consist of things, nor of things and people added together, because understanding ourselves in a world is the condition of the possibility that we can meet any kind of beings at all. Least of all can the world itself have the character of a real thing. When we ask What is world? we are already blocking the way to a genuine understanding of this phenomenon, because with the "what" we are usually on the lookout for a thing or the essence of a thing. The world is not a thing, but Da-sein himself is worldish. He is, at the bottom of his being, world-disclosing, world-forming. Da-sein alone is such that he foregoingly, a priori, understands his own being in a relation-whole, in which and from which he can meet other beings and understand them in *their* being.

The disclosure of world thus proves to be an essential constituent of Da-sein's understanding of being, and as such belongs to the central problem of *Being and Time*, namely, How is it possible for Da-sein to understand being? What does being mean? The fundamental constitution of being-in-the-world is not, as it is sometimes thought to be, an *answer* to Heidegger's question, but is a sharper and fuller formulation of the question to be answered. In this formula, ". . . the-world" is a vast question mark, whose meaning has been briefly indicated in the preceding paragraph, but which must now be more fully explained as follows.

Da-sein, as the finite being he is, cannot himself make the beings he needs, and cannot therefore know anything in advance of their real qualities and properties, which are vital to him for his own existence. Unable to create anything, Da-sein must be able to receive what is already there, and not merely anyhow, in an unintelligible jumble of impressions, but in such a way that these things become accessible as the things they are, understandable in their being. This is only possible if they can show themselves in a coherent whole, which is not merely an empty frame, like an iron hoop holding a jumble of things together, but is a whole that has a definite structure of its own, so that in it and from it the multitude of beings are in advance understandable in an *articulated* coherence. This structural whole (world), which Heidegger will show to be a complex of references or relations, must enable Da-sein to refer himself to other beings in a purposeful way, and, conversely, to relate them to himself in their relevance to and bearing upon his own existence.

The articulated **whole** of a world, as was indicated above, is always understood by us in **advance**, and cannot be retrospectively glued together from any number of sense impressions and perceptions of actual things, events, or people. On the contrary, if these perceptions did not take place in a previously disclosed whole, any coherent and intelligible experience would be impossible.

The disclosure of world necessarily goes before experience, and one possible explanation is that the world must be "formed" in and with Da-sein's own being. Da-sein himself is "world-forming," or, as it may also be expressed, "world-imaging" (*weltbildend*. WG, 39, W, 55, G9, 158, ER, 89, P, 123). This "world-image," of course, must not be thought of as a sort of advance copy of a flesh-and-blood world, but as a wholly insubstantial horizon of meaning, a whole of reference in which we always move with so much familiarity that we do not even notice it. The ontological problem is to show and explain in detail how Da-sein himself must be in order to be capable of "fore-imaging" a world to which experience has contributed nothing. This is the problem that Heidegger formulates with the fundamental constitution of Da-sein as being-in-the-world.[1]

How does Heidegger propose to solve his problem? What is the basic thought that guides him? It may be summed up in the following thesis. The very finiteness of Da-sein makes it both possible and necessary for him to "form" a world. It is because his own being is in advance disclosed to him in its dependence that there lies in it already a disclosing reference to the being of other beings.

This basic thought is clearly hinted at in the reference complex "by means of . . . in order to . . . for . . ." that was briefly mentioned in the first paragraph of this chapter.This complex is a simplification of a much more elaborate structure worked out by Heidegger in his world analysis (SZ, Div. One, chap. 3). For our purpose, which is not to follow up the details of Heidegger's analysis, but to get an insight into his fundamental idea of world, it is sufficient to grasp that this relational complex, only more elaborately articulated, forms the structure of world, and it is with its help that Da-sein in advance refers himself to . . . , directs himself toward . . . , anything that might appear within his horizon.

For the point we are considering, the "by means of . . ." is especially illuminating: it is in itself a document of Da-sein's finite being. If Da-sein were a perfect substance, distinguished by independence and self-maintenance without recourse to anything apart from itself, he would not need to refer himself to a thing as the "means by which. . . ." More than that, it would be inexplicable how, as a perfectly self-contained being, he could even understand that something might be needful or useful for accomplishing something else.

It is because Da-sein's being is disclosed to him in its jeopardy and dependence that it must in advance refer him to the possibility of meeting other beings and prescribe the ways in which they can bear on his own existence, for example, by way of dangerousness, usefulness, harmfulness, and so on. To solve the problem of world, Heidegger must show in detail how this disclosure takes place and what are those existential structures capable of performing the task of disclosure.

Of the basic structures that have a specifically disclosing function, Heidegger names three: *Befindlichkeit*, which may be rather inadequately rendered as "attunement"; *Verstehen*, understanding; and *Rede*, discourse. The last will not enter into the discussion at present, and, since it may easily confuse the reader, it should be noted that by "discourse" Heidegger does not mean the ontic phenomenon of language, but an existential structure that makes language possible.

The existential concept of *Befindlichkeit* cannot be adequately expressed by any single English word. The common German phrase, *Wie befinden Sie sich?* means: How do you feel? How are you? *Sich befinden* generally means how one is, how one feels. Important also is the core of the word, *sich finden*, to find oneself. The whole expression may be explained as follows: Da-sein is a priori so that his being manifests itself to him by the way he feels; in feeling, he is brought to himself, he finds himself. The ontic manifestations of *Befindlichkeit* are familiar to everyone as the moods and feelings that constantly "tune" Da-sein and "tune him in" to other beings as a whole. To avoid having to coin some clumsy expression for *Befindlichkeit*, it is convenient to call it "attunement."

In Heidegger's interpretation, attunement must on no account be taken for a "lower" faculty which is at war with the "higher" faculty of understanding. For one thing, neither attunement nor understanding are faculties, but existentials, that is, ways of being. Each has its own character and way of disclosing that is not only not opposed to the other, but is in advance "tuned in" to the other. Attunement always has its understanding; understanding is always attuned. Each has a specific disclosing function in the whole of care.

The moods and feelings, which are apt to be dismissed by us as accidental and meaningless, are ontologically of great importance, because they originally bring Da-sein to himself as the factical self he already is. Each mood reveals in a different way—for example, in joy Da-sein is manifest to himself as he who is enjoying himself, in depression as he who is weighed down by a burden, and so on. Tuned by moods and feelings, Da-sein finds himself in his thrown being, in the inexorable facticity "*that* I am and have to be," delivered over to myself to be as I can, dependent upon a world for my own existence.

Moods and feelings rise from Da-sein's thrownness and bring him face to face with it. By "thrownness," Heidegger does not mean that Da-sein is cast into the "natural universe" by a blind force or an indifferent fate, which immediately abandons him to his own devices, It means that his own "real" existence is manifest to Da-sein in the curious way that he can always and only find himself *already* here, and can never get behind this *already* to let himself come freely into being. But although he can never originate his being, yet he is "delivered over to himself": he *has* to take over his being as his. Da-sein's fundamental impotence and dependence, that he cannot make and master his own being, are originally and elementally revealed by attunement.

But moods and feelings tune Da-sein not as an isolated self; on the contrary, they bring him to himself in such a way that he finds himself there, in the midst of other beings. With this "in the midst of ...," Da-sein is already lifted into a world, surrounded by beings that are always manifest in a certain wholeness. *Why* this is so cannot yet be shown, but *that* it is so is not an accident; it lies in the structure of attunement itself to refer Da-sein to the possibility of other beings as a whole. Moods and feelings, far from being "inarticulate," have a distinctively articulated structure. This can best be demonstrated by Heidegger's analysis of fear as a specific mode of attunement (SZ, § 30), which we shall now consider as far as it is relevant to this discussion.

In the mood of fear, three main articulations can be distinguished: "fear of . . . ," "fear itself" (fearing, being afraid), and "fear for. . . ."

In fear as "fear of . . ." there lies already a disclosing reference to other beings, which can approach from the world in the character of the fearsome. Fear in advance refers itself to something definite, whether it is another Da-sein, or a thing, or an event, which can approach by way of a threat from a definite direction. It should be observed that in fear as "fear of . . ." there must already be disclosed something like a relation-whole, something like a neighborhood, from which some definite thing can approach as the fearsome.

"Fear itself," the fearing (being afraid), discloses the fearsome by opening itself to its fearfulness, by letting its threateningness strike home. It is not that some future evil is first discovered as an objective "fact" and then feared, but fear itself discovers something in its fearsomeness. It is only because Da-sein himself is constantly tuned by latent fear that he can "in fact" discover something as threatening. A detached observation and investigation of an object could never find out that it is fearful.

Existential attunement is the condition of the possibility of what Heidegger calls *Angänglichkeit*. *Angänglich* means in the first place approachable, capable of letting something come near. *Angehen*, as in the phrase, *es geht mich an*, means: it is my business, it is my concern, it touches me, it strikes me, moves me. On the ground of attunement, Da-sein is approachable, concernible, touchable, strikable, capable of being affected and moved by whatever may approach him from the world. Da-sein could never be affected through the senses, if attunement did not in advance throw him open to be affected in various ways; for instance, something like resistance could never be discovered by the sense of touch, if Da-sein were not in himself already "touchy."

For Heidegger, affection and perception through the senses are not primary, "ultimate" phenomena, but are founded in—that is, require for their necessary foundation—the more original phenomenon of attunement. It is clear also that in Heidegger's interpretation, receptivity through the senses is not a pure receptivity, a mere passive soaking up of what is given, but is grounded in the spontaneous activity of attunement, which throws Da-sein open and constantly keeps him open to whatever may approach from the world.

The same thought is expressed by Heidegger in the phrases "letting be" (*Seinlassen*) and "letting meet" (*Begegnenlassen*), which the reader constantly meets in *Being and Time* and are often felt to be obscure and confusing. These phrases imply that Da-sein's finite being-in-the-world is neither the creativeness of an infinite Being, who can make actual, concrete beings, nor, on the other hand, is it the pure passivity of something made. It is a spontaneously active receiving of what is already there, in the course of which things are set free in their being (*freigeben, Freigabe*); they are delivered from their hiddenness and given the possibility to be disclosed in their being. This disclosure happens when Da-sein "throws a world" over things, within which they can show themselves as and for the things they are.

But, as far as our discussion has gone, it is still not clear how the world itself is disclosed, or, to speak more precisely, how Da-sein's own being is manifest to him as being-in-the-world. It is true that in Heidegger's hands a mere mood has already revealed more than would have been thought possible, but so far, the "wholeness" of a world has always been presupposed. Let us now turn to fear as "fear for . . ." to see what further light it can throw on our problem, and whether attunement, taken by itself, can make the disclosure of being-in-the-world fully understandable.

Fear is always "fear for. . . ." In being afraid, Da-sein is afraid for himself. Da-sein is capable of fear, because in his being it is this being itself which is at stake. The threat to his ability-to-be makes manifest to Da-sein his deliverance over to himself. Even when the fear is not directly and immediately for his own being, but for property and possession, Da-sein still fears for himself, because his access to things, his "being near to things" essentially belong to his being-in-the-world. Similarly, when Da-sein is afraid for someone else, he still fears also for himself, being threatened in the most fundamental relational possibility of his existence, his being with others like himself (*Mitsein*).

What has this summary of Heidegger's analysis of fear brought to light? What and how does attunement disclose? It discloses Da-sein in his existence (self) *as* already thrown into a world, in the midst of other beings, upon which he is dependent. Attunement not only throws Da-sein open to the possible thereness (thatness) of other beings, but different moods in advance prescribe *how* their thereness can show itself: joy discovers it as joyful, pleasure as pleasing, fear as fearsome, and so on. Attunement is itself a way of being-in-the-world. It rises from the depth of Da-sein's thrownness and reveals, more elementally and far-reachingly than any thinking can overtake, that he is and has to be, dependent upon a world and being borne in upon by what might befall him from it.

But although attunement reveals elementally and far-reachingly, it yet fails to illuminate fully the meaning of what it reveals. Attunement itself constantly delivers Da-sein over to the beings in the midst of which he finds himself. In his thrownness, Da-sein falls captive to his "world"; he is enthralled and bemused by the things that are; he is pressed in upon and hemmed in by them (*benommen*). To achieve freedom of movement and full illumination, Da-sein must somehow free himself from his thralldom to what is, he must transcend beings as a whole, among them first and foremost himself. But what is it to which Da-sein can transcend? He transcends to the *possibilities* of his being. Not from how he is, but from how he can be, does Da-sein become transparent to himself as the thrown self he already is.

The disclosure of possibilities *as* possibilities is the achievement of existential understanding. In Heidegger's interpretation, understanding is not a cognitive faculty, like comprehending or explaining, but is a basic way of existing. It is, in fact, nothing other than the "fore-structure" of care, whereby Da-sein is constantly before himself, ahead of himself. Since understanding is a structure of the original whole of care, it must necessarily be "tuned" by attunement. All the possibilities of Da-sein's being that understanding can disclose must hence be possibilities of a thrown and dependent being as disclosed by attunement. Keeping this important thought in mind, let us now examine in greater detail the "fore-throw" structure of understanding and see how it helps to "fore-form" the relational-whole of world.

Heidegger characterizes understanding as an *Entwurf*. *Entwerfen* means to throw forth, to throw forward and away from oneself: *to project*. Similarly, the noun *Entwurf* has the same meaning as a project, something that has been thrown forward, projected. *Entwurf* in the pregnant sense, however, does not mean just any kind of project, like going for a picnic tomorrow, but means the ground plan, the first basic design, the all-embracing conception that in advance encircles the whole and so makes it possible for any details in it to "hang together," to "make sense." Conversely, the fore-throw of an all-embracing whole has its meaning in referring back to all that it embraces. This gives us a clue to the essentially two-way structure of understanding: it throws forward possibilities, but, at the same time, it holds out toward itself what it has fore-thrown. This can be easily tested by us, simply by thinking of some possibilities we are planning to carry out. A little imagination will show that while we throw these possibilities forward, they at the same time turn round and seem positively to look at us.

But the original possibilities which existential understanding throws before and toward itself are not possibilities of empirical things and happenings; they are the possibilities of Da-sein's being as a whole. They can be a whole only because they are in advance manifest from the possibility of a *not*, which ends all his possibilities and thus in advance closes them. The understanding of this not reveals to each Da-sein his being as singly and solely his, and so brings him to himself in the uniqueness of his finite self. But this self is already tuned by attunement to find itself dependent upon a world in which and from which the thereness of other beings presses in and bears upon itself. Hence the possibilities of this self must necessarily be of existing-in-the-midst-of . . . , existing-in-relation-to. . . . The fore-throw, in which attuned understanding brings the whole of the possibilities of Da-sein's thrown being before itself, is the original happening of being-in-the-world.

In going out beyond all "that" and "there," understanding throws open the horizon of the possibilities of Da-sein's being as the world, in which Da-sein can be a factical self among other beings. Understanding thus throws a world over beings as a whole, among them Da-sein himself as he already is (*Überwurf*. WG, 39, W, 55, 158, ER, 89, P, 123). The horizon of world is transcendental. It in advance encompasses the whole of Da-sein's being. Understanding thus opens up a distance between the factical self Da-sein already is and the utmost limit of his possibilities. Only from this distance to himself can Da-sein become fully illuminated as a self that can be himself only and always as the thrown self he already is, referred to beings he has not made and cannot master, but with the essential difference that he can be this self either in the mode of flight and covering over, or he can take over his finite possibilities as fully and wholly his own.

It has now become possible to clear up a puzzling question that the reader may already have asked himself: How can Da-sein "disown" himself to the world and yet exist for the sake of himself? The world, as interpreted by Heidegger, is not something apart from Da-sein, but is Da-sein himself in the whole of his possibilities, which are essentially relational. It is for the sake of these that Da-sein exists: the *for the sake of* is the primary and basic character of world. It is from this horizon that things are first opened up in their possibilities, that is, are understood as the things they essentially are. The essence of things in our ordinary, everyday world (*Umwelt*) is to be means to ends, because the world-horizon that is primarily "meaning-giving" has the basic character of the *for the sake of* Da-sein's own existence.

It has now been shown that an attuned understanding is capable of "fore-forming" a world that not only precedes experience but is far more than a vague, inarticulate wholeness. Attunement not only throws Da-sein open to the being (thatness) of other beings, but in advance prescribes *how* their being is discoverable—for example, as threatening, as joyful, or whatever. The understanding fore-throw of Da-sein's possibilities of being not only embraces them in advance as a whole, but with the *for the sake of* gives a fore-image of how the things discoverable within it can "hang together," how they can "make sense." The relational complex of "by means of . . . in order to . . . for . . . ," whereby Da-sein in advance refers himself to whatever may appear within his horizon, is only possible in an original unity with the *for the sake of*, and constitutes the ontological structure, the worldishness of Da-sein's primary and basic world (*Umwelt*).

This structure, however, as Heidegger explicitly remarks (SZ, 65), is modifiable into the worldishness of specific "worlds"—that is, there are other ways in which Da-sein can relate himself to beings as a whole. It appears, then, that the ontological meaning of the relational structure of world has not yet been fully brought into view, and needs further elucidation.

Heidegger interprets the essentially relational way in which Da-sein understands his being as a *signifying*. The *for the sake of signifies* a *for*, an *in order to*, a *means by which*. Understanding holds out the familiar whole of these relations before and toward itself in an originally disclosed unity, and lets itself be referred by these relations themselves. In his familiarity with these relations, Da-sein signifies to himself, gives himself originally to understand how he is and can-be-in-the-world. The relation-whole of this signifying is interpreted by Heidegger as significance. The ontological structure of world, the worldishness of world as such, is *significance* (SZ, p. 87).

Heidegger's interpretation of the ontological structure of world as a significance-whole makes it understandable that Da-sein's primary world can be modified into specific "worlds," by taking other relational complexes as "significant." Moreover, it completely justifies Heidegger's bald refusal to acknowledge any real connection of real things as world in the genuine sense. The coherence of a world made possible by an understanding of significance is of a totally different order from the real connections of things that persist regardless of whether there is Da-sein to discover them or not. If Da-sein disappears from the face of the earth, things will not fly off into space but will go on gravitating toward the earth, even though there is no one to discover and understand something like gravity. But the *significant* reference complex "by means of . . . in order to . . . for . . ." obviously cannot persist except insofar as there is Da-sein who relates himself to things in this signifying way. Significance—that is, world—only "is" in the understanding of Da-sein, to whom his own being is disclosed as being-in-the-world.

The basic idea that guides Heidegger's interpretation of world was set out earlier in the thesis that the very finiteness of Da-sein makes it both possible and necessary for him to form a world. It is because his own being is disclosed to him in its dependence that there lies in it in advance a disclosing reference to the being of other beings. This thesis has now been elucidated in as much detail as the aim of this chapter requires. Has the discussion brought us to the answer to Heidegger's question, How is it possible for Da-sein to understand being? Not yet. Some important steps toward it have been taken. It has become evident that the original disclosure of being must happen through attunement, which reveals the "that I am," and that the "fore-imagings" of understanding must already be tuned by this disclosure. But as to the innermost possibility of these events, no explanation has yet been given, nor can Heidegger be expected to give it until the end of his inquiry.

For the present, the most urgent task is to get a more concrete grasp of what has emerged so far. This is all the more important because Heidegger's ideas are far removed from our accustomed ways of thinking, and even when all due allowance has been made for the remoteness of ontological interpretations, it may be rightly felt that these must be relevant to our concrete experience or else be banished into the sphere of abstract speculations. Is there any way in which Heidegger's idea of world can be brought nearer to us? Are there any obstacles that obscure its relevance to our experience and which can be removed at this stage?

There is at least one obstacle that can be easily removed. This lies in the strictness of Heidegger's thought and language, essential to philosophy but unnecessary to our everyday existence, as a result of which we often fail to recognize in what Heidegger says the perfectly familiar experience of our own being-in-the-world. For instance, we usually equate being with living, so that we rarely think or speak of being in a world, but rather of living in, or staying in, or moving in a world of a specific character. We do not, for example, say of a woman that she is in her domestic world, but that she lives in it. What we mean by this phrase is nevertheless one specific concretization of being-in-the-world in Heidegger's sense: the possibilities of this woman's existence, we imply, are gathered up in family and home, on which she habitually spends herself. She holds out these possibilities before herself *as the world* in which she is at home. It is in and from these possibilities—from her world—that she understands herself in relation to other beings; and, conversely, it is by reference to her world that she understands other beings in their relevance to and bearing upon her own existence.

This example not only shows the connection between Heidegger's ontological idea of world and the world we "live" in but also helps us to understand one of the most puzzling features of the expression *being-in-the-world*. At first sight, the word *in* almost irresistibly suggests a spatial relation, so that the image formed of the world is that of a vast spatial container in which we occupy an insignificant spot. Heidegger is well aware of this danger, and that is why on introducing the concept of being-in-the-world his first concern is to discuss the meaning of the "in" (SZ, 54). The word, Heidegger explains, cannot have the same spatial-categorial meaning as it has when we speak of an extended thing being *in* an extended spatial container, "as water is 'in' the glass, the dress is 'in' the closet." Da-sein cannot be "in space" as an extended thing but only in the way appropriate to himself as being-in-the-world: he discloses space in relating himself to things by way of undistancing them and directing them to. This existential spaceishness is only possible on the ground of, and as an essential constituent of, Da-sein's fundamental worldishness. Something like space must, therefore, belong to a world, but it is not primarily, let alone exclusively, constitutive of world (SZ, Div. One, chap. 3, B and C).

That the "in" does not have a spatial-categorial meaning was concretely shown by our example. A woman does not live in her domestic world by occupying space in it but by keeping herself to these familiar possibilities of her existence. Similarly, we are not thinking of a spatial relation when we say of a man that he moves in the artistic world or that he is at home in the society world. What Heidegger, in a strictly ontological sense, calls "being-in" is concretely experienced by us as "living-in," or "moving-in," or "being-at-home-in." All these phrases express the same meaning: staying near-to . . . , being-familiar-with . . . , in-habiting (both in the sense of habituation and dwelling) . . . a world of this or that specific character.

Why is it that the world we "live" in is familiar to us always in this or that specific way? Because our possibilities are essentially finite, not only in the sense that they are in fact limited, but because possibilities in themselves have a not-character. These finite possibilities, moreover, are manifest to each one of us as the possibilities of *my* being; the world is therefore always essentially *my* world.

But does this mean that each Da-sein is locked into a world of his own from which he may never truly get across to another Da-sein's world? Any such thought is obviously alien to Heidegger, to whom the world itself is nothing but the reference-whole in which Da-sein understands himself among other beings. Insofar as these other beings are fellow men, they also are-in-the-world in the same way as himself. Da-sein is not only not locked into a world of his own, but the world is his in such a way that he in advance shares it with others like himself.

Da-sein's relation to other Da-seins is shown by Heidegger to be fundamentally different from his relation to things. Being-with others like himself (*Mitsein*) belongs directly to Da-sein's existence (self) and helps to constitute its world-forming character, whereas his being-near-to things (*Sein-bei*) is founded upon his thrownness and factical dependence on a world. Da-sein cannot be with things in a mutually shared world, because things are only innerworldly (*innerweltlich*); they are discoverable *within* the world, but are unable to disclose their own being *in* a world.

When Heidegger speaks of "world" (nature) in quotation marks, he usually means purely an ontic connection of *things*, because beings who exist as Da-sein can never merely occur in nature like things, which have the character of reality. The fundamental difference between the way Da-sein relates himself to fellow existences and the way in which he refers himself to things also helps to explain why Heidegger cannot work out both relations at the same time in his world-analysis (SZ, Div. One, chap. 3). The theme of fellow existences is introduced into the analysis only briefly; its detailed elucidation is left over to a subsequent chapter (Div. One, chap. 4). The ontological structure of world is worked out by Heidegger exclusively from the relation-complex ("by means of . . ." etc.) whereby Da-sein refers himself to things. Following Heidegger's own trend, the theme of Da-sein's everyday self in relation to other selves will be dealt with separately in this book, after the discussion of world and of the reality of things within the world has been concluded (Part II, chap. 4 of this book).

Accordingly, we will at this stage confine our attention to Da-sein's being-near-to things, or, as it may also be expressed, his staying-close-to the "world" (*Sein-bei*). How are Da-sein's dealings with things characterized by Heidegger? Since Da-sein inhabits the world by way of care, each of his fundamental relations must have a specific care-character: he is near to things by "taking care" of them (*besorgen*). "Taking care" is an existential-ontological term whose meaning may be explained as follows. A basic way in which Da-sein inhabits his world is to reckon with things, to take account of things. With Da-sein's factical existence, his taking care of things splits itself up into an extraordinary variety of ways, of which Heidegger gives a long list of examples: "to have to do with something, to produce, order and take care of something, to use something, to give something up and let it get lost, to undertake, to accomplish, to find out, to ask about, to observe, to speak about, to undermine . . ." (SZ, 56). Among the deficient modes of taking care, Heidegger mentions desisting from something, neglecting (an opportunity), taking a rest, and so on.

Da-sein is near to things primarily in a practical way by using and handling them. A deficiency of careful (care-taking) having-to-do-with things makes possible an important modification whereby Da-sein's primarily practical approach becomes modified into the only-looking-at things of theory. Although theory, just as much as practice, is a taking care of things, the theoretical approach represents a profound modification of Da-sein's original understanding of reality, whose consequences are so far-reaching that it requires a discussion on its own (see the next section of this chapter).

Before going on to consider theory and practice, however, the main conclusions reached so far may be briefly summarized as follows.

The world is not a thing, nor does it consist of things. The coherent whole of a world cannot be explained from the real connections of real beings but only from the way in which Da-sein a priori understands his own being in the whole of its possibilities. These possibilities belong to a finite and dependent being and are hence necessarily relational. They are disclosed by attuned understanding in anticipation of possible other beings. The articulated reference-whole (significance-whole), in which and from which Da-sein in advance refers himself to any possible beings he might meet, constitutes the ontological structure, the worldishness of world. It enables Da-sein a priori to understand the being of other beings and is disclosed in co-original unity with Da-sein's own being as the primary *for the sake of*. On the ground of his fundamental constitution of being-in-the-world, a world essentially belongs to Da-sein and its basic character is therefore *the* for the sake of. This prescribes the significance-structure of Da-sein's nearest everyday world in which he takes care of things primarily in a practical way by using and having-to-do-with them. This original way of taking care of things is capable of being modified into a theoretical only-looking-at things. In view of the predominantly, if not exclusively, theoretical approach of Greek-Western philosophy and of the positive sciences that have sprung from it, leading ultimately to the present Atomic Age, Heidegger's elucidations of this problem have a much wider than purely philosophical interest.

2. The Theoretical and Practical Ways of Taking Care of Things

What does Heidegger mean when he characterizes theory as an "only-looking-at" things? Negatively, it must be remarked that the "only" should not be understood in a derogatory sense, although it must be confessed that Heidegger's language would sometimes almost justify such an interpretation. Taken in a strict sense, however, the "only" has a purely ontological meaning. It indicates that something that originally belonged to Da-sein's approach to things has been stripped off, leaving the "only-looking" as the dominant and supposedly the only appropriate way to approach them.

What is it that disappears when Da-sein's practical having-to-do-with things turns into theory? Is it the making and doing which now give place to observation and thinking? Or is it that the sense of touch and the other senses drop into the background, leaving the sense of vision the predominant role it has undoubtedly played in Greek-Western thinking? There is certainly some truth in these suggestions, but in themselves they cannot explain the difference between theory and practice. As Heidegger points out, it is not even possible to draw a clean demarcation line between "doing" and "thinking," between "touching and handling" and "only-looking-at" (SZ, 358). A purely practical man, say a small-scale craftsman, may be doing nothing, only looking at his workshop, thinking of the work to be done the next day, the materials to be bought, and so on. This looking and thinking are yet purely practical. A theoretician, on the other hand, still uses his tools, paper and pen, if nothing else, not to speak of the elaborate manipulation of instruments that may go into an experiment; yet this doing and handling stand in the service of theory. Heidegger takes great care to emphasize these points, but he still insists on calling theory an only-looking. What is missing from this approach to things, and, in the first place, in what way is theory a "looking" at all?

Theory, Heidegger explains in the lecture "*Wissenschaft und Besinnung,*" ("Science and Reflection") comes from the Greek *theôreô* and originally means a reverential gazing upon the pure aspect in which a thing shows itself. "Aspect," in this connection, is to be understood in the Greek sense of the *eidos*, idea, the form in which something shows what it is—its essential being. Theory in the highest philosophical sense means a gazing upon the truth, which takes the truth into its keeping and guards it (VA, 53, QCT, 164).

Theory thus turns out to be the same as, or closely akin to, the apprehending, the "seeing," which has of old been called *noein*, the pure, nonsensuous apprehension of beings in their being. This has been traditionally regarded as the only proper ontological approach to things. Why, then, is it an "only-seeing"? What is missing from it that makes it radically different from the practical way of "seeing" things? It is nothing less than the world. The things that are originally understood as belonging to a world and having their place within it are now stripped of their boundaries; they no longer meet Da-sein in the horizon of the primary *for the sake of*, but in an indifferent world-all, a natural universe, where they occur in space as purely substantial bodies. Theory is an only-looking which strips things of their world-character and objectivizes them into mere material substances to be found somewhere in an indifferent universal space (SZ, 358ff.; also 112).

The incalculable importance of this fundamental modification in Da-sein's understanding of things is that it is from things as mere substances that Greek-Western philosophy takes its start. The consequences of this start for Western science and technology are a constantly recurring theme in Heidegger's later works and deserve serious study. In *Being and Time*, however, the ontological theme predominates, and this is our concern at present.

What are the philosophical consequences of the theoretical start from things as pure substances? The first and most decisive consequence is that the world, in Heidegger's sense, is passed over from the beginning and cannot become even a problem. Nature, the all of beings, is substituted for the genuine phenomenon of world, giving rise to perennial problems of cognition and knowledge, for whose solution countless "theories of knowledge" have been constructed.

Traditional problems of cognition, Heidegger points out, have their source in an insufficient interpretation of Da-sein's being (SZ, 59ff.). The puzzle which hosts of theories of knowledge set out to explain is how a supposedly isolated self, a subject, can get out from his "inner sphere" to an object, the "world" outside himself. But, as Heidegger shows, the completely unjustifiable assumption on which all these theories are based is that Da-sein is first of all a "worldless subject" who has subsequently to transcend himself in order to take up a relation to his object, the "world." In Heidegger's interpretation, on the contrary, Da-sein is never worldless, and the world is not an object to which he has to "get out." Da-sein is such that his own being is in advance manifest to him in a significant reference-whole (world), in which and from which he directs himself toward . . . , relates himself to . . . whatever specific beings he may meet. Only this a priori worldishness of Da-sein makes it possible for him to "take up relations" to things in a secondary and derivative way, for example, in explicitly investigating and explaining them, in widening and developing knowledge in various directions, and so on.

It is the world-forming character of man's being that is presupposed in all theories of knowledge which take their start from the "subject-object relation" as the supposed "ultimate" that cannot be further elucidated. According to Heidegger, on the contrary, it is precisely this "subject-object relation" that demands a fundamental inquiry, so that its inner possibility can be brought to light. All problems of cognition lead back to the existential constitution of Da-sein as being-in-the-world from which they originally spring and on the basis of which alone they can be solved. A deeper inquiry, it is true, will reveal that even this fundamental constitution is insufficient fully to define Da-sein's being, but it is the structure from which the analysis and interpretation must start.

Accordingly, the whole of Division One of *Being and Time*, except for one introductory chapter, consists of an analysis of the fundamental constitution of Da-sein as being-in-the-world, leading toward an exposition of Da-sein's being as care. It has already been shown, however, that Da-sein never is-in-the-world in a vague generality but exists always in one or another of the definite modes or manners (*Seinsarten*) possible for him. In the first place and for the most part, Da-sein exists in the everyday manner of taking care of his "world." The full theme of Division One can therefore be defined as being-in-the-world in the mode of everydayness. The ontic world from which Heidegger's analysis starts is the nearest workaday world of everyday existence (*Umwelt*), and this now requires some further consideration.

3. THE ONTIC BASIS OF THE ONTOLOGICAL INQUIRY INTO WORLD: THE *UMWELT* OF EVERYDAY EXISTENCE. THE MEANING OF *UMWELT*

The term *Umwelt*, together with two other key words, *Umgang* and *Umsicht*, has so essential a meaning in Heidegger's world-analysis that it well deserves a short discussion on its own.

It is not by accident that each of these key words begins with *Um*. This word is already familiar to us as the *for* of *for the sake of*. A second meaning of *Um* now appears for the first time: it indicates the spatial relation of round-aboutness, nearness, in the sense of immediate surroundings. From what we have learned so far, it is evident that for Heidegger the primary meaning of *Um* is *for*, but, since something like space essentially belongs to a world, the secondary meaning of round-aboutness must also prove to be relevant.

We shall first consider *Umwelt* in its secondary meaning, because this is how in ordinary usage the word is generally understood. Accordingly, *Umwelt* means a world that is round-about us, a world that is nearest, first at hand. There is no appropriate single word in English for *Umwelt*. For most purposes, it can be quite adequately rendered by "environment," but this rendering will not be adopted here. Owing to its biological and sociological flavor, "environment" seems alien to Heidegger's thought and might perhaps with advantage be reserved for an ontology of life, where the "world" of plants and animals could fittingly be called environment or surroundings.

One suggestion that Heidegger undoubtedly intends to convey with *Umwelt* is of a world that is closest and most familiar to Da-sein, a world in which he in the first place and for the most part lives. We shall paraphrase *Umwelt* by "surrounding world," with the sense of "the first and nearest world." It becomes immediately evident how excellently Heidegger's "exemplary" world has been chosen; it is, in a sense, a universal world, since no matter in what age or society, or under what particular conditions Da-sein may live, he cannot, as it were, bypass a world that is first and nearest to him.

For his own illustrations, it is true, Heidegger goes by preference to the world of the small-scale craftsman, but this is only because a small workshop is peculiarly suitable for demonstrating all the essential feaures of Da-sein's everyday world. For instance, the reference complex of "by means of . . . in order to . . . for . . ." can be vividly shown by the use of tools on the work in progress; "nature" enters as the source of materials needed for the work; the "others" are also there as the merchant who delivers the materials or the customer for whom the clothes, the shoes, and so on, are "made to measure"; with the others, the common, public world is also indicated. For purposes of illustration, the little world of the craftsman could hardly be bettered; but it would be a complete misunderstanding to think that Heidegger has only this specific type of world in mind. All that essentially belongs to Da-sein's nearest world must be the same regardless of class or age or social-economic developments; its significance-structure must be the same regardless of whether anything is produced in it or not: we only need to think, for instance, of the world of the "idle rich" or of the bedridden invalid.

There is, moreover, a definite way in which Da-sein in his everyday existence inhabits his world, and this is what Heidegger calls *Umgang*: Da-sein goes about the world and goes about his business with the things he meets within it. *Umgang* basically means the practical, using and handling way of taking care of things, whose difference from a theoretical only-looking-at things has already been indicated. It must not be thought, however, that the practical having-to-do-with things is blind: it has its own way of "seeing," that is, of understanding, which Heidegger calls *Umsicht*, meaning literally, *looking around, circumspection.*

Having taken the *Um* in its spatial sense, the three key words have now come into view as: the *world round-about us* (the first and nearest world); *going about* the world and *about* our practical business with things; looking around, *circumspection*. Suggestive as all this is in itself, what Heidegger intends to say comes fully to light only when we turn to the *Um* in its primary sense of *for*.

Da-sein's first and nearest world is evidently the for-world, in the strict sense that the form, the "how" of its coherence is given by the *for the sake of* his own existence. This prescribes the character of significance, the specific for-worldishness of the everyday world, by the relational complex "by means of . . . in order to . . . for. . . ." Da-sein inhabits his nearest for-world by going about his business in it: his going about is *for* something, whether the something is directly for his own sake, or for the sake of others or whether it is in order to achieve something else to be taken care of. Da-sein's going about his business for something is in advance guided by a circumspect for-sight, which discovers what things are *for*, under what circumstances they can be used as means. What circumspect for-sight has "its eye on" in advance is the primary world-form of *for the sake of*, with which the whole significance-structure of "by means of . . . in order to" is disclosed in an original, indivisible unity. With the concept of circumspect for-sight, Heidegger gives an existential-ontological explanation of what is familiar to us as common sense. The Da-sein of common sense sees things in advance in the light of their possible utility, harmfulness, relevance, or irrelevance to circumstances. The commonsense view is only possible on the basis of an existential understanding, which fore-throws the possibilities of Da-sein's existence as his world, in the "light" of which alone the possibilities of things in their relevance to . . . , their bearing upon . . . this or that situation become understandable.

But now the inevitable question arises. Is this everyday understanding of things not merely "subjective"? Is the only-looking of theory not truer, because it is more "objective"? These questions will be dealt with in the next chapter, where the reality of beings within the world will be our theme.

III

The Reality of Beings within the World

The preceding chapters have already shown that reality has a much more restricted meaning in *Being and Time* than in traditional ontologies. Not only Da-sein's being is taken out of the sphere of reality but also all existential phenomena, such as, for instance, time and world. These only "are" when a disclosure of being happens. There is one phenomenon of a rather ambiguous character, however, which requires some consideration, and this is language. The existential foundation of language is, indeed, obvious, and yet it is readily overlooked. The reason is that the words of a language can be collected and preserved in books, in which they acquire a certain reality within the world; they become accessible just like things. Hence one can get the impression that language consists of word-things to which meanings are added. The truth, according to Heidegger's interpretation, is exactly the opposite: Da-sein's factical existence discloses world as a significance-whole that can be articulated into those "significances" for which words grow (SZ, § 34, esp.161).

The sphere of reality is thus restricted by Heidegger to those beings that are independent of a disclosure of being—for example, plants, animals, the earth, the seas and the stars. All these real things, with their ontic properties and connections, are independent of the disclosure that happens with Da-sein's existence. They are there, regardless of whether they are discovered or not. Their being, their reality, on the other hand, is only understandable to Da-sein and can never be independent of his existence.

But, as we have seen, things can be approached and discovered in different ways. The two main possibilities we have considered are the practical and the theoretical approach, and of these two, Heidegger maintains, the practical is primary, while the theoretical is secondary and derivative. Things are originally discovered and understood in their reality by the circumspect for-sight of everyday care. This discovers things not as mere substances that happen to be there in a universal space but as utensils that are handily there within the world. Reality thus shows itself in the first place not as the substantial presence of indifferent things but as the handy presence of useful things. The ontological character of the things that meet us within the everyday world is handiness (*Zuhandenheit*).

But, it may be objected, even granted that Heidegger is right in saying that we first understand the reality of things as handiness, these things must already be there in nature before Da-sein ever comes on the scene. Are metaphysics and the sciences, each in its own way, not objectively truer, do they not come nearer to things as they are in themselves, just because they understand them in their substantial reality? Is handiness, after all, not merely a subjective coloring we impose on things?

These objections may be briefly answered in the following way. It is certainly true, Heidegger would say, that things must already be there for us to find, otherwise we could never find them. But this is not the point in question. The point is how it is possible for us to understand the "being there" of things at all. We primarily understand that things are handily there, not for any accidental or arbitrary reasons, but because they can become accessible in their being only within a world. Everyday care understands the being of things from their relevance (*Bewandtnis*) to a world, and this is the way in which they can be discovered as they are "in themselves." It is quite erroneous to think that handiness is a "subjective coloring" we cast over things: it is a mode of being prescribed by the significance-structure of world, which enables us to understand things as they are "in themselves." Our everyday having-to-do-with things could never decree the apple tree to be handy if it were not "in itself" handy, at hand, and if its fruit were not "in itself" handy for eating. It is only from long tradition and habit of thought that we almost automatically dismiss what we call "merely subjective" as untrue. If we could not discover things "subjectively"—if we could not let them touch us, concern us, be relevant to us—we could not discover them at all.

Only on the basis of the already discovered handiness of things does their merely substantial presence become accessible. The change from the one to the other comes about by a break in the intimate, completely taken-for-granted reference complex, from which things are understood as things for. . . . Owing to this break, Da-sein takes a new look at things, which now show themselves as merely substantial things of such and such qualities and properties. It is only now that the mere whatness of things comes to the surface and hides what they are for. With this change, things are cut off from the *for the sake of* by reference to which they were originally understood as utensils. They "fall out of the world," they become unworlded (*entweltlicht*), and now present themselves as mere products of nature occurring in an indifferent universal space (SZ, § 16 and § 69). The traditional idea of being, drawn from this secondary mode of reality, may therefore be called *substantial reality* or *objective presence* as against the *handy reality* of things that belong to a world (*Vorhandenheit*, as against *Zuhandenheit*).

That this is how we *in fact*, though not in theory, understand the things we use in our everyday world is shown by our propensity to ascribe all kinds of "values" to them. The simplest utensil—a knife, for instance—cannot be grasped in its being as a merely substantial thing. The knife is essentially "more" than a material body of such and such properties, of such and such appearance, size, and weight. It is this "more" we try to explain when we ascribe a "usefulness value" to the knife. What happens, in fact, is that, standing, as we do, in a long ontological tradition, we unquestioningly take it for granted that the knife is merely substantially real, thereby covering over our original understanding of its being as relevant to . . . , handy for. . . . We first strip the thing bare of what belongs to it as a utensil, then try to restore what we have taken away by adding to it a value.

But, it may be asked, does Heidegger's interpretation not apply only to manmade utensils? These, admittedly, are "more" than mere substances, but what about the material bodies that are simply there in nature? These also, according to Heidegger, are originally understood by us in their handy-being. What, for instance, could be more handily there than the sun, and what could be less manmade? It is not primarily our labor that makes things into utensils; it is the significance-structure of our world that enables us to understand things as utensils. Only on the ground of this understanding are we able to improve on what we find, and so make tools that are even handier, even more "valuable" for some specific purpose.

As to the philosophical concept of values, and the elaborate theories of values that have been worked out in the modern era of philosophy, these are considered by Heidegger to be highly questionable and rootless phenomena. They have arisen because the existential constitution of being-in-the-world, on the ground of which Da-sein in advance understands the things he meets as "valuable"—handy for something—has been completely overlooked. Once the original whole of being-in-the-world has been passed over, philosophy finds itself compelled to try to glue it together from bits and pieces, by superimposing values on the substances that have fallen out from the significance-whole of a world, just as it is obliged to construct ingenious theories to explain the commerce between a supposedly worldless subject and a cognized "world."

Why is it that in Greek-Western thinking so fundamental a structure as being-in-the-world has been overlooked, and with it the primary ontological character of things as handy reality has been consistently missed? It cannot be an accident, nor a failure on the part of the great thinkers of this tradition. The reason lies in the fundamental "fallenness" or "falling" of Da-sein's being, whereby he is whirled away from himself to the things within the world. Instead of interpreting them from his understanding of being-in-the-world, Da-sein tries to understand his own being from their reality.

The elemental trend toward the "world" which carries Da-sein away from himself cannot fail at the same time to affect the relation most essential to him: his being with other Da-seins in a mutually shared world. The radical difference between being-with others and being-near-to things was pointed out already in earlier discussions, and our next task is to examine in some detail Heidegger's ideas on this important theme.

IV

Being-with-Others and Being-One's-Self

1. The Basic Concept of Being-with

Da-sein is able to relate himself to his fellow men only because his own being is in advance disclosed to him as being-with. This fundamental structure of Da-sein's self is the existential foundation of all that we usually speak of under the title of personal relations and human society. If, as a matter of common experience, Da-sein constantly enters into all kinds of associations with other men, this is not the result of the "fact" that he is not the only one of his kind in the world, but the other way round: he can recognize others like himself in the world and enter into relations with them because his own being is disclosed to him as being-with. When there are "in fact" no others, when Da-sein is alone, he does not thereby cease to-be-with others, and this fundamental character of his being manifests itself with peculiar intensity in his loneliness, in his missing the others. Even when Da-sein thinks he does not need the others, when he withdraws from them and has nothing to do with them, this is still only possible as a privative mode of being-with.

To our usual way of thinking, it seems the most obvious fact that Da-sein can understand others in their being, both as like himself and as other than himself. Ontologically, this fact is a problem that is neither obvious nor easy to explain. In Husserl's phenomenological school, to which at one time Heidegger belonged, the solution of this problem was thought to lie in "empathy" (*Einfühlung*), literally: "feeling oneself into another." Heidegger rejects this solution, because it assumes that the other is "analogous" to oneself, is a "double" of oneself, and leaves unexplained precisely the most difficult problem: How is it possible that this "double" of myself is yet manifest to me as the "other"? (SZ, 124ff.).

This is the problem to which Heidegger offers the solution of *being-with*. Just as Da-sein is never a worldless subject, but in advance refers himself to the possible presence of things within a world, so he is never an isolated, otherless "I," but in advance understands himself as I-myself-with-(possible other selves). The "with" already refers him to the other as a self; that is, as one who exists in the same way as he himself and yet is the "other" *with* whom he can be together in the same world.

The basic structure of being-with cannot be reduced to or explained from anything else. The articulated whole of being-myself-with-(another-self) cannot be melted down into an "inarticulate," isolated "I," which then somehow finds its way to another, equally isolated "I." Da-sein does not have to find his way to another Da-sein, because with the disclosure of his own being as being-with, the being of others is already disclosed and understood. It is true that in everyday being-together-with-others, this primary understanding of the other, as well as of oneself, is often covered over and distorted, so that to know each other requires a "getting-to-know-one-another." Necessary and unavoidable as such special and explicit efforts may be to disclose oneself to another self, they do not originally constitute being-together-with-one-another but are only possible on the ground of the primary being-with.

Being-with others is a basic structure of each Da-sein's self, for the sake of which he exists: Da-sein therefore exists essentially for the sake of others. He understands them in advance as the selves who are in the world in the same way as himself: their being has the same character of *for the sake of* as his own. On the ground of the irreducible with-structure of his being, Da-sein is essentially with-worldish. His world is in advance a world he shares with others; his being-in-the-world is in itself a being-with-others-in-the-world.

But just because being-with is a fundamental constituent of Da-sein's own self, it can be modified according to the basic possibilities of existence; that is, Da-sein can be with others in an "owned" ("authentic") or a "disowned" ("inauthentic") way. These possibilities are first hinted at by Heidegger when he introduces the concept of "solicitude" "concern-for," or "care-for," (*Fürsorge*) as the way of care appropriate to being-with other existences in a mutually shared world (SZ, 121ff.). The meaning of this specific way of care has now to be briefly considered.

"Care-for" is a literal translation of Heidegger's word *Fürsorge* and is adopted here to preserve the connection with care and taking-care, but the German word, it should be noted, has a range of meaning which is much better conveyed by *solicitude*. Another way to suggest the general meaning of *Fürsorge* would be to render it by charity (*caritas*). Social charitable institutions, Heidegger remarks immediately after introducing his concept of *Fürsorge*, are grounded in the existential care-for, and the need for them is made urgent by the deficient and indifferent ways in which Da-seins care for each other in much of their everyday being-together. Passing-by-on-the-other-side and being-of-no-concern-to-each-other are the indifferent modes in which everyday care-for usually keeps itself. But, it should be observed, even the most indifferent way of being-with others is still another order of being from the simultaneous occurrence of a number of objects together.

As to the positive modes of caring-for, Heidegger shows that there are two extreme possibilities; and in these, the owned or authentic and disowned or inauthentic way of being-with others comes to light. (SZ, 122). On introducing this topic, Heidegger treats it with a brevity that seems surprising, until it is realized that it cannot be made genuinely understandable without the interpretation of owned existence which is to follow some two hundred pages later.

In the first of its positive modes, care-for, so to speak, "jumps in" (*einspringt*) for the other; it takes the "care" off the other, usually by taking care of things for him. In so doing, however, it throws the other out of his place by stepping in in his stead, so that the other takes over ready-made what he should have taken care of for himself. In such caring-for, the other can easily become dependent and dominated in so unobtrusive a fashion that it may often pass unnoticed by him. This mode of caring-for is widespread in everyday being-together and concerns primarily the handy things that have to be taken care of.

In its second positive mode, care-for, so to speak, "jumps ahead" (*vorausspringt*) of the other in his ability to be himself, not to take the "care" off him but to give it back to him properly, as his own. Such caring-for is not primarily concerned with what the other does but with his existence as a self, and it may help to make him transparent to himself in his own being as care.

Between these two extremes, there is a wide range of varied and mixed modes of caring-for, whose discussion, as many readers of *Being and Time* note with some regret, is not essential to Heidegger's central theme and is consequently passed over. Instead, Heidegger turns to give a brief indication of the way of "seeing," of understanding, by which care-for is guided. Parallel to the circumspect for-sight (*Umsicht*) which guides everyday taking-care, care-for has its own ways of "seeing"; these are called by Heidegger *Rücksicht* and *Nachsicht*.

The usual meaning of *Rücksicht* is considerateness, or, if the "seeing" (*Sicht*) is to be emphasized, it might be rendered as a *considerate regard* for someone. *Nachsicht* is excellently rendered in the Macquarrie and Robinson translation of *Being and Time* as *forbearance*.[1] Both these concepts are highly suggestive and could be interpreted in several ways, especially since Heidegger gives no further explanation of their precise meaning. There are, however, some illuminating comments on *Rücksicht*, and its extreme deficiency, ruthlessness, to be found in Heidegger's essay on Anaximander (HO, 331ff., G5, 359ff., EGT, 46ff.), but to discuss these would lead us too far away from our theme.

The interpretation to be given here keeps in view that the concepts under consideration are analogous to *Um-sicht*, for-sight. The first component of *Rück-sicht* means "back-"; *Rücksicht* therefore means an understanding that lies in looking back. What does this understanding look back on? On thrownness and dependence upon a world that has to be taken care of. But thrownness is in itself a thrownness-with and for other; the world has to be taken care of with and for the other. This "back-looking" understanding is evidently the guide of the "jumping-in" mode of caring-for.

Nach- means after, toward, to. *Nachsicht* is accordingly an understanding that lies in looking toward or to something. What does this understanding look to? To the possibility of being a self, for the sake of which Da-sein bears his being as care. But to be a self is only possible with another self. Da-sein thus bears care for the other self; in looking to this, he may help the other to bear his own self as care. This forbearing looking-to the other self is evidently the guide of the "jumping-ahead" way of caring-for.

Both these ways of "seeing" are capable of a wide range of modifications, of which the ruthless disregard of the other's thrownness is an extreme form of deficiency. The indifferent mode of forbearance is called by Heidegger *Nachsehen*. This is not a looking-to, but an overlooking of the other self, a taking-no-notice-of-it; it is not genuine forbearance, but an uncaring toleration, which largely guides the indifferent modes of everyday being-together.

Ultimately, however, all modes of being-together, whether genuine or not genuine, whether they spring from an owned or disowned existence, are made possible by the structure of being-with, which is constitutive of each Da-sein's self and which cannot be ironed out so as to leave an undifferentiated identity called an "I." It is because traditional philosophy has always had a worldless, otherless "I" in view that it has been forced to interpret the essence of Da-sein, his self, as though it were a substance: a recognizable identity which underlies (is present to) a constantly changing stream of experience.

As against the traditional attempts to explain the self with the help of an idea of being drawn from the reality of things, Heidegger takes the idea of being-with-others-in-the-world as the only basis from which an ontological analysis of Da-sein can even start. This fundamental constitution is not merely a rigid framework, but it itself determines the way in which Da-sein is together with others, and even the way in which he himself is a self. In the first place and for the most part, Da-sein is captivated and taken in by his world (*benommen*). Hence it comes about that his first meetings with others have a predominantly worldish character: the others meet him in their occupations in the world, of which he himself is also taking care. How does this meeting concretely take place and how does it determine the way in which both the others and one's own self first become understandable?

In his everyday existence, Da-sein stays predominantly in his nearest world, in which the others are also busy in their care-taking worldishness. The others are there not merely accidentally, and in addition to what one does with things, but are there in one's occupations from the start, as, for example, the customer for whom the clothes and shoes are "made to measure," as the merchant who delivers the materials for the work, as the friend who gave a present of the book one reads; the field along which one walks shows itself as owned by so and so, decently cultivated by him, and so on (SZ, 117f.).

The others meet us not only in our "private" occupations but also in the common with-world; for example, in the use of public means of communications, in undertakings which take care in common of the mutually shared world, as in the upkeep of the facilities provided by a community, and so forth. To an overwhelming extent, everyday being-together does not get beyond the business pursued in common and beyond the average understanding of the others and of oneself which grows from what they do and from what oneself does in the world.

In his average everydayness, Da-sein finds the others in their care-taking being-in-the-world and finds himself among them as taking care with them (SZ, 118). Far from being an encapsulated I who has to go "out" of himself to another I, Da-sein first finds even himself in coming back to himself from "out there," where he is busy taking care of the world among the others. In this common absorption in the world, the "I myself" is not even clearly differentiated from all the other selves; the others are those among whom I also am, among whom I also find myself. In his self-forgetful everydayness, Da-sein is in the first place and for the most part not himself.

What does Heidegger mean by the startling announcement that, in his everyday existence, Da-sein is not himself? Negatively, he clearly cannot mean that Da-sein suddenly loses his I-character and ceases to be a self altogether; he can only mean that Da-sein exists as a self in one of the definite ways that are open to him. How this way of not-being-oneself is to be positively understood will become clear in the next section, where we shall consider Heidegger's answer to the question *Who is the self of everydayness?*

2. THE EVERYDAY SELF AND THE "THEY"

The most salient point that has emerged from Heidegger's analysis can be briefly stated as follows. In the everyday world, the others meet us as *what* they are in their makings and doings: "They *are* what they do" (SZ, 126).

What Heidegger emphatically says in the sentence "They *are* what they do" seems at first sight easy to understand. When someone asks us "Who is so and so?" we almost automatically reply, "He is a surgeon, a businessman, a student of philosophy," or whatever. But, when we come to think of it, is this habit easy to explain just because it is familiar? Is it so "natural" that the self each Da-sein is should be manifest to us from his profession? How is it possible for us to characterize Da-sein's self from what he does? This is the question Heidegger goes on to answer in the paragraph which immediately follows the sentence "They *are* what they do"—a short paragraph that is not only the decisive step taken in the present analysis but is one of the key passages of *Being and Time*, and, as such, is not fully comprehensible where it stands. It is only about halfway through Division Two that this passage will retrospectively come to clarity. Meantime, let us see how far we can understand at present the existential-ontological explanation Heidegger gives of "who's who" in the everyday world.

In the first place, how does Da-sein understand himself as a self at all? Primarily, as has been shown in our discussion of existence, from the *possibilities* of his being. These are originally manifest from the possibility of a *not*, which belongs to each Da-sein singly and uniquely. In the finiteness of his being, each Da-sein is sheerly uninterchangeable; no one can stand in for him there, no one can take his being off him and bear it for him. But in everyday being-together, Da-sein turns away from the possibility that is most his own and understands himself from his worldish possibilities among other selves. In his everydayness, Da-sein in advance measures his own self by what the others are and have, by what they have achieved and failed to achieve in the world. He thus understands himself in his difference from the others by the *distance* that separates his own possibilities from theirs. "Being-with-one-another is, unknown to itself, disquieted by the care about this distance" (SZ, 126). Everyone measures his distance and so "stands off" as himself from the others. This existential "distantiality" or "stand-offishness" (*Abständigeit*) can concretize itself in many different ways. It is there, for instance, in the care to catch up with the others, to "do as the Joneses do." Or it may manifest itself in the opposite way, in going all out to consolidate some privilege or advantage one has gained and so keep the others down in their possibilities. All kinds of social distinctions, whereby Da-sein understands his own existence by his distance from others in class, race, education, and income are grounded in the existential stand-offishness, which means: in the first place and for the most part, Da-sein understands his existence by "standing off" from the others and not by the genuine possibilities that lie in the uniqueness of his finite self. In his everydayness, Da-sein looks away from the true distance, the limit of his finite being, from which alone he can become truly transparent as the self he is, and measures his self in advance by his distance from what the others are and do.

This existential stand-offishness implies that in everyday existence Da-sein draws the possibilities of his being from what is prescribed and decided on by others. He is thus delivered over to the subservience of domination (*Botmässigleit*) by the others and disburdened of the being that is singly and solely his. In everyday being-together, Da-sein is not himself; the others have taken his being away from him (SZ, 126). But who are the others? They are not this one or that one, not anybody or the sum of all: "they" are just "people," the people of whom we say "people think so," and "people don't wear that any more." We call them "they" and "people" to hide that we essentially belong to them, not by what we in fact think and do but in being as we are, measuring the possibilities of our own existence from what "they" say one can be and do.

Since in everyday being-together, "they," the others, are not any definite others, they are essentially interchangeable; anyone can stand in for everybody else, anybody can represent and substitute anyone else, almost like a thing which can just as well represent its genus and species as any other thing. With this, the ontological character of Da-sein's being, which is always singly and uniquely *my* being, comes into a mode of not-being in the sense that it is *not* itself according to its ownmost possibility. This is the strictly ontological meaning of Heidegger's thesis that, in his everyday being-in-the-world, it is *not* Da-sein himself who *is there*, but it is "they," people, who *are there*, oneself among them. In the first place and for the most part, the *who* of everydayness, the everyday self, is the "they" (*Das Man*).

Because of their interchangeability, it is in principle impossible to pin down who "they" are to any definite persons. It is precisely in their inconspicuousness that "they" exercise a dictatorship that can never be brought home to anyone, so that no one can be made responsible for it. There are many social-historical forms in which the dictatorship of "them" can concretize itself. It would be a complete misunderstanding of the existential-ontological idea of a "they-self" to think that it applies only to modern society in some specific political-social forms. If Heidegger is right at all in saying that to exist as a they-self is one of the possibilities of Da-sein's finitely free being, then this possibility is open to Da-sein by virtue of his own being and not by the accident of this or that form of society.

Indeed, no specific oppression is needed to establish the power of "them," because the tendency to level down and average out the distinctiveness of each self is there already in being-together-in-the-world. The reduction to uniformity happens simply in taking care of a mutually shared world; in using its public facilities, newspapers, entertainments, and the like. Here everybody is like everybody else. The existential tendency to average out and level down all differences is commented on by Heidegger in the words: "Overnight, everything primordial is flattened down as something long since known. Everything gained by a struggle becomes something to be manipulated. Every mystery loses its power" (SZ, 127).

Heidegger goes on to explain how and why this happens. Standoffishness, averaging-out and levelling-down constitute the "publicity" (*Öffentlichkeit*) of an average understanding of being. This public understanding in advance leads and determines all explanations of self and world, not because it goes deeply into things but, on the contrary, because it is insensitive to differences of genuineness and *niveau*. In this average, public understanding, everything becomes accessible and commonplace, and no one is responsible for having made it so. It is "they" who have understood and decided how things must be. "They" thus disburden everyday existence of responsibility, for "they" are strictly speaking *nobody* who could be taken to account for anything said and done; it is always the "others" who have said and done so. In everyday being-together, "Everyone is the other and no one is himself" (SZ, 128).

It is in "them," who are nobody, that the everyday self finds its first stability (*Ständigleit*): it stands as not-itself. This "standing," of course, is not the sheer lastingness of a thing. Although scattering himself into a they-self, Da-sein can never become a pure "what"; even to-be-not-himself and nobody is still only possible to a self.

"They" must therefore never be thought of as a genus of which each everyday self is a sample, but as a basic way in which Da-sein can exist as a self. It is for the sake of the they-self that Da-sein in the first place and for the most part exists. This primary *for the sake of* articulates the significance-whole of the world in which Da-sein lives and prescribes the average possibilities of being-in-the-world. But just because these possibilities are understood from what "they" are and do, the everyday self covers over its own unique character. It is from the average, public understanding of being that traditional ontology took its start and has been consistently misled by it to ascribe to Da-sein's essence, his self, the ontological character of a substance.

The "owned" self of a resolutely disclosed existence is not a different order of being, not some exception or genius that hovers over "them," but is a modification of "them," a resolute gathering of one's self from its scatteredness into a they-self. "They" are a fundamental existential and not some ontic quality of Da-sein produced by external conditions. Even less are "they," as is often thought, a contemptible figure of ridicule, although, it must be confessed, Heidegger's language in speaking of the they-self would sometimes almost justify such a conclusion. As against this, Heidegger's own ontological tendency must be held fast. Properly considered, indeed, "they" are far from ridiculous, but a more shattering document of man's finite being than the "owned" self of a resolutely disclosed existence can ever be.

3. The Publicity of Everydayness

(a) Discourse and Language: Everyday Discourse as Idle Talk

The theme of the present discussion is the publicness or public disclosedness of everyday being-together, insofar as it is constituted by discourse and language. It has already been mentioned that, in Heidegger's interpretation, discourse (*Rede*) is a fundamental existential which is co-original with attunement and understanding. These latter have in themselves a definite and intricate structure, so that the being disclosed by them is always already articulated. What is understandable is therefore always expressly articulable. Discourse, as an existential, is the articulation of understandability: of existence and fellow-existence, of the significance-whole of world and of the being of beings within the world. Hearing, listening, and being silent essentially belong to speech and make up its full ontological structure. Da-sein hears not because he has ears; he has these organs of hearing because by virtue of his own being he is a hearer. Hearing, listening, and being silent are existential possibilities that belong to Da-sein as a speaker. A stone cannot speak and therefore cannot be silent.

On the ground of his existential constitution, the factually existing Da-sein always "speaks out," and it is this "spoken out" speech that Heidegger interprets as the ontic phenomenon of language. It may well be seen from this that the actual languages we have cannot be those "ultimates" for Heidegger from which all explanations have to start. To suppose that they are is all the less feasible because each language already hides in itself one definite interpretation (*Auslegung*) of what it articulates, an interpretation which is usually so unobtrusive that it remains unnoticed. Thus, for instance, each language loosens up the significance-whole of world into "significances," which explain in a specific way the everyday world in which Da-sein is together with "them," the others.

In everyday being-together, the spoken-out discourse, language, has the character of a communicating talk, whose function is to share with the listener the disclosedness of the things talked about. The listener himself is thus brought into a disclosing relation to the things that are the subject matter of the talk.

Since, however, language itself already gives a certain explanation of the world, it is in itself understandable. In everyday talking-together, there is a strong tendency on the part of the listener, not so much to bring himself into a genuinely disclosing relation to the things talked of—that is, to understand them for himself from the things themselves—as rather to understand the talk itself. This is possible because both the talker and the listener already understand the language in the same average way.

With the omission of going back to the things themselves, whose disclosedness is the soil from which language grows, there is a constant danger that language, solely by virtue of its own potentialities, uproots itself. What is shared is not the primary and immediate disclosure of self and world but an average understanding of the talk itself. Everyday being-together moves largely in a mutual talking-together and in repeating and handing on what has been said. In the course of this the talk loses, or has perhaps never gained, a genuinely disclosing relation to being and beings. The unique gift of speech, "of gifts the most dangerous" (Hölderlin), can itself become the medium for uprooting Da-sein from his primary understanding of existence and his nearness to things.

Discourse has thus always the possibility of becoming what Heidegger calls *Gerede*, a word for which we have many approximations, none of which hits the target clean in the center. Chatter, gossip, idle talk, groundless talk, bottomless talk, hearsay, all hover on the circumference. "Hearsay," although it is not a translation of *Gerede*, can perhaps best convey what Heidegger means, but because it is a literal translation of *Hörensagen*, a word Heidegger uses several times in *Being and Time*, we shall follow the widespread practice of translating *Gerede* as "idle talk"; it is the kind of talk that hears, that is, understands what is said, then passes on (says on) what has been learned by hearing without "getting to the bottom" of what the talk is about.[2] Writing, as a mode of communicating discourse, can bring a further uprooting into everyday existence. Like genuine talk, so genuine writing can degenerate into an idle scribbling (*Geschreibe*), which is not so much a "hear-say" as a "read-say," feeding itself on what has already been written and passing it on as a supposed contribution toward keeping the disclosedness of world open. "The average understanding of the reader will *never be able* to decide what has been drawn from primordial sources with a struggle, and how much is just gossip" (SZ, 169).

Groundless hearsay or idle talk thus helps to "publish" an average explanation of existence and world in everyday being-together. It offers the possibility of understanding everything without going into anything. It develops an average understandability to which nothing remains hidden, so that it in advance hinders and closes a deeper and more genuine approach to things. It is in itself a disguising and covering-over, although, as Heidegger emphatically points out, there is no intention in it to deceive or falsify. Idle talk, simply by omitting to discover things in themselves, is a falsification of speech in the genuine sense, whose whole function is to be discovering, that is, to be true, according to Heidegger's interpretation of truth, as we shall see in a later chapter.

All of us grow up in and draw our first understanding of things from the average explanation of being and beings "published" by everyday hearsay. Much that is useful is learned from hearsay, the common basis on which, and from which, and against which, all genuine understanding and communicating and rediscovering take place. No Da-sein can ever keep himself "untouched and unseduced" by the explanations made public in hearsay (SZ, 169). It decides in advance even the possibilities of attunement—that is, of the basic way in which Da-sein lets the world touch him, concern him. "They" have always already prescribed what one sees and how one feels about the world and oneself.

In everyday being-together, whose openness is essentially constituted by hearsay, Da-sein's existence is cut off from its primary relations to itself, to fellow existences and to the world. Its roots are slackened and it sways uncannily in its hold on the disclosedness of self and world (*Schwebe*). Yet, even the uncanniness of this swaying is hidden by the self-assurance and bland matter-of-courseness of an everyday understanding (SZ, 170).

(b) The Everyday Way of Seeing: Curiosity

Among the different ways of "seeing," that is, of understanding, by which our specific "cares" are guided, we have come across two: care-for others is guided by a considerate looking-back on thrownness and a forbearing looking-to the self (*Rücksicht* and *Nachsicht*), while everyday taking-care of things is guided by circumspect for-sight (*Umsicht*). The latter, as we have seen, can modify itself to a theoretical only-looking-at things. In everyday being-together, however, circumspect for-sight has another possibility of modification or, perhaps it would be more correct to say, of degeneration. Just as genuine talk can degenerate into idle talk, so the circumspect for-sight of everyday care can degenerate into idle curiosity. This is called by Heidegger *Neugier*, an expressive word in common use, which literally means greed for the new. This curiosity is in the strictest sense of the word "idle," because it arises when everyday existence has nothing more at hand that needs to be taken care of. The care of circumspect for-sight to discover and bring near the handy things to be attended to now detaches itself from its proper task and becomes the care of looking around, merely for the sake of looking.

The idleness of curiosity must on no account be confused with the leisureliness of a theoretical "only-looking," which stays with things in order to understand them, and which, in the highest sense, is an admiring gazing on beings in their pure essence. The curiosity of circumspect for-sight which has broken free of its proper boundaries is exactly the opposite. It roams far and wide out into the world, not in order to understand things but simply to see how they look. In this greed for novelty lies the care of everyday existence to provide itself constantly with new possibilities of delivering itself over to the world.

As against the leisureliness of a "theoretical" staying with things, the idleness of curiosity is characterized by a constant jumping off from the new to the still newer. Curiosity is a not-lingering with things, that gives itself always fresh opportunities for scattering and distracting itself and leads to a new uprooting of man's being as being-in. It will be remembered that "being-in" means dwelling-in . . . , staying-near-to . . . , in-habiting . . . a world familiar to us in this or that way. The not-staying and self-scattering of curiosity drives Da-sein's being-in to a loss of dwelling (*Aufenthaltslosigkeit*).

Idle talk and roaming curiosity are not merely two different ways of everyday being-together, but one drags the other with it. They decide together what one must have seen and heard. Idle talk leaves nothing unexplained, curiosity nothing undiscovered, and so they offer to everyday existence the guarantee for a supposed genuineness and vitality of "living." This supposition brings to light a third phenomenon constitutive of the public disclosedness of everydayness (SZ, 173).

(c) Ambiguity

The ambiguity that characterizes everyday being-together spreads not only over the explanation of world and of the things within it but, most importantly, over the possibilities of one's own existence together with other existences. It is not only that the all-knowingness of idle talk and curiosity makes it impossible to distinguish what is genuinely known from what is not, but it also publishes in advance what is to happen and what can and will be achieved. The broadcasting in advance of what can be done is usually a good enough reason not to throw oneself into the necessarily slow business of actually carrying it out. Supposing someone does carry out something, then the ambiguity of idle talk and curiosity has already taken care that the achievement, the moment it is finally realized, looks already obsolete. The ambiguous "fore-knowing" and "fore-seeing" of all possibilities make out that the action and the actual achievement are something belated and secondary. Consequently, people are as a rule misguided as to what are, and what are not, the genuine possibilities of their factical existence.

The ambiguous openness (disclosedness) of being-in-the-world spreads itself over the way in which people are together in their everyday business and social intercourse. This has often the character of a tense and secretive watching and questioning of one another. "Under the mask of the for-one-another, the against one another is at play" (SZ, 175). But Heidegger immediately goes on to add that the ambiguity does not spring from an intention to deceive, nor is it primarily produced by the insincerity of individuals; it lies already in a thrown being-together in a world.

The three constitutive characters of public disclosedness—idle talk, curiosity, and ambiguity—show an ontological connection with each other that points to a basic mode of Da-sein's being. This is analyzed by Heidegger just before the opening of the sixth and last chapter of Division One. The place of this analysis, which is entitled "Falling and Thrownness," already indicates its methodological importance to the whole first division of *Being and Time*, providing, as it will turn out, the basis for the exposition of Da-sein's being as care.

4. FALLING AND THROWNNESS

The phenomena of idle talk, curiosity, and ambiguity have brought into view a peculiar "movement" in Da-sein's being, which is called by Heidegger *Verfallen*. This concept has so far been usually alluded to in this book as *fallenness*, in order to avoid presenting the reader with a puzzle until the time came when it could be explained. Now it is becoming evident that what Heidegger means by this concept is not a fallen state of Da-sein, fallen perhaps from a state of grace into corruption, but the *movement* of falling. This movement, moreover, is not one of the accidents that can befall Da-sein in his factical existence but is one of the basic ways in which Da-sein can-be-in-the-world: in the way of disowning himself. This event cannot be explained as the result of external causes and circumstances but only as a positive possibility of being-in-the-world, which in its finite freedom can move away from itself, can disown the utmost illumination of which it is capable.

But if being-in-the-world essentially tends to "move away," to "err away" from itself, and this cannot be ascribed to any extraneous causes, then the temptation to "err" must lie in the very structure of being-in-the-world itself. Indeed, as Heidegger proceeds to show (SZ, 177), the temptation is there already in the fore-throw structure of understanding. Its specific function, it will be remembered, is to bring before and toward itself the whole of the possibilities of being, to which being-with-others-in-the-world essentially belongs. Accordingly, understanding constantly throws out before and toward itself possibilities of being-with "them" in the way of idle talk and boundless curiosity. Purely and simply by its own fore-throw of possibilities, understanding constantly tempts itself to stray away, it literally seduces itself (leads itself off) to seek its own fulfillment in the explanations of self and world made public by "them." Being-in-the-world, as essentially constituted by understanding, is thus in itself "seductive" or "tempting" (*versucherisch*).

But why does understanding seduce itself to seek its possibilities among "them"? Because "their" self-assured all-knowingness reassures it of the fullest and most genuine possibility of being-in-the-world. The care of understanding, which in its own nature is a looking-out for possibilities, is thus offered the calm reassurance (*Beruhigung*, "tranquillizing") that "they" hold the secret of the true life, that is, of one's ownmost possibility for being-in-the-world.

The calm of this reassurance, however, does not bring being-in-the-world to a haven of peace, but, on the contrary, it increases the impetus of the fall. Tempting itself to err away from its own genuine possibilities, which can become transparent only in a single self, understanding tends to uproot itself further and further, until it becomes estranged or alienated from itself (*Entfremdung*). Among the many possible concretizations of self-estrangement, some of which are especially acutely felt in our own age, Heidegger singles out as an example the opinion that

> understanding the most foreign cultures and "synthesizing" them with our own may lead to the thorough and first genuine enlightenment of Da-sein about itself. Versatile curiosity and restlessly knowing it all masquerade as a universal understanding of Da-sein. [. . .] When Da-sein, tranquillized and "understanding" everything, thus compares itself with everything, it drifts towards an alienation in which its ownmost potentiality for being-in-the-world is concealed. (SZ, 178)

This alienation, however, as Heidegger emphasizes, does not mean that Da-sein is "in fact" torn away from himself, but, on the contrary, he is driven into the extremest self-analysis and self-interpretations of all kinds in which he finally "catches" himself, that is, becomes completely caught and entangled in himself (*Verfängnis*). But far from genuinely finding himself in this entanglement, it finally closes all possibilities for an understanding that springs genuinely from his own self. In this seductively reassuring, estrangingly entangling way of being-in-the-world, Da-sein so to speak casts his moorings and plunges away from himself, not to fall into some abyss which is not himself, but to fall into the disowned way of being himself (*Absturz*).

The movement in Da-sein's own being constantly drags him away from the fore-throw of genuine possibilities and drags him into the opinion that "they" dispose of the fullness of life. The constant "dragging away from . . ." and "dragging toward and into . . ." finally reveals the movement of falling as a whirl or eddying (*Wirbel*).

The steps of Heidegger's analysis, briefly summarized in the preceding paragraphs, have so far clearly followed from the initial step, namely from the fore-throw of possibilities, whereby understanding constantly leads itself astray. But now Heidegger proceeds to take a new step whose connection with what has gone before is not at all evident and seems even to contradict it. The whirling movement of the fall, Heidegger says, characterizes not only the existential constitution of being-in-the-world but at the same time makes manifest the "throw" of thrownness. Da-sein's thrownness is never a finished fact, which happens once at birth and is then left behind: as long as Da-sein in fact exists, he "remains in the throw," which whirls him away into disownment to "them" (SZ, 179).

But how is it, we ask ourselves, that the "falling," which was first explained from the fore-throw of understanding, suddenly turns out to arise from the "throw" of thrownness? How do these two hang together? Presumably, the connection would be clear if we understood exactly what Heidegger means by saying that Da-sein "remains in the throw," but this suggestive phrase fails to convey any precise meaning at the moment. Or is it perhaps wrong to take it for granted that the phrase must have a precise meaning? Should it not be regarded rather as a figure of speech, suggestive, and inevitably blurred at the edges? This would go against all that we have come to know of Heidegger's thought, a thought that is incomparably strict and translucently clear, provided, of course, that the grave difficulties of penetrating to it are overcome, and even more, that the clarity proper to an inquiry into being is not expected to be of the same kind as the clarity proper to a mathematical theorem or to a report of a football match. On the basis of what our previous discussions have shown, we can confidently expect that Da-sein "remains in the throw" in a strict and precisely understandable sense that will come to light when all that is most basic to Heidegger's thought has been brought into view. Much of it still remains to be discovered. The next chapter, while it cannot take us the whole way, will take us an important step nearer to clarifying the connection between the fore-throw of understanding and the throw of thrownness.

V

The Basic Mood of Dread (Angst) and the Being of Da-sein as Care

1. THE DISCLOSURE OF BEING THROUGH DREAD

Heidegger's analysis of "falling" or "falling prey" as the disowned way of being-in-the-world, brings him to the climax of Division One. Its last chapter has the central task of elucidating the originally whole structure of Da-sein's being as care. The extraordinary difficulty of this task will be best appreciated by those readers who have already grappled with the full text of *Being and Time*. The complexity of Da-sein's being, as it is brought to light by Heidegger in Division One, is considerable. It is not surprising, therefore, that Heidegger should announce that in order to penetrate to the phenomenon of care, an approach to Da-sein must be found through which his being will become accessible in a certain *simplified* way (SZ, 182). Nor is it surprising that Da-sein is to be brought face to face with his being in the mood of dread, for the most original and most far-reaching possibility of disclosure lies in attunement, of which dread will prove to be a preeminent mode. What is surprising is that Heidegger should propose to take for the basis of his analysis the *falling*, the disowned or inauthentic way of being-in-the-world. The proposal to confront Da-sein with himself in a way of existing in which he turns away from himself seems strange indeed, until the reasons for it are explained by Heidegger. These may be briefly indicated as follows.

Disowned existence, as a movement "away from . . . ," makes manifest a threat from which Da-sein flees. Although the threat is not fully faced, yet it is there, disclosed in the very recoil from it. This threat, as Heidegger's analysis will show, is revealed by dread, on the ground of which Da-sein flees from himself into his occupations with things within the world. The preceding inquiry has shown, however, that the flight of disowned existence is not an occasional, isolated act, but a basic way in which Da-sein is-in-the-world. This implies that dread also cannot be an occasional, isolated experience, but must constantly tune Da-sein and reveal to him a threat to his existence. Dread is the basic mood that lies at the ground of Da-sein's being, although it rarely rises to the surface and few of us might recognize it as fully and explicitly experienced by us. Nonetheless, the threat it reveals is attested precisely by Da-sein's flight from it, so that the disowned way of existing may very well serve as a basis from which Heidegger's analysis can start.

Heidegger's first concern is to distinguish sharply dread from fear, which is evidently akin to it and yet radically different. Fear as "fear of . . ." always discovers some definite threat approaching from a definite direction in an already disclosed neighborhood. The whereof of fear, the fearsome, has the character of some handy thing or real thing or another Da-sein approaching from the world. But in disowned existence, it is *from himself* that Da-sein turns away. The threat cannot come from beings within the world, because it is precisely to these that he flees. The threat revealed by dread cannot therefore strike at Da-sein from this or that definite direction, from this or that definite thing, but strikes at him solely from himself. It is not beings within the world that dread dreads, but *being-in-the-world as such.*

The whereof of dread, the dreadsome, is being-in-the-world as such. This thesis is put by Heidegger at the head of the main body of his analysis, to be substantiated in detail by what follows. The first step Heidegger takes is to consider the wholly indefinite character of what dread dreads. How does this differ from the definiteness of a fearsome thing discovered by fear? The difference is not one of degree: the dreadsome is totally other than any possible thing can be. It is not as though dread as "dread of . . ." merely left it vague and uncertain what particular things were to be dreaded: dread (*Angst*) makes manifest that things *as such* are wholly irrelevant to it.

> Nothing of that which is at hand and objectively present within the world, functions as what *Angst* is anxious about. The totality of relevance discovered within the world of things at hand and objectively present is

completely without importance. It collapses. The world has the character of complete insignificance. In *Angst* we do not encounter this or that thing which, as threatening, could be relevant. (SZ, 186)

This short passage from Heidegger's analysis of dread already shows that here we are face to face with something which cannot be fully understood by even the most serious and sustained effort of thinking—naturally so, since the way in which a mood reveals is completely different from any thinking about it. But, if Heidegger is right in saying that a genuine experience of dread is rare, it seems that most of us are doomed not to understand this central piece of the first division of *Being and Time*. Is there not, we ask, some experience common to us which could at least give us a hint of what Heidegger is analyzing here?

Perhaps we could get a hint of it by considering what the things, which Heidegger says "collapse" or "shrivel up" in dread, normally mean to us. They are primarily the useful and indispensable things "by means of which" we can do this and that. But it is not only that we can do this and that with things; they are also primarily what we can do something about. No matter how fearsome a thing is, we may not be totally helpless before it; we can at least try to run away or try to do something, as we say, to help.

But the dreadsome must evidently be of a nature we cannot do anything about. Most of us experience in one way or another, at one time or another, the total impotence and helplessness of "I can do nothing to help," in the face of which the things we can do something about shrink into utter insignificance and irrelevance.

The unique power of dread lies precisely in bringing things into the mood of total insignificance, and so making manifest that the dreadsome is not a thing, it is not of the character of any beings at all: it is nothing. Consequently, it cannot be found anywhere within the world, it cannot approach from any definite place or direction in a certain neighborhood. The dreadsome is nowhere and nothing. But, as Heidegger goes on to point out, the nowhere and nothing are not mere nothings: in them lies the disclosure of place itself, of world itself.

This passage, it may be said without exaggeration, is a key to Heidegger's whole thought, provided that it is understood precisely and not in a vague, general way. Let us first consider what Heidegger means when he says that the nowhere of dread discloses place itself. In our everyday experience, a place is a definite here and a there where we ourselves and things are at a certain distance and in a definable direction from each other. But in every definite here and there something like a where, or more precisely, whereness, must already be understood. In order to fix the place of a thing "over there" at such and such a distance and in this or that direction from us, we must be able to relate ourselves to it, so to speak, in a "whereish" fashion. What enables us to do so is the disclosure of whereness (place) itself. This happens directly and elementally in the nowhere of dread. The nowhere does not arise from thinking of all possible places together and then negating them. On the contrary, the very indefiniteness of the nowhere brings to light purely the where, or more exactly, the whereness solely by itself. It is only because whereness is always manifest to us that we can and must relate ourselves to the things we meet by giving them a definite *where*, a place. Far from being a negation of all possible places, the nowhere is the possibility of place. It makes possible the discovery of the place and space that essentially belong to and help to constitute the world.

The world itself is directly revealed in the nothing of dread. This nothing is not an absolute, total nothing, nor is it an absence or negation of all things, but the sheer other to things as such. It is only because we in advance look beyond things to the nothing revealed in dread that things can and must show themselves to us as a whole, *as* things and not nothing. Only from the disclosed *whole* of things can any single thing stand out and show that it stands in itself as the thing it is. The solid, stable standing-in-itself of a tree, a house, a mountain is precisely what we mean when we point to it and say It really *is* there, it really exists.

Heidegger's interpretation of dread complements his earlier world-analysis. In working out the worldishness of world, Heidegger showed *how* the world is as a coherent reference-whole in which Da-sein understands himself among other beings. This understanding is only possible if beings are given the chance to show themselves in their bodily presence, in what is traditionally called their real existence. It is primarily the function of attunement to disclose the presence of beings as a whole. Each mood, it was said earlier, lifts Da-sein into the midst of beings, which are always manifest in a certain wholeness. How and why this is so could not be explained earlier, because it is only in his analysis of dread that Heidegger takes up this problem and offers his solution of it. It is the nothing of dread that opens up the horizon from which and against which beings stand out as a whole. Far from being a negation of all things, the nothing is the possibility of things: it gives things the possibility to show themselves as they are in themselves. This possibility, in Heidegger's interpretation, is the world itself.

Hence the world cannot be a thing, a reality that exists independently: the world is only a fundamental way in which Da-sein himself exists. When, therefore, dread brings Da-sein face to face with the world itself, it brings him directly before his own being as being-in-the-world. What dread dreads, the dreadsome, is *being-in-the-world itself* (SZ, 187).

The revelation of Da-sein's own being in dread does not happen in a thinking and judging and making propositions about an object to be dreaded, but in the way proper to attunement. Dreading itself reveals to Da-sein elementally and purely his thrown being-in-the-world.

As a mode of attunement, dread is at the same time "dread for. . . ." This cannot be for a definite possibility of a factical existence, which is threatened by this or that definite thing or event. Any such definite threat is in advance excluded by the nature of dread itself.

> What *Angst* is anxious for is being-in-the-world itself. In *Angst*, the things at hand in the surrounding world sink away, and so do innerworldly beings in general. The "world" can offer nothing more, nor can the *Mitda-sein* of others. Thus *Angst* takes away from Da-sein the possibility of understanding itself, falling prey, in terms of the "world" and the public way of being interpreted. It throws Da-sein back upon that for which it is anxious, its authentic potentiality-for-being-in-the-world. *Angst* individuates Da-sein to its ownmost being-in-the-world which, as understanding, projects itself essentially upon possibilities. Thus along with that for which it is anxious, *Angst* discloses Da-sein as *being-possible*, and indeed as what can be individualized in individuation or its own accord. (SZ, 187–88)

The passage just quoted, and what follows immediately after, will prove to be of central importance to the inquiry into the "owned" way of existing to be carried out in Division Two of *Being and Time*. It is dread as "dread for . . . ," as Heidegger points out, which makes manifest to Da-sein his *freedom for* being his own self as a possibility. The preeminent revealing power of dread lies in bringing Da-sein before the finite freedom of his being-in-the-world, as the same being into which he is already thrown and delivered.

With the exposition of the full structure of dread, Heidegger has brought its strange and unique character into view. *What* dread dreads is a thrown being-in-the-world. This has proved to be the same as what dread is *for*: the ability-to-be-in-the-world. But not only that. As Heidegger emphatically points out, the sameness extends even over dreading itself, which, as an attunement, is a fundamental way of being-in-the-world. The sameness of the disclosing with the disclosed world, to our usual way of thinking, appears to be something in the nature of an empty tautology, a "going round in a circle" that can produce no results. Ontologically, however, it is precisely the sameness that is pointed out by Heidegger to be of utmost importance. Dread reveals Da-sein's being purely and wholly in itself as a thrown possibility of being-in-the-world. It is true that the function of every mood is to disclose Da-sein's being in all its essential articulations, as existence (self), world, and being-in (dwelling in . . . , inhabiting . . .). But while other moods refer Da-sein to beings other than himself, dread detaches him from them and brings him purely to himself as a single being-in-the-world.

But the uniqueness of this mood, it might be thought, is perhaps only "read into it" by ontological interpretation. To prevent such a suspicion from arising, Heidegger calls to testimony the explanation of dread given by everyday common sense, which, as Heidegger often says, no one would accuse of any hankerings after philosophy. How does everyday experience explain this mood? In dread, it is commonly said, "one feels uncanny." The German word for uncanny, *unheimlich*, literally means *unhomely*. The seriousness of the discussion that Heidegger goes on to devote to this word indicates that what may seem to be merely an afterthought to the analysis of dread will later prove to be its very core. What does Heidegger show as coming to light in this commonly attested feeling of uncanniness?

First, it is the peculiar character of indefiniteness, the nothing and nowhere of the dreadsome that is expressed by the *uncanny*. But at the same time, the uncanny is the *unhomely*, the not-being-at-home. The everyday familiarity with and at-homeness in the world is suddenly broken in dread. The usually taken-for-granted at-homeness comes into the existential mode of not-at-home. This brings into view what it really is *from* which the disowned way of being-in-the-world flees. It flees *from* the uncanny not-at-homeness that lies at the ground of a thrown being-in-the-world. It flees to the reassured at-homeness made public in the explanations given by "them." This flight, however, has been shown to be not merely accidental and occasional; it is constant and basic. This means that "Tranquillized, familiar being-in-the-world is a mode of the uncanniness of Da-sein, not the other way around. *Not-being-at-home must be conceived existentially and ontologically as the more primordial phenomenon*" (SZ, 189).

In view of the extraordinary power and penetration of Heidegger's analysis of dread, which may absorb the reader's whole attention, it must be stressed that the conclusion just quoted is its most important result for Heidegger's central question, How is it possible for Da-sein to understand being? What does being mean? It is already beginning to emerge that the manifestness of the *not* is most fundamental to our understanding of being, and so to our existence as Da-sein. The *not*, it now appears, is not originally disclosed by understanding as Da-sein's ultimate possibility: it is revealed from the beginning by dread which already tunes all fore-throw of the possibilities of a finite being. Da-sein is not finite because he does not "in fact" last forever. In this sense, a stone or a tree are equally finite, whereas Heidegger means by finiteness the fundamental and unique character of Da-sein's being. Da-sein exists finitely because dread in advance reveals to him a *not* in his impotent and uncanny not-at-homeness. This *not* is said to each Da-sein alone, and only in hearing it can he understand "that I already am." This understanding, into which a latent dread constantly tunes Da-sein, is nothing else than the throw of thrownness. As soon as and as long as Da-sein factually exists, he "remains in the throw."

These reflections, while they do no more than unfold some of the implications of Heidegger's analysis of dread, do in fact run far ahead of what can come explicitly into view at the end of Division One. Our present aim is only to understand the basic trend of Heidegger's thought, whereas Heidegger himself has to give the strictest evidence for every step he takes. This makes the unfolding of his main theme necessarily slow and laborious. Even the concept of care that Heidegger is able to work out at the end of Division One is still a provisional concept, showing the ontological structure of only the disowned (falling) way of being-in-the-world. It is, one might say, the "disowned" care of being. Its main articulations into existence (self), thrownness (facticity), and fallenness have already been discussed by us above (Part Two, chap. I, sec. 1, subsec. a). Much of what was then obscure has since become clear. At this stage, therefore, a short discussion of the concept of care will be sufficient for our purpose.

2. The Structure of Da-sein's Being as Care

In approaching the climax of Heidegger's "Preparatory Fundamental Analysis," it is helpful to remind ourselves of two points. The first is that the word *man* gives only the ontic meaning of the essentially two-dimensional, ontic-ontological term *Da-sein*. Taken in its primary and most important ontological sense, *Da-sein* means the disclosed thereness of being. When, therefore, Heidegger says that the being of Da-sein is care, he does not mean *only* that the original whole of man's being, which we express simply by saying "I am," is to be interpreted as care. He means at the same time, and much more importantly, that being can only be there as care; only as a factually existing being-in-the-world (care) does the illumination of being happen.

This brings us to the second point to remember. If care is the name for the "actual" thereness of being, it must be the originating source, the gathering place, of any understanding whatever of being. It stands to reason, then, that care must have an extremely complex structure; and this is expressed by Heidegger in the formula "being-ahead-of-itself-in-already-being-in (the-world) as being-together-with (innerworldly beings encountered)" (SZ, 192).

Since even this formidable concept of care will later prove to be incomplete, the first point to clarify is what is still missing from it. This can best be done by recalling the idea of being as such—that is, what- and how-being, something, nothing, and notness. As we have seen, the what- and how-being of things, and things as such, something, are disclosed from the world and are clearly accounted for in the care formula. The mysterious nothing has proved to be the world itself. On the other hand, the notness that most fundamentally determines Da-sein's existence cannot yet be made explicit in the present formula. That is why in the course of his further investigations Heidegger will have to complete and reformulate the concept of care in a new way.

Let us now examine the complicated structure with which Heidegger presents us at the end of Division One. It is so unlike any care we have ever experienced that it always remains strange and hard to grasp: ahead-of-itself-in-already-being-in (the world) as being-together-with (innerworldly beings encountered). At first sight, the whole formula looks extremely clumsy and alienates with its abundance of hyphens and its parentheses. More attentively considered, however, it will be seen to gather into itself in the most compact way possible all that Heidegger's inquiry has so far shown to be fundamental to Da-sein's being-in-the-world. The "ahead-of-itself" obviously indicates the ontological character of existence. On the ground of the fore-throw of possibilities, Da-sein is never merely here and now like a thing, but is constantly out beyond himself, relating himself, in the first place, not to other beings, but to his own ability-to-be. This way of being, in strictly ontological terms, is a being toward an ability-to-be: Da-sein constantly relates himself to, bears himself toward, a possibility of his existence in a definite way. Since the care-structure we are considering at present is that of disowned existence, the "self" which care is "ahead of" is always the scattered they-self.

But, it will be remembered, the evidence on which Heidegger is basing this interpretation was gained from the phenomenon of dread. How and where did dread show the "ahead-of-itself" structure of care? In what dread dreads *for*, namely for Da-sein's ownmost ability-to-be. At the same time, dread brought elementally into view that the ability-to-be is only possible to a being *already* thrown into a world. The whereof of dread, the dreadsome, showed itself as a thrown being-in-the-world. The "already" expresses the inexorable facticity of thrownness, the impotence to undo the "that I already am." The meaning of the whole phrase "already-being-in " may be summed up as follows. Da-sein dwells in the world in such a way that his own dwelling manifests itself to him always as an already accomplished fact; he can never go behind the "already" to originate his own being.

But, it will be noticed, "the world" now stands in parentheses. The reason is that care, in the strict sense, is the structure of what would traditionally be called the "real existence" of Da-sein, whereas the world is only an existential character of his being. If Heidegger were writing an ontology of the traditional style, the world would function as a category defining Da-sein's being.

Similarly, "innerworldly beings encountered" also stands in parentheses, but for a different reason. These beings are not Da-sein himself, nor are they purely ontological structures like the ahead-of, already-being-in, and being-together-with. They are concrete, ontic beings that must be distinguished from the strictly ontological concept of care, to which they nevertheless essentially belong: the structure of being-together-with directly refers Da-sein to other beings within the world.

It is to these beings that Da-sein constantly flees on the ground of a hidden and latent dread. In the concept of care we are considering, the being-together-with (innerworldly beings encountered) means the fundamentally falling way in which Da-sein loses himself in his occupations with things. In this mode of existing, Da-sein's being-with others like himself has a predominantly worldish character. Hence the "innerworldly beings encountered" imply other existences as well as things. It may be noted that the structure of being-with others is not made explicit by Heidegger: it is implied both in the "ahead-of-itself" and in "already-being-in."

But apart from leaving the "being-with" others implied, Heidegger's formulation of care shows with unparalleled compactness the disclosure of self, world, and beings within the world as it is made possible by the structure of Da-sein's being. The philosophical significance of the concept of care is difficult to grasp at a glance. This is one reason why the last chapter of Division One does not close immediately after the exposition of care, but goes on to show how the perennial problems of philosophy gather themselves in Da-sein's being as care as the "place" of their origin. In Greek-Western ontology, these problems were posed and their solution attempted on far too narrow a base, leading to such senseless problems as the demand for "proving" the reality of the "external world." But, as Heidegger is now able to show, all disclosure of reality and world is grounded in and made possible by Da-sein's being as care, which it is senseless to try to "prove" to itself.

Above all, it is only now that Heidegger can turn to the most fundamental and central problem of all philosophy, the problem of truth. In the course of Division One, this central problem has been discussed only incidentally, lacking the basis on which it could become the main theme of interpretation. With the exposition of care, the required basis has been gained. Accordingly, Heidegger now turns to give an existential interpretation of truth, which it will be our next task to consider. Strange as this will seem in comparison with the logical theories of truth to which we are accustomed, Heidegger claims that it is no more than the interpretation demanded by the oldest insights into truth that were once alive in our philosophical tradition but now lie buried under logic.

VI

Truth, Being, and Existence: Heidegger's Existential Interpretation of Truth

The oldest name for truth in Greek-Western philosophy is *alêtheia*. For Heidegger, the central meaning of *a-lêtheia* lies in *lêthê*: hiddenness, concealment, coveredness, veiledness. The *a-* has a privative function. The whole word can be faithfully rendered in English by expressions like un-hiddenness, un-concealment, dis-closure, dis-covery, re-velation. Although the elemental Greek experience of truth as a violent and uncanny spoliation, whereby things are wrenched from hiddenness and brought out into the light to show themselves as the things they are, has long since been neutralized and made harmless by theoretical definitions of truth, a reflection of the original insight still lingers in the English words no less than in the Greek *alêtheia*.

The sense in which truth is to be understood in *Being and Time* is unhiddenness, disclosure, and discovery. This makes it immediately evident that the whole treatise, even when it does not mention the word, is an inquiry into truth—necessarily so, because truth and being belong together. The disclosure of being that happens in and with Da-sein's being as care is the original phenomenon of truth itself. This original truth, often called by Heidegger *ontological* truth, is the condition of the possibility of all ontic truth; that is, of the discovery of beings within the world in various ways and degrees of explicitness and exactness.

According to Heidegger's interpretation, truth is not some reality that hovers over and apart from Da-sein but is the fundamental event that happens with Da-sein's disclosing way of being. "To be true," for Heidegger, primarily means "to be disclosing," and this is the basic way in which Da-sein exists. The truth of owned existence will prove to be the most original phenomenon of truth, but this cannot be shown until the inquiry has been carried a stage further in Division Two. Co-original with the disclosure of Da-sein's own being in a world is the discovery of beings within the world. These beings are "true" in a secondary sense: they are not discovering, but discovered, and thus able to show themselves as and for the beings they are. A proposition, statement, or judgment is true insofar as it discovers things, takes them out of hiddenness, and lets them be seen in and from themselves. But whereas traditional philosophy has for so long regarded the proposition as the primary locus of truth, Heidegger shows it to be a far-off derivative of original truth, whose "locus" is the existential constitution of Da-sein's being as care. The essence of propositional truth has traditionally been thought to lie in the correspondence of the proposition or judgment with the state of affairs that is judged to obtain. Heidegger does not reject this theory as wrong or false; his aim is to demonstrate its derivative character (SZ, 223ff.; also WW, 7 ff., W, 75ff., G9, 179ff, P, 137ff., BW, 119ff.).

At first sight, it might seem to be a mild kind of criticism of the traditional definition of truth to say merely that it is derivative. But, it must be remembered, Heidegger is not talking about just any kind of study; he is talking of philosophy, whose business is to go to the original source. In its sphere, any derivation is in itself a de-generation. How is the derivative propositional truth, which Heidegger holds to have usurped a dominant place in philosophy, further elucidated by him?

Propositions, statements, judgments, or pronouncements of any kind are ontic phenomena that belong to language. Language, as Heidegger's previous inquiries have shown, requires for its foundation existential discourse (*Rede*), which has been defined as the articulation of understandability. The function of communicating pronouncements is to share the already disclosed being-in, self, world, and beings within the world with the listener and so bring him into a disclosing relation to the things talked about. Among the many possible kinds and modes of pronouncements, the propositions that logical theories of truth have in view are far from being primary. This is interestingly shown by Heidegger in a simple but illuminating example. He compares the everyday pronouncement "The hammer is too heavy" with the theoretical-physical proposition "The hammer is heavy." Between these two pronouncements, there is literally a world of difference. In the first, the discoveredness (truth) of the hammer is in advance understood from the workaday world. In the second, the world in which Da-sein lives has disappeared: this massive thing, the hammer, is now only-looked-at from the horizon of the substantiality of substantial bodies, which can be defined, among other things, by mass (weight) (SZ, Sec. 69b). The proposition par excellence that traditional logic has in view is of the second type. Its truth is clearly several stages removed from the original discoveredness of things as handy utensils, not to speak of its derivative character insofar as it necessarily rests on existential-ontological foundations that make the discovery of things first of all possible.

The proposition can be communicated both in speech and writing, preserved, handed down, and handed round. It thus acquires a certain handy reality within the world. It is there when it is needed and relieves us of the trouble of bringing ourselves into a primarily disclosing relation to things themselves. It is only now that the possibility of everyday hearsaying idle talk becomes fully understandable. It lies in the nature of propositions that they preserve the discoveredness (truth) of things and so maintain, albeit in a secondary and derived way, a certain disclosing relation to the things themselves.

As Heidegger's previous analysis has shown, there is a tendency in the hearsay of everyday idle talk to let the handy proposition entirely take over and carry the function of disclosing and discovering, which it does by preserving the "discoveredness of. . ." this and that. So it comes about that when the need arises to demonstrate the truth of something, that is, when recourse is had to things themselves to attest that they are such and such, what they are compared with are the propositions whose "property" truth has become. If what the handy proposition says is found to agree with, to correspond with, how the real thing shows itself to be, then the proposition is confirmed as being "really" true. In accordance with the basic trend of traditional ontology, the whole of the relation "proposition-corresponding-with-real thing" is understood to be something "real." The truth, which is thought to be the distinctive "property" of the proposition, itself acquires the character of reality, and its original "locus" in the existential structure of Da-sein's being is forgotten.

In Heidegger's interpretation, however, truth cannot exist somewhere by itself like a thing, and cannot have the ontological character of reality. Truth, as disclosing and discovering, can only be when and as long as Da-sein factically exists. Understood in this way, it may be said that truth is "relative" to Da-sein's being. But does this "relativity" mean that truth is delivered over to the arbitrary invention of a subject and to the fallibility of his thinking? This is far from what Heidegger intends to say. Original truth as the disclosure of being, Heidegger says, a priori determines Da-sein's being through and through. His own way of being is the last thing Da-sein could ever invent or think out for himself. Truth is anything but the achievement of a subject or a product of his thinking faculties; it is the existential structure of care that is in advance so "organized," so "laid on," as to make Da-sein open both to himself and to other beings. If Da-sein is able to discover any truth by his own efforts, this is only possible for him because he himself is let into the original happening of truth, for which he is used and needed, and only in being so used and needed is he able to exist as Da-sein (GE, 34ff., 59ff., DT, 62ff., 81ff.). It is not Da-sein who disposes of truth, rather is it truth that disposes of Da-sein.

Just because truth is not the property or invention of Da-sein, it in advance assigns to him the way and direction in which disclosing and discovering can proceed. For instance, as we saw earlier, the articulated significance-whole of world (ontological truth) already prescribes definite ways in which the things discoverable within it can "hang together," can "make sense." The predisclosed whole of significance itself directs Da-sein toward . . . , refers him to . . . , other beings in certain ways, and so enables Da-sein to take his direction from . . . , to keep himself right by . . . , the things themselves that meet him within his world. The discovery of things (ontic truth) is not arbitrary and lawless, because it is in advance directed to bind itself to the things themselves. This is why ontic truth must prove and verify itself in and by the things that it brings to light.

Since, however, all the ways in which Da-sein exists are grounded in his finite freedom, in his disclosing relation to things, he can omit verification, he can refuse to let them show themselves as they are in themselves, he can force them into horizons of explanation that are completely alien to them. The seemingly obvious principle that, in an explicit inquiry into any specific kind of beings, the way of approach, the method of investigation and verification, must be drawn from their way of being and not from some preconceived notion of scientific truth, is frequently stressed by Heidegger, who is never afraid of saying the "obvious" where it is necessary. In view of the widespread desire today to approximate every explanation to the exactness of mathematics, Heidegger lays emphasis on the following points.

1. The exactness of cognition is not necessarily synonymous with essential truth. For instance, the measurements of time and space in

our everyday world are ludicrously inaccurate compared with the scientific measurements of events that happen to substances in an indifferent universal space (SZ, § 23). Nevertheless, statements like "It's a stone's throw away," or, "You can walk there in half an hour," are definitely understandable and perfectly appropriate to a world inhabited by everyday care. The paths on which Da-sein carefully goes about his business are different every day, but it is precisely in this way that the "real world" is originally discovered and is truly at hand. It is, therefore, not a priori certain that when we have exactly measured, say, the distance of the sun from the earth, and measured the sun itself as a complex of moving particles, we have understood it more truly than when everyday care discovers its handiness for warmth and light, for growth and life.

2. The prevalent tendency to regard the exactness of mathematics as the standard for the strictness of scientific truth is vigorously contested by Heidegger. Exactness, he maintains, is not synonymous with strictness (SZ, § 32, esp. 153). Mathematics is not stricter than history, it is only more exact, and it can be so only because the existential foundations relevant to it are much narrower than those required for history. As for philosophy itself, the strictness of thought it demands cannot be approached by any ontic science, yet its findings are in principle not susceptible of the kind of proof and demonstration that are possible to the ontic sciences. Its method and mode of verification, as we shall see in the next chapter on phenomenology, must be drawn from the unique nature of its own subject matter.

Since philosophy concerns itself with being, whose disclosure is truth itself, Heidegger assigns to philosophy the highest place among all explicit, "thematic" inquiries into truth. At the same time, he vigorously insists that no philosophy can in principle claim to be absolute or the only possible one. Like all explanation and interpretation, it is one of the finite possibilities of Da-sein's existence, and as such it stands at the same time in truth and in untruth.

As a factually existing being-in-the-world, Da-sein stands co-originally in truth and untruth. Just as the disclosing way of existence cannot be of Da-sein's own making, so the possibility of hiding, erring, and covering over cannot originally be in Da-sein's own power. Da-sein errs, not only and not primarily because his intellect is fallible and he cannot in fact know everything, but because hiddenness and concealment essentially belong to the event of unhiddenness and disclosure. It is paradoxical, and yet understandable, that the most original truth lies precisely in revealing the hidden as hidden. It is the recoil from this abyss of truth that sends Da-sein back to beings, at the same time whirling him away from himself to the things within his world. Da-sein errs away from himself, not by a conscious or subconscious act of self-deception, nor even aware of a desire to cover over the finiteness of existence, but because it belongs to his thrown and falling way of being. Untruth as hiddenness, erring, and covering over originally belongs together with truth as unhiddenness, disclosure, and discovery; the two are one and the same event.

The existential interpretation of truth, Heidegger maintains, is the necessary interpretation of the insight into truth that lies in our oldest philosophical tradition and is expressed in the word *alêtheia*. The goddess of truth leads Parmenides before the ways of discovery and concealment, between which the thinker has to choose by under-standingly distinguishing the two and deciding for one. This means that Da-sein stands co-originally in truth and untruth. The same tradition, moreover, has always brought together truth and being. Parmenides said: *to gar auto noein estin te kai einai* (Fragment 5, quoted in SZ, 212, and very often in Heidegger's later works), "The same namely are apprehending and being." Although this oldest insight into the essence of truth begins to be covered over already in Greek philosophy, it reasserts itself at its end with Aristotle, who can still identify truth with being and beings, calling the latter "the unhidden," "the self-showing," "the true."

The logical definitions of truth that later become dominant in Western philosophy also have their roots in Greek thought. The theory of propositional truth is an offspring of the traditional inquiry into beings as beings and has its rightness and validity concerning the definition of the substantial being of things. This truth, however, is not only limited and derivative but is not the most important kind of truth. Far more important to us than a correct cognition of things is the openness or pretence that concerns our own existence, on the basis of which we make our vital decisions and which determines the genuineness of our relations with other human beings (WW, 22f., W, 196f., G9, 196f., P, 150f., BW, 135f.).

But it is not enough merely to define the limits of logic and its truth, nor is it enough to go back to an older tradition and revive it. The *alêtheia* has not merely to be rediscovered, but has to be more originally understood than was possible at the beginning (US, 134, G12, 126-27, OWL, 39). The hiddenness at the heart of the *alêtheia*, although elementally experienced, did not become a problem for Greek thought. Attention turned not to the remarkable event that the unhiddenness had happened, but to what had come to light through this event: beings as beings. Truth, as a coming to light from concealment, has been thought to belong to being. In Heidegger's interpretation, it is rather the other way round: being belongs to the event of truth, which happens with the existence of Da-sein. Truth, being, and existence are a single event, to which original untruth, as hiddenness and erring, essentially belongs.

Finally, one point may be raised and briefly considered: the concrete bearing of Heidegger's interpretation of truth on his own inquiry. It has clearly emerged from the preceding discussions that, in a fundamental analysis of Da-sein's being, the truth of existence has to be *wrested* from the covering over that characterizes the everyday and disowned way of existing. Hence the urgency of finding the right approach to Da-sein and the proper method whereby the existential analysis can proceed. The importance of the phenomenological method for *Being and Time* is evident on every page. It is no exaggeration on Heidegger's part when he writes that his investigations "would not have been possible without the foundation laid by Edmund Husserl" (SZ, 38).

VII

The Concept of Phenomenology

Husserl's pure or transcendental phenomenology must be sharply distinguished from all other methods or disciplines that bear the same name.[1] In a general sense, phenomenology means the study of the forms in which something appears or manifests itself, in contrast to studies that seek to explain things, say, from their causal relations, or from evolutionary processes, and the like. The method of phenomenology is sometimes characterized as "descriptive," but this is considered by Heidegger to be tautologous, since the concept of phenomenology, properly understood, already implies description.

In § 7 of the introduction to *Being and Time*, under the title "The Double Task in Working Out the Question of Being," Heidegger gives a preliminary concept of phenomenology, leaving the full concept to be elucidated in Division Three. Because this division is missing, Heidegger's discussion of phenomenology remains not only short but also incomplete. It is, moreover, restricted to Heidegger's own aims and needs. His interpretation of phenomenology as primarily a method that prescribes only *how* an investigation is to be carried out, but not *what* is to be investigated, would be contested by the most distinguished exponents of Husserl's thought, and above all by Husserl himself.

Heidegger introduces his discussion of phenomenology by explaining Husserl's well-known maxim "*Zu den Sachen selbst!*": "To the things themselves!" The "things" referred to in this maxim, as we shall see presently, are not concrete, material things, but the "phenomena" themselves. The maxim formulates the demand that no time-honored concepts or theories, however well proven they may seem to be, must be taken over and made the starting point of some constructed evidence. Only phenomena that have been originally brought to light and been directly demonstrated as "self-evident" can satisfy the phenomenological demand for truth and claim to hold a place in the investigation.

After this first, broad characterization of the method, Heidegger proceeds to examine in detail the two components of the concept of phenomenology: phenomenon and *logos*. To begin with, *phenomenon* is a word that has been used in so many senses both in philosophy and outside it that a strict, unambiguous definition of its meaning has become necessary.

The Greek word *phainomenon* means the manifest, the self-showing. Heidegger defines the basic meaning of phenomenon as "what shows itself in itself." The Greeks occasionally identified the *phainomena* with *ta onta*, things, beings. There are, however, various ways in which things can show themselves; it is even possible that they show themselves as they are *not*, but only seem to be. Seeming is a self-showing in which things look as if they were such and such, but are not truly so. Seeming is thus a privative modification of phenomenon. Only the positive and original meaning of phenomenon, however, is to be admitted into its definition: that which shows itself in itself.

Both *phenomenon*, in the strict sense, and *seeming*, as its privation, must be distinguished from other ways in which things can appear. "Appearing" and "appearance," come from *adparere*, to come forward, to show oneself—that is, originally they mean the same as "phenomenon." This is why "appearing" and "appearance" (*Erscheinung*) are often used to define "phenomenon"—a practice that can lead to hopeless confusion in view of the manifold and ambiguous meanings of "appearance." A symptom, for instance a feverish flush on the patient's face, appears, shows itself, but in so doing it points away from itself to something else, to a disturbance in the organism. The disturbance, the illness, is often said to "appear" in the symptom, and yet the illness does not in the strict sense appear at all, it merely announces itself in and through the symptom. All signs, symptoms, symbols, or indications of any kind, in which something announces itself without directly appearing, must be distinguished from phenomena in the strictly defined sense if confusion is to be avoided.

The situation is further complicated by yet another sense in which "appearance" (*Erscheinung*) can be understood. It can mean an emanation of something that itself remains essentially hidden. In this case, "appearance" means an effect, a product, which indicates a producer, but in such a way that in showing itself it constantly conceals the true being of the producer: it is a "mere appearance." Kant uses the term *Erscheinung* in a twofold sense. In his thought, the word means in the first place simply "the objects of empirical intuition." But these appearing, self-showing objects—phenomena in the original and genuine sense—are at the same time emanations of something that essentially hides itself in them—they are "mere appearances."

Without going into still further complications mentioned by Heidegger, it is abundantly clear that his definition of the phenomenon as that which shows itself in itself is both necessary and right. It is, however, as Heidegger immediately points out, only a purely formal concept of phenomenon. The formal concept can be deformalized by determining what are to be taken for phenomena par excellence. One such possible deformalization has already been mentioned with Kant's "objects of empirical intuition." These objects are phenomena in the strict and genuine sense; they satisfy what Heidegger calls the "vulgar concept of phenomenon."

The phenomena which phenomenology seeks to bring to light, on the other hand, are of an entirely different order. Before they are concretely defined, however, Heidegger examines the second component of phenomenology, the *logos*. In the history of philosophy, the *logos* has been interpreted in widely different senses, as speech, reason, proposition, judgment, concept, definition, ground, relation. Heidegger renders the *logos* in its basic meaning of *discourse* (*Rede*) but warns that this translation can only justify itself when it has been shown what discourse itself means.

Aristotle explains the function of discourse as *apophainesthai*: to make manifest that which is spoken of (*De interpretatione*, chaps. 1-6, *Metaphysics*, Z, chap. 4, *Nicomachean Ethics*, chap. 6). The inner connection of phenomenon with *apophainesthai* jumps to the eye. The speaking *phainesthai* lets something be seen, shows something; *apo* . . . , from itself. That is: insofar as the speaking is genuine, it draws what it says from that which is spoken of. Speech is a demonstration, not in the derived sense of reasoning and proving; it demonstrates in the original sense, it points to . . . , it directly lets something be seen. This "demonstrative" way of making manifest, however, is not the character of every form of speech. Begging for something, for instance, also makes manifest, but in a different way.

Since the function of the *logos* as *apophansis* is to show something, it can have the form of a synthesis. But synthesis does not mean a connecting of ideas, a manipulating of psychical events. The "syn" has a purely apophantic meaning: it lets something be seen in its *togetherness* with something, it shows something *as* something.[2]

The generally accepted view that Aristotle assigns truth to the *logos* (proposition, judgment) as its original locus, Heidegger points out, is quite unjustified, because it overlooks that Aristotle is thinking of the *logos* in contrast to a more original way of discovering, of being true: the *aisthêsis* and *noein*. The *aisthêsis*, the simple, sensuous perception of beings, always discovers, insofar as it aims at something that is genuinely accessible only through it and for it. Thus, vision always discovers color, hearing discovers sound, and so on. In the purest and most original sense true, that is, always discovering, so that it can never cover over, is the *noein*, the pure "seeing" of beings in their simple essential being. This seeing can never be false, never cover over, although it can remain an un-seeing, inadequate to fulfill its disclosing function.

The possibility of falsehood arises with the synthesis-structure of the *logos*. When the showing of something is no longer simple and direct, but has to have recourse to something else and show the thing *as* something (e.g., the hammer *as* heavy), then a covering over becomes possible. The propositional truth is only the opposite of this covering over—a distant offspring of original truth.

The meaning of *logos* has now been sufficiently elucidated for a formal definition of phenomenology. *Logos* says: to let something be seen from itself. *Phenomenon* says: that which shows itself in itself. Taking the two together, phenomenology means: to let that which shows itself in itself be seen from itself. The concept of phenomenology, Heidegger says, is different from other sciences to which it bears an outward resemblance, such as theology, biology, and sociology: the sciences of God, of life, of human community. These latter name the subject matter that is to be investigated. Phenomenology, on the other hand, only names the way in which the matters to be investigated are to be brought to "show themselves," and this way has already been indicated by the maxim "To the things themselves!"

But what are the "things" that phenomenology lets us see? What are, for it, the phenomena par excellence? They are *not* the real things we meet within the world, which are always directly accessible to us and do not need a difficult and intricate method to bring them to light. The phenomena of phenomenology must be such that they are usually half-hidden, disguised, or forgotten, so that they in themselves demand a special approach. These phenomena are not beings but the being of beings. What phenomenology shows is always "being," its structures and characters, its meaning, its possible modifications and derivations. Phenomenology is the method, the way, in which being, the subject matter of ontology, can be approached and brought to self-showing.

Just because being and its structures are usually half-hidden, or covered over, or disguised, the phenomena have to be *wrested* from the objects of phenomenology. Hence the proper method is needed to secure the starting point of an analysis, the access to the phenomena themselves and the penetration through the prevailing disguises, the most dangerous of which, according to Heidegger, are those ossified concepts within a system that claim to be crystal clear, self-evident, and requiring no further justification.

Since being is always the being of some kind of beings, these beings themselves must first of all be secured in the mode of approach proper to them. This is a preparatory, prephenomenological step that is indispensable for the analysis proper. Here the phenomena in the vulgar sense, the concrete, ontic beings, become relevant. They are the "exemplary beings," the prephenomenological soil for the inquiry whose proper theme is being.

The prephenomenological soil of *Being and Time* is, of course, first and foremost man himself in his concrete existence. But the aim of *Being and Time*, as has been repeatedly said, is not merely to produce a regional ontology of man. Its method is entirely adapted to its own aim as a fundamental (existential) ontology, and is sometimes called "hermeneutic phenomenology" to distinguish it from the same method applied to other philosophical purposes.

Those readers to whom phenomenology has so far been perhaps hardly more than a name will no doubt look for some more detailed explanations from Heidegger as to what his method is and how it works. In the course of unfolding his theme, especially when the inquiry enters into a new phase (e.g., at the beginning of the interpretation of time, SZ, § 63), Heidegger does in fact stop to explain in detail the methodological steps about to be taken. Heidegger's elucidations of his method are always important and illuminating, but they do not, of course, aim at giving a simple, overall picture of phenomenology. The broad principles laid down in the "Exposition," on the other hand, are too general to be of much practical help to the reader who does not have at least an elementary knowledge of phenomenology. Such knowledge, although not explicitly demanded by Heidegger, is in fact required to make his treatise fully comprehensible. Without it, the peculiarly phenomenological way of "seeing," whereby such ungraspable phenomena as being and the structures of being are brought to "show themselves," remains a constant puzzle to the reader.

At this point, therefore, we shall turn away from *Being and Time* and attempt to take a few steps toward Husserl's thought. This diversion is necessary not only for a better understanding of phenomenology, but, above all, for indicating the point at which Heidegger radically departs from Husserl. This departure has a profound influence on the style of *Being and Time*, many of whose passages are incomprehensible without some insight into the controversial issues within the phenomenological movement itself.

The divergence between the two thinkers shows itself already in the concept of intentionality, which is the starting point and guiding principle of Husserl's thought. This concept can perhaps be best approached from the formal definition of phenomenon: that which shows itself in itself. Taken by itself, a phenomenon is evidently incomplete: the self-showing needs something to which it can show itself. The "something" which the phenomenon needs as the place of its appearing is thought by Husserl to be transcendental consciousness. This must not be confused with empirical consciousness, which is accessible to us in simple reflection, and which is the sphere studied by the empirical science of psychology. Consciousness—which must always be understood as transcendental consciousness—is in turn dependent on the phenomenon, since it is its very essence to be consciousness of . . .— that is, it always goes out for an object, it aims at something, it means something, it intends something. This basic character of consciousness is called by Husserl "intentionality." In his thought, especially in later years, "intentional" and "transcendental" tend to become the same. The unique and peculiar character of consciousness is that the phenomena, the objects which it intends, are constituted by its own activities in respect of whatness (essence, "meaning") and in respect of thatness (existence in the traditional sense).

It will be immediately evident to the reader that the disclosure of being that Husserl ascribes to consciousness belongs to the existential way of being in Heidegger's thought. The difference is not a matter of terminology: it is radical, and all the sharper because of the common ground between the two thinkers. Both agree that the metaphysical start from beings is not fundamental enough, and that the home ground of philosophy can only be the transcendental ground where the disclosure of being happens. Further, they are in complete agreement that the "place of the transcendental" cannot be simply one of the realities among other realities in the world, but that the "transcendental subject" must exist in a totally different way from the merely real object. It is at this point that the two thinkers radically diverge. Heidegger strikes out on his own interpretation of the "transcendental subject." Each thinker works out his problem in so different a way that, in spite of many similarities and in spite of Heidegger's incalculable debt to Husserl, a comparison between their thought is difficult to make. Perhaps the best way to indicate the difference is to look a little more closely at Husserl's problem and the way in which he sets out to solve it.

The task of philosophy, as Husserl sees it, is to unfold all the implications that lie enclosed in the intentional structure of consciousness. The first indispensable requirement for accomplishing this task is to develop a reliable method for gaining access to consciousness itself, a method that will enable us to "see" the immensely complicated contents and activities of consciousness just as immediately as we see the "real word" in an act of sense perception.

A sense perception is, of course, itself an act of consciousness. But all our naive awareness of the real world is already, as it were, an end product of the activities of pure consciousness. These activities lie "anonymously" in all our empirical experience, both of things and of ourselves as the concrete beings we are. Husserl therefore proceeds to suspend, to "put into brackets," to put out of action, everything that we normally accept ready-made from consciousness, and so to turn the phenomenological "eye" to consciousness itself. The method proceeds step by step, by way of a series of "reductions," one of which is called the "phenomenological reduction." In this, the reality of the world, as it is naively experienced by us, is suspended, put out of action, not because the reality is in the least doubtful or uncertain but because it is a product of consciousness, and the aim is to get those activities into view which first of all constitute this reality.

What is it, then, that Husserl suspends in the phenomenological reduction? Nothing less than the *is*. But not only the *is* of things is suspended; the *am* must also be put out of action, because what we naively experience in the *I am*, is the "empirical subject," the concrete beings we are in the real world. The *am* is no less a ready-made product of transcendental consciousness than the *is* of a thing, and must therefore be neutralized to get the contents of consciousness itself purely into focus.

But, it may be asked, does Husserl intend to say that everything in the world, ourselves included, is a sort of invention, a figment of imagination on the part of consciousness? Any such thought is as alien to Husserl as it is to Heidegger. It is not real beings that are constituted by consciousness, but their being in respect of what and how. This achievement of consciousness, moreover, is so little arbitrary that it proceeds by the strictest laws, to discover which is part of the task of phenomenology. Nor does consciousness simply invent the what and how of things, but is dependent on receiving the "stuff" (Greek: *hylê*) on which it can go to work. The first problem, indeed, phenomenology has to solve is how consciousness can receive the "stuff" it needs in order to be able to work on it.

This problem is much more puzzling than it might seem to be at first sight. Let us consider a real thing; for example, a red apple. A moment's thought will show that "this red apple" is totally different from "my awareness of this red apple." The real apple is solid, hard, of such and such a color and shape, extended in space, and so on. My awareness of the apple, on the contrary, is neither solid, nor hard, nor colored, nor shaped, nor extended in space in any way. It is evident that this real apple, with its real qualities and properties, can never bodily "get into" my consciousness, and yet must be able to present itself to it *as* real, *as* rounded, *as* red, *as* solid, and so on. How is this presentation possible?

It is possible through sensations, or sense data (hyletic data), which themselves are of the nature of consciousness and present its activities with the "stuff" it works on. As Husserl's careful and detailed analyses show, these sensations or sense data are already in themselves extremely complex: they are fluid, they shade off, are variable, are accompanied by an escort of potential sensations. These manifold and variable sense data, however, would in themselves remain meaningless if they were not caught up by the so-called noetic (from *nous*) activities of consciousness, which explain their meaning (*Sinn*) by assigning to them the appropriate formal categories—for example, substance, quality, and the like. The noetic activities thus explain the sense data for what they are, for example, *as* the color of a material thing. In other words, they constitute the whatness, the essence of the object present to, intended by, consciousness. But the "what" already implies being (existence, thatness) of some sort: this is determined by the so-called thetic activities of conciousness, which set the mode of being of the object as, for instance, "certainly there," as well as its time-character, for instance, as "actual, now, present." These manifold and complex activities, in a process of continuous synthesis, bring forth the unified, identical "noema," the "intended," the "meant" object itself in its whatness and thatness. The noema is, of course, not the material thing itself, which could never be "produced" by consciousness; it is the way in which a material thing can be present to consciousness.

Even this oversimplified sketch will certainly suggest to the reader some similarities with Kant, just as Husserl's "reduction" may have reminded him of Descartes's method. To give Husserl's comments on these resemblances in a few words: Descartes was the first to turn toward the sphere of transcendental subjectivity (consciousness), but he got stuck halfway. He did not develop his method nearly radically enough (i.e., he suspended the reality of the world, but not the *I am*). His "thinking subject" remained a merely empirical subject, who exists in exactly the same way as the extended object, so that it is precisely the transcendental achievement of subjectivity that is left unexplained. Kant, on the other hand, penetrated further than perhaps any other thinker into transcendental consciousness but without fully realizing the peculiar nature of the "promised land" he had entered, which he could not therefore fully explore; nor could he develop the necessary method for its exploration. Kant's great achievement is the achievement of the intuitive leap of genius, which could not complete the arduous, painstaking, and enormously extensive tasks involved in a systematic exploration of consciousness.

One of the first tasks of phenomenology must be to analyze all the essential components, structures, and functions of consciousness itself. In its first phase, this inquiry has necessarily the character of a so-called static analysis. For the purpose of study, it must bring consciousness, which is essentially a Heraclitean flux, to a standstill. This freezing of a temporal event into immobility, while indispensable, is artificial, and must be complemented by a genetic analysis of consciousness, whose task is to show the generation of its activities in time, and the generation of time itself in consciousness.

This rough sketch of only a small corner of Husserl's phenomenology is all that can be given here without going altogether beyond the bounds set to this discussion. Seen in comparison with Husserl, the parallels in Heidegger's thought are as striking as the differences; it is as if a landslide had occurred, shifting everything onto another plane.

Nevertheless, it is precisely by venturing his own interpretation of "transcendental subjectivity," and by adapting phenomenology to the needs of his own question, that Heidegger most dramatically shows the potentialities of Husserl's method. The whole of *Being and Time* is a demonstration of phenomenology at work. It strikes the reader at once with its air of vigor and self-reliance, which is in no small measure due to the demand for original experience and self-evidence made by phenomenology. No method, of course, can produce genius, but where the two meet, the results are bound to be out of the ordinary. Heidegger can cut through centuries of encrusted and seemingly unchallengeable "truths" by asking one simple question about them. At the same time, as our exposition of Heidegger's basic thought has already shown, he is not out to destroy tradition. Heidegger is very far from declaring the

118   Part Two: Basic Features and Problems of Being and Time

whole of metaphysics to have been one vast mistake, arising from an ambiguous use of language. He shows how and why metaphysics had to be as it is, why its language had to be ambiguous, and where the limits of its truth lie. A further, perhaps incidental, but nonetheless delightful result of phenomenological thinking is that it brings alive those technical terms and concepts into which the original insights of past thinkers have hardened, by showing how and from where they had originally been drawn. As to Heidegger's own concepts, they are not abstract generalizations; they explain by making explicit what already shows itself, and the only way to understand them is for each one to see for himself what they are "letting him see."[3]

VIII

A Preview of the Tasks and Problems of Division Two

The preceding exposition of Heidegger's leading themes has moved mainly on the level of the "Preparatory Fundamental Analysis." The difficulties of bringing Division Two into the framework of a general introduction to *Being and Time* have already been mentioned. Not only does Heidegger's inquiry enter into a new phase, but the intricacy of this division calls for a much more closely knit study than has been made in this book of Division One. Before moving to that more detailed study of Division Two a short outline of the course Heidegger's inquiry takes in that division and an indication of the answer toward which it strives will be given in this concluding chapter of the second part of our guide. Its aim is not only to give an introductory survey of how Heidegger goes on to develop his main theme, but primarily to indicate the perspective in which alone the fundamental ideas and problems raised in Division One can be fully understood.

An extraordinarily important feature of a phenomenological inquiry is its point of departure. How and where does the new phase of *Being and Time* set in? It can only set in at the result achieved by the "Preparatory Fundamental Analysis": the exposition of man's being as care. The incompleteness of the formulation that Heidegger can give to this concept on the basis of his preparatory investigations begins to show itself already on the last page of Division One. The complexity of the care-structure leads Heidegger to ask whether the results so far reached are radical enough. Have they penetrated to the last intelligible ground of the unity and wholeness of Da-sein's being? Has the whole of Da-sein's being been brought into view at all? Evidently not. Being-in-the-world is, after all, ended by death and begun, at the other "end," by birth, whereas the "Preparatory Fundamental Analysis" has considered only the everyday happening "in between." Moreover, it is the essential character of Da-sein that to each one his being is manifest as *mine*. This is the ground of the possibility of owned and disowned existence; but the "Preparatory Fundamental Analysis" has only brought the average and disowned way of existing into phenomenological view. The incompleteness of the first phase of the inquiry has to be remedied before it can be shown that time is the deepest originative ground of the wholeness of Da-sein's being as care, and thus the meaning of being as such.

The starting point of Division Two proves to be the question as to how the whole Da-sein is and how he wholly is. It is the question of the extremest possibilities of Da-sein's existence, in contrast to his everyday mode of being. These extreme possibilities appear to lie, on the one hand, in the two "ends" of being-in-the-world that constitute its wholeness, and, on the other hand, in owned existence, constituting the way in which Da-sein can be wholly himself, according to his ownmost possibility. The question of wholeness and owned existence, however, is nothing other than the problem of a finitely free being.

But no sooner is this problem formulated than grave difficulties begin to present themselves. In the first place, how can Da-sein be a whole at all? Certainly not as a sum, or a thing, or even as a merely living being is a whole. Da-sein can only be a whole in the way of care, whose essence lies in its disclosing character. The task facing the existential analysis, therefore, is to show whether and how Da-sein can disclose to himself the whole of his being.

This task, however, seems at first sight to be impossible to accomplish, not for accidental but for essential reasons. We seem to be able to get direct evidence only of the fact of the birth and death of others. As to his own being, Da-sein cannot get behind his own thrownness, he can only find himself already there as a thrown fact; while, at the other end, in experiencing his own death, he already ceases to be.

These peculiar difficulties make necessary a completely different approach to the problem from the one used in Division One. There the existential-ontological problem was approached from the existentiell-ontic basis of the factically existing Da-sein; here the method has to be reversed. The first task is to find out whether it is existentially possible for Da-sein to be a whole at all, in the way proper to his own being.

This task is completed by Heidegger in a series of detailed and closely integrated analyses, which lead to the conclusion that Da-sein cannot be made into a whole by having an end tacked on to his existence in death, but that his being is in itself a being-toward-an-end; as soon as and as long as a Da-sein is, he already exists in and from the disclosed possibility of the end of his existence, to which he relates himself in this or that definite way.

How is death, as the disclosed end of Da-sein's being, to be characterized existentially? It is the extreme possibility of the sheer *im*possibility of being-anymore. This possibility can never be transcended by the fore-throw of further possibilities; it is sheerly unrelational, being singly and uniquely each Da-sein's own; and it is certain, though indefinite as to the "when." Care thus reveals its ontological character of a being-thrown-into-death, as Da-sein's extremest possibility.

This existential-ontological concept of death—so far, it is only a concept—now demands an examination of whether a disclosure of death is ontologically possible. It is possible, as Heidegger proceeds to show, to an understanding which opens itself to a constant threat that rises from the ground of Da-sein's being, his thrownness into his "there." This threat is elementally revealed in the basic mood of dread. Understanding runs forward to this threat, fully disclosing it as the extreme possibility of not-being-able-to-be-there-anymore. The disclosure of death is thus seen to be ontologically possible on the basis of attunement (mood) and forward-running understanding.

But all this is, so far, merely an ontological construction and remains worthless unless Da-sein himself, in his ontic existence, confirms that the disclosure which has been postulated is possible in concrete experience. Where can such confirmation be found? Heidegger finds it in what is usually called "the voice of conscience." That this "voice" cannot be found as an observable "fact" by an objectively orientated investigation, that its "reality" cannot be proved, does not make it meaningless for the existential inquiry; on the contrary, it shows that in conscience we have a genuine and original existential phenomenon.

The task now is to analyze and interpret existentially the concrete, well-attested experience of conscience. Differently as this may be understood and explained by each Da-sein, there is general agreement that it is a voice that has something to say to oneself. It is, therefore, completely in accord with experience when Heidegger sees the ontological function of conscience in disclosing something, in giving something to understand, not to Da-sein in general, but to a Da-sein singly and individually.

All the stranger is Heidegger's interpretation of conscience as the call of care and of what this call gives man to understand. To mitigate its strangeness, it must be emphasized that Heidegger's interpretation is neither psychological, nor ethical-moral, nor religious, but existential-ontological. Its task is not to find out what circumstances may bring about an experience of conscience, or how its voice is heard and understood by each Da-sein, but to show how Da-sein must a priori be, that is, how he must be manifest to himself in his being, so that in his factical existence he *can* hear a voice of conscience at all, and *can* understand himself convicted of a debt (*Schuld*), or summoned to fulfill some obligation he owes.

According to common experience, conscience discloses something like a *debt*. Like the English word, the German *Schuld* has a wide range of meaning: guilt, sin, owing a debt or a duty, being indebted, being responsible for (guilty of) some deficiency or harm. After analyzing the concept of debt, Heidegger comes to the conclusion that a *not* is essentially implied in it. What conscience gives to understand has, in a formal-existential sense, an essential not-character, it is *nichtig*, it is determined by a *not*.

The central problem, therefore, is how this *not* is disclosed to Da-sein, so as to make it possible for him to be convicted of a debt or of an owing of any kind. This is only possible, as Heidegger shows, because Da-sein is fore-goingly revealed to himself as owing his being. He can never go behind his thrownness and let himself come, of his own accord, into being. *Not* as thrown by himself but only as a thrown fact can Da-sein ever find himself already there. It is to this *not* that care calls Da-sein back from his scatteredness into the they-self and from his lostness to things, giving him to understand that he *owes* it to take over his being and be the impotent (*not*-potent, *not*-determined) ground of an impossibility (the possibility of *not*-being-able-to-be-anymore). Strictly ontologically, Da-sein's being as care must be defined as being the *not*-determined ground of a *not*ness, as "being the (null) ground of a nullity" (*Das (nichtige) Grund-sein einer Nichtigkeit*, SZ, 285).

In this new formulation of care, the "being-the-ground," or "ground-being" (*Grund-sein*) comprehends in itself the whole provisional care-structure worked out at the end of Division One. This, however, cannot be shown in detail in the present short preview of Division Two. We must follow up, instead, Heidegger's interpretation of conscience, for, so far, the full phenomenon of conscience has not yet come into view. If conscience is the call of care, then hearing this call essentially belongs to it. And how does Da-sein hear this call? Simply by being wanting-to-have-conscience (*Gewissen-haben-wollen*), by being willing to be called back to his thrown self and summoned forward to his utmost possibility of not-being. Resolutely disclosed to himself from the ground of his being in the possibility of his end is the way in which Da-sein *can* exist wholly as an owned self.

The phenomena of conscience and owing not only provide Heidegger with the required ontic-existentiell basis for his inquiry, but show at the same time that the two apparently separate problems of how Da-sein can be a whole properly, and how he can exist as an owned self, are one and the same. Existing in the resolute disclosure of his thrown being-toward-an-end is the way in which Da-sein can-be-a-whole properly, that is, in the way appropriate to his own being (*eigentliches Ganzseinkönnen*).

Although the exhaustive inquiry into wholeness, end, death, and conscience may be regarded as only preparatory to Heidegger's time-interpretation, it is important enough to occupy almost exactly half of the more than two hundred pages of Division Two. There is good reason to think that its importance does not become fully explicit in this division. The phenomenon of conscience and the new formulation of care prepare the ground for finding the answer to the question, How is it possible for man to understand being? Although Heidegger does not expressly say so, the internal evidence compellingly points to the conclusion that here is the basis from which Division Three would have to start.

The immediate function of the long preparatory inquiry, however, is to lead up to the second half of Division Two. What contribution has it made to this most important part of what we have of *Being and Time*? What problem has it solved and what problem has it raised? It has solved the problem of the extreme possibilities of Da-sein's being. In so doing, however, it has shown that the structure of care is even more complex than had been suspected, comprehending in itself the phenomena of death, conscience, and owing. This increased complexity makes it all the more urgent to lay bare the ontological meaning (*Sinn*) from which the unity of the whole care-structure becomes understandable.

The meaning of care—the most original and fundamental form of its unity—is *time*. Its exposition needs for its basis the fully unfolded structure of care, because the phenomenon of time can be *originally* experienced only in owned existence. The care of everyday existence is, of course, also grounded in time, but the time that shows itself there is not the original phenomenon but a disowned modification of it.

Heidegger introduces his time-interpretation through the existential structure of death. How is it possible that Da-sein can understand himself, whether in an owned or a disowned way, in the utmost possibility of his existence? This is possible only if Da-sein is such that he *can* come toward himself in his possibilities at all. The coming, in which Da-sein comes toward himself in his ownmost possibility, is the original phenomenon of the future (*Zu-kunft*: coming-toward, or coming-to, SZ, 325). But Da-sein can only come toward himself in his possibilities insofar as he already is; that is, *is* as having-been. The original coming-toward himself is thus in itself a coming-back-to the thrown self that Da-sein is as having-been. The coming-back-to is the original phenomenon of the "has-been" or "having-been" (*Gewesen*) which springs in a certain way from the future. Coming-toward himself in his possibilities as back-to the thrown self he is as having-been, Da-sein is at the same time meeting beings within the world: this is only possible insofar as Da-sein is able to *present* them to himself (*gegenwärtigen*). The present is an offspring of the future and past.

The primary ecstasis (standing-out-of-itself) of time is the future. The ecstatic unity of future, past, and present is called by Heidegger "timeishness" or "temporality" (*Zeitlichkeit*). Timeishness *is* not (i.e., it is not the presentness of a thing), but brings itself to ripeness. It brings itself to ripeness in bringing forth possible modes of itself as time, in the threefold unity of future, past, and present. Original time is the time of owned existence which comes toward itself from the *end* that closes all other possibilities. Original time is thus itself closed: it is finite time.

As against the original, finite time of owned existence, how does it stand with the time of everydayness? It is from this existential phenomenon, Heidegger tells us, that the vulgar concept of time is drawn. Losing himself to his world, Da-sein understands himself not from his own utmost possibility, but from his makings and doings in company with other people, from the successes and failures he expects or fears. In the first place and for the most part, Da-sein comes toward himself in his worldish possibilities. The time that shows itself in this mode of existing is not a Da-sein's own, it is the public time, or, more precisely, the published time of the they-self. It belongs to anybody and nobody; that is why it is endless. The traditional concept of time as an in-finite succession of now-points is derived from the disowned time of disowned existence, levelled down and deprived of its ecstatic character, until the original phenomenon becomes well-nigh unrecognizable.

From Heidegger's interpretation of Da-sein's being as "existent timeishness" grow the manifold and complex tasks that occupy the second half of Division Two. These require a close study, as indeed does Heidegger's whole time-analysis, of which only the first few steps have been roughly indicated here. By way of preparation let us summarize the main problems whose solution is assigned by Heidegger to the three long chapters (chaps. 4–6) that compose the second half of Division Two.

The first task facing Heidegger is to show that the wholeness and unity of all the main structures of care—that is, existence, facticity, and falling—are only possible on the ground of Da-sein's timeishness. All the essential findings of the "Preparatory Fundamental Analysis" are once more analyzed and interpreted in terms of time. The timeishness of understanding and attunement, of falling and of the everyday taking care of things, of the fundamental constitution of being-in-the-world and the temporal-horizontal structure of world, and many other themes are worked out by Heidegger in a long chapter entitled "Temporality and Everydayness" (chap. 4).

The next chapter begins with an analysis of the owned self and its ontological interpretation. This leads to an existential exposition of history from the "happening" of owned existence, illuminating, at the same time, the possibility of a genuine being-with others which springs from one's own self. The problem of the first "end" of Da-sein's being, its beginning with birth, which seems to have been unduly neglected in favor of its ultimate end, now reemerges with the important theme of taking over one's thrownness and historical heritage as one's own. While in the context of *Being and Time* the existential interpretation of history stands primarily in the service of Heidegger's fundamental ontology, it has undoubtedly a wider than purely philosophical interest and is considered by many readers as the central piece in Division Two.

In the sixth and final chapter, Heidegger takes up the problem of the vulgar concept of time, the world-time in which things come into being and pass away and in which the happenings within the world take place. As against the views expounded by some modern philosophers (e.g., Bergson), Heidegger interprets world-time as a perfectly genuine time-phenomenon, grounded in Da-sein's everyday being-with others and taking care of things. One of the tasks of this chapter is to show in detail how the concept of a featureless, "unecstatic" time has been derived from the "significant" time of the worldishness of everyday care. Parallel to Division One, where Heidegger sets off his existential interpretation of world against Descartes's "extended world," he now sets off the connection between timeishness, man's factical existence, and world-time, against Hegel's interpretation of the relation between time and spirit.

In the last short section of Division Two (§ 83), which is the last section of *Being and Time* as we have it, Heidegger comes back once more to the central theme of the whole fundamental ontology: the question of the meaning of being as such. Up to the point reached in the inquiry, the question still awaits an answer. The last page of *Being and Time* moves to its close with a series of questions. "How is the disclosive understanding of being belonging to Da-sein possible at all?" (SZ, 437). This question will be answered by laying bare the horizon from which something like being becomes understandable. The original whole of Da-sein's existential-ontological constitution is grounded in timeishness. This is where the possibility of an understanding of being must be sought. Heidegger brings the division to an end by asking: "Is there a way leading from primordial time to the meaning of *being*? Does *time* itself reveal itself as the horizon of *being*?" (SZ, 437).

PART THREE

❦

Division Two of Being and Time: *Da-sein and Temporality*

INTRODUCTORY

Heidegger's first concern is to survey the "hermeneutic situation," that is, the conditions required by the interpretation, as it stands at the beginning of Division Two. This proves to be insufficient not only for the ultimate interpretation of temporality as the meaning of being in general but even for working out the timeish structure of Da-sein's being as the meaning of care. Since the results so far reached are not radical enough, Heidegger's first task will be to make good the twofold deficiency of the present hermeneutic situation.

The first deficiency was already indicated in the last chapter of Division One. It lies in the almost complete obscurity of owned existence. This came into view only for a moment in the analysis of dread; both its existential structure and its concretization in a factical existence remain to be demonstrated in detail.

The second deficiency is perhaps even more serious. The whole of Da-sein's being has not yet come into focus at all. The Preparatory Fundamental Analysis considered Da-sein only as he exists every day between birth and death. These extreme "ends" have so far been left out of consideration altogether. The omission is all the more serious because the beginning and end of being-in-the-world are not mere incidents that have nothing to do with what happens "in between" them; on the contrary, they constantly reach into and determine the whole of care. Da-sein as care *is* this beginning and this end, as well as the "in between." It remains to be shown in detail that care is in fact capable of carrying Da-sein's extremest possibilities—in contrast to his average, everyday mode of being—in itself. Until this is done, the thesis that care is the original whole of Da-sein's being remains an empty assertion.

The problem of Da-sein's wholeness and of his ability to be his own self, will take up nearly half of Division Two. It may well be asked why Heidegger added this preparatory half to Division Two, when its subject matter would seem to assign it to Division One. A close study of the subject, however, will reveal that it belongs much more immediately to the problem of time than to that of everyday being-in-the-world. Everyday being-in-the world draws Da-sein away from himself and turns him to his worldish relations to other beings; hence the problem of space comes to the fore already in the third chapter of Division One. Something like place and space evidently belongs to Da-sein's worldishness. The world-time, however, in which things are and move, change and endure, will turn out to spring from a more original primordial time. This is the horizon from which being, in any way in which it is understandable ("meaningfull") at all, manifests itself. All explicit interpretations of beings must ultimately originate in this horizon of time, and hence the formal concept of being as such, with all its possible articulations and modifications, must have a temporal meaning. It is evident therefore that the more original primordial time must be the hinge on which Being and Time "turns round" to Time and Being.

The absence of the solutions that Time and Being (Division Three) promised to bring vitally affects the interpretation of Division Two. It cannot look forward to the answers from which the obscurity of unanswered questions could be, as Heidegger intended, retrospectively cleared up. What is even more important, the very problem raised by *Being and Time* remains obscure, for it is in the nature of philosophy, in contrast to science, that the solutions it offers never leave its problems behind, but only show them in their perennially problematic character. It is not surprising that in later years Heidegger frequently has occasion to refer to the lack of comprehension that the problem raised in *Being and Time* met with in the philosophical world, and to ascribe the main reason for it to the decision to hold back Division Three from publication. Whether Heidegger's reasons for this decision can be regarded as adequate or inadequate will be considered in our penultimate chapter.

Our most immediate concern is how to overcome, as far as possible, the obscurities of Division Two. The first step the present interpretation proposes to take is to make explicit how far Heidegger carries the exposition of specific problems and where he breaks them off. This negative side of the interpretation is important because it will prevent the illusion of conclusiveness and finality from arising, when in fact not one specific problem raised in *Being and Time* is carried to a conclusion. On the positive side, however, the interpretation will go beyond what the text explicitly says and suggest what solution may be intended by Heidegger, or is at least compatible with his thought, provided that sufficient evidence is available for doing so. Supplementary evidence will be drawn mainly, though not exclusively, from two short works that immediately follow *Being and Time* (WG and EM) and that are generally considered to belong immediately to its problematic.

IX

The Articulation, Language, and Method of Division Two

1. The Articulation of Division Two

The theme and development of Division Two was briefly outlined in chapter 8 of this guide. Our present aim is to single out some important details for further discussion.

One such detail is the unusually long preparatory part of Division Two, which cuts the division into two nearly equal halves. To be quite precise, the first part covers ninety-four pages, while the second part, which carries the main theme, is only eighteen pages longer. Moreover, the relevance of the long introduction to the main theme is not at all easy to see. As a result, the reader who comes to it unprepared often works through its ninety-four pages with a growing impatience and irritation. What, he asks himself, has all this to do with temporality? What possible bearing can conscience, owing, ground, opened existence, and so on, have on the problem of time? Consequently, the first thing he may rightly demand from an exposition is to be shown that these phenomena are in fact connected with Da-sein's timeish way of existing and with the time that springs from it.

Let us approach this problem in a seemingly round-about way. Let us first ask a preliminary question. Why is it, we ask, that time, the most fundamental character that unifies and defines all being, enters so late into Heidegger's inquiry? Why is it that in his world-analysis

(Div. One, chap. 1), where an exhaustive discussion is devoted to space, we do not hear a word about time? This omission is all the more strange because in our usual thinking we tend to couple space with time. We talk about the spatiotemporal universe as a matter of course. The events of nature obviously happen in space and time. Both are equally fundamental for defining how things are and move, change and endure. Why is it, then, that in Heidegger's existential analysis space and time are set so far apart?

The reason is that Heidegger is not concerned with describing events in space and time, but with the origin of these phenomena in the existential constitution of our being. The existential origin of space clearly lies in our worldishness. The world *wherein* we dwell and stay near to things has in itself an essentially "whereish" character. But is not time also fundamental to world? Certainly it is, but the world is not fundamental enough to originate time. Its place of origin does not primarily lie in our relation to other beings, but in our nearness to ourselves. Timeishness is the most fundamental way in which a finite existence comes near to and affects himself, in which he brings himself to himself. This is why it cannot be made explicit in the first division of *Being and Time*, where Da-sein's existence is investigated only in the mode of falling away from himself to the world. Before the phenomenon of time can be made explicit, its place of origin in Da-sein's relation to himself must be fully laid bare.

This is the task carried out in the long preparatory part of Division Two. Attentively examined, its analyses of the extremities of birth and death, and of the call of conscience to a resolute existence in these extreme possibilities, all strive toward the sole end: to bring man back to himself from his lostness to the world. They thus clear the source and ground from which time springs. Once this is clearly seen, the relevance and necessity of the introductory part of Division Two no longer stands in doubt.

2. The Language of Division Two

The aim of this section is not to list all the new terms we shall meet in Division Two, but to select a few important ones for preliminary study. But before coming to them, a word must be said about some concepts already familiar to us from Division One. There is sometimes a new emphasis, a slight shift in their meaning as they enter into the differently orientated inquiry of Division Two. This does not call for a new German terminology, for Heidegger's concepts are in advance so chosen that they cover the whole range of meaning required of them. Unfortunately, the range of the English translations rarely coincides with that of the original. Hence the terms most suitable for Division One may not always be the best for Division Two and may have to be reconsidered.

Two cases in point may be mentioned. The first is the *Da* of *Da-sein*. It can best be expressed by "there" in Division One, whose main theme is Da-sein in his worldish existence, in which he finds himself "there" among the things in his world. Division Two, on the contrary, takes owned existence for its main theme. In this way of being, Da-sein no longer understands himself from the world, but relates himself to the world from his own resolutely disclosed self. In this context, the *Da* can be more appropriately expressed by "here."

The second case arises from the difficult concepts of *das Man* and *Man-selbst*. The German *man* has a range of meaning that we cannot express in a single word: people, they, one, and the passive voice (e.g., *man sagt*, it is said) are possible ways of translating it. Before deciding which of these might be most suitable for Division Two, let us briefly recall what it is we want to express. According to Heidegger, Da-sein can exist as not properly himself, a possibility arising from his being-with-others in the same world. In his everydayness, Da-sein is mostly not himself, but *one-of-them, one-of-the-others* (*das Man*). It is they, the others, who explain and make public how people commonly exist, *oneself-among-them* (*Man-selbst*).

The composite expressions are introduced here to show that Heidegger's German *das Man* comprehends in itself both "one" and "them" in an organic unity, impossible to express in a single English word. The translator is forced to choose between several inadequate alternatives. Much can be said in favor of "one" and "oneself," in spite of their regrettable ambiguity, for in English "being oneself" usually means "being one's *own* self"—exactly the opposite of Heidegger's meaning. In the first division, however, "they" seems to be the better choice, for there the stress undoubtedly falls on the constitutive function of "them," of "people." In the second division, the emphasis shifts. The pull toward the owned self becomes so strong that it affects even the disowned self. In fact, it is only in contrast to owned existence and in the face of the extremity of death that the "oneself" emerges from its obscurity among "them" and begins to distinguish itself from "people," from "others," at all. In Division Two, many passages clearly demand the use of "one" and "oneself," while others clearly insist on the use of "them," and sometimes of "people." All these expressions will be used in accordance with the demands of the text.

Other terms familiar from Division One which may need rethinking will be discussed as they occur in the text. We shall now proceed to examine some new concepts of Division Two. The discussion does not aim merely at giving a dictionary definition of them, but at showing something of the direction in which Heidegger's thought moves. It will at the same time give us an opportunity to gather up the results reached in previous studies. As Heidegger always reminds his readers, these must be firmly kept in mind in the new phase of the inquiry.

(a) Timeishness

Although this term has already been repeatedly used, no attempt has so far been made to justify it as a translation of Heidegger's *Zeitlichkeit*. Considering that it is the central concept of Division Two, a smoother rendering into English would certainly have been desirable. "Timeliness" had to be ruled out as completely unsuitable, but "temporality" provided a possible alternative. In spite of several points in its favor, the word has not been adopted here, because Heidegger has assigned a definite role to it: the "temporality of being" (*Temporalität des Seins*) was to have been elucidated in Division Three. There is both a connection and a difference between the timeish way in which man exists and the temporal character of being as such. To show this in an easily surveyed form, two tables are set out below.

Figure 9.1 shows the main modes of being with which we have become familiar in Division One, figure 9.2 the distinctive time-character that belongs to each.

Students of German philosophy may find it useful to recall that *Realität* generally means the pure thereness (*existentia*) of things; that is, its usual meaning is very near to Heidegger's *Vorhandenheit*. The differentiation between handy reality and substantial reality, at-handness or objective presence at hand, it must be remembered, came into philosophy only with Heidegger's *Being and Time*. The originality of his analyses has led to a tendency greatly to overstress the importance of "handy reality" in Heidegger's thought as a whole. For Heidegger himself, the philosophical importance of everyday utensils lies solely in their belonging to a world, so that the reference-structure of world can be directly demonstrated from their handy-being. This was not possible when the start was made from the substantial reality of mere substances, the common practice in Western philosophy.

For students of Kant it is especially important to note that the German use of *Realität* as pure thereness (*existentia*) is comparatively modern. As Heidegger points out, Kant himself still uses *Realität* in its

FIGURE 9.1

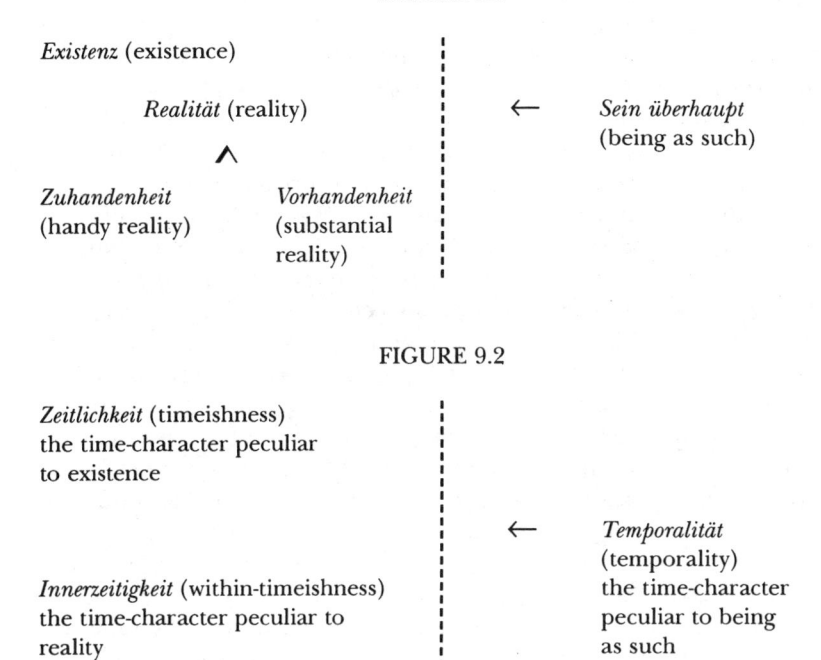

Existenz (existence)

    Realität (reality)   ←   Sein überhaupt
         ∧   (being as such)

Zuhandenheit   Vorhandenheit
(handy reality)   (substantial
                     reality)

FIGURE 9.2

Zeitlichkeit (timeishness)
the time-character peculiar
to existence

                                  ←   Temporalität
                                         (temporality)
Innerzeitigkeit (within-timeishness)   the time-character
the time-character peculiar to   peculiar to being
reality   as such

medieval sense of whatness, essence, or, to use Kant's term, concept (KPM, 84, G3, 86–87, KPM(E), 59; FD, 164–65, WT, 212–13; W, 296, G9, 469, P, 355). Kant's famous thesis that "Being is obviously not a real predicate" (*Critique of Pure Reason*, A 598, B 626) thus means that when we ascribe being (*existentia*) to things, we are saying nothing about *what* the thing is. For instance, the whatness of a merely possible spoon is exactly the same as that of an actually existing spoon.

These tables show that the two main ways in which actual, concrete beings can be—namely existence and reality—are unified and determined by their specific timeishness. Being as such, on the other hand, is not a way in which concrete beings are, but a purely formal concept of being. Its "temporal" character can therefore only be a purely formal concept of time. Hence it seems that timeishness is a better rendering of *Zeitlichkeit*, in spite of the admitted awkwardness of the expression.

(b) The Tenses of "To Be"

A difficulty far more serious than the clumsiness of single terms arises from the grammatical structure of English and German. In English, the perfect of *to be* is formed with the auxiliary verb *to have*. In German, the corresponding tense is formed with *to be*. What has this to do with Heidegger's inquiry into being and time? Simply this: if our existence is fundamentally timeish, this must in some way always be understood by us and articulated in our language. Without any philosophy, without any Heidegger, we are always saying "I shall be" and "I have been," and we understand as a matter of course our future-being and our past-being in these words. How we can understand something like a future and a past, and how these basic modes of time originally manifest themselves in our existence, are questions we do not normally ask. For Heidegger, however, these questions are central. It is in their discussion that the grammatical difference mentioned above will prove to be an insuperable difficulty. No amount of ingenuity can transform our "I have been" into "I am been" (*Ich bin gewesen*). We are forced to resort to circumlocutions like "I am as having been." This is obviously a much less telling way of saying that the "past-being" expressed in the "been" is not something passed away, gone away from me, but that I am constantly "present" to myself only in and from having been. To show even more vividly how I am my own "past," Heidegger even goes to the length of making a present participle out of the "been" (*gewesend*). Ludicrous and impossible as it would be in English to say "I am been-ing," in German the construction is entirely natural and immediately understandable. Some of the opaqueness the reader must expect in Heidegger's time-analysis arises from the unalterable fact that German is pliable in a different way from English.

(c) Heidegger's Tautologies

Next we may take a characteristic expression of Heidegger's: *Zeitlichkeit zeitigt sich*. The unusually long discussion that follows in *Being and Time* is not devoted solely to this phrase, but to the whole problem that it represents. This problem does not concern Heidegger alone, but the whole of philosophy. It is this: how can we speak of being in an appropriate way, when being is totally "other" than beings? If we rightly say of a tree that "it is," can we claim equal rightness for "being is"? The "is" means being; we might as well say "the is is"—obviously a flagrant tautology. An equally embarrassing situation arises when we try to speak of the characters of being. How are these to be distinguished from those ontic characteristics that belong to beings? In our usual descriptions of a person, for example, we say that he is fair, raw-boned, slow in thinking, and the like. But we also say "man is temporal." We are compelled to employ the same form of speech when the meaning is totally different. The sentence "Man is temporal" does not predicate an ontic characteristic of man; it means that he *exists in a timeish way*. It does not describe what certain beings are, but how existence is, how being is.

This whole problem is touched upon by Heidegger when he warns his readers that timeishness (*Zeitlichkeit*) does not belong to the order of beings, and therefore all "is" should be kept away from it. "*Zeitlichkeit*," Heidegger says, "is" not, but "*zeitigt sich*" (SZ, 328). *Zeitigen* means to bring to ripeness, to mature, to let arise, to bring forth. As we shall see later, what timeishness brings forth is not beings, but purely and solely various modes of itself. Long before we come to understand precisely what this means, we can and do notice something peculiar about the phrase "*die Zeitlichkeit zeitigt sich*." Both the noun and the verb have *Zeit*, time, at their root. What we have before us is evidently a tautology, which unfortunately is lost in translation. It might just be possible to say "timeishness timeifies," and the meaning would not be very far off Heidegger's, but the expression is too forced to be used, except perhaps in extremity. (In their translation of *Being and Time* Macquarrie and Robinson have been somewhat more successful. They have adopted "temporality" for *Zeitlichkeit*, which enables them to say "temporality temporalizes.")[1]

Helpful as a well-turned translation undoubtedly would be, the really important thing is to understand why Heidegger deliberately adopts a tautology where it could be avoided. Is it out of a childish delight in playing with words? Or is there a sober, well-founded reason for it? Certainly there is. Heidegger thinks that meaningful tautology is the only way in which we can express that being is not something, but the sheer "other" to all beings. It may be asked, however, what in fact this "other" can be? If it is not something, not anything, must it not be nothing? Indeed, Heidegger maintains like Hegel, only for quite different reasons, that being and nothing are the same. All the more important for us to remember that this "nothing" is not a total, absolute hiddenness. It must be manifest to us in its own way, otherwise we could not even say "it is nothing." How the nothing "is" can be expressed with precision only in a tautological way: the nothing negates (*das Nichts nichtet*. WM, 34, W, 11, G9, 114, P, 90, BW, 105, EB, 369). Similarly formed phrases can be found scattered throughout Heidegger's works, such as: "the world worlds" (*die Welt weltet*), "place places" (*der Raum räumt*), "speech (language) speaks" (*die Sprache spricht*), and so on.

Although these tautologies are introduced here for the first time, they are not altogether strange to us. Especially the phrase "the nothing negates" strikes a familiar note, because what it says is so basic to Heidegger's thought that, in a different form, it had to be considered already in our study of Division One. A fuller explanation of this phrase will therefore give us the best chance of seeing that the tautologies quoted above are in fact eminently meaningful.

If Heidegger rightly maintains that being and nothing are the same, then the first task must be to show that the nothing negates in such a way as to make something—that is, beings as such, understandable in their being. This happening is possible only because the negation differentiates between nothing and something: Nothing not Something, and conversely, Something not Nothing. The capital letters are introduced here solely to emphasize the differentiating function of the negation (the *not*). It holds the nothing and something apart, so that from the difference between them each can show itself, the nothing as nothing, the something as something. At the same time, the difference holds them together in their sheer "otherness," for the nothing can only show itself as the other to something, as the "not something," while the something can only show itself as the other to nothing, as the "not nothing."

This difference, however, is what we familiarly call the difference between being and beings. For when we assert of something that "it is," the "is" means purely that the something has become manifest in and as itself. This is possible only because the something can show itself in its difference from nothing, as "not nothing." This reflection enables us to see in what sense being and nothing are the same, and in what sense we may rightly distinguish between them. When we consider being purely with regard to beings—that is, as the manifestness of beings in and as themselves—then we rightly speak of the being of beings. But when we consider being purely with regard to its possibility, then indeed being and nothing are the same.

At this point, however, a doubt may arise. If both nothing and something can only appear from the difference between them, does Heidegger rightly insist that the nothing negates? Would it not be equally true to say that the something negates? This thought proves to be untenable as soon as we realize that something can never disclose nothing. All the beings in the world can never make the nothing understandable. The possibility lies only the other way: the nothing must be disclosed to us in advance, and only from it can something come to light *as* something, beings *as* beings.

Metaphysics, on the other hand, starts from beings. Its basic question, "What are beings as beings?" Heidegger rightly insists, can never radically formulate, let alone solve, the problem of being, for beings can never explain being, something the nothing.

Heidegger's tautological way of expressing how the nothing "is," has so far proved to be not only meaningful but eminently precise: the nothing negates by introducing the first differentiation between nothing and something, being and beings. In so doing, however, it in advance drives beings on to the same plane: they must and can only show themselves *as* beings, not nothing. The nothing negates by unifying beings *into a whole*. That is why Heidegger usually speaks of beings in the whole (*das Seiende im Ganzen*), and not, as would seem more natural to us, of beings as a whole.

Hence when there are beings like ourselves in whose existence an understanding of being becomes a fact, we must necessarily find ourselves amidst beings in the whole. Moreover, we do not merely indifferently occur among other beings, but are in advance referred to them. The nothing repels us and so turns and directs us toward beings. This repelling and referring is grounded in a negation as denial and withdrawal. The nothing denies us any further progress, it utterly forbids any further penetration into itself. The nothing denies itself as "something" we can grasp and hold on to; it withdraws itself from us as a ground we can stand on. In this denial of penetrability and ground lies the initial thrust that throws us into a world, referring us to beings that we *can* grasp and hold on to, among which we *can* find firm ground. The nothing negates as the inner possibility and necessity of world, which essentially belongs to our being. When we ask about the "world itself," we are asking precisely about the last intelligible ground of its possibility and necessity.

But the world of a factical existence, as we know from Division One, has a richly differentiated structure and is altogether a highly defined phenomenon. Has this anything to do with the central event that the nothing negates? We may say in anticipation that it has, although it cannot yet be shown how and why. As the following study will try to show, the nothing negates in certain definite ways, and all these ways have the character of notness, that is, of denial and withdrawal. The nothing gives us no ground to stand on, no place to stay in, no time for further possibilities. As we shall see, in these various ways of negating, denying, and withholding, lies the ultimate disclosure of these irreducible characters—time the most fundamental among them—whereby we can articulate and define being.

What we do know already is that the world, as a highly articulated and defined phenomenon, has a unique function in the disclosure of being. This function is that only in and from the world can any concrete beings meet us and be distinguished according to what they are and how they are. The articulations of "what" and "how" were first brought to our attention by Heidegger's idea of being: what- and how-being, something, nothing, and notness. The something, or more precisely, to-be-something, can be further differentiated into how-to-be and what-to-be. But, as we can now see more clearly, all these articulations of being are still only empty, formal concepts, devoid of any real content. To enable us to fill these empty forms with concrete content—that is, to enable us to find ourselves among other beings and so distinguish ourselves from them, our own mode of being from theirs—is the unique function of world. It is the uniqueness of world that finds expression in the phrase "the world worlds."

Heidegger's tautologies, which at first seemed forced or meaningless, have now proved to be highly appropriate to those phenomena that belong to the disclosure of being. These are not an absolute nothing, nor, on the other hand, can they "be" in the same way as beings are. Each of these phenomena, moreover, has a distinctive and unique function in unifying, articulating, and defining being, which cannot be replaced by anything else. They are identical only with themselves; they are the strictly understood "identities." But there is still a further point that Heidegger expresses by his tautologies. This can best be exemplified by the last two tautologies, which were mentioned above but which we have not yet discussed.

Heidegger says *der Raum räumt*, "place places." First of all a word must be said about the English rendering, for it could be objected to on the ground that *Raum* means space, while the German for place is *Ort* or *Platz*. Nevertheless, the paraphrase comes as near as possible to Heidegger's meaning, because the everyday world, where something like space first becomes accessible to us, has primarily a place-character. This is very different both from the levelled-down space of a theoretically defined nature, and from the formal space accessible to a pure intuition (looking-at). What a geometrician "looks at" are not things in space, but purely space itself and its properties. The everyday world, on the other hand, is primarily "placeish," for the essential reason that our being-in-the-world is a staying-in, a dwelling-in. Hence the world, as the wherein of our everyday staying and dwelling, is familiar to us as the dwelling place, the home.

Granted, then, that the phrase "place places" comes close to Heidegger's meaning, what does it tell us? It tells us that only because something like place belongs to the disclosure of being can we understand ourselves as occupying a place in a world and direct things to their places within it. Place itself, as a character of being, "gives" us place, that is, makes the discovery of place and space first of all possible.

Similarly, it is speech that articulates our understanding of being and brings it to word in language. Primarily, therefore, it is language that speaks, and we speak only because we are in advance called into voicing the disclosedness of being. Language is not a tool, not an instrument of the subject, not a human invention. It is the other way round: we can be human only because the gathering and preserving of truth in language is our uniquely human vocation.

Let us sum up briefly what has emerged from our discussion of Heidegger's tautologies. First, they are called for by the phenomena themselves, insofar as these belong to being and cannot therefore "be" in the same way as beings. Second, each of these phenomena has a distinctive and unique function that can best be expressed in a tautology. Third, the tautologies impress on us that these phenomena, although they manifest themselves only in our existence, are not the arbitrary invention of a subject or in any way the product of our "subjectivity."

The whole of this discussion arose from the still obscure phrase "timeishness brings itself to ripeness" ("timeifies," "temporalizes"). Its aim was to prepare an understanding for this phrase when we meet it in the text of Division Two. At the same time, it helped to clarify the problem of how being "is," and to carry forward the exposition of the central problem of the "nothing."

(d) Primordial Time (Ursprüngliche Zeit)

Heidegger calls the timeishness of owned existence "primordial" or "original" time. In Heidegger's usage, *ursprünglich* has a twofold meaning.

First, it is applied to what originates, what gives rise to something. Second, it is applied to something that springs straight from the origin and remains near its source. Accordingly, owned existence originates the time that remains near its source in the finiteness of man's being. In contrast to this, disowned existence originates the time that falls away, runs away from its finite origin, giving rise to the vulgar concept of an infinite now-time.

How all this happens will gradually come to light in Division Two. What can be usefully done at this point is to remove the misgivings we all feel in the face of an interpretation that denies an "objective existence" to time and explains it as a "subjective," that is, an existential phenomenon. It is interesting to note that in his introduction to the second edition of the *Critique of Pure Reason* Kant points to this difficulty as the stumbling block that even his most attentive readers found hardest to surmount. The difficulty can be simply stated as follows. The natural universe, we would argue, was there long before man and presumably will be there long after man has disappeared; it is completely independent of him. But how can the universe endure and change except *in time*? If time were merely our "subjective" way of apprehending, unifying, and ordering events, the independent existence of an "objective world" would be completely inexplicable.

This difficulty arises, in the last resort, from our tendency to confuse being with beings. Let us ask once more, What does it mean that a thing, for instance, that tree over there, is (exists)? It means that it is manifest to us precisely as that tree, a thing completely independent of us, a thing in its own right. Hence when no man exists and an understanding of being is no longer possible, the tree itself will not cease to endure and change, but it will no longer have the chance of *manifesting* itself as enduring and changing, that is, as being in time. The objections to an existential interpretation of time prove to be untenable when time is understood as a fundamental character that defines being, and being means the *manifestness* of beings in and as themselves.

(e) The "Originality" of an Ontological Interpretation

In introducing Division Two Heidegger explains that he is not yet ready to interpret the meaning of being as such, or even able at this stage to interpret the meaning of Da-sein's being (care), because the analysis carried out in Division One lacks *originality*. If we understood "originality" in the vague sense of "novelty," the professed lack of it would indeed be surprising. As things are, Heidegger clearly means that Division One has not yet penetrated deeply enough into the structure of care. In order to do so, the inquiry must show that care is capable of explaining the whole of Da-sein's being, from its beginning with birth to its ending with death. Further, the concept of care must be able to explain the unity of Da-sein's being—that is, how such very different ways of existing as owned and disowned existence can both originate in and receive their possibility from the one basic structure of care. When all this has been shown, Heidegger's existential inquiry will have gained the required "originality."

3. THE METHOD OF DIVISION TWO

The phenomenological demand for evidence puts Heidegger's powers to a severe test in Division Two. Its very subject matter seems to deny any concrete foothold to the inquiry. To take only one example, Heidegger's task is to work out the difference between the owned and the disowned (falling) ways of existing. This difference is not of the same order as, say, the psychological one between timidity and aggressiveness, introversion and extroversion, and so on. These psychological dispositions can well be documented by characteristic modes of behavior. The basic ways of existing, on the contrary, can never be so concretely demonstrated. It is doubtful whether in any specific instance we can know with any certainty in what way Da-sein exists.

How, then, does Heidegger set about his task? His main foothold lies in those characters of everyday existence that have already been analyzed and secured in Division One. In this way of existing, as has been shown, Da-sein *falls away* from himself by *fleeing from* a threat that constantly pursues him. Owned existence, therefore, must lie in a resolute *turning toward* the threat that overtly or covertly determines Da-sein's being. The basic characters of owned existence can be shown by going *counter to* the trend dominant in the falling way of existing, somewhat on the principle that by going against the stream we are bound to arrive at the source.

This method, it may be remembered, is first employed in the exposition of Da-sein's being as care (Div. One, chap. 6). There it is deeply impressive because it is based on the elemental experience of dread. If it becomes less impressive in the analysis of owned existence, the weakness lies not so much in the method as in the basis from which Heidegger is compelled to start. In working out the existential concept of death, for instance, much emphasis is laid on the everyday tendency to explain away death by making it into a fact like other facts. What troubles us is whether it is the whole truth, whether Heidegger is not forced to underplay everyday existence in order to show how owned existence must be.

On the other hand, it must be recognized that the basis on which the inquiry must rest is strictly prescribed by Heidegger's aim. The aim is to explain the meaning of being by penetrating to the inmost possibility of our understanding of being. All the ways in which we can experience ourselves, other beings, and things in general, are in advance determined by that understanding. The ground of its possibility can therefore only lie in our being itself and not in any circumstances extraneous to it. The solid facts and conditions in which other kinds of inquiries can find a firm footing are not only irrelevant but inadmissible to Heidegger's. All his evidence must be drawn purely from Da-sein's existence and how this is manifest in his understanding.

A few words have to be said about the method to be adopted for the exposition of Division Two. Generally speaking, the importance of following the development of the main argument cannot be overstressed. This implies a corresponding firmness in passing over details of great interest that are not absolutely essential to the main movement. This principle of exposition, however, is greatly affected and modified by the overriding consideration that *Being and Time* is an unfinished work that demands unusual methods. The normal and simple way would be to take the reader through to the end, then come back to those difficulties and obscure passages that can be illuminated only from the end. Since the absence of Division Three makes this impossible, the expositor is forced to devise ways of mitigating its absence as far as possible. The method adopted in this guide is to pay special attention to those central themes that Heidegger leaves half finished in Division Two, obviously intending to complete their interpretation in the third division. These will be discussed in great detail and, where it is possible, suggestions will be made about their final place and function in the solution of Heidegger's ultimate problem.

X

Da-sein's Possibility of Being-a-Whole and Being-toward-Death

1. CAN DA-SEIN BE EXPERIENCED AS A WHOLE?

At the end of Division One, Heidegger formulated the unity of existence, facticity, and falling in the single concept of care. According to this, Da-sein is ahead-of-himself-already-being-in (a world) as being-together-with or being-near-to (beings met within the world). The primary structure of care, the "ahead-of-himself" now raises the doubt whether Da-sein can ever be a whole in the sense of having reached completeness. The "ahead-of-himself" seems to say clearly that Da-sein, as long as he factically exists, is essentially "beyond" himself as he already is. Existing for the sake of himself, he constantly relates himself to his possibilities, to what he is not yet but can become. Even when Da-sein is sunk in hopelessness, when he expects nothing more from "life," when he is ready for anything, he is still not cut off from his possibilities. Hopelessness, despair, and disillusionment are specific ways in which Da-sein can relate himself to his possibilities. His ability to become what he is not yet belongs so essentially to his being that when he is no longer "ahead of himself," he is no longer here at all. The moment there is nothing more "lacking" or "missing" from his being-in-the-world, he has already ceased to be. His ontic existence in a world can then no longer be experienced and so the necessary basis for an existential interpretation cannot be secured.

Nevertheless, the problem of Da-sein's wholeness must not yet be given up as hopeless. It is possible that what appears to be the essential "unwholeness" of care arises from a notion of completeness and end which may be appropriate to things, or even to other living beings, but not to Da-sein. Two problems have therefore to be examined. First, whether Da-sein can indeed be a whole in his ontic, factical existence, and how his wholeness can be understood from his end in death. Second, how Da-sein's "end" and "wholeness" are themselves existentially constituted.

2. Experiencing the Death of Others

The wholeness Da-sein reaches in death is the transition to his no-more-being-here. Death itself denies him the possibility of experiencing this transition and understanding it from his own experience. But although this is his situation with regard to himself, all the more impressive and deeply experienced is the death of others. Since Da-sein is essentially in a world with others, does death not become "subjectively" accessible through them? Can the death of others not provide the phenomenal basis for ontological interpretation?

The death of another is undoubtedly his end and the transition to his no-longer-being-in-the-world. For those who are left behind, however, he has not totally vanished. His body is still with them in their world. It is taken care of and honored in funeral rites and the cult of the burial ground. Even in death, Da-sein is "more" than a material thing or the lifeless body of a merely living being. The bereaved stay with him in sorrowful remembrance and care for him in reverence. But in such remembering and staying with the dead, the dead person himself is no longer factually in "our world." Experience of another's death reveals it as a loss suffered by those who are left behind, *not* as the loss of *his* being suffered by the dead himself.

A careful analysis shows that another's death is incapable of providing the genuine experience on which alone an ontological interpretation could be based. What this interpretation wants to get into view is solely the death of the dying, his coming to the end of *his* being, not the affliction this brings to others, nor the way he may still be with them in this world.

The attempt to find a substitute for a genuine experience has failed because it has overlooked the way of being that distinguishes Da-sein from other beings. It is assumed that a Da-sein could be substituted and replaced by another, so that what he could not experience in himself could become accessible in and through another.

In the everyday world, it is true, one Da-sein can and often must substitute for another. In the business of taking care of the world, one is what one does. The interchangeability of one with another in a mutually undertaken making and doing is not only possible, but is constitutive of the everyday self. But all substitution fails when it comes to dying. A Da-sein can die for another, but this does not in the least relieve the other of *his* dying. Each Da-sein must take his death upon himself. It is his utmost possibility in which his sheer ability to be is at stake (*es geht um*). Death is a purely existential phenomenon, constituted by existence and mineness. Existence is the being that is manifest to each of us as *mine*. This being that is mine is for me constantly at stake. Death *is* only as the end of my existence; it is essentially *my* dying. It can therefore never be a happening, a within-worldish occurrence. That is why the substitution of another's death for mine had to fail.

Nevertheless, the outcome of the preceding analysis is not negative. It shows positively that the wholeness constituted by "ending" in death is an existential phenomenon. It can be explained only from the existential structure of an existence, which is essentially *my* existence. If the "end" itself is to be appropriately grasped, it can only be done in an existential concept of death. Concepts of "end" and "wholeness" drawn from other modes of being are incapable of explaining the ending of an existence. Even the extinction of life in a purely living being must be distinguished from the existential phenomenon of death.

3. Incompleteness, End, and Wholeness

The principal results of the preceding analyses are summed up by Heidegger in three points: 1. An "unwholeness" essentially belongs to Dasein, insofar as he is *not yet* what he can become. The not-yet indicates something like a constant "lack" in his existence. 2. The not-yet is eliminated only when Da-sein himself comes to his end. This has the character of a no-longer-being-here, i.e. of a sudden and total overturning of his mode of being. 3. His coming to an end is a way of being in which each Da-sein is sheerly uninterchangeable.

Further analysis will reveal, however, that some of the interpretations that first suggested themselves are not tenable. To begin with, does the not-yet that belongs to existence truly imply the "lack" of something that can be fetched from elsewhere outside Da-sein himself? Can this "something" be gradually added to him so that his incompleteness is, by and by, filled up? This sort of completing belongs only to things that are made up of parts; for example, a required amount of money is not yet put together. The money at hand is not sufficient to pay a debt. The amount still lacking is not simply nonexistent: it is a handy thing in the mode of unhandiness. When it becomes available and the whole sum is put together, it still retains the character of handiness. Da-sein, on the other hand, is not "all together" when his not-yet has been completely "filled up." On the contrary, he is then no longer here at all. Clearly, Da-sein cannot be made into a whole like a handy thing whose wholeness is the sum of parts.

But even among things, the not-yet may indicate different ways of incompleteness. The moon, for example, is not yet full. With the gradual withdrawal of the covering shadow, the not-yet diminishes until the moon is full. But obviously, the full moon has been there all along, and the not-yet-full applies only to our perception, not to the moon itself. As for Da-sein, however, his not-yet is not only inaccessible to perception, it is not yet "there" at all.

The problem of Da-sein's wholeness is whether he himself can be his not-yet, that is, be what he becomes. A comparison must therefore be drawn with other living beings, to which a "becoming" evidently belongs. An unripe fruit, for example, goes toward its ripeness. That it is not-yet can in no way be added to it from outside. The fruit itself brings itself to ripeness. This "bringing itself" is the way of its being. If the not-yet-ripe fruit could not of itself come to ripeness, nothing outside it could ever eliminate its not-yet. In contrast to this, the incomplete sum can only be completed by having parts brought to it. According to its own way of being, the sum is totally indifferent to what is still lacking from it, or more precisely, it can neither care nor not care for its own completeness. The fruit, on the contrary, cannot be indifferent toward its ripeness, for only in ripening can it *be* unripe. The not-yet is already drawn into its being. Similarly, Da-sein is, as long as he is, already his not-yet.[1]

But although the comparison with the fruit has brought out essential similarities, there are also important differences that arise from the "end" that constitutes the wholeness. Ripeness as an end is not analogous to death as an end. In ripeness the fruit fulfils itself. Death, on the other hand, does not necessarily mean that Da-sein has come to the end of his specific possibilities. Da-sein may die unfulfilled long after he has reached and passed the maturity possible for him. End does not necessarily imply fulfilment. In what sense, then, can dying be understood as an ending?

Things can end in different ways, according to their specific ways of being. The rain ends: it stops, it vanishes. The road ends: it stops, but it does not vanish. On the contrary, its end shows the road to be precisely this one and no other. Then again, end may mean being finished: with the last stroke of the brush, the painting is finished. The bread is at an end: it is used up, no longer available as a handy thing.

Dying is not an ending in any of these senses. In death Da-sein is neither fulfilled, nor has simply vanished, nor is finished, nor at an end like a handy thing that is no longer available. For just as Da-sein is constantly his not-yet, so he is always already his end. Ending as dying does not mean that Da-sein is at an end, but that he is to (or toward) an end (*Sein zum Ende*). Death is a way of being that Da-sein takes over as soon as he is. "As soon as a human being is born, he is old enough to die right away" (SZ, 245).

The obscurity of Heidegger's *Sein zum Ende*, later to be defined as *Sein zum Tode*, is aggravated by the difficulty of rendering it into English. The exact translation, "being to the end," and "being to death," must remain ambiguous (and even misleading) until its meaning can be more fully grasped. The alternative rendering of "being toward an end" ("being toward death") is less exact but perhaps less misleading, and can be used with advantage in many contexts.

At the present stage, nothing could be gained from further verbal explanations. Heidegger's own phrase, though verbally clearer, is hardly less obscure than the translation. It cannot be more at the moment than an empty formula, a statement of the problem: How can man *be* his end? How can his wholeness be constituted by his end? This new formulation of the problem nevertheless represents an important turning point in Heidegger's inquiry. It closes the first stage of a tentative approach. The attempt to grasp Da-sein's wholeness by starting from his possibilities, from what he is not yet but can become, has ended in failure, for Da-sein cannot become a whole by having bits and pieces added to him. It is now clear that if Da-sein can be a whole at all, he can be so only *from* his end. All his other possibilities which lie before his death can be understood only from the ultimate possibility of his end.

The direction of the inquiry must therefore be entirely reversed. It must start from the end that constitutes the wholeness. How strange and radical the course that Heidegger now proposes to take is best seen from the fact that Da-sein's beginning in birth has so far not even been considered. What would seem to us the natural course to take, to start from the beginning, is tacitly passed over by Heidegger. The implication is that even the beginning, the birth, can be understood only by coming back to it from the end.

The results of the inquiry alone can show whether the course on which Heidegger sets out is justified. What has been shown so far is that Da-sein's end in death and the wholeness constituted by it cannot be explained except from his own way of being. The inquiry is thus compelled to turn to the fundamental structure of care for guidance. Nothing else can offer a basis for the solution of the problem, assuming that it is soluble at all.

4. The Existential Analysis of Death in Contrast with all Other Kinds of Interpretation

The existential analysis of death is preceded by a short preparatory section. Its task is to make explicit what this analysis aims at and what does not belong to its sphere, and so to contrast it with other inquiries into the same phenomena.

First and most obviously, death is investigated by those ontic sciences which concern themselves with life—biology, physiology, medicine, psychology, and so on. Death in the widest sense is a phenomenon of life. Living must be understood as a way of being to which a being-in-the-world belongs.[2] Its ontology must start from an ontology of Da-sein and proceed by a privative (reductive) method. Da-sein himself can be regarded purely as a living being, and enrolled into the plant and animal world. His death may then form part of the subject matter of those sciences for which the end of life, its connection with growth and procreation, its causes and ways, and so on, is a relevant study.

In all such ontic inquiries, however, definite ideas of life and death are already at work. These must be existentially analyzed and interpreted. A first step is to make a strict distinction between the various ways in which life can end. A purely living being ends in perishing (*Verenden*). Da-sein himself has an ontic-physiological end, which may be called "decease" (*Ableben*). Dying in the strict existential sense, on the other hand, must be understood as the way of being in which Da-sein *is* to his end. Accordingly, Da-sein never perishes, and he can cease to live (decease) only as long as he *is* dying. The medical-biological investigation of decease can be ontologically relevant, but only if the basic existential analysis of death has first been secured. Or must all illness and death be regarded as primarily existential phenomena, even from the medical point of view?

Furthermore, the existential interpretation of death goes before all biographical-historical and anthropological-psychological investigations. All of these necessarily presuppose a definite concept of death. It is revealing that psychological studies of the problem of death, anthropological investigations of primitive death cults, and so on, usually throw far more light on the life of the living than on the death of the dying.

But just because of its ontological precedence, the interpretation of death as the "end" of being-in-the-world does not and cannot make any ontic decisions about what happens "after death," whether a higher or lower way of being is then possible, whether Da-sein lives on or some kind of immortality is possible for him. It is as much outside the sphere of an ontological interpretation to come to ontic decisions about a "world beyond" as it is to come to such ontic decisions about this present world. It remains entirely "this worldly" in the strict sense that it interprets death solely insofar as it constantly stands before and reaches into the factical existence in the world.

Finally, the sphere proper to an existential analysis of death excludes questions which Heidegger sums up under the title of a "metaphysics of death." Such questions are, for example, how death "came into the world," and what meaning it has in the all of beings as evil and suffering. Metaphysical deliberation about these questions already presupposes not only an existential concept of death, but also an ontological understanding of the all of beings, and especially of evil and negativity.

From an ontic point of view, the results of the following analysis will show the peculiar formality and emptiness that characterizes all ontological interpretations. On the other hand, the rich and complex structure of the"end" as the preeminent possibility of existence will come all the more sharply to light. The urgent problem facing the analysis is how to guard against arbitrary and preconceived ideas of death. It proposes to meet this danger by keeping in view how death concretely reaches into Da-sein's everyday existence, whose essential characters have been analyzed and secured in the first division.

5. A Preliminary Sketch of the Existential Structure of Death

Dying as a way of being is grounded in care. Care is the unity of Da-sein's existence (ahead-of-himself), facticity (already-being-in-the-world), and falling (being-near-to-things). These fundamental characters of Da-sein's being, as the present analysis will show, come most sharply to light in death.

The preceding inquiry has conclusively established that in being ahead-of-himself (not yet), Da-sein is not "lacking" in anything that could be added to him from outside. His utmost not-yet has the character of something to which Da-sein relates himself (*sich verhält*). Here Heidegger gives us a first hint of how the obscure phrase "being to (or toward) an end" should be understood. The "to" or "toward" indicates a relation: Da-sein constantly bears himself toward, brings himself before, a possibility of his being which is its utmost. In English, we might simply say that Da-sein constantly comes face to face with his end. The ultimate not-yet has the character of something that stands before man (*Bevorstand*).

This, however, is not a precise enough definition of death, for many other possibilities can "stand before us"—for example, the rebuilding of a house, the arrival of a friend. These are handy or real things, or other existences. In a different way, a journey may stand before us, or a showdown with others, or the renunciation of something we ourselves could be, possibilities of our own that are grounded in our being together with others. None of these is comparable with death.

The positive characterization of death, which Heldegger now proceeds to give, is so important that it will be rendered almost in full in the next three paragraphs, with the addition of a few explanatory remarks.

When it comes to dying, it has already been shown, each Da-sein is sheerly uninterchangeable. In death, therefore, each Da-sein stands before himself in the possibility that is most his own. It is his sheer being-in-the-world that is at stake. His death is the possibility of his no-more-being-here. This belongs solely to his own self and refers him wholly to his own ability-to-be. Standing before himself in this way, all his relations to other beings are loosened. His ownmost, unrelational possibility is at the same time his utmost. Da-sein cannot pass—that is, outstrip, outdistance—the possibility of death in his own abilitv-to-be. Death is the possibility of the sheer impossibility of being-able-to-be-here. Death thus reveals itself as the ownmost, unrelational, unovertakeable possibility. As such, it stands before Da-sein in a *preeminent* way. It is existentially possible only because Da-sein is disclosed to himself in the way of being ahead-of-himself. This primary structure of care concretizes itself most originally in a being toward death as the preeminent possibility of existence.

This ownmost, unrelational, and impassable possibility, however, is not acquired by Da-sein incidentally in the course of his being. On the contrary, when Da-sein exists, he is already thrown into this possibility. That he is delivered over to death is not in the first place a matter of an explicit or theoretical knowledge, but reveals itself more originally and penetratingly in the mood of dread. The dread of death is dread of Da-sein's ownmost, unrelational, and impassable possibility. The "whereof" of dread is being-in-the-world itself. The "for" of dread is the sheer ability-to-be-in-the-world. Fear and dread, as Heidegger has already shown in Division One, are not the same. A distinction must be sharply drawn between fear of the ontic, biological "end of life" (decease), and dread as the basic mood which discloses that Da-sein as a thrown being exists to his end. The existential concept of dying can now be more fully defined as a thrown way of being toward an utmost, unrelational, unovertakable possibility. As such, it is radically different both from a pure vanishing and a mere perishing, as well as from a ceasing to live.

Coming face to face with death is not an occasional "attitude" in certain individuals, but essentially belongs to Da-sein's thrownness, which reveals itself in attunement (feeling, mood). Attunement discloses always in this or that definite way. Hence a factical existence can relate himself to his death in different ways. The fact that many do not "know" about death is no proof that Da-sein does not universally relate himself to it, but only that in fleeing from it, he usually hides it from himself. Da-sein factually dies as long as he exists, but mostly in the everyday way of falling captive to his "world." His absorbed occupation with things reveals the flight from his uncanny not-at-homeness, that is, from his being toward death. This being is constituted by existence, facticity, and falling. The ontological possibility of death is grounded in Da-sein's being as care.

But if a being toward death originally belongs to care, then it must manifest itself already in everyday existence, albeit in a disowned way. The connection between death and care, which has so far been outlined only in a preliminary way, must be confirmed by its first concretization in Da-sein's everydayness.

6. BEING-TOWARD-DEATH AND EVERYDAYNESS

The average, everyday self is constituted in the publicity of being-with-others in the same world (SZ, Div. One, chaps. 4 and 5 B; and see above Part Two, chap. 4, sec. 1). "They," the others, find an explanation for everything and "publish" it in idle talk. All explanation is drawn from and founded upon an attuned understanding. The problem now to be examined is this: How does the attuned understanding that underlies everyday idle talk disclose a being toward death? How does the everyday self relate to its ownmost, unrelational, impassable possibility? Which mood discloses to it its thrownness unto death and in what way?

In everyday being-together, death is "known" as a constantly occurring event. Friends and acquaintances die. People die daily and hourly. Death is a familiar happening within the world. "They" have already found an explanation for it. In talking about death, they say: one oneself also dies some day, but in the meantime, one is still spared.

The everyday saying "one dies" unmistakably reveals how "one" is toward death. In such talk, death is understood as an indefinite something that must come from somewhere, but for oneself it is not yet here and therefore not yet threatening. Under cover of "one dies" everybody else and one oneself can indulge in the illusion that death strikes at "one," and not at myself. Death is thus levelled down to a within-worldish occurrence that happens to people but does not belong to any Da-sein as his own, for the "one" of everydayness is *nobody*.

The ambiguity that characterizes everyday explanations twists death into one of the "realities" of the world and so conceals its true character as the ownmost, unrelational, impassable possibility. In this way, it helps to *seduce* Da-sein into losing himself *precisely in his ownmost self* by covering over the possibility that preeminently belongs to him.

The evasive concealment of death goes so far that the nearest friends of the "dying" often persuade him that he is going to escape death and return to the reassured everydayness of his worldish occupations. Such talk is meant to console the "dying," but it does just as much for the "consolers" themselves. They thus help the "dying" to hide from himself the possibility that is most his own and provide a constant *reassurance* about death.[3] And when it comes to an actual decease, the public must be as little incommoded by it as possible. The death of others is not infrequently looked upon as a social inconvenience, which should not be inflicted on the public.

The publicity of everydayness tacitly regulates the way in which "one" has to relate himself to death and prescribes the mood that should determine "one's" attitude to it. The mere "thinking about death" is already branded as cowardly fear and a morbid escape from the world. The everyday self suppresses the courage to dread death. Dread brings Da-sein before himself as delivered over to his last possibility. The publicity of everydayness turns this dread into the fear of a coming occurrence. Ambiguously disguised as fear, it is then explained as a weakness which a self-assured existence must not know. The proper mood is decreed to be an indifferent calm in the face of the "fact" that one dies. Such "superior" indifference estranges Da-sein from his utmost, unrelational ability-to-be.

Seductiveness, reassurance, and estrangement, are characters of Da-sein's falling way of being. The falling being toward death is a constant flight from it. But the flight itself testifies that even the everyday self is a thrown being into death. Even in his average everydayness, his ownmost ability-to-be-in-the-world is constantly at stake for Da-sein, albeit in the mode of an imperturbable indifference toward the utmost possibility of his existence.

A more penetrating interpretation of the everyday evasion of death will bring more sharply into view what it is from which Da-sein flees. This method was first employed by Heidegger in the analysis of dread (SZ, 184; see above Part Two, chap. 5, sec. 1). This will put the inquiry into a position to define the full existential concept of death.

7. Everyday Being toward an End and the Full Existential Concept of Death

The positive results of the inquiry carried out so far may now be summed up. Death as the end of Da-sein has been formally defined as the ownmost, unrelational, impassable possibility. In his factical being, Da-sein brings himself before this possibility as the sheer impossibility of existing. In his everydayness, Da-sein relates himself to this possibility by concealing and evading it.

Two important points still remain to be elucidated. The first is how the certainty, the inescapability of death reveals itself. The second is whether it is possible for Da-sein not merely to relate himself to his death in the evasive, everyday way, but properly to free it as his own.

The theme of the present section is the certainty of death. In the everyday saying, "Death comes to us all," something like a certainty is already admitted. The question is, however, whether the admission is adequate to the way in which death is certain. This question makes a short examination of certainty and of the criterion of its adequacy necessary.

Certainty evidently belongs to truth. In the existential interpretation, "to be true" has a twofold meaning. Primarily it means "to be disclosing and discovering," which is the basic character of existence. I am disclosed to myself and am discovering things within the world. The thing itself, insofar as it is discovered, is true in a secondary sense. Certainty has the same twofold meaning. Primarily, it is I myself who am certain, and secondarily, the discovered (true) thing is certain.

The primary meaning of certainty is defined by Heidegger as *Fürwahrhalten*, to hold something for true. The excellence of this expression can be appreciated only when it is carefully thought over. I hold, I keep, something for true when I can hold myself to it; I do not vacillate and tumble about in this truth as I do in a baseless opinion, for the thing itself is discovered in such a way that it gives me a firm hold, it binds me to itself. An eminent mode of certainty, according to Heidegger, is conviction (*Überzeugung*). This seems at first sight surprising, because in ordinary use the word often means merely a strongly held personal opinion, but Heidegger interprets it in the opposite way: I am convinced of something when I let myself be overcome, vanquished (*convincere*) solely by the testimony (witness, *Zeugnis*) of the discovered thing itself and let it wholly determine my discovering relation to it.

A certainty is adequate, therefore, when it is grounded in the discovered (true) thing itself and the discovering relation to it is appropriate to the thing in question. According to the differences among beings and the varying intentions, direction, and range of our investigations, the ways of truth and the certainty adequate to them are variable. For the present Heidegger is concerned solely with the way in which we are certain of death. This will turn out in the end to be a preeminent certainty of our being-here.

In his everydayness, Da-sein covers over the preeminent possibility of his being. Covering over, concealing (untruth) originally belongs to the disclosing way of existing. The certainty that belongs to the concealing (untrue) way of being toward death is not an uncertainty, a doubt, but an *inappropriate* way of being certain. If one understands death as an event within the world, then the certainty that belongs to such events is inappropriate to the way death "is."

They say: it is certain that death comes. But in order to be certain of death, not "they," not "one," but each Da-sein himself must be certain of his own dying. What is the basis, the evidence for the everyday certainty of death? It is not merely hearsay, for one experiences daily the death of others. Death is undeniably a "fact of experience." But as this "fact of experience," death (decease) has merely an "empirical" certainty. As far as one knows, everyone dies.

Death is in the highest degree probable, but, to a cautiously "critical" view, it lacks the absolute, apodeictic certainty that distinguishes certain theoretical truths.

The "merely" empirical certainty of decease as an occurrence, however, does not decide about the certainty of death. The actual decease of others may provide the occasion on which Da-sein in the first place becomes aware of the "fact" of death, but from such experience he cannot become certain of death as it is. Even the everyday self, however, is at bottom differently certain of his death from the way certainty of death is admitted in public talk. It is precisely this "difference" that is evaded and covered over. But the evasion itself testifies to what it evades, namely the certainty of the ownmost, impassable possibility of existence.

They say that death comes certainly, but in the meantime, not yet. The "but" whittles away the certainty of death. "In the meantime, not yet" refers the everyday self to the urgency of the business that "in the meantime" can still be taken care of. Death is pushed off and away to a "sometime later" whose probability depends on the "average expectation" of life. In this way, the everyday self covers over the certainty peculiar to death, namely that it is *at any moment possible*. The indefiniteness of the "when" of death goes hand in hand with its certainty. Everyday being toward death evades the indefiniteness, not by calculating when decease might take place, but by pushing in front of it the definite, calculable urgencies and possibilities of everyday care.[1]

The full existential concept of death may therefore be defined as follows. Death as the end of Da-sein is the ownmost, unrelational, certain and indefinite, impassable possibility of his existence. In the existential sense, death is not a "fact," an occurrence within the world; there is death only in the being of a Da-sein to his end, which in one way or another is constantly disclosed to him.

Dying is a way of being in which Da-sein can be a whole. Already the everyday flight from death shows that the end that concludes and determines Da-sein's wholeness is nothing to which Da-sein comes only at the end of his life in decease. Even everyday Da-sein *is* to his end— that is, comes constantly to grips with it, albeit only "flightily." The uttermost not-yet of his self, before which all his other possibilities are piled up, is always already drawn into his being. The not-yet lies in the primary constitution of care, according to which Da-sein is constantly ahead-of-himself. At first, it raised the doubt whether Da-sein could be a whole at all. But now it has turned out that, far from preventing the wholeness of a factical existence, the not-yet makes the wholeness of his being toward an end first of all possible.

As a thrown being-in-the-world, Da-sein is already delivered over to his death and relates himself to it in a definite way. The everyday evasion is a *disowned* being toward death. Although disownment is the way in which Da-sein for the most part exists, it need not necessarily and always be so.

But can Da-sein understand his ownmost possibility *properly*, that is, be toward his end in the way of owned existence? Until this question is worked out and answered, the existential interpretation remains deficient. Owned existence is a possibility of a factically existing Da-sein. This must be ontologically explainable from the structure of care. To work out this explanation is the task of the last section of the present chapter.

8. THE EXISTENTIAL STRUCTURE OF AN OWNED, AUTHENTIC WAY OF BEING-TOWARD-DEATH

Heidegger introduces his analysis by stressing the methodological difficulty of his task. Is it not a "fantastic undertaking," he asks, to outline the existential structure of a proper, authentic, owned being toward death, when perhaps in fact no Da-sein ever exists in this way, or if he does, it must remain hidden to others? Must such a questionable "structure" not remain an arbitrarily invented construction?

Fortunately, there are two phenomenally secured resources on which the present interpretation can draw. First, the existential concept of death has been fixed. Second, the disowned way of being toward death has been characterized. This shows privatively how an owned existence does *not* relate himself to his end: he *cannot evade* it, he *cannot cover it over* in flight and ambiguously explain it. How, then, must a proper understanding of death be constituted?

Understanding is the way in which Da-sein *is* toward his possibilities. "Being toward a possibility" can mean being out for something possible, seeking it, in order to bring about its realization. In everyday taking care, we are constantly out for possible things. In all making and doing and producing there lies the tendency to destroy the possibility of the possible handy or real thing by leading it over into actuality.

It is evident that being toward death as a possibility cannot mean that we are *out for it*. For one thing, death is nothing real or handy. For another thing, in bringing about the "actuality" of decease, we would pull the ground from under our feet for being toward death as a possibility.[5] It follows from this that we cannot relate ourselves properly to death by dwelling on its possibility, by thinking about how and when it might become "actual." Such brooding over death weakens its possibility-character by wishing to make it into something calculable and disposable. A genuine understanding of death, on the contrary, must disclose it *as a possibility*, must make it explicitly its own *as a possibility*, and must hold it out before itself and endure it *as a possibility*.

Such an understanding of possibilities would seem to lie in expecting them. A tense expectancy undilutedly discloses the possible in its "whether it comes or not, or whether it comes after all." But, on a closer view, expecting the possible proves to be similar to being out for it. The possible is in advance understood from the actual and in relation to it, namely how and when it might become realizable. Even in expecting, one jumps away from the possible, takes a firm foothold in the actual and is essentially waiting for it.

The proper way to understand death, on the other hand, is to run ahead to it as a possibility (*Vorlaufen in die Möglichkeit*). Before considering how Heidegger develops the concept of "running ahead" or "running forward," or "anticipation," we may note that it is not essentially new. Understanding, as Division One has shown, discloses possibilities by throwing them forward and throwing itself into them. It is this "forward movement" of existence that is formally espressed in the "ahead-of" structure of care. There, however, it is still left entirely open whether Da-sein can be ahead-of-himself in different ways, and if he can, how these ways may be constituted. What Heidegger now sets out to show is that running ahead is the extremest way in which Da-sein can be ahead-of-himself, and hence it alone is capable of fully disclosing his extremest possibility.

> In running ahead to this possibility, it becomes "greater and greater," that is, it reveals itself as something which knows no measure at all, no more or less, but means the possibility of the measureless impossibility of existence. Essentially, this possibility offers no support for becoming intent on something, for "spelling out" the real thing that is possible and so forgetting its possibility. As anticipation of possibility, being-toward-death first makes this possible and sets it free as possibility. (SZ, 262)

In this important paragraph Heidegger has shown that a preeminent understanding is required to disclose Da-sein's preeminent possibility and so *makes it* first of all *possible.* What does this mean? That unlike real things, which are there independently of our discovering them, a possibility stands before us *as a possibility* only insofar as it is disclosed and understood. Running ahead discloses the utmost possibility and gives it to Da-sein to understand as his own. To stand before himself in his utmost, ownmost ability-to-be, however, is nothing other than to exist as his own self.

Running ahead thus makes possible the owned way of existing and so sets Da-sein free for his finite freedom. The freedom of a finite being lies in the different ways in which he can relate himself to his finiteness. Disowned being toward death is one way in which Da-sein can and usually does bear his finiteness. Running ahead gives Da-sein to understand that he *can* free himself from his lostness to "them" and exist primarily from the utmost possibility of his own self. Only when it becomes transparent to him that this is something he can do and could always have done, does his lostness in the everyday "oneself" among "them" become fully manifest.

But Da-sein's ownmost possibility is at the same time unrelational. Running ahead to it gives Da-sein to understand that he must take it over solely from himself. Death does not merely indifferently belong to each Da-sein, but claims him singly. It individuates Da-sein into a single self, and makes it manifest that all caring for others and taking care of things fails when it is his own sheer ability-to-be that is at stake. But the failure of these ways of being-in-the-world to support Da-sein in the face of death does not cut them off from himself, for they are an essential condition of existence as such. Da-sein exists fully as his own self only insofar as in being-with others and being-near-to things, he throws himself primarily into his ownmost ability-to-be, and not into the possibilities of oneself in the everyday world.

The ownmost, unrelational possibility is impassable. It stands before Da-sein as the extremest possibility of his existence. Running ahead to death does not evade its impassability, but "sets it free for it," that is, opens itself to be moved and affected by it, suffers itself to be struck to the core by it. When Heidegger speaks of a "passionate anxious freedom for death" (SZ, 266), he is not thinking of a quickly evaporating emotion of enthusiasm, but of a soberly steadfast, suffering openness to an end that cannot be surpassed by the forethrow of further possibilities. This alone can set Da-sein free from his dependence on those chance possibilities that lie before his utmost possibility, by enabling him genuinely to understand them as finite, and to let him choose his own from among them, instead of letting others prescribe the average possibilities for the everyday "oneself."

The extreme possibility of existence to give itself up shatters all rigid insistence on what has already been reached and achieved, and so saves Da-sein from the danger of falling behind himself and "becoming too old for his victories (Nietzsche)" (SZ, 264). Free for his ownmost possibilities, which are determined from the *end*—that is, are understood as finite—Da-sein will not misunderstand the possibilities of others which are overtaking his own or try to force them back into the limits of his own. Death as the unrelational, impassable possibility individuates Da-sein into a single self only to make him understanding toward others in *their* ability-to-be.[6] Since running ahead to the utmost possibility at the same time discloses all other possibilities that lie before it, it in advance encompasses the whole of a Da-sein's existence; that is, it enables Da-sein to be a whole in his factical existence.

The ownmost, unrelational, impassable possibility is certain. The way to be certain of it is determined by the corresponding truth (disclosedness). Da-sein holds death for true—is certain of it—by running ahead to it as his ownmost ability-to-be. He himself makes the certainty possible for himself, and what enables him to do so is the anticipatory forward-running way of existence. The certainty of death cannot be calculated from statistics of actually occurring deceases. It belongs to a totally different order of truth from the disclosedness of things or from the formal objects accessible to a pure intuition (looking-at). The certainty of death—death *is* only and always as my own—is far more original than those, for in it I am certain of my own being-in-the-world. It demands not merely one definite disclosing relation to things, but the whole of Da-sein in the fullness of an owned existence. Only by running ahead to death can he make certain of his ownmost being in its unovertakable wholeness.

The certain possibility of existence is indefinite. How can this constantly certain possibility be disclosed in such a way that it remains constantly indefinite *when* it will become an impossibility? In running ahead to his indefinitely certain death, Da-sein opens himself to a constant *threat* which rises from his thrownness into his "here." This is existentially possible because all understanding is attuned. Moods and feelings bring Da-sein before the thrownness of his "that-he-is-here." The mood which is capable of keeping open the sheer threat rising from his ownmost single being is dread. In dread, Da-sein finds himself face to face with the nothing of the possible impossibility of existence. Dread is dread for the ability-to-be of a factical existence already thrown into death. Because running ahead individuates Da-sein into a single self and in this singleness makes him certain of his whole ability-to-be, the basic mood of dread essentially belongs to his understanding of himself from his ground.

In this paragraph, Heidegger has shown that the preeminent understanding that lies in running ahead, and the preeminent attunement that is concretely experienced in dread belong together and constitute the possibility of an owned existence. Dread, no less than running ahead or anticipation, individuates Da-sein into a single self by bringing him back to himself from his lostness to things. Both bring Da-sein before the nothing of his possible inability-to-be. Even in the absence of Division Three, we can be reasonably certain that in this extremest disclosure lies the answer to Heidegger's question, How is it possible for Da-sein to understand being?

These implications, however, are at this point only hinted at by Heidegger and are, in fact, not fully worked out even at the end of Division Two. The analysis so far carried out is only sufficient to show the existential structure of an owned being toward death, which is summed up by Heidegger as follows:

> *Anticipation reveals to Da-sein its lostness in the they-self, and brings it face to face with the possibility to be itself, primarily unsupported by concern taking care of things, but to be itself in passionate anxious* freedom toward death *which is free of the illusions of the they, factical, and certain of itself.* (SZ, 266)

The existential structure of anticipation or running ahead—that is, of an owned way of being toward death—shows that it is ontologically possible for Da-sein to be a whole. It should, therefore, be possible for a factically existing Da-sein to be "in fact" a whole. And yet, the working out of this existentially possible wholeness remains a fantastic assumption until its concretization in an ontic existence has been demonstrated. Does any Da-sein in fact ever throw himself into an owned being toward death? Does he in fact *bear witness* to his ability to do so? Does he ever *demand* it from himself that he ought to exist wholly as himself?

These questions already indicate the theme and task of the next chapter. They also suggest that quite apart from Heidegger's principal theme, this second chapter of Division Two should be of unusual interest, since in it Heidegger must lay bare the ontological source and ground of ethics and morality. While our freedom lies in our understanding of possibility as such (I can be, I am able to be) this is obviously not sufficient to explain what we usually call "moral freedom." For this, we must be able to understand not only that "I can be this way or that," but also to understand that "I ought to be this way and not that," and be able freely to submit or not submit ourselves to the implied demand. Further, it is evident that the demand must be made by ourselves to ourselves, for no externally imposed command could make the free submission to an "I ought" possible.

XI

Witness to an Owned Existence and Authentic Resolution

1. Conscience as the Call of Care

Since owned existence is an essential possibility of Da-sein as Da-sein, it cannot be the result of extraneous circumstances or of favorable influences, but his own being as care must be capable of showing him his everyday lostness and of calling him back to his own self. This eminent "showing" or "witnessing" happens in conscience. Heidegger's first task is to determine which are the existential phenomena in whose sphere conscience belongs. Guidance is given by the ontic experience of conscience as a "voice" that has something to say to us : it discloses something, it gives us something to understand. Conscience thus belongs among the phenomena which disclose to us our hereness. These phenomena are attunement, understanding, and discourse or *Rede*. The fact that conscience manifests itself as a voice indicates that it is a mode of discourse.

As an existential constituent of Da-sein's being, discourse articulates what is understandable. It enables us *expressly* to articulate an already disclosed significance-whole and so to explain it and make it *explicitly* our own. Existential discourse "comes to word," it "voices itself" in our ontic languages. The concrete "voicing" of speech, however, important as it is in being-together and in public communication, is not always essential. Silence is also a mode of speech, and it is the preeminent mode in which conscience speaks to us. This does not conflict with the everyday experience of it as a "voice," because what is really meant by the "voice" is not an audible sound, but its function of giving us something to understand.

There is indeed no need for conscience to be generally audible, because it does not speak to mankind at large, but solely to myself. It is purely the self of the everyday "oneself," bemused by the noise of public talk, whom conscience *calls*. The demanding and summoning character of conscience is pregnantly expressed by Heidegger when he speaks of it as a *call*, rather than as an indeterminate voice.

Whom conscience calls is indubitably a Da-sein in his own single self. What he does and who he is in the publicity of the everyday world is mercilessly ignored and passed over by the call. Just as dread overturns the relevance-whole of things into complete irrelevance, so conscience pushes the vanity of "one's" public position into total insignificance. It thus deprives Da-sein of his habitual hiding place and brings him to himself.

But what is it that conscience calls to the self? Strictly speaking, Heidegger maintains: nothing. The call gives no information about worldish affairs, has no objective facts to relate. The self who has been called is not told about anything, but is summoned to himself. According to the existential interpretation, the primary and proper task of conscience is not to tell us *what* we are to *do*, but *how* we are to *be*.

As a summons, conscience calls Da-sein forward into the possibility of his own self. Hence it is that the call need not bring itself to word and sound. "Conscience speaks solely and constantly in the mode of silence" (SZ, 273). It thus forces Da-sein into the "reticent stillness" of himself. The absence of words does not mean that the call is vague and incomprehensible, but that it demands a different kind of "hearing"—that is, understanding—from communicating talk.

But, it may be asked, does the wordlessness of the "silent call" not imply that it is a deficient kind of discourse compared to, say, a fully expressed logical proposition? On the contrary, Heidegger implies that it is more fundamental than any logical proposition can be. In one of his later works, he calls language "the sounding of stillness" (*das Geläut der Stille*. US, 30, G12, 27, PLT, 207). The stillness in which conscience speaks is the most fundamental and original speech: it is the way in which *Da-sein calls himself* from the depth of his being.

But is it not premature to decide that in conscience *Da-sein calls himself?* Where is the phenomenal evidence to show that the caller and the called are the same? What are the phenomenal characteristics of the caller that would make Heidegger's interpretation at least a possible one, even if it could not be proved to be the only possible one?

In the first place, Heidegger points out, the caller is characterized by the same indefinability in worldish terms as the called. This seemingly negative character has a positive meaning for Heidegger. It indicates that the caller fulfils himself purely in calling and wishes to keep all curious and importunate examination away from himself. But does this not mean that to question who the caller is must be inappropriate to the very nature of conscience? It is certainly inappropriate, Heidegger says, in the case of an ontic-existentiell hearing of the call. An "introverted" self-analysis is the last thing conscience demands from us, because it only weakens the proper response to its call. But things are different for an existential-ontological inquiry. Its task is to discover how Da-sein himself must be in order to be able to experience a summons to himself at all.

Beyond his essential indefiniteness, what further characteristics of the caller are accessible? Without any doubt, each of us experiences the call as coming from myself, and not from anyone else who is with me in the world. This shows that the caller and called may be (though need not necessarily be) one and the same. At the same time, it indicates that they must nonetheless be in some way differentiated. Must the calling self not be differently "here" from the self who is called? Is it not Da-sein in his extreme possibility who calls the lost self of everydayness?

Before coming to a final decision on this point, let us consider the third characteristic of the caller. This seems in a way to contradict the preceding one, for just as certainly as the call comes *from* me, it is neither planned nor decided upon *by* me. "'It' calls, against our expectations and even against our will. . . . The call comes *from* me, and yet *over* me" (SZ, 275).

This characteristic is undoubtedly the strangest feature of conscience: the summoning of Da-sein to the most fundamental decisions he can make, cannot itself be decided upon or disposed of by Da-sein himself. It is this phenomenal feature of the call, Heidegger points out, that has given rise to the most divergent interpretations. On the one hand, conscience has been explained as the manifestation of a strange power, of God, which reaches into Da-sein's existence. At the other extreme, the "reality" of conscience has been denied and the whole phenomenon has been "explained away" as merely psychological or even biological. The latter attempt finds its support in the implicit, but all the more dogmatic ontological assumption that what is "in fact" there, must be substantially real, and what cannot be proved to be substantially real (*vorhanden*), cannot exist at all.

Both extremes of a theological and a scientific explanation are rejected by Heidegger on the ground that neither takes sufficient account of Da-sein's existential-ontological constitution. If Da-sein's being as care is in itself capable of originating the call of conscience, then there is no ontological need to go outside for an explanation, nor is there any justification for denying conscience just because its facticity cannot be proved in the same way as the fact of a substantial thing.

How does Heidegger proceed to show that the call can indeed originate in care? He has recourse to the suggestion that was made earlier; namely that Da-sein as caller is "here" in a different way from Da-sein as the called. As the called, Da-sein is here in the mode of a falling being-in-the-world, who disowns himself to "them," the others. The caller is the same Da-sein, but in the mode of an uncanny not-being-at-home-in-the-world, dreading the nothing of world into which he has been thrown in the dread for his single ability-to-be. Da-sein calls himself from the deepest ground of his radical singleness, in which he faces the naked "being that has to be as it is and can be" (SZ, 276). The caller is unfamiliar to the everyday self lost in the noise and talk of the varied business of the world. Something like a strange voice, coming from a single self thrown into the nothing of world, the call has no useful information to give about worldish affairs. "But what should Da-sein even report from the uncanniness of its thrown being? *What* else remains for it than its own potentiality-of-being revealed in *Angst*? How else should it call than by summoning to this potentiality-of-being about which it is solely concerned?" (SZ, 277).

The call must speak in the uncanny mode of silence, since it has nothing to report that could be communicated in public talk. On the contrary, it calls Da-sein back from such talk into the reticent stillness of his existence. The certainty with which this silent voice nonetheless addresses itself to *myself* arises from the fact that in his radical singleness each Da-sein is sheerly unmistakable to himself. It is clear, therefore, that conscience in its very nature does not disclose an "ideal of existence" that is universally valid for everyone, but discloses to each Da-sein his single, concrete situation, which he is summoned to take over as his own. This is why the existential analysis must resist any attempt to formulate a universal ideal existence (SZ, 266, 279); such an attempt would go against the meaning of conscience. On the other hand, the definition of the concrete possibilities of an individual existence is equally outside its sphere, for these are necessarily varied and always in part determined by the specific world in which a Da-sein lives. The task of the existential analysis is purely to show what are the conditions of the possibility that Da-sein can exist in the way he does; so, in the present instance, how it is possible that he can be called by conscience at all.

How has the preceding discussion helped to solve the problem whether conscience can be explained from care? It has brought to light that what conscience "gives to understand" is nothing but care itself in the mode of its possible authenticity.

> *Conscience reveals itself as the call of care*: the caller is Da-sein, anxious in thrownness (in its already-being-in . . .) about its potentiality-of-being. The one summoned is also Da-sein, called forth to its ownmost potentiality-of-being (its being-ahead-of-itself . . .). And what is called forth by the summons is Da-sein, out of falling prey to the they (already-being-together-with-the-world-taken-care-of . . .). The call of conscience, that is, conscience itself, has its ontological possibility in the fact that Da-sein is care in the ground of its being. (SZ, 277–78)

The analysis has now brought to light that the full structure, or more precisely, movement of conscience, is that of a *forward-calling recall* (*vorrufender Rückruf*). It calls *from* the depth of thrownness *forward into* the utmost possibilities of existence and calls Da-sein from his everyday lostness *back to* his own thrown self. This circling movement belongs to the call of care, because care itself, in its whole structure, has the same "circularity."

The existential interpretation of conscience will, of course, be unacceptable not only to the scientific, but even more to the theological explanations of the same phenomenon. With regard to the latter, it must be borne in mind that Heidegger neither asks nor answers the *ontic* question of who conferred on Da-sein his way of existing. An indispensable precondition for asking such a question is that we must already understand being. To find out how such an understanding is at all possible is Heidegger's sole concern. This fundamental-ontological aim is dominant in the whole analysis of conscience, and will come to special prominence in the next section. Its task will be to determine the existential meaning of the *Schuld* (debt, guilt, owing), which is universally heard and understood in every concrete experience of conscience.

2. Understanding the Call and Owing

In ordinary usage, *Schuld*, *Schuldigsein*, and various composite phrases that can be formed from them, generally carry the idea of owing a debt, of being under an obligation, of being at fault or culpable, of being guilty of (the cause of) some deficiency or harm. The everyday sense of the word will usually be rendered here by "debt" or "guilt." Its existential sense, on the other hand, will be expressed by the ethically more neutral word of *owing*. Heidegger himself keeps the ambivalence of *Schuld* constantly in play, the ethical concept of guilt providing an overtone to the existential concept of owing. This is quite deliberate, for in his interpretation the ontological condition of the possibility of "moral guilt" will turn out to lie in the existential "owing."

What can be meant by an *existential* concept of owing is, of course, still obscure. It cannot be merely a general term for the different kinds of debt, failing, and guilt familiar to us in everyday experience, but means an "owing" that lies already in our own being. Before I can load myself with guilt by specific acts of commission and omission, *I am owing* already insofar as I simply *am*. Otherwise, I could never understand that I am owing something to someone in my factical being together with him. The existential analysis must bring to clarity the original meaning of the owing that makes its appearance as a "predicate" of the "I am."

The familiar concepts of debt and guilt, on the other hand, are drawn from everyday explanations of existence and cannot function as the last criteria for the existential interpretation because they are derivative and arise from an understanding to which a proper ontological approach is foreign. Nonetheless, even a misexplanation can give a pointer to an original phenomenon, and that is why the ontological interpretation of phenomena like owing, conscience, and death must start from what everyday commonsense says about them.

What guidance do the vulgar concepts of debt and guilt give us toward the existential concept of owing? In the first place, debt is understood as an owing that arises by withholding or taking away from someone something to which he has a claim, by not fulfilling a demand in the sphere of a mutual taking care of things. In so doing, one can become culpable of an offence against a public rule or requirement and punishable by law.

In the idea of being culpable or guilty of something (*schuld sein an*) there lies further the idea of being the ground and origin of something. This meaning is expressed in English by "owing to"; for example, owing to me (because of me), another has been led astray, damaged, or even broken in his existence. This kind of moral guilt is summed up by Heidegger in a very condensed formal definition, which may be explained as follows: 1. To be the ground (cause, origin) of a deficiency in the existence of another. 2. The ground itself is deemed to be defective through the deficiency caused in the other. 3. The (moral) defectiveness of the ground has the character of the nonfulfilment of a demand made on Da-sein in his being-together with others.

It must be observed that Heidegger's definition of the everyday concept of moral guilt is questionable in several respects. For one thing, it suggests, without explicitly saying so, that the defectiveness of the "ground" is usually accounted for by the actual damage or harm caused. This, however, runs counter both to common sense and law, not to speak of religious-ethical teaching. The "moral defect" is generally considered to lie in the "ground" itself, in the intention of evil, prior to and regardless of the actual damage caused. Heidegger further suggests that the "moral demands" are usually conceived as rules or norms that somehow exist in and by themselves like things, and are imposed on Da-sein from outside. But does this do justice either to everyday understanding or to traditional ethics? Conceptions of a substantially existing norm or standard, laid on as a yardstick to measure Da-sein's conduct, have undoubtedly been and are widely held. But they are by no means the only ones, as is shown by Kant's idea of morality as a free self-submission to a self-given moral law. Even everyday understanding is not as crudely uncomprehending in ethical respects as Heidegger makes out, following what may well be no more than an ancient philosophical prejudice. It is perfectly true, of course, that everyday understanding is neither capable of nor intent upon giving a philosophical explanation of its ethical insights. These may be, nonetheless, perfectly genuine and penetrating. Heidegger asserts, on the other hand, that they are entirely drawn from a calculating taking-care of things in whose horizon morality becomes a balance sheet of deeds that ought or ought not to be performed and a settling of accounts in respect to mutual demands and obligations. Hence the way in which everyday existence relates himself to conscience, Heidegger alleges, is to bargain and negotiate with it. But, we ask, is this a full "phenomenal" characterization of the everyday experience of conscience? Is it not rather a one-sided and distorted caricature of it? A "bargaining" with conscience is certainly familiar to all of us, but it is by no means a constant or necessary concomitant of the experience. Even less is it blindly accepted as right and appropriate. On the contrary, the everyday talk of "paying conscience money" clearly shows that it is rejected by common sense itself. It knows, far better than Heidegger would allow, the difference between manipulating things and ethical conduct. Heidegger deals with the practical and ethical sphere in precisely the same way as he dealt with the everyday understanding of death. But while he may be perfectly right in saying that the latter arises from a fleeing and disguising way of being unto death, he seems to forget that the practical ethical question What ought I to do? cannot be evaded; it presses on us too constantly and urgently in everyday existence. In this sphere, common understanding can hardly be as obtuse as Heidegger, admittedly in company with many other philosophers, tries to make out.

Nonetheless, Heidegger takes two pointers toward the existential concept of *schuldig* from the much-despised everyday concepts of debt and guilt. These concepts show, in the first place, a definite not-character or negativity. So, for instance, the everyday notion of debt has its not-character insofar as it means a denying or withholding of something from someone. Similarly, the concept of moral guilt shows a negativity insofar as it means a deficiency, a not-fulfilling of a demand or a law. In the second place, the notion of moral guilt implies the idea of being the ground (cause, origin) of something which is itself deficient, that is, is determined by a *not*. Heidegger therefore defines the formal-existential concept of *schuldig* as "being-the-ground of a being which is determined by a not—that is, being the ground of a nullity" (*Grundsein einer Nichtigkeit*. SZ, 283).

The existential concept of *schuldig* can be approximately expressed by the word *owing*. "To be owing (to)" expresses in the first place that something is denied to and withheld from Da-sein's being, apart from and prior to any nonfulfilment of a demand made on him. This manifest denial and withholding is constitutive of the finiteness of Da-sein's existence. A completely self-sufficient being, a "perfect substance," could not possibly "be owing to" anything in any respect. In the second place, the "owing" expresses that Da-sein himself is the ground, not only of his own free actions and decisions, but above all of his own becoming. It is *owing to* how Da-sein already is that he can and must throw himself forward into his possibilities and so exist as the ground of himself. Da-sein's ability-to-be (coming-to-be) has, in turn, its own ground-character since it is *for its sake* (owing to it, on account of it) that Da-sein as care is constantly ahead-of-himself. As the original *for its own sake*, Da-sein's ability-to-be is in turn determined by a *not*, which reveals itself in the extremest way In the possibility of not-being-here-anymore. This possibility is the complete withdrawal of Da-sein's own being-here, which thus reveals itself as a being sheerly determined by a negativity. To be the *not*-determined ground of a negativity is Da-sein's being as care.

It is evident that the existential concept of owing is not a simple category of causality. It expresses the manifold ways in which the "nothing negates"—denies and forbids, withdraws and withholds—in Da-sein's being as care, which has at the same time the character of "ground." The existential owing permeates the whole of care in its essential articulations of facticity (thrownness), existence (forethrow), and falling.

The first and deepest manifestation of owing lies in Da-sein's thrownness. Thrownness means that Da-sein has *not* brought himself into his being; he can only find himself already here. He can *never* go back behind the fact of thrownness so that he could originate his "having to be as he is and can be" from his own self. Da-sein is thus revealed as *impotent* to be the ground of himself: he owes the very being which is handed out to him as his own. Although Heidegger does not make it explicit, it is clear that Da-sein "owes" both in an ontic and an ontological sense. Just as he can never bring himself forth as a concrete, ontic self, so he is powerless to confer on himself his disclosing way of existing. But "Because it has *not* laid the ground *itself*, it rests on the weight of it, which mood reveals to it as a burden" (SZ, 284). This weight can never be shaken off or left behind, for solely as the thrown being he already is can Da-sein exist as the ground of his own coming-to-be.

> And how *is* this thrown ground? Only by projecting itself upon the possibilities into which it is thrown. The self, which as such has to lay the ground of itself, can *never* gain power over the ground, and yet it has to take over being the ground in existing. Being its own thrown ground is the potentiality-of-being about which care is concerned. (SZ, 284)

Da-sein thus constantly lags behind his possibilities, not only and not primarily because in fact he cannot realize all of them, but because as the not-self-originated or not-self-grounded ground he is already behind the possibility of being his own ground. "Da-sein is never existent *before* its ground, but only *from it* and *as it*" (SZ, 284). His beginning thus manifests itself to Da-sein from a nothing of himself, that is, from his never having been here before his thrownness. This accomplished fact, however, in itself discloses the possibility of not-being-here. When, therefore, Da-sein dreadingly runs forward to the possibility of death, he is not disclosing anything "new" to himself, but only lets the possibility into which he is already thrown "stand" before him as a possibility, in the full clarity of its certainty and unchangeability. The deepest owing manifest in one's finite being is "*never* to gain power over one's ownmost being from the ground up" (SZ, 284).

It must be noted that in the short passage we have been considering, the word *never* recurs three times, twice in italics. This cannot be passed over as an accident, but must be taken as a hint that the negativity which permeates care as the not-self-grounded ground comes to light in an eminent way in the *never*. The hint, however, is not further elucidated by Heidegger when he sums up the owing character of Da-sein's thrownness as follows:

> Being *a self,* Da-sein is the thrown being *as* self. *Not through* itself, but *released to* itself from the ground in order to be *as this ground.* Dasein is not itself the ground of its being, because the ground first arises from its own project, but as a self, it is the *being* of its ground. (SZ, 284–85)

The positive ground-character of owing therefore lies in Da-sein's existence as a factical self. But this selfhood must not be understood as the enduring self-sameness of a substance that "underlies"—lies to the ground of changing qualities—nor of a subject that maintains itself in a recognizable identity and is thus constantly "present" to a changing stream of experience. Da-sein's selfhood is constituted by the way he exists, by the way he throws himself forward to his possibilities, in which he understands himself. Since, however, the structure of care is "free" to modify itself in two basic ways, Da-sein constantly stands in one or another of his possibilities:

> Da-sein [. . .] is constantly *not* other possibilities and has relinquished them in its existentiell project. As thrown, the project is not only determined by the nullity of being the ground but is itself *as project* essentially *null.* Again, this definition by no means signifies the ontic property of being "unsuccessful" or "of no value" but an existential constituent of the structure of being of projecting. This nullity belongs to the being-free of Da-sein for its existentiell possibilities. But freedom *is* only in the choice of the one, that is, in bearing the fact of not having chosen and not being able also to choose the others. (SZ, 285)

This passage repeats, only a little more fully, what was already said in the analysis of dread. Da-sein's "free-being for the freedom of choosing and taking hold of himself" is ontologically grounded in the modifiable structure of care. This can *concretize* itself only in the definite choice of one possibility and the renouncing of the other. And it is only because Da-sein is in the first place *choicelessly* thrown into the negativity of *dis*ownment that conscience calls him back to his freedom for his utmost, outmost possibility. Since conscience essentially belongs to Da-sein, *not* to follow its call, *not* to decide, is in itself a choice. Da-sein's freedom to decide in itself necessitates a choice. It is the seal of its finiteness that freedom can only and must bind itself to *one* end and renounce the other. Only this finite freedom can make something like necessitation, bindingness, and responsibility at all understandable.

According to the existential interpretation, morality requires the whole of Da-sein's being for its ontological foundation. Da-sein as care is the not-determined, not-self-grounded ground of a negativity. Only a being who is manifest to himself as determined by a denial and withholding can understand that in his factical existence he may be "owing" something. Only because Da-sein is the ground of his own becoming in such a way that he understands himself in his possibilities, can he demand from himself that he ought to exist in this way and not that. Only this can enable him to bind himself to a freely chosen way of being as a responsible self. The existential roots of morality thus reach down to the deepest depth and most far-reaching disclosing structures of care. It is Heidegger's great merit, in contrast to modern positivist tendencies, to show that the disclosure (truth) that makes morality possible is even more fundamental and original than the discovery (truth) that makes our cognition of things possible. The dogmatic positivistic assumption that the reality of things is the only "true" being about which "meaningful" statements can be made, must relegate the far more profound questions concerning how I ought to be to the sphere of "mere" emotions, which, equally dogmatically, are assumed to have nothing whatever to do with truth. Heidegger, to be sure, also says that conscience makes no "statements," but for exactly the opposite reason: it calls in the uncanny mode of silence, because it is the most originally disclosing mode of speech possible.

On the other hand, it may be asked whether, in taking back the phenomena of conscience and owing to their ontological foundation, Heidegger has not lost sight of morality altogether. For, we may wonder, where is the specifically "moral" character of conscience unless it gives us some direction or guidance to what is good or bad. Nowhere does Heidegger's interpretation give us the slightest hint of how good and evil may be distinguished and decided upon. Since the "good" is thought to have the character of "for its own sake," it may be that the possibilities of Da-sein's existence as the original "for the sake of" are intended to give us a hint of the source from which our ideas of the good are drawn. But if this is Heidegger's intention, he nowhere makes it explicit. This problem will be further commented on later, when we will be in a better position to see whether Heidegger has any more to contribute to questions of ethics.

For the present, we turn back to our central preoccupation with the fundamental-ontological problem of *Being and Time*. The interpretation of conscience and owing has taken some vital steps toward the solution of this problem. But just as the analysis of dread in Division One breaks off at a vital point, so the present analysis stops tantalizingly short of where it undoubtedly intends to lead us. To mention only one matter, the eminent way in which negativity, nullity, and the nothing come to light in the *never* remains a bare hint, which, in the absence of Division Three, leaves us wondering whether the *never* might not be the hinge on which the question of Being and Time turns round to the question of Time and Being. Heidegger himself is fully aware of the host of unanswered questions he has raised in the present analysis, for he explicitly draws attention to its incompleteness.

> Still, the *ontological meaning of the notness* of this existential nullity remains obscure. But that is true also of the *ontological essence of the not in general*. Of course, ontology and logic have expected much of the not, and thus at times made its possibilities visible without revealing it itself ontologically. Ontology found the not and used it. But is it then so self-evident that every not means a *negativum* in the sense of a lack? Does its positivity get exhausted by its constituting the "transition"? Why does every dialectic take refuge in negation, without grounding it *itself* dialectically, without even being able to locate it *as a problem*? Has anyone ever made the *ontological origin* of notness a problem at all, or, before that, even looked for the conditions on the basis of which the problem of the not and its notness and the possibility of this notness could be raised? And where else should they be found *than in a thematic clarification of the meaning of being in general*? (SZ, 285–86)

This unposed question of traditional philosophy is explicitly answered by Heidegger's lecture "What Is Metaphysics?" which we shall briefly consider in the next section. According to it, all negativity and no-saying, down to the last logical *not*, is grounded in the nothing originally disclosed by dread. The above paragraph gives notice, however, that this whole complex problem can only be clarified from the meaning of being as such, from the temporal character of being. (This compels us to wonder once more whether the *never* is not meant to give us a hint as to how the nothing becomes "meaningful" to us.) Unfortunately, the lecture gives us no hint of any temporal meaning of negativity.

Even more incomplete than the present exposition of negativity is Heidegger's elucidation of ground and ground-being. How precisely, we must ask, do care as the not-determined ground-being and the previously worked-out care-structure hang together? Is the one somehow superimposed on the other? If not, how is the connection to be envisaged? And if the self is *not* to be understood as a constantly underlying self-sameness, how is its "constancy" and "self-standingness" and "ground-being" to be positively understood? These questions, it is true, will be taken up later in Division Two, but without their essential connections being brought sharply enough into focus. This is one of the main reasons why the important chapter 5 on Da-sein's "historicity" (*Geschichtlichkeit*) remains as obscure as it is. Its connection with self-standingness and ground-being may be unnoticed by the most careful readers. Even a distinguished interpreter like Beda Allemann remarks that chapter 5 is "pushed in between the temporal analyses" of chapters 3, 4, and 6 of Division Two. "It is methodologically only loosely connected with the other chapters. . . . The whole (fifth) chapter appears as an excursus, whose theme, it is true, is most closely linked up with the aim of the investigation, without however necessarily belonging to the sequence of the explication of Da-sein's temporality."[1]

As against this view, it may already be pointed out that it is Da-sein's *owing*, his not-being-self-grounded, which refers him to other beings among which he can take root, gain a stand (stability and continuity), and so come to rest on a "ground" which carries and holds him. One way in which Da-sein brings himself to a stand is in delivering over to himself his tradition. This is constitutive of his "historical-being." Its time-structure and event-character are not loosely connected with the elucidation of the whole time-character of care, but are central to it. This, however, remains obscure unless the connection between owing, ground, and self-standingness is grasped in advance. In the present exposition we have arrived at one of those points where Heidegger brings the investigation to the verge of a most important explanation, only to break it off before it becomes truly understandable. Following the method adopted in this book, this is where the interpretation must step in and try to make explicit what the fragment of *Being and Time* leaves unsaid.

3. INTERPOLATION: GROUND-BEING AND NOTHING

Shortly after the publication of *Being and Time*, when its completion was still fully envisaged by Heidegger, two short but important works appeared: "What Is Metaphysics?" (WM, 1929) and "On the Essence of Ground" (WG, 1929). The first takes up the problem of negativity, left unfinished in the section above, while the second elucidates the "being of ground." Although both these short works still fall far short of accomplishing the task assigned to Division Three, they carry their problems an important step further forward than Division Two. The separateness of these two works, however, is in itself a pitfall. Both deal with the structurally indivisible *transcendence* of Da-sein's being, the first in the direction of thrownness, the second in the direction of forethrow (possibility).

Let us first consider briefly the lecture, "What Is Metaphysics?" It repeats, although from a different starting-point, the main steps taken in the analysis of dread in Division One. The phenomenological description of dread is much less detailed, and takes us in a few hasty steps to the point where beings as a whole, ourselves among them, sink away into complete insignificance, and we are overcome by an uncanny not-at-homeness. In the withdrawal and gliding away of beings, we are left with no hold. What is left and overcomes us is only this "*no.*" In this "no," dread has made manifest the nothing.

So far, no addition has been made to the former analysis of dread, except perhaps that the lecture lays even greater stress on the circumstance that the nothing is disclosed not in and by itself, but together with (at one with) the sinking away beings as a whole. From here, however, Heidegger proceeds to take a new step.

> In dread lies a shrinking back from . . . , which, of course, is no longer a flight, but a mesmerized stillness. This back from . . . takes its origin from the nothing. It (the nothing) does not attract to itself, but is essentially repelling. The repulsion from itself, however, is as such the relegation to the sinking-away beings as a whole, which the nothing lets glide away. (WM, 34, W, 11, G9, 114, P, 90, BW, 105, EB, 369)

The cardinal point in this passage is that our "shrinking away from . . ." or "back from . . ." *takes its origin from the nothing*. This positive repulsion by the nothing *originates* the movement or, more precisely, the movedness (*Bewegtheit*) of Da-sein's being as the *thrown forethrow*. The repulsion is nothing other than the throw of thrownness.

Is the positiveness of negativity exhausted by its forming the transition in dialectics? This question was asked in Heidegger's analysis of conscience and owing. The question now receives an answer: The nothing disclosed in dread is in the highest sense "positive," for its repulsion throws us into our forethrowing way of being.

But how can the nothing press in upon us in such a "positive" way? Heidegger does not explicitly say, but this need not prevent us from trying to unfold the implications of his thought. In confronting us with the nothing, dread brings us to an impassable limit which forbids us any further penetration into our having been thrown. The nothing repels us not by putting any obstacles in our way but by offering us "nothing" that we could hold on to and know; it totally denies us any access to itself. This denial and forbiddance of the nothing is the repulsion that refers us to beings as those which we *can* know and among which we *can* stand on a firm ground. This "repulsing relegation to beings as a whole" is the very essence of the nothing, its "negating." It is not we who "deduce" the nothing from beings by negating them as a whole. According to Heidegger, the opposite is the truth: all our negativity and no-saying is possible to us only because the nothing of beings is originally revealed and experienced in dread. The nothing itself "negates."

> The negating is not just any occurrence, but as a repulsing relegation to the sinking-away beings as a whole it makes manifest these beings in their full, previously hidden strangeness as the sheer other—to the nothing.
>
> In the clear night of the nothing of dread first arises the openness of beings as such: that they are beings—and not nothing. What is an addition in our speech, "and not nothing," is however not a subsequent explanation, but makes foregoingly possible the manifestness of beings as such; the essence of the originally negating nothing lies in this: it brings here-being, Da-sein, first of all before beings as such.
>
> Only on the ground of the original manifestness of the nothing can human Da-sein turn toward and become familiar with beings. insofar, however, as Da-sein essentially relates himself to beings that he is not and to the being he himself is, in his Da-sein as such he comes always already from the manifest nothing.
>
> Da-sein means: being held out into the nothing.
>
> Holding himself out into the nothing, Da-sein is always already beyond beings as a whole. This being out beyond beings is what we call *transcendence*. Did Da-sein not transcend at the ground of his being, did he not in advance hold himself out into the nothing, he could never relate himself to beings, hence not even to himself.
>
> Without original manifestness of the nothing, no self-being and no freedom.
>
> With this, the answer to the question concerning the nothing has been gained. The nothing is neither an object nor any being at all. The nothing neither occurs by itself nor side by side with beings to which as it were it hangs on. The nothing makes possible the manifestness of beings as such for human here-being. The nothing does not in the first place give us an opposite concept to beings, but belongs originally to being itself. In the being of beings happens the negating of the nothing. (WM, 34–35, W, 11–12, G9, 114–15, P, 90–91, BW, 105–106, EB, 369–70)

This passage has been quoted at length because it brings the most explicit answer Heidegger gives anywhere to the central question of *Being and Time*: How is an understanding of being at all possible to Dasein? The answer, however, is by no means complete nor is it detailed enough to be without serious difficulties and obscurities. It does not explain, for instance, how dread individuates Da-sein and brings him *singly* before the nothing, and how this is revealed as the nothing of himself. The whole stress of the present passage falls on how the nothing makes manifest *beings as a whole* (*das Seiende im Ganzen*, literally: beings in the whole). Beings show themselves "in the whole" from their sheer otherness to the nothing. Against the nothing, any possible beings are in advance driven together into a unity, into a wholeness, from which they must show themselves *as* beings, not nothing. The "not" of the "not nothing" expresses the manifest difference between beings and nothing. In understanding this difference, we understand *that* beings *are*. The disclosure of the nothing in dread as the sheer "other" to beings is therefore the disclosure of being as the *that-to-be*.

According to Heidegger, Da-sein alone exists in such a way as to be brought directly face to face with the nothing. This implies that being itself—the original disclosure of being—must necessarlly be finite. While *beings* can exist in and by themselves, their being, that is, their difference from the nothing, can manifest itself only when there are beings like Da-sein who hold themselves out into the nothing in their finite here-being. *That* Da-sein directly confronts the nothing of himself *is* his finiteness. His "that I am" is therefore a radically different way of being from the "that they are" of other kinds of beings. They do not directly face the nothing of themselves; it is we who hold them out into their possible nothingness, from which they become manifest *as* the beings they are. It is evident, therefore, that the being of beings, that is, the ontological difference, requires the *mediation* of Da-sein's being-in-the-world for its disclosure. It is at this point that the incompleteness of "What Is Metaphysics?" becomes obvious. It tells us only of the transcendence that happens in dread, and of the "throw" initiated by the nothing as a repulsion or relegation to beings as a whole. This, however, forms a single, indivisible unity with the "forethrow," the transcendence to possibilities. The, whole of transendence constitutes the structure of being-in-the-world, which mediates between the original disclosure of being (nothing) in dread and the being of beings within the world. This problem—the problem of the ontological difference—is dealt with in the essay "On the Essence of Ground." Its essential connection with "What Is Metaphysics?" is somewhat obscured by the historical recollection with which Heidegger introduces the problem of "ground." We will not follow up the whole of Heidegger's elucidations, but will try to see in what way "ground-being" is the same as being-in-the-world, and first of all, how the forethrow of possibilities— the transcendence to world—forms an indivisible unity with the "throw" of the nothing.

As we have seen, the repulsion of the nothing throws Da-sein into the midst of beings as a whole. His thrownness concretely manifests itself in attunement. Except for the basic mood of dread, attunement turns Da-sein toward beings and throws him open to them in different ways, while at the same time it brings him back to himself, since in every feeling Da-sein "feels himself," and thus feeling, finds himself in the midst of beings. Attunement constitutes the "world-openness" of Da-sein's here-being. But, as "On the Essence of Ground" proceeds to elucidate, it does not constitute the whole world-structure, for in his thrownness Da-sein is entirely thronged about and pressed in upon by beings; he lacks any distance to them from which they could become fully understandable in what they are. Even Da-sein himself cannot come to full clarity as the self he is unless he can open up a distance to himself as he already is. This distance, this free dimension of movement, is opened up by the forethrow of the possibilities of how he *can* be in the midst of beings. In this, Da-sein once more transcends, goes out beyond beings as a whole, among them first and foremost himself. The forethrow of the whole of his possibilities of being is the original opening up of world.

Now, how does this forethrow form a structural unity with the throw of thrownness? The throw initiated by the nothing does not come to a standstill when Da-sein finds that be is already here; it elicits the forethrow by driving beyond all "that" and "here." It is the constant threat of the nothing which duly drives Da-sein into going out beyond what already is by an anticipating projection of what can be. In dreadingly facing the nothing, he dreads for his own ability-to-be. The anticipating forethrow of his possibilities is therefore *for the sake* of himself. The world as the whole of his possibilities of being has therefore the primary and basic character of the *for the sake of* (*Umwillen*).

At this point, it is helpful to remind ourselves that the German *Umwillen* literally means "for the will of." This makes it more explicit that the understanding forethrow of possibilities is originally not a theoretical thinking out of what can be or might be, but a "willing" going out for it.

This is, of course, perfectly familiar to us from experience. What makes Heidegger'a talk of the "forethrow" strange is only that we do not ordinarily consider the ontologlcal conditions which make our daily decisions possible. What lies, for instance, in the decision of my buying a certain house next year? "I will buy this house" means that I throw this specific possibility ahead of myself without, however, letting go of it: I hold it out before and toward myself *as* a possibility. But what is it precisely that is thrown forward in my willing to buy this house? Obviously, I cannot bodily remove this house or myself into a still nonrealized possibility; what I throw forward is my *possible being* in relation to the *possible being* of this house a year hence. This makes it clear that all understanding anticipation of possibilities transcends, oversteps beings as a whole as they are "here and now." On the other hand, it is also clear that this whole transcendence to possibilities is grounded in and made possible by the original disclosure of being from the nothing as the sheer "other" to beings. Were being not already manifest as the that-to-be, it could never be thrown forward as the can-be.

Now what is it precisely that is "willed" in my "willing" to buy this house? Not this handy thing, the house itself, which stands there "in itself" independently of my willing, but my possible relation to it. This possibility, however, is not "there" in itself like a thing, but is formed only in and by my "willing" it, by my "being out for it." Further, I am not out for the house for its own sake, but as a place for living in; handiness of the house is constituted precisely by its being for something else than itself. The specific "what for" of the house, its "essence," becomes understandable only from the dependent "for the sake of" living in it. Since our existence is an "owing" staying and dwelling in a world, it in advance refers us to such things that may prove to be suitable for dwelling places. It is therefore, from the forethrow of possibilities that the beings disclosed as a whole in thrownness become differentiable in what they are, and we ourselves come to clarity both in our connectedness with and dependence upon them, and in our essential difference from them.

The whole structure of being-in-the-world is thus constituted by thrownness into the midst of beings as a whole and the forethrow of possibilities. But what is it, Heidegger asks, which in its own nature forms the *for the sake of* as such? It cannot be a specific "act of will," but is *freedom* itself.

> The transcendence to world is freedom itself. Accordingly, freedom does not butt into the "for the sake of" as something like a substantial value or aim which is there in and by itself, but freedom holds out—*as freedom*—the "for the sake of" toward itself. In this transcending *holding-out* the "for the sake of" *toward itself*, man's here-being comes to pass, so that in his existence he can be essentially bound to himself, that is, can be a free self. Herein, however, freedom at once reveals itself as the source of bindingness and obligation. *Freedom alone can let a world rule and world in man's being-here*. A world *is* never, but *worlds*. (WG, 43-44, W, 59-60, G9, 163-64, ER, 102-103, P, 126)

The tautological phrase "the world worlds" impresses on us that the world is not of the same order as beings, nor is it the totality of beings, but is a pure ontological horizon constantly "formed" by the forethrow of Da-sein's possibilities of being. These are, essentially: being-with others like himself, being-near-to things, and being himself. All specific, "provisional" possibilities, however, are in advance encompassed by the ultimate possibility of death as the sheer impossibility of being-here-anymore. In this impossibility lies the extreme negativity of Da-sein's owing-being; but whereas the nothing of dread reveals itself as the sheer other to *beings* (*das Nicht-Seiende*), it negates in death as the other to being, as not-being (*Nichtsein*). This impassable not-to-be not only brings all forethrow to a stand, but turns the forward-movement of Da-sein's being back upon itself. In the extreme negativity of death there lies once more a "positive" repulsion, which throws Da-sein back upon himself and directs him to existence within the limits of his factical being-in-the-world. The movement of "back-to-himself" initiated by the impenetrable nothing of death will prove to be, as we shall see presently, the movement of "primordial time."

The freedom (transcendence) that "forethrows" a world as the whole of Da-sein's possibilities, is thus essentially finite. The "bindingness" that it makes possible is not an accidental addition to it, but belongs to its finite structure. Not only is the *for the sake of* which freedom holds out before itself for the sake of being-here-to-the-end, but even in every provisional possibility freedom must "end" itself, that is, direct itself to an end in which it gathers itself, brings itself to a stand, finds a firm hold to which it binds itself. Without this self-gathering, self-binding nature of freedom, Da-sein could never steadfastly endure against the onrush of change in his factical being-in-the-world.

The finite structure of freedom, however, remains opaque in the essay "On the Essence of Ground." Even less explicit is the temporal meaning of ground as standing and staying, a self-gathered enduring or constancy. The latter is hinted at only in a single remark that is easily passed over unnoticed by even the most attentive reader. Once it is realized that freedom (transcendence) is a going out for an end (for the sake of) in which it gathers itself, brings itself to a stand, while ground has the temporal character of standingness, constancy, enduringness, gatheredness, the connection between the two becomes evident at a stroke. It may now be appreciated why Heidegger maintains that freedom is not merely one specific kind of "ground" or "cause," as in Kant's thought, where the spontaneity of free-will is contrasted with the causality of nature. According to Heidegger, freedom is the "origin" of ground as such (WG, 44, W, 60, G9, 165, ER, 104, P, 127). This means that something like ground or cause could not be understandable at all without the disclosure that happens in the transcendence of being-in-the-world.

The "original"—that is, the originating relation of freedom to ground—is called by Heidegger "grounding," (*Gründen*). This is scattered into three specific ways: 1. grounding as founding (*Stiften*); 2.

grounding as taking ground or gaining ground (*Bodennehmen*); 3. grounding as proving or accounting for (*Begründen*). This threefold scattering or strewing of ground is not accidental but corresponds to the three modes of time—future, past, and present—for transcendence (freedom) itself is rooted in the timeish structure of care.

The first grounding is nothing other than the "founding" of world in the forethrow of the *for the sake of* as such. The horizon of possibilities formed in and by transcending freedom opens up the distance between how Da-sein already is and how he can be. This distance is the dimension of "free play" (*Spielraum*) in which a free existence can hold himself. It gives Da-sein not only the dimension into which he can advance at all, but in holding out the *for the sake of* before him, it gives him a direction and end (the ground, the reason for) to which he can keep himself. Thus the transcending of beings, of what already is, is not a blind, directionless stumbling forward into "unbounded" possibilities of being, but is in advance guided by the *for the sake of* as the primary "ground" (reason for).

Furthermore, the forethrow of possibilities is in advance grounded in thrownness. Attunement makes manifest to Da-sein his "that I am" in the midst of beings which surround him, press in on him, occupy him, and tune him through and through. Da-sein's attuned finding himself among beings belongs essentially to his transcending way of being; it constitutes the "soil," the firm base for all forethrow. In belonging among beings as a whole, freedom "takes ground," gains a firm stand, so that human Da-sein gains a steady foothold in the fact of what already is and has been. Facticity and possibility constitute the single structural whole of transcendence as freedom.

In facticity, however, there lies an essential denial or withdrawal of certain definite possibilities; for example Da-sein has been thrown into one definite "historical situation," and so on. The indefiniteness that essentially belongs to the possibilities of Da-sein's existence has been limited by facticity, which has always already decided for a this and not that, a so and not otherwise. This withdrawing and limiting function of facticity is overreached and exceeded by possibilities, which are in their nature "richer" than what is already possessed. In the essential interplay between facticity and possibility there is thus a constant tension and discrepancy. From this tension springs the question Why? Why this and not that? Why so and not otherwise? Why anything at all and not rather nothing? With these questions, Da-sein addresses himself to making manifest beings in themselves, that is, to ontic truth. In all these questions, however, there lies already the foregoing understanding of what-being, how-being, and being (nothing)—ontological truth, which makes all ontic truth first of all possible. This understanding of being is formed and articulated in transcendence. It gives the foregoing *answer*, the first and last "ground" (reason) to all whyquestions. Transcendence is thus in itself a "ground-giving," for in it is revealed being, which is the ultimate ground and origin of the whyquestion we ask in the ontic discovery of beings. The transcendental origin of the "why" in advance directs Da-sein to ask beings to "prove themselves," to "give an account of themselves," by showing the "ground," or "cause" for being as they are. In being "proved" and "accounted for," beings come to stand on a firm ground; their wellfounded truth is stable and holds good, it can be counted on and relied upon amidst the pressure of uncertainty and change. But just because all ontic "proving" and "giving the reason for" springs from the freedom of Da-sein's finite transcendence, he can also throw evidence to the wind, he can suppress the demand for justification and proof, or distort and disguise it (WG, 48–49, W, 64–65, G9, 169–70, ER, 114–15, P, 130–31).

The preceding interpretation of freedom as a threefold grounding has made it much more explicit than the rest of the essay does that in all grounding there lies the tendency to hold and stabilize, to gather and bind into a steadfast enduringness. This interpretation, far from being arbitrary, only follows up the easily overlooked hint the essay itself gives us. At this point, Heidegger himself raises the question of whether the three very different ways of grounding have not been arbitrarily brought together under the title of "ground." Do they have anything more in common than an "artificial and playful community of the sound of words? Or are the three ways of grounding at least in one respect—although each in a different way—identical?" Indeed they are; though, as Heidegger hastens to add, their common meaning cannot be elucidated on the "level" of the present treatise. Nevertheless, Heidegger proceeds to give us a brief but invaluable hint: each of the three ways of grounding springs from "the care of endurance and stability" (*Beständigkeit und Bestand*, WG, 51, W, 67, G9, 171, ER, 122, P, 132).

It is important to note that the core of both of Heidegger's words comes from *stehen*, to stand. In an ontological-temporal sense, "to stand" means both the "standing-there," the immediate presence (*existentia*) of something, and its "staying in presentness," its constancy, enduringness as itself. It is easy to see that these are the basic characters of the traditional idea of the substance, or what is for Heidegger the same thing, of the subject. "*Standing presentness*" (*ständige Anwesenheit*) is, according to Heidegger, the temporal meaning of the central concept of being in traditional ontology (EM, 154, G40, 211, IM, 168).

Basic to the idea of substantiality (*ousia*) is an enduring self-sameness, an identity that maintains itself through movement and change and so "underlies"—that is, lies to the ground of and is constantly present in—all alteration and becoming. This traditional idea of being, as we can now see, has its existential origin in the freedom (transcendence) of Da-sein's being-in-the-world.

But just because Da-sein's being-in-the-world is care, he cannot "stand as himself" merely in the indifferent duration of a self-same substance or subject. His "self-standingness" is constituted by the whole transcending movement of care as the thrown forethrow. His thrownness into his "here" already throws him forward into the ultimate possibility of not-being-here; he stands as already stretched out between the extreme limits of his being, which throw him forward and back upon himself. The "care of endurance and stability" is therefore not of a sheer changeless duration but of a self-gathered steadfastness in the movement of a thrown being. All the three ways in which freedom is a "grounding," as we can now see more clearly, are ways in which care gathers and limits itself, finds a hold and steadiness in the movement of its finiteness.

The traditional idea of substantiality, on the other hand, has grown from a question of being which, according to Heidegger, is not original and fundamental enough and which, in the course of history, has run further and further away from its source. Heidegger'a well-known attacks on the idea of "substance," most particularly in the "second phase" of his thought, are directed especially against its degenerate and impoverished form in the modern age of technology, which has reduced the being of beings to a sheer calculable persistence for a calculating-representing subject. The bitterness of Heidegger'a attacks may indeed easily give rise to the impression that he wants to "eliminate" all notions of "standingness" and "presentness" from the idea of being. This impression, however, must be treated with great caution, for neither Heidegger nor any other thinker has the power to "eliminate" what belongs to being itself; he can only try to lead it back to its origin and show it within its proper limits.

Something like constancy and self-standingness, however, evidently belongs to being, for it alone can make beings identifiable in what they are. The identifiability of beings, according to Heidegger's own interpretation, belongs to the disclosing function of world. This can be unambiguously documented by the following passage.

"Da-sein transcends" means: he is in the essence of his being world-forming [*weltbildend*], and that in several senses: he lets a world come to pass, and with the world gives himself an original view (image, *Bild*), which is not itself grasped, but which nonetheless functions as a pre-view [*Vorbild*] of all manifest beings, among which each existing Da-sein himself belongs. (WG, 39, W, 55, G9, 158, ER, 89, P, 123)

This sentence is not only obscure, but is surprising, for until now we have heard only that the world is "formed" by the forethrow of the *for the sake of* the possibilities of Da-sein's being. But now this sentence—obscure as it may be in all other respects—clearly tells us that the world itself gives us a kind of "pre-view," an "original image" of beings, from which they become recognizable as beings. How this happens, Heidegger does not explain. A certain pointer, however, may be found in Heidegger's Kant-interpretation, especially of the "transcendental object" and of the principle of the "anticipations of perception" (KPM, 113ff., G3, 121ff., KPM(E), 82ff; FD, 167ff., G41, 217ff., WT, 214ff.). Since, however, Kant's thought moves in the dimension, albeit transcendental dimension, of subjectivity-objectivity, its interpretation must on no account be directly identified with Heidegger's own thought. Nonetheless, with due precautions and reservations, we can take a hint from it to explain the above passage in the following way.

In the forethrow of the *for the sake of*, freedom gives itself a direction in which to advance, and at the same time, gathers itself, brings itself to a stand in an "end." Every near and far "aim" forms a kind of limit within the direction of advance, but at the same time indicates the possibility of further advance. So, for instance, my intention to buy a house forms a provisional limit, but it already invites further progress in the same direction; for example, planning how to furnish the house after buying it. All forethrow of such provisional, "realizable" ends, however, is in advance encompassed by the ultimate possibility of not-being-here-anymore. This not-to-be stands before us as a constant and impassable limit to any further advance. In forming an unchanging, impenetrable horizon to all our coming and going, it gives us an original "view" of an impenetrable, standing "something." It is only because we always already have an impassable horizon in view as a "something" that resists us that we can recognize and identify a concrete something *as* something when it meets us within the world.

Although this interpretation cannot be "proved" to correspond to Heidegger's intentions, it can be at least indirectly confirmed. In his analysis of dread, Heidegger calls the world the most original, primordial "something" (SZ, 187). Since the world as a pure horizon certainly cannot "originate" concrete, ontic beings in the sense of "producing" them, it can only give us an "image" from which they become understandable as the beings they are. This is only possible if the horizon itself shows itself in its constancy and standingness as the original "something."

A further confirmation for this interpretation may be found in Heidegger's "idea of being as such (what- and how-being, something, nothing, and negativity)" (WG, 52, W, 69, G9, 175, ER, 125, P, 133). This "idea of being" is evidently the same as the "clarified concept of being" to which repeated reference is made in *Being and Time*, and which was to have been finally "clarified" in Division Three. What is immediately striking in it is the apparent incongruity of the "something." What can the "something" be if it is not a formal concept of beings as such? But if it is a concept of beings, what business does it have in the idea of being as such?

It would certainly have no business there if it were merely an ontic concept, a generalization abstracted from the concrete beings that happen to be accessible to us. Its only justification to be in the "idea of being" at all is that it is not an ontic but an ontological concept which in advance lies in all our meeting with concrete beings, and makes them first of all understandable as the "self-standing" beings they are.

How has this interpolation helped to clarify Heidegger's elucidations of "owing"? It has shown that "ground-being" and being-in-the-world are the same, insofar as care is the care of stabilizing its own movement as the thrown forethrow. Further, it has unfolded the "positive" function of the nothing which makes Da-sein's being as care possible. What has not come into view so far is the emphatic recurrence of the *never*, which we have noted in Heidegger's elucidation of Da-sein's owing being. On this point, unfortunately, Heidegger gives us no help at all. Nonetheless, we have every justification to think that if the *never* has a real significance in the context, it must have an important bearing on both the constitutive characters of "owing," namely on its negativity and its "standingness," which has turned out to be the temporal meaning of ground.

Nothing could be more obvious than the negative character of the *never*, for it sheerly denies us any "when." Yet just as the nothing does not "annihilate" beings, but brings them to light in their sheer "otherness," so the never does not annihilate time, but brings the sheer "whenness" purely to light. And just as we cannot "deduce" the nothing from beings, it is even more impossible to "deduce" the never from the usual concept of time as an endless succession of nows. To do this, we would have to think of time as a whole and then negate it; but since the "flow of nows" is beginningless and endless, it is in principle impossible to think of it as a whole. Indeed, as soon as we begin to consider the never, we are led to the surprising conclusion that it cannot be explained from the usual conception of an endless, "linear" time at all, but must belong to a more original time.

Further, is not the never something like a "standing" time? Does it not show the "standing of its self" in a much more original way than the constantly present "now" in an endless succession of indifferent nows? The never does not give us an "image" of an indifferent, unchanging presence, but brings instantly home to us *unchangeability itself*. It is the never that gives us originally to understand our unchangeable impotence to be the origin and master of our own here-being. It has, therefore, the same repelling character as the nothing. It totally repels any attempt to go "past it" or "beyond it," and so turns us to the definite "when" of our factical staying in the world. It is precisely the unmovability of the never that "moves" us to grasp our factical, finite, measurable possibilities. The never itself is immeasurable in the same way as the nothing: it keeps our finite "measuring" sheerly away from itself.

As even these few reflections show, the never must indeed have an important bearing on the problem of Da-sein's owing-being as the not-determined ground of a negativity. The fact that Heidegger does not elucidate it any further in the course of his analysis of temporality in Division Two seems to indicate that a special role was reserved for it; perhaps it was intended to be the hinge on which Being and Time "turns round" to Time and Being.

4. Owing, Guilt, and Morality:
The Authentic Hearing of the Call of Conscience and the Existential Structure of Owned or Authentic Existence

The "free will" that is the precondition of Da-sein's "moral self" has now been shown to lie in the transcending structure of being-in-the-world. The finite freedom of this transcendence forms and articulates the manifold ways in which Da-sein "owes"—that is, is the not-determined ground of a negativity. The "owing being" to which conscience summons Da-sein has therefore a positive ground-character, which makes possible a responsible decision and is at the same time permeated with negativity, which in advance refers Da-sein to others than himself, as those to whom he is "owing." The finite freedom of this positive-negative ground-being is the existential condition of the possibility of the moral "good" and "bad," that is, of morality as such and of the concrete forms morality can take in Da-sein's factical being-in-the-world (SZ, 286).

188   Part Three: Division Two of Being and Time

How the various forms of morality arise and how Da-sein gains a concrete insight into the being of the good and bad are problems to which Heidegger takes up a strikingly evasive position. He merely repudiates the traditional concepts of the "good" and of "values," as well as the concept of the bad as a "privation of the good," on the ground that they have been drawn from the traditional idea of being as substantial reality (*Vorhandenheit*). But any positive indication of how good and bad may be distinguished is remarkably lacking in *Being and Time*. It leaves it open to us to suppose that the "good" comes to light with the original disclosure of being, which "throws" us into our being-in-the-world, and that is why the possibility of being-in-the-world has the basic character of the *for the sake of*. But in this disclosure, the nothing "negates" in the extremest way, and this, presumably, brings the "bad" cooriginally to light. These suppositions seem to be confirmed by Heidegger's "Letter on 'Humanism'" published twenty years after *Being and Time*, assuming that we can identify what Heidegger calls the *Heile*, the wholesome, the healing, the holy, with the source of the "good," and the *Grimmige*, the grim, with the source of the "bad" (HU, 112ff., W, 189ff., G9, 359ff., P, 272ff., BW, 237ff.). But even if we can justifiably draw on this later work for explaining what *Being and Time* leaves unsaid, it still gives us nothing more precise than the widest of generalizations. Just because the *for the sake of* being-in-the-world comprehends in itself all the ways in which Da-sein can factually be, and these ways are capable of a wide range of modifications, we need a much more precise guidance as to which of these ways we ought to bind ourselves to as "good" and which we are to reject as "bad." According to the "Letter on 'Humanism'," insofar as Da-sein ek-sists—"stands out into the truth of being"—being itself allots to him those "directions" (*Weisungen*) that must become law and rule for him (HU, 114, W, 191–92, G9, 360–61, P, 274, BW, 238–39). Here Heidegger himself admits the necessity for "law and rule," which manifests itself in Da-sein's being as the "care of standingness and stability." He contradicts himself, therefore, when in his analysis of conscience he rejects the demands for concrete ethical "norms and rules," which, Heidegger here says, arise from an everyday understanding, incapable of anything more than business dealings, and which demands a handy rule and norm in the mutual settling of accounts and obligations (SZ, 288, 292ff.). But, on Heidegger's own showing, the necessity of rules and laws does not arise merely from disowned existence and its supposed incomprehension, but from the original "directions" of being itself, which "directs" us to bind ourselves to something that holds and steadies us.

In view of the fundamental-ontological aim of *Being and Time*, it is true, we cannot demand from it a fully worked out "ethics" any more than a "physics." But what we can demand from it is to show us the bridge on which we can cross from the original disclosure of being, as the ultimate foundation of morality, to the concrete ethical principles that are binding on us in our factical existence. It is this bridge that is so strikingly lacking in *Being and Time*.

Even Heidegger's later works show the same reluctance to enter concretely into the problem of ethics, which leads him into renewed contradictions. So, for instance, in the "Letter on 'Humanism'," Heidegger seeks to justify his own negative position by referring to the early Greek thinkers, who also knew no philosophical discipline called "ethics," and yet were anything but "unethical." As an illustration, Heidegger quotes a story about Heraclitus, who, on being found by visiting strangers warming himself in front of a baking oven, encouraged them to enter with the words, "Also here the gods are present" (HU, 107ff., W, 185ff., G9, 355ff., P, 269ff., BW, 233ff.). But this story, far from supporting Heidegger's position, only shows up its weakness. It is just because the present technical age, as Heidegger himself stresses, is characterized by a growing rootlessness and a complete absence of "the God," that even the most makeshift norms and rules of conduct must be carefully nurtured and preserved (HU, 105, W, 183–84, G9, 353–54, P, 268, BW, 231–32).

But, it may be asked, does Heidegger not give us in *Being and Time* at least one example of a positive ethical decision? If conscience calls Da-sein back from his disownment and summons him to take over his existence as his own, this cannot be a merely abstract, theoretical disclosure, but is a call to the most basic ethical decision Da-sein is capable of making. Indeed, Heidegger himself explicitly acknowledges that his ontological interpretation of existence is based on a definite ontic conception of owned existence, on "a factical ideal of Da-sein." This fact, moreover, has a positive necessity, considering that it is Da-sein's being that is the thematic subject of the inquiry (SZ, 310). It can be easily understood why, from the philosophlcal point of view, owned existence must be the "highest," the "worthiest" way of being: because in it Da-sein most completely fulfills his "essence," his "destiny" of existing as the "place" in which the disclosure of being, that is, original truth, concretizes itself. Standing-in-the-truth has of old been the philosophical "ideal" of the highest kind of "life."

As against this ideal the self-disguising flight of everyday existence into disownment to "them" must necessarily be a lower and less worthy way of existing. But, here again, Heidegger constricts himself into contradictions, for instead of acknowledging this necessity, he explicitly disclaims any intention of a "moralizing criticism" of everyday Da-sein (SZ, 167). The disclaimer notwithstanding, we must maintain that Heidegger is in fact making a concrete ethical distinction between owned and disowned existence; the very tone of rejection and contempt in which he speaks of the disowned "oneself" (*Man-selbst*) is itself an ethical indictment. The fact that Heidegger makes such ethical judgments is in itself perfectly in order, and indeed unavoidable; what is objectionable is that it leads him into a onesided and tendentious representation of the everyday self and his understanding. Practically all the examples selected by Heidegger show everyday being-together as a scene of, at best, indifference, at worst, back-biting, malice, and cowardice, not to speak of the exaggerated lack of comprehension Heidegger ascribes to the common understanding. While Heidegger's illustrations cannot be rejected as untrue, they certainly present only one side of the picture. Nowhere does the onesidedness of Heidegger's presentation come more jarringly to the fore than in his descriptions of the everyday experience and understanding of conscience. Let us consider briefly a few points from the "criticisms" which, according to Heidegger, may be raised against the existential interpretation from the side of everyday experience.

In the first place, the objection might be made that the essential interpretation makes no distinction either between the "reprimanding" and the "warning" conscience, or between the "good" and "bad" conscience. Heidegger first considers the last objection, pointing out that in all interpretations conscience is primarily "bad"—a sign that conscience is to be understood as something like a "being guilty" (owing). But how is this "being guilty" to be understood.

> The "experience of conscience" turns up *after* the deed has been done or left undone. The voice follows up the transgression and points back to the event through which Da-sein has burdened itself with guilt. If conscience makes known a "being guilty," this cannot occur as a summons to . . . , but as a pointing that reminds us of the guilt incurred. (SZ, 290)

In this interpretation, Heidegger observes, the whole experience of conscience is presented as a series of occurrences which take place one after the other, so that the "voice" has its own "place" after the event. What Heidegger has in view here is the time-structure of real happenings, which occur as a sequence in a linear, one-dimensional now-time. This time-structure, however, is not the original one of care, in which Da-sein is constantly ahead-of-himself in such a way that he at the same time is turned back toward his thrownness. How does Heidegger explain the undoubted experience of the "voice" as *following* the deed? He maintains that the actual guilty deed is only the *occasion* for hearing the call, for wakening the conscience that sleeps. The everyday explanation, however, does not get the full existential phenomenon into view, but stops halfway when it sees only a series of happenings one after the other. Conscience, to be sure, calls back, but beyond the committed deed back to the original owing-being which lies in Da-sein's thrownness. At the same time, it calls him forward to the ability-to-be-owing of his existence, which he is summoned to take over as his own. It is only as this forward-calling recall that conscience shows the original structure of care.

As against Heidegger's criticism of the everyday interpretation of conscience as existentially insufficient, we may ask whether he himself gets the *whole* ontic-existentiell experience into view. We must answer No, because the "voice" does not merely castigate us for a committed deed; it calls for something like restitution and a firm resolution to become better in the future. The call for restitution and resolution to change ourselves essentially belongs to a genuine and full experience of conscience. Both common understanding and religious-ethical teaching reject an experience which is a mere, often self-indulgent, wallowing in remorse, and insist that the proper "hearing" of the voice lies in how we act on it. This will turn out to be not vastly different from Heidegger's own interpretation of the "authentic" hearing of the call. Furthermore, when the *whole* ontic-existentiell phenomenon of conscience is taken into account, as a call for a repenting and restituting resolution, its "structure" turns out to be nothing other than a forward-calling recall. It is only because Heidegger takes hold of merely a fragment of the genuine experience that he can find it to be so deficient in comparison with the existential interpretation. Similarly, his criticism of the "warning" conscience as being merely a reference to some future deed will not hold water, because it again ignores the full phenomenon. He does not ask how conscience "warns" and how it alone can warn. It can warn solely by bringing us to ourselves as we already are and have been and by accusing us of being already guilty of and responsible for intending evil. Here again the forward-calling recall structure of conscience comes to light, as indeed it must do in every concrete experience, if Heidegger's existential interpretation is true and not merely an arbitrary invention.

One fundamental difference between existentiell experience and the existential interpretation must certainly be admitted. The latter aims at exposing the last ontological foundations that make the concrete experience first of all possible. The former have no such intention, and it is questionable whether it can be rightly accused of shortcomings because of this. The proper sphere of everyday understanding is the concrete situation and the action it demands. This seems to be a much truer reason for its preoccupation with "what ought I to do?" than its incapability, as Heidegger avers, to comprehend anything beyond a businesslike taking care of things. Besides, here again Heidegger contradicts what he himself says elsewhere. In his analysis of everyday being-together, he showed that Da-sein's caring-for other existences has a completely different character from his taking care of things. While the latter is guided by *Umsicht*, a circumspection that discovers what things are *for*, the former is guided by *Rücksicht*, a considerate regard for the other's thrownness, and by *Nachsicht*, a forbearing looking-after the other as a self (SZ, 123). These ways of "seeing"—of understanding—which guide Da-sein's relations to other selves, must be alive already in his everyday existence and must disclose to him in some way that his "dealings" with other existences are different from his makings and doings with things. Insufficient and even wrong as the explicit explanations given by everyday understanding may be from the existential-ontological point of view, there is no evidence to show that it cannot distinguish at all Da-sein's relation to himself and to other selves from his relation to things. And the further question arises whether everyday understanding can be justifiably criticized for its ontological shortcomings when its own proper sphere lies in the concrete situation. Heidegger himself seems to feel that some kind of distinction is necessary, for at the end of his criticisms he suddenly adds that the *existential* insufficiency of the everyday understanding of conscience is no judgment on the *existentiell* "moral quality" of the self who holds himself to it.

> Just as existence is not necessarily and directly jeopardized by an ontologically insufficient understanding of conscience, the existentiell understanding of the call is not guaranteed by an existentially adequate interpretation of conscience either. Seriousness is no less possible in the vulgar experience of conscience than is a lack of seriousness in a more primordial understanding of conscience. (SZ, 295)

The clear distinction Heidegger draws in this paragraph, though somewhat belated, will prove to be helpful when we come to consider the precise nature of the change that is brought about by an authentic hearing, that is, understanding of the call. In what does this authentic understanding lie? Before answering this question, Heidegger proceeds to gather up the results of the whole preceding investigation. The following paragraph is the final summary of *what* conscience gives Da-sein to understand and *how* it gives him to understand it.

> The call is the call of care. Being guilty constitutes the being that we call care. Da-sein stands primordially together with itself in uncanniness. Uncanniness brings this being face to face with its undisguised nullity, which belongs to the possibility of its ownmost potentiality-of-being. In that Da-sein as care is concerned about its being, it calls itself as a they that has factically fallen prey, and calls itself from its uncanniness to its potentiality-of-being. The summons calls back by calling forth: *forth* to the possibility of taking over in existence the thrown being that it is, *back* to the thrownness in order to understand it as the null ground that it has to take up into existence. The calling back in which conscience calls forth gives Da-sein to understand that Da-sein itself—as the null ground of its null project, standing in the possibility of its being—must bring itself back to itself from its lostness in the they, and this means that it is *guilty* [*owing*]. (SZ, 286–87)

It will be noticed that in this paragraph Heidegger refers twice to the "standing" of Da-sein. As the preceding interpolation has shown, this "standing" is the basic temporal character of "being the ground." What, then, does it mean that in his not-at-homeness, Da-sein stands primordially together with himself? It means that the *authentic* way in which Da-sein "grounds himself" and grows firm roots in his thrownness is not by turning away from it and disowning himself to other beings, but by steadfastly enduring its threatening negativity as belonging to his own self and setting it free for its possibilities. And how does Da-sein authentically "stand" in the possibility of his being? Not by "standing off" from others and measuring himself by the distance that separates his possibilities from theirs, but by opening up the distance between himself and his *own* utmost possibility, which reveals his extremest "guilt" or "owing." Only this can give him the final certainty of himself and the end that can steadily guide him in the choice of the "realizable" possibilities of his single being-in-the-world.

The cited paragraph first defines what conscience is and *what* it calls. It then tells us *how* it calls: it does not inform Da-sein of his owing-being as of an indifferent fact, which he can acknowledge or ignore, but calls to him that he *shall*, that he *owes it* to bring himself back from his lostness, and so to gather himself, to come to "stand in himself" as his own ground.

It would seem, then, that in summoning Da-sein to a decision about how he is to be, conscience itself gives him his first "ought." Although Heidegger does not explicitly say this, the "ought" is clearly implied in the "zurückholen soll," "must bring (himself) back," for the German "sollen" expresses our "ought." This is the justification for translating the "schuldig ist," which follows the "soll" as an explanation of it, by "he owes it," instead of by [as in the translation cited here] the more usual "he is guilty"—a rendering that can be fitted into the context only with the greatest difficulty. But apart from the always disputable translation of a somewhat ambiguous text, it is evident that conscience must bring Da-sein before the original "must" or "ought," and this for two reasons. First, because conscience does not merely inform Da-sein of his owing-being, but summons him, demands from him to take it over for himself. It is in this demanding character of the call that the "ought" lies. Second, because the proper understanding of the call cannot lie merely in cognizing "what" it says, but lies in a decision. This decision first of all enables Da-sein to exist as a fully moral being, whose "I ought" springs from his own self and not from a half-hearted submission to what is prescribed for him by others. Without this response to the summons of conscience, Da-sein cannot become even properly "guilty" in his factical existence, for he has failed to accept full responsibility for his not-self-given self. Only when his aboriginal, inalienable "guilty"—that is, the negativity of his finiteness—has been accepted, can he be authentically good or bad within the limits of his finiteness.

> Then the correct hearing of the summons is tantamount to understanding oneself in one's *ownmost* potentiality-of-being, that is, in projecting oneself upon one's ownmost authentic potentiality for becoming guilty. When Da-sein understandingly lets itself be called forth to this possibility, this includes its *becoming free* for the call: its readiness for the potentiality-of-being summoned. Understanding the call, *Da-sein listens to its ownmost possibility of existence.* It has chosen itself. (SZ, 287)

This is the first time that something like a concrete choice, an "I will," becomes explicit in *Being and Time*. In view of the controversial question of whether there is a radical change or only a development between Heidegger's "early" and "late" thought, it is helpful to note that already in *Being and Time* the first ontic choice, the most basic concretization of Da-sein's freedom, is an answer to a call which Da-sein cannot choose and dispose of. This is emphasized by Heidegger when he proceeds to unfold the meaning of the authentic response to the call:

Understanding the call is choosing, but it is not a choosing of conscience, which as such cannot be chosen. What is chosen is *having* a conscience as being free for one's ownmost being-guilty [owing]. *Understanding the summons* means: *wanting to have a conscience*. (SZ, 288)

This passage makes explicit what was already remarked in passing; namely that the decision, the choice, is not something in addition to and subsequent to a "theoretical" understanding of the call, but that the understanding is in itself the choosing, the "willing." This "willing understanding" is indeed nothing other than the concretization—in an authentic way—of the freedom which transcends to a world and a "willing going out for" the possibilities of existence.

At this stage, an important point must be briefly mentioned. In the modern metaphysics of subjectivity, the will-character of being has come to ever greater predominance, from Kant onward through German idealism and Nietzsche to its final embodiment in the present age of technology, whose naked "will" to unlimited control and mastery over beings as a whole has become unmistakable. In view of this dominant trend, it cannot be sufficiently emphasized that in Heidegger's thought the "will-character" of man's transcendence (freedom) to world is not the "ultimate," but is itself grounded in the throw of the nothing which throws him into his forethrowing way of being. Insofar, therefore, as his transcendence to world is a "willing" going out beyond beings as a whole, it is itself made possible by a throw that does not have a will-character.

But if the ontological will-character of care is not its dominant and ultimate constituent, even less is it subject to any ontic choice on Da-sein's part, for his own being is the last thing he can will or dispose of. This is what is meant by Heidegger when he points out that conscience itself cannot be chosen—for it belongs to Da-sein's being as care. Da-sein can only be willing to *have* conscience. The "having" implies a holding, a keeping; an authentic understanding of conscience does not let go of its call as though it were a mere occurrence, but keeps itself in constant readiness, is steadfastly willing to be called forward to the owing which lies in his own existence. This readiness to be summoned to himself, however, represents phenomenally the *owned way of existing*. Its ontic possibility has now been attested by conscience, to which an authentic hearing of the call essentially belongs.

In his willingness to have conscience, Da-sein's here-being is disclosed in a preeminent way. Disclosedness (truth), however, is the most fundamental essential character of care. The disclosedness which lies in an authentic understanding of the call is constituted by the forethrow of Da-sein's ownmost possibility of owing, by the basic mood of dread which reveals the not-at-homeness from which care calls, and by the silence in which it calls as the original mode of speech. The call "comes from the soundlessness of uncanniness and calls Da-sein thus summoned back to the stillness of itself" (SZ, 296). He who is willing to have conscience understands the call appropriately in a reticent silence. This eminent, authentic disclosure of his being-there—the reticent, dreading self-forethrow to his ownmost owing-being—is called by Heidegger "resoluteness" (*Entschlossenheit*). More precisely, Heidegger's word means both resoluteness and utmost disclosedness. The ambivalence is essential, for it expresses that the authentic mode of care is the most original *truth of existence*, and that this can concretize itself only in the resolute choice on the part of a factically existing Dasein. The truth of his own existence is not a distant and hidden piece of knowledge which he has to find through long researches and intellectual efforts; on the contrary, it is *given* to him by conscience. What is demanded from each Da-sein is the resoluteness to open himself to the call, to let himself be told of himself.

This interpretation of resoluteness makes a clear distinction, a distinction unfortunately not explicitly made by Heidegger in this connection—between an existentiell-ontic and an existential-ontological understanding. According to our interpretation, a resolute hearing of the call requires only the former, which, of course, always includes an implicit, untheoretical understanding of being. This can be perfectly genuine and sufficient without any explicit, theoretical-ontological insight. The latter is the business of the philosopher, and philosophy is always the concern of the comparatively few. Owned existence, on the other hand, is the possibility of Da-sein as Da-sein; it would be absurd to suppose that it depended on any specific theoretical interests, nor does Heidegger's analysis in the least lead to such a conclusion. But the height of absurdity would be to assume that a specific *existential* philosophy is the precondition of owned existence—an assumption which nonetheless seems to be tacitly made by numerous existentialistic writers, who appear to imagine that a "philosophizing" about choice, self, nothingness, and so on, no matter how facile and half-baked it may be and often is, is the hallmark of an authentic self.

Heidegger's elucidation of owned existence is sober and bare in the extreme, and almost inevitably, something of an anticlimax. There is no outward drama in turning from disownment to the most "primordial truth of existence," nothing that could be depicted as a startling happening. Heidegger's first concern is to recall to his readers what precisely is to be understood by the "truth of existence." As has already been shown in Division One, truth in the existential sense is not primarily a quality of judgments (propositions), nor of any specific ways in which Da-sein relates himself to beings (e.g., as in a theoretical-scientific approach to them), but is primarily a fundamental character of being-in-the-world itself. The constitutive moments of this structure, namely the world, the being-in, and the self as the "I am," are cooriginally disclosed by an attuned-articulating understanding. From the significant reference-whole of the world, Da-sein already refers himself to the things which meet him within it. These things are originally discovered in their interconnected relevance, their handiness for this and that. The significance-structure of the world is, indeed, nothing but the understanding anticipation (forethrow) of how the beings to be met within it can be related both to each other and to Da-sein's existence. The *for the sake of* Da-sein's own existence is the ultimate ground from which the whole significant chain of references spring and to which they lead back. The possibilities of finding shelter, livelihood, and advancement, for the sake of which Da-sein is constantly ahead-of-himself, are in the first place guided by "one's" lostness among "them," who have always already decided about these average possibilities of existing in the mutually shared "world" upon which each Da-sein is dependent.

Now, what happens when the lost "oneself" is summoned by conscience and the call is resolutely answered? Apparently, nothing happens; the factical world in which Da-sein lives is not changed, his daily occupations, his circle of friends and acquaintances are not exchanged for others, and yet his care-taking being-near-to things and his caring-for being-with others are now primarily determined not by the possibilities prescribed by "them," but from the resolutely grasped possibilities of his own self.

Resoluteness as authentic self-being does not cut Da-sein off from his world, does not isolate him from others, but, on the contrary, first of all enables him genuinely to-be-in-the-world. The resoluteness to himself makes it possible for Da-sein to "let the others be" in their own existence and to help to disclose it to them in a "liberating" caring for them which "leaps ahead" of them (*vorspringend-befreiende Fürsorge*). The resoluteness of an owned existence can become the "conscience" of others. The authentic being-together-with-others can only spring from owned existence, and not, as Heidegger remarks with his usual acerbity, from the "ambiguous and jealous stipulations and talkative fraternizing in the they and in what they wants to undertake" (SZ, 298).

While no one would dispute the insufficiency and lack of genuineness of the kind of "stipulations" or agreements Heidegger has evidently in mind, the crucial question is whether there is anything better that could concretely take their place. An absolutely free, "presuppositionless" meeting with others, unbounded by any mutually accepted standards, is impossible, not only as a matter of fact, but because freedom itself is finite; on Heidegger's own showing, it is not only grounded in thrownness, but has to bring itself to a "stand" by gathering itself in a binding end. If an authentic being-together is concretely possible—and if it is not, it cannot be a genuine possibility at all, but is a mere ontological invention—it can be imagined only as a resolutely free self-submission to a mutually binding end. What such an end could be and how it could be conceived at all if each Da-sein exists primarily for the sake of himself, is of course a big question. Would an authentic being-together not require an end which each accepts as greater than himself? Short of that, would the kind of mutual agreements Heidegger derides not be the best that could be aimed at in practice?

In the important problem of how to bridge the gulf between theoretical "insights" and the ways to their concrete achievement, Heidegger leaves us without any definite guidance. It cannot be urged in excuse that his own interest is purely theoretical in these matters; on the contrary, he is very well aware that the whole idea of owned existence, and with it, of an "authentic morality," is nothing without its possible concretization. Indeed, the whole inquiry into conscience has been conducted for the express purpose of "attesting" owned existence as a factical possibility of Da-sein. The construction of an abstract "resolute existence" could claim no place in *Being and Time*. That is why Heidegger emphasizes that resoluteness "exists" only as a "self-forethrowing resolution," a concrete act of resolve. This concrete resolution is not merely the acceptance of ready-made and recommended possibilities, but is the forethrow and determination of the factical possibility an existence chooses for his own. *What* is chosen cannot therefore be prescribed and defined in advance. On the other hand, the choice is never entirely unbounded and directionless: its sphere and range is ontologically prescribed by existentiality itself as a thrown ability-to-be in the way of a care-taking caring-for. Its ontic range, in turn, is limited by the specific world into which a factical existence has been thrown.

Uncertain as it is what Heidegger really thinks about an authentic being-together, he leaves us in no doubt on one point: even resolute existence can never escape from "them" and "their" world. Disclosed to himself in his "here," Da-sein stands cooriginally in truth and untruth. The untruth of erring and disguising is not simply left behind, but is first of all recognized and resolutely taken over as essentially belonging to Da-sein's falling being. The "irresoluteness" of everyday existence, which delivers Da-sein over to the ambiguous explanations of "them," always remains in dominance, although it may not be able to assail a resolute self. Nonetheless, he remains always dependent on "them" and "their" world, just because his own possibilities which are disclosed and determined by resolution, must necessarily be drawn from the factical world of his thrownness. It is precisely a resolute existence who becomes wholly transparent to himself in his limitation. He does not withdraw himself from "reality," but first of all discovers what is factically possible and grasps it as his ownmost ability-to-be among "them." By contrast, the irresolutely disowned existence drifts along with the opportunities publicly offered by "them," never truly deciding for himself on the possibilities that are to be his own.

The existential phenomenon of a resolutely disclosed "hereness" is called by Heidegger the "situation." In a brief discussion of this phenomenon, Heidegger points out that there is a "spatial" meaning in "situation," just as there is in the "here" of being-here. This is rather surprising, because the spatial reference is not what we would primarily or predominantly think of in a "situation." Heidegger, however, takes this opportunity to remind his hearers that Da-sein is never merely "in space" in the same way as an extended thing, but "gives himself space" (*einräumen*) or, one might say, "allocates himself a place," by reference to the things of which he is taking care. As Division One has shown, the significant reference-whole of the world has an essentially "spaceish" character constituted by an orientating-bringing-near of things. The existential "spaceishness" of Da-sein's "hereness" is grounded in the disclosure of his being-in-the-world. The "situation" is nothing but the resolutely disclosed "here" of a factical existence an authentic self is "resolved" to be. To the disowned "oneself," on the other hand, his situation is closed; he knows only the "general position" in which be loses himself to the next-best "opportunities" and fills up his existence by calculating what might "fall to him" from circumstances.

It has become clear, Heidegger proceeds to say, that the call of conscience is not merely critical and negative, nor does it hold out an empty "ideal of existence" before Da-sein, but positively calls him forward into his situation. Further, it is clear that the authentic hearing of the call does not merely "cognize" the situation, but brings itself to stand resolutely in it—that is, it is already "acting." The reason Heidegger usually avoids contrasting "action" and "practice" with "theory" is that these distinctions are not ultimate; both are grounded in care. The most detached, theoretical investigation is no less a careful taking-account of things than is the grossest manual working with them. To contrast the resolute "action" of owned existence with a "theoretical attitude" would, therefore, be completely misleading. Resoluteness is nothing but the authentic mode of care, which concretizes itself in a resolutely grasped "situation."

It would be idle to pretend, however, that the existential concept of the "situation" has now come to full clarity. Especially puzzling is Heidegger's initial emphasis on its "spatial" meaning, which seems to have little to do with the concrete situation of a resolutely owned existence. It may well be that Heidegger intended to develop this theme later on, for instance, by showing that the world as the familiar dwelling-place of man's everyday staying and dwelling is originally disclosed by the dreading not-at-homeness in which the situation of a resolute existence has its foundations. If such was Heidegger's intention, however, it is certainly not worked out in Division Two.

The present chapter has brought us a first delineation of owned existence which conscience summons Da-sein to become. So far, the owned self remains something of a shadow beside the vulgar vigor of "them." Only when Heidegger begins his time-interpretation as the "meaning of care" will the authentic self come fully into his own. Before that, the essential connection between resoluteness and the anticipatory forward-running understanding of death will have to be worked out in detail. This will be the first task of the next chapter.

XII

Authentic Ability-to-Be-a-Whole and Temporality as the Meaning of Care

The decisive task of the present chapter is to take a step that Heidegger calls *grund-legend*. This step will "lay the ground" for all that has so far been brought to light by the existential analysis. The "ground" to be laid—the temporal constitution of care—is "ground" in the sense that it makes the unity of care originally possible. On no account must it be understood as a "producing cause," a *causa efficiens*. Before this decisive step can be taken, certain problems that have an immediate bearing on it must still be elucidated. The first of these is the inner connection between resoluteness and anticipatory running forward into death. A forward-running resoluteness will prove to be the concretization of the authentic mode of care, in which its temporal structure first becomes phenomenally accessible. This is why its elucidation has been deferred to the present chapter instead of being carried out in the preceding one, where it may seem logically to belong. The second problem to be dealt with is the methodical basis of the whole existential analysis. The third is the ontological constitution of the self. These preparatory discussions will now be considered in turn.

1. ANTICIPATORY FORWARD-RUNNING RESOLUTENESS AS THE AUTHENTIC WAY OF BEING-A-WHOLE

Chapter 1 of Division Two showed that Da-sein can be a whole in an authentic being unto death. This is constituted by running forward unto death as the ownmost, unrelational, impassable, certain, and yet indefinite possibility of existence. As the extreme possibility of the impossibility of being-here-anymore, death in advance *closes* Da-sein's ability-to-be and thus constitutes its wholeness. All this, however, remains a purely ontological construction, whose possible concretization in a factical existence must still be attested. This attestation is satisfactorily achieved if it can be shown that the resoluteness of an owned existence in its own nature tends to become a *forward-running resoluteness*. The tendency can already be seen in a general way when it is considered that resoluteness means the readiness of a factical existence to take over his owing-being wholly as his own. This "owing," however, determines Da-sein's being as care from beginning to end; it is precisely in the extreme negativity of death that this "owing" character of care comes fully to light. An authentic existence, therefore, must resolutely take over his own being unto death. This happens in a forward-running resolution, which *modalizes* the whole structure of the owned way of existing.

The call of conscience reveals Da-sein's lostness among "them" by calling him back to his own ability-to-be-himself. Da-sein becomes wholly transparent in his own ability-to-be only in resolutely taking over his being unto death as his ownmost possibility.

The call of conscience ignores all Da-sein's "worldish" achievements and his position among others. It singles him out and individuates him into his own owing-being. His singleness strikes most sharply into his conscience when a forward-running resoluteness discloses death as his ownmost, *unrelational* possibility.

The "owing" to which a resolute existence is constantly ready to be summoned *goes before* every factical indebtedness and *stays after* its annulment. The constancy of his owing becomes wholly manifest only from the possibility that is sheerly *impassable* for each existence. In resolutely running forward into death, Da-sein has taken his "owing" wholly into his own existence, for no further "owing" can then overtake him.

The phenomenon of resoluteness has brought the investigation before the most original *truth of existence*. It may not be superfluous to remark that the truth of existence is *not* equivalent to the truth of being, for the latter means all the ways and modes in which being can disclose itself at all, whereas the former means the specific way in which we understand and relate ourselves to our own ability-to-be. Although care is the "place" where the disclosure of being as such concretely happens, this does not mean that Da-sein's own existence *exhausts* the whole of the truth of being.

For the present, however, the *truth of existence* is Heidegger's especial problem, as may well be seen from the length of the analysis devoted to it. Since this is one of the trickiest passages in *Being and Time*, we shall go over it step by step.

The analysis is introduced by the sentence "Resolute, Da-sein is revealed to itself in its actual factical potentiality-of-being in such a way that it itself *is* this revealing and being revealed" (SZ, 307). This sentence reemphasizes the peculiar nature of our understanding our own existence. This understanding is not a "faculty" we possess in addition to existing, but is the way in which we exist. We ourselves *are* this understanding and our own being *is* the understood. Existential concepts and existential analysis are nothing but an explicit bringing-into-word and explaining of this "revealing revealedness"—of the truth of existence.

All truth, however, as chapter 1 of Division Two echoed, has a corresponding certainty. The original truth of existence demands a correspondingly original certainty. Now, how does resoluteness reveal existence? "It *gives* itself the actual factical situation and *brings* itself into that situation" (SZ, 307). The situation is not a ready-made mixture of conditions and opportunities that are "there" and merely await cognition; it is the understanding forethrow of *my* possibilities in the particular world into which I have been thrown. In the forethrowing opening up of its own possibilities, resoluteness "gives" itself the situation. This "giving," however, is not the theoretical thinking out of a plan that might be carried out or pushed aside; the resolute choice of definite possibilities is in itself an active throwing oneself—that is, "bringing oneself" into them. The owned way of existing, far from being a withdrawal and estrangement from the world, is an active taking-hold of a fully revealed "hereness," of a situation in a world.

In its very nature, however, a situation cannot be calculated in advance like the calculable, self-same presence of a substantial thing; the situation can be disclosed only in a free, previously undefined, but nonetheless definable resolution.

> *What, then, does the certainty belonging to such resoluteness mean?* This certainty must hold itself in what is disclosed in resolution. But this means that it simply cannot become *rigid* about the situation, but must understand that the resolution must be *kept* free and *open* for the actual factical possibility in accordance with its own meaning as a disclosure. The certainty of the resolution means *keeping oneself free for* the possibility of *taking it back*, a possibility that is always factically necessary. This holding-for-true in resoluteness (as the truth of existence), however, by no means lets us fall back into irresoluteness. On the contrary, this holding-

for-true, as a resolute holding oneself free for taking back, is the *authentic resoluteness to retrieve itself*. But thus one's very lostness in irresoluteness is existentially undermined. The holding-for-true that belongs to resoluteness tends, in accordance with its meaning, toward *constantly* keeping itself free, that is, to keep itself free for the *whole* potentiality-of-being of Da-sein. This constant certainty is guaranteed to resoluteness only in such a way that it relates to that possibility of which it can *be* absolutely certain. In its death, Da-sein must absolutely "take itself back." Constantly certain of this, that is, *anticipating*, resoluteness gains its authentic and whole certainty. (SZ, 307–308)

This paragraph has been quoted at length because it gives rise to new perplexities each time it is read. Only one obvious point emerges from it with any clarity; namely that resoluteness must keep itself open to changing factual possibilities. But, apart from the consideration that Heidegger would hardly waste a long paragraph on stating such a banality, the point by no means exhausts the meaning of the passage. To understand it at all, the precise meaning of certainty must first of all be recalled. Certainty means, primarily, *to be certain*. I am certain of something when I hold it for true; that is, when I can hold myself in its truth, stay in it, can be constantly bound by it. Now, what resoluteness must be certain of is not the true (discovered) presence of an object, but the revealedness of existence, revealed precisely by resoluteness itself. This certainty is gained by resoluteness not by clinging to a momentary situation "here and now," but by revealing existence wholly to its end. It is only by running forward to the certain possibility of not-being-able-to-be-here-anymore that the "I-am-able-to-be-here" itself is eminently revealed. This certainty, moreover, is not the momentary conviction of existence in the "moment" of dying, but holds and binds Da-sein *constantly* and over the *whole* of his existence. It reveals the whole of Da-sein's being by throwing him back on to his thrownness. The resolute taking-over of existence lets itself be called back to its not-self-chosen ground in thrownness. Resoluteness is the constant readiness to be dreadingly brought before the throw of the nothing that originally reveals the "that I am." Resoluteness brings itself back again to the original revelation that happens in this throw and brings the throw back into a factical existence by freely choosing to be this thrown being.

The certain truth of existence, for which resoluteness "holds itself free," is thus the very opposite of the certain, actual presence of a substantial thing. Resoluteness follows the movement of the call of care as a forward-calling recall: forward, into the certain possibility of not-being-here-anymore, from which the "I am here" becomes certain, and back, to the nothing of a not-self-grounded self, which throws him into his factical being-in-the-world. Only in running forward to the extreme limit of its ability-to-be-here, can resoluteness gain the authentic certainty of a whole existence.

Some of the deepest obscurity of our passage has now been lifted. It gains further clarity, however, when it is contrasted with Descartes's *cogito ergo sum*, a contrast that Heidegger almost certainly, though only implicitly, intends to draw. The Cartesian conception of truth as the certainty of representation (*Vorstellung*), Heidegger maintains, dominates the modern age even where it is apparently refuted. The certainty of this truth lies in the always calculable representability of an object by a subject. The *cogito ergo sum* is the absolute, unshakable ground of this truth. But what guarantees the unshakability, the indubitable certainty of the ground itself? It is the at all times necessary presence (am) of the thinking-representing subject (I) in all his representations (I think). The presentness of the subject (I am) can be absolutely and always counted upon (calculated) in every I think. With this, however, the meaning of the "I am" is perverted into the calculable self-sameness and persistent presentness of a substance. The certainty of the Cartesian "I am" is not drawn from the original truth (disclosedness) of existence, but from an objectivized, always presentable and present, thinking thing. The temporal structure of a forward-running coming-back-to is totally lost in the calculable presentness of a persistently present subject. *Me cogitare=me esse*, according to Heidegger, is the basic equation of the modern age, on which all truth is to be based (HO, 100, G5, 109, QCT, 150). The indubitable presentness and presentability of the *esse* in every *cogitatio*, however, is not the certainty appropriate to the original truth of existence. The unshakable foundation of the modern conception of truth is itself lacking an original foundation.

The perversion of existence into a wholly different mode of being (substantiality), however, is not an accident but arises from the irresoluteness of a fleeing-concealing disownment. Da-sein stands cooriginally in truth and untruth. It is precisely the forward-running resoluteness that gives an owned existence the original certainty of concealment, for without an authentic disclosure the concealment of a disowned way of being could not be discovered. Da-sein's lostness into the irresoluteness of "them" rises from the ground of his being and can never be completely overcome. Forward-running resoluteness, therefore, holds itself open to the constant possibility of concealment, of which it is certain.

It may not be superfluous to emphasize once more that the concealment Heidegger has in mind is not a conscious and deliberate self-disguise and self-deception. It springs from the negativity that permeates Da-sein's owing-being. One important way in which this negativity concretizes itself is the essential *indefiniteness* of Da-sein's ability-to-be. The indefiniteness can define itself in a resolution for a particular situation, but it can never be eliminated. It reveals itself wholly in an authentic being unto death. A resolute running-forward brings itself before the possibility that is constantly certain and yet *indefinite* as to *when* it will turn into the impossibility. In resolutely disclosing the indefiniteness of his extreme situation, an existence wins his authentic ability-to-be-a-whole.

The indefiniteness of the "when" of death is originally revealed in dread. Resoluteness endeavors to demand from itself the courage to dread. It removes all disguise from the deliveredness of Da-sein to himself. The nothing before which dread brings Da-sein reveals the negativity that determines his here-being from the ground (SZ, 308).

The analysis has now shown the tendency that lies in resoluteness itself to be *modalized* by an authentic being unto death. It is authentically and wholly what it can be only as a forward-running resoluteness. And conversely, the authentic being unto death finds its ontic-existentiell concretization in *forward-running resoluteness*. Until now, it could only pass for an ontological construction. Now, however, its concrete possibility has been attested by resoluteness as the authentic mode of itself. At the same time, a forward-running resoluteness is the existentiell possibility of an authentic being-a-whole. The ontological problem of Da-sein's wholeness is not merely a theoretical-methodical problem, as it appeared to be at the beginning. The way the problem of wholeness was raised in chapter 1 of Division Two is justified only because it is grounded in an ontic possibility of a factical existence.

The phenomenal demonstration of a way of being in which Da-sein can bring himself before and to himself—can be authentically a whole—may nonetheless be far removed from the everyday, commonsense understanding of existence. This, however, is no proof that it is not a genuine, concrete possibility of a factical existence. Heidegger rejects any suggestion that an understanding that grows from a falling mode of being can be the judge of its own authentic possibilities. On the other hand, Heidegger does not deny that a factical "ideal" of owned existence underlies the whole existential-ontological analysis. On the contrary, he stresses that

> not only is this fact one that must not be denied and we are forced to grant; it must be understood in its *positive necessity*, in terms of the thematic object of our inquiry. Philosophy will never seek to deny its

"presuppositions," but neither may it merely admit them. It conceives them and develops with more and more penetration both the presuppositions themselves and that for which they are presuppositions. This is the function that the methodical considerations now demanded of us have. (SZ, 310)

2. Justification of the Methodical Basis of the Existential Analysis

Heidegger must now make explicit the evidence on which the whole existential analysis is based and justify its method. This justification is all the more urgent because the "violence" of Heidegger's method has by now become unmistakable. Since the disowned mode of care itself covers over the original, authentic mode of Da-sein's being, the existential interpretation is compelled to execute a *countermovement* against this trend inherent in care. It must try to *conquer* Da-sein's being from and against its own self-disguise. How can such a "violent" method be justified?

To a greater or lesser extent, Heidegger points out, *all* interpretation is "violent," because the understanding that unfolds itself in it has a forethrowing (projecting) structure. But just because all interpretation necessarily sustains itself in and from an anticipatingly projected horizon (meaning), it must be all the more securely *guided* and *regulated*. Leaving other kinds of interpretations aside, from where does an *ontological projection* draw the evidence for its appropriateness? Ontological interpretation projects the already "given" beings on to their being, whose structure is to be explained in explicit concepts. But where are the indicators that point the way to being? More specifically, what are the pointers that guide and regulate the steps of the existential interpretation of care?

The evidence to which Heidegger now has recourse is nothing new, but a summing up of what has already, though more incidentally, appeared in the course of the investigation. The existential interpretation draws its evidence from the *self-interpretation* that essentially belongs to Da-sein's being. All that Da-sein is and does is infused with an understanding of his own being. His own care-taking being-near-to things, for instance, is always in sight together with his circumspect discovery of them. In all factical existentiell possibilities, existence itself is at least implicitly understood and in some way explained. An ontological explanation of Da-sein's being is therefore already prepared by the way Da-sein *is*.

Nonetheless, how does Da-sein's usually untheoretical, "preontological" self-explanation lead the conception of an authentic existence?

Who is to say what makes an existence "authentic"? As far as Da-sein's ontic existence is concerned, Heidegger disclaims any pretensions to setting up an "ideal" that would be binding and obligatory on everyone. As far as the existential interpretation is concerned, on the other hand, he claims that it is entirely justified in basing itself on those existentiell possibilities that are most properly Da-sein's own. For Da-sein is essentially his ability-to-be and free for his ownmost possibilities, or exists in unfreedom against them. The interpretation is bound to take the ontic ways in which Da-sein *can* exist and project them on to their ontological possibility. And if Da-sein usually explains himself from his lostness to things, then his authentic possibilities, discovered by moving counter to his lostness, first of all brings the "undisguised phenomenal content" of his being fully to light (SZ, 313).

It may be objected at this point that Heidegger does not really justify his interpretation of owned existence, because the distinction between owned and disowned existence is already presupposed in the justification. But Heidegger is perfectly well aware of this. Such "presuppositions," as we shall see below, are precisely the "projections" essential to an interpretation. The important point is whether their choice has been properly guided or whether it is arbitrary and accidental. There is nothing arbitrary, Heidegger claims, in the stress that falls on the forward-running resoluteness that constitutes "owned existence," since Da-sein himself demands it from himself from the ground of his being. The way in which Da-sein relates himself to his eminent possibility in death has not been assigned a central role by accident, but because being-in-the-world has no higher instance of its ability-to-be than death.

But granted all this, the *existential* interpretation of these phenomena has not been justified. On the contrary, it becomes more and more evident that a "presupposed" idea of existence as such has guided the whole interpretation. Even the first steps of the analysis of everydayness were already regulated by a "preconceived" notion of existence. Otherwise it could not have been said that Da-sein "falls" into disownment, so that his "ownmost" possibilities must be wrested from his self-disguise. What has guided the first projection of the idea of existence?

> Our formal indication of the idea of existence was guided by the understanding of being in Da-sein itself. Without any ontological transparency, it was, after all, revealed that I myself am always the being which we call Da-sein, as the potentiality-of-being that is concerned to be this being. Da-sein understands itself as being-in-the-world, although without sufficient ontological definiteness. Thus existing, it encounters beings of the

kind of being of things at hand and objectively present. No matter how far removed from an ontological concept the distinction between existence and reality may be, even if Da-sein initially understands existence as reality, Da-sein is not just objectively present, but has always already *understood itself*, however mythical or magical its interpretations may be. For otherwise, Da-sein would not "live" in a myth and would not take heed of its magic in rites and cults. The idea of existence which we have posited gives us an outline of the formal structure of the understanding of Da-sein in general, and does so in a way that is not binding from an existentiell point of view. (SZ, 313)

This idea guided the whole preparatory analysis up to the first conceptual formulation of care, which, in turn, provided the basis for an explicit ontological distinction between existence and reality. But how could these two different modes of being be distinguished from each other unless an idea of being in general or as such were already "presupposed"? Indeed even a bare, formal idea of existence must already "presuppose" an idea of being as such (*Sein überhaupt*), in whose horizon alone it can be differentiated from and contrasted with reality.

Here Heidegger touches on a paradox that must be constantly kept in view. On the one hand, being manifests itself only in care, but on the other hand, the range of its manifestness is "immeasurably" wider than merely Da-sein's own being. It must be so if being becomes understandable to us from the "immeasurable" nothing. Its repulsion in advance refers us to beings as a whole, that is, throws us into our being-in-the-world. Together with ourselves, the nothing must make manifest all other beings as *not nothing*, as beings that are. The disclosure of being in advance reaches beyond ourselves, although its concrete happening takes place only in our own being as care.

But if both existence and reality already presuppose an idea of being as such, should the latter not be the first to be clarified? The clarification could be achieved through the concrete analysis of Da-sein's understanding of being. This, however, demands a prior interpretation of Da-sein's being guided by the idea of existence. Is it not obvious, then, that the whole fundamental ontological problem goes round in a circle? The idea of existence and of being as such are first "presupposed," and Da-sein's being is interpreted in the light of this "presupposition" in order to win from it in the end the idea of being as such.

The circular movement of the fundamental ontology is indeed much more obvious than that of many a "deductive proof" where it is subtly disguised. But, as Heidegger points out, the existential analysis has a totally different character from a deduction that starts from an axiom or a premise and proceeds by logical rules to prove further propositions from it. The charge of a "circle in proof" cannot apply at all to the existential analysis, because it does not start from an axiom that we have "pro-posited" (*angesetzt*), but from the way in which *we ourselves are*. Nor does the analysis "deduce" propositions about Da-sein, but proceeds to lay bare what must already lie at the ground of our being. The "presupposed" idea of existence is an understanding-anticipating projection of Da-sein's ontological constitution. This understanding is then unfolded in such a way that it lets Da-sein himself have the last say whether the formal outline of his projected constitution is appropriate to him or not. In no other way can beings of any kind be made accessible in respect of their being. The so-called circularity to which objections may be raised is nothing less than the fundamental structure of care. Da-sein as care is constantly ahead-of-himself. In the existentiell forethrow of his possibilities he has always already projected, if only preontologically, existence and being in general. It is the "forethrowing" structure of care that lies in every explicit "presupposition" of the existential analysis.

> But the "charge of circularity" itself comes from a kind of being of Da-sein. Something like projecting, especially ontological projecting, necessarily remains foreign for the common sense of our heedful absorption in the they because common sense barricades itself against it "in principle." Whether "theoretically" or "practically," common sense only takes care of beings that are in view of its circumspection. What is distinctive about common sense is that it thinks it experiences only "factual" beings in order to be able to rid itself of its understanding of being. It fails to recognize that beings can be "factually" experienced only when being has already been understood, although not conceptualized. Common sense misunderstands understanding. And *for this reason* it must necessarily proclaim as "violent" anything lying beyond the scope of its understanding as well as any move in that direction. (SZ, 315)

In the circular structure of care lies the possibility of any understanding of being whatever. The fundamental ontology must therefore "aim at leaping into this 'circle' primordially and completely, so that even at the beginning of our analysis of Da-sein we make sure that we have a complete view of the circular being of Da-sein" (SZ, 318). Previous ontologies of Da-sein, Heidegger implies, have fallen short precisely because they have failed to "presuppose" the whole of his being in its peculiarly "circling" movement. They have started from an all too meager worldless "I" and proceeded to procure for it an "object," with an ontologically groundless relation to the object. Or where "life" is made the theme of the inquiry, it is not enough to take account of death merely occasionally. As for the practice of restricting the inquiry first to a "theoretical subject," later to be amplified on the "practical side" by a tagged-on ethics, this is branded by Heidegger as to "*artificially* and *dogmatically* cut out" the original subject matter, which is the *whole* of Da-sein's being.

By way of contrast, the existential analysis has put its preparatory effort into securing the authentic wholeness of Da-sein's being. With the working-out of forward-running resoluteness, the previous inadequacy of the hermeneutic (interpretatory) situation has been overcome and the methodical requirements for a further progress of the investigation are now fulfilled.

Heidegger closes his reflections on method with an important paragraph in which he reminds us that forward-running resoluteness brought us to the phenomenon of the original and authentic truth. In Division One, however, it was shown that the everyday understanding of being covers over original truth insofar as it understands being only in the sense of substantial reality (*Vorhandenheit*). Truth and being, however, belong so inseparably together that the revelation of original truth must at the same time modify our understanding of being. The authentic truth of forward-running resoluteness must vouchsafe us the understanding of the being of Da-sein and of being as such. The possibility of this understanding is what the existential analysis seeks to discover. Its "ontological truth" is grounded in an original existentiell truth, *whereas the latter does not necessarily need the former*. This last remark of Heidegger's, apart from its methodological importance, should remove any lingering doubt whether an authentic existence is dependent on an explicit philosophical understanding. As we said in the last chapter, an existence can be perfectly "authentic" in Heidegger's sense without any philosophy. Finally, we shall glance at the second-last sentence of this closing paragraph, because it is so ambiguously constructed that it may easily lead to serious misunderstandings. "The most primordial and basic existential truth, for which the problematic of fundamental ontology strives in preparing the question of being in general is *the disclosure of the meaning of being of care*" (SZ, 316).

The most obvious way to read this sentence is that the "problematic of fundamental ontology" is merely preparatory to the "question of being in general." According to this reading, the temporal analysis of being in general or as such, which was to have been carried out in Division Three, would be something different from the fundamental ontology of the first two divisions. This, however, is quite untenable, for the temporal interpretation of being as such is the very goal of the fundamental ontology; it is the concrete answer to the "question of being" as it is raised and worked out in *Being and Time*. To get the meaning of Heidegger's awkwardly phrased sentence, it may be paraphrased in the following way: The most original, ground-laying existential truth that the fundamental-ontological problematic strives to reach is the disclosedness of the ontological meaning of care. This (namely the temporal meaning of care) is preparatory to the question of being as such (namely to the question of the temporal meaning of being as such).

3. CARE AND SELFHOOD

The section immediately preceding the first steps of the temporal analysis deals with the problem of the self. Why does Heidegger assign a place of such methodological importance precisely to this problem? There are two reasons. Firstly, the self will prove to play an eminent part in the succeeding investigations, especially in the interpretation of Da-sein's "historical-being." Secondly, and more immediately, it leads directly to the problem that the temporal analysis is designed to solve, namely the problem of what makes the unity of care possible.

The first two chapters of Division Two have made us aware of the increasing complexity of the structure of care, which has been shown to comprehend in itself the phenomena of death, conscience, and owing. The original unity of this complex whole has by now become an urgent problem. Heidegger, it is true, has stressed from the start that care is an "original whole" and not an aggregate put together from existence, facticity, and so on. But the wholeness of care has not yet been followed back to its foundations; the *ground* of its unity still remains to be demonstrated.

Is the "ground" of this unity not self-evident? The complex modes and possibilities of care, after all, do not exist in and by themselves, but only as possible ways in which concrete beings are. It is *I myself* who exist as care; it is *I* who exist in the various ways and possibilities of my being. "The 'I,'" Heidegger remarks, "seems to 'hold together' the totality of the structural whole. The 'I' and the 'self' have been conceived for a long time in the 'ontology' of this being as the supporting ground (substance or subject)" (SZ, 317).

It is only with reservations, we must observe, that Heidegger introduces the notion that the "I" "holds together" the structure of care. It "seems" to do so, Heidegger says, implying that a thorough examination is needed before a decision can be reached. Until now, the existential-ontological problem of the self has not been raised in a positive way. Division One showed only negatively that the "who," the "self" of everydayness, is not the authentic "I myself," but the disowned one-self-among-others. Even this disowned one-self, however, could not be ontologically grasped with the help of the categories of substance (*Vorhandenheit*).The phenomenon of the self is comprehended already in care, which cannot be "constructed" from the categories of reality. The ontological problem of selfhood lies in the existential "connection" between care and self.

According to the method outlined in the last section, the existential interpretation of selfhood takes its "natural" start from the self-explanation of everyday existence. Da-sein expresses himself "about himself" in his "I-saying." The "I" means only myself and nothing further. Hence the content of this expression has been held to be absolutely simple. In its simplicity, the "I" does not define other things, it is not itself a predicate, but is the "absolute subject." The "subject" that is pronounced in every I-saying is always found to maintain itself as the self-same—that is, it underlies (*substare*), lies to the ground of continuously changing experiences—and further, it is conscious of its own numerical identity at different times; it is what the old "rational psychology" defined as a "person."

> The characteristics of "simplicity," "substantiality," and "personality," which Kant, for example, takes as the foundation for his doctrine "The Paralogisms of Pure Reason" (*Critique of Pure Reason*, A 348ff.), arise from a genuine "prephenomenological" experience. The question remains whether what was experienced in such a way ontically may be interpreted ontologically with the aid of the "categories" mentioned. (SZ, 318)

Kant himself, Heidegger points out in the important passage which now follows, although he repudiates the *ontic* theses about a "soul-substance" that have been derived from the phenomenal content of the I-saying, fails to reach a proper *ontological* interpretation of selfhood. On the contrary, "he does, after all, slip back into the *same* inappropriate ontology of the substantial whose ontic foundations he theoretically rejected for the I" (SZ, 318-319). In support of this contention, Heidegger now proceeds to give a short summary of the Kantian analysis of the "I think."

> The "I" is a bare consciousness that accompanies all concepts. In the I, nothing more is represented [*vorgestellt*] than a transcendental subject of thoughts. "Consciousness in itself (is) not a representation . . . , but a

form of representation in general" [*Critique of Pure Reason*, B 404]. The "I think" is the "form of apperception that adheres to every experience and precedes it" [A 354]. (SZ 319)

The phenomenal content of the "I," Heidegger concedes, is rightly fixed by Kant as "I think," or, "if the relation of the 'practical person' to 'intelligence' is also considered—in the expression 'I act.'"[1] Saying I must be grasped in Kant's sense as saying I think. The "I" of the *res cogitans* is called by Kant the "logical subject." By this he means that the "I" is the subject of logical activity, of "connecting." All connecting is "I connect." The "I" already lies at the ground of (*hypokeimenon*) all connecting and relating. Hence it is "consciousness in itself" and not a representation or perception, but rather the "form" of it—that is, it is the formal structure of representation or perception as such. This formal structure makes all representation or perception and perceived first of all possible. The "I" as the form of perceiving and as "logical subject" mean the same thing (SZ, 319).

Heidegger finds two positive results in Kant's analysis: first, it shows the impossibility of an ontic derivation of the "I" from a substance, and second, it fixes the phenomenal content of the "I" in the "I think." Nonetheless, the "I" is still conceived in an inappropriate sense. For, Heidegger says, coming to the crux of the matter,

> the ontological concept of the subject does *not* characterize *the selfhood of the I qua self, but the sameness and constancy of something always already objectively present* [*Vorhandenes*]. The being of the I is understood as the reality of the *res cogitans*. (SZ, 320)

But why is it, Heidegger asks, that Kant could not exploit his genuine start from the "I think" and had to fall back into the inappropriate ontology of the substantial? The answer to this question makes explicit the steps that lead from Kant's transcendental analysis of Dasein's "inner nature" to the existential analysis of *Being and Time*. Heidegger begins his answer by pointing out that the full phenomenal content of the "I" is not merely "I think," but "I think something." To be sure, Kant also sees perfectly clearly that the "I" is constantly related to its representations and is nothing without them. For Kant, however, these representations are the "empirical" that are "accompanied" by the "I"; they are the "appearances" to which the I "hangs on." Kant fails to explain the manner of this "accompanying" and "hanging on," but it is clear that he understands them as a constant "being present together" of the I with its representations. This means, however, that the being of the I and the being of the represented are not in principle distinguished; that is, the being of the I is understood as the presentness of a substance.

But it is not only that Kant failed to fix the full content of the I as "I think something"; more importantly still, he did not see what must be ontologically already "presupposed" in the "I think something." For if the "something" is understood to mean "beings within the world," then the "something" necessarily presupposes a *world*, and precisely this phenomenon helps to determine the fundamental constitution of the "I," if it is to be able to "think something."

With the ontological "presupposition" of world, which is demanded by the "I think something" as a necessary condition of its own possibility, Heidegger can now fix the full phenomenal content of the everyday saying-I: this "I" means the concrete being I am as "I-am-in-a-world." It is because Kant did not see the phenomenon of world as an essential constituent of Da-sein's own self, Heidegger maintains, that he had to keep away the "empirical" perceptions from the a priori content of the "I think." This, however, must lead to a restriction of the I to an *isolated* subject that "accompanies" perceptions in an ontologically undefined way (SZ, 321).[2] "*In saying-I, Da-sein expresses itself as being-in-the-world*" (SZ, 321). The everyday self-interpretation, however, tends to understand itself from a care-taking preoccupation with beings *within* the world, so that the basic structure of being-in-the-world is constantly covered over. Da-sein usually flees from himself into being one-of-them. Thus it is *not* my own self that speaks in the "natural" saying-I, but the lost one-self. In the variety of everyday happenings and in chasing after things to be taken care of, the self of the self-forgetful "I-take-care" appears in a simple, indefinitely empty, constant self-sameness. In the everyday world *one is what* one takes care of. Thus the problem of the self is in advance forced into the inappropriate categorial horizon of "what one is," of an unchangingly present self-thing in the stream of changing events and experiences.

By now it has become unmistakable that Heidegger's elucidations of the self circle round the problem of its *temporal structure*, although this remains at the present stage necessarily implicit. Heidegger does not diverge from the traditional view that the self has the character of *ground*; the question is only and always how the ground-being of the self must be interpreted. As the interpolation in the last chapter showed, the temporal meaning of ground lies in its "standingness" (*Beständigkeit*). In other words, ground means being in the mode of continuity, standing, steadiness, enduringness. The different ways of "grounding," in which our being-in-the-world " "steadies itself," "gains a firm stand" in thrownness and forethrow, all spring from the "care of stability and constancy." The traditional notions of substance and subject are certainly, if only implicitly, derived from this temporal meaning of "ground," but they explain it as a duration, a permanence in presentness. This, however, as Heidegger constantly impresses on us, is not the way in which the self "stands." It is not that the self lacks continuity and endurance, but these have a character of their own that can be explained only from the whole structure of care. For every saying-I as "I-am-(already)-in-a-world" cooriginally implies "I-am-near-to" the handy things that meet me within the world, and "I-am-ahead-of-myself." I am the being who is concerned for my own ability-to-be, for the sake of which I constantly throw myself forward to my possibilities. In every ontic saying-I the *whole of care* voices itself, though mostly in the falling mode of I-take-care (of things). The most frequent and loudest "saying-I" comes from the disowned oneself, who evades his authentic ability-to-be. In this mode of being, however, I "stand" as not-myself (*Unselbst-ständigkeit*).

The selfhood of an authentic self cannot be explained from the disowned not-I, but only from an authentic ability-to-be, from a forward-running resoluteness. Its existential structure is constitutive of the *authentic mode of care*. This alone can explain the "standingness of the self" (*Selbst-ständigkeit*) in the twofold character of an *enduring steadfastness* (*beständige Standfestigkeit*). To put this in terms that are more familiar: the continuing identity of ourselves of which we are aware through all the movement and change of our whole existence is to be interpreted from the temporal structure of care.

Closely connected with the problem of a self-maintaining identity is what traditional philosophy has formulated with the title of "independence," "being-in-itself" (*An-sich-sein*). Independence has always been a basic character of substantial being, although the precise meaning of "independence" may vary greatly according to what is to be independent from what or from whom. This problem is not explicitly raised in the present section, but is clearly implied in Heidegger's expressions "*Selbst-ständigkeit*" and "*Unselbst-ständigkeit*," which have the secondary meaning of "independence" and "lack of independence" respectively. Although this problem is not made explicit, Heidegger presumably intends to suggest that it has its place in the present ontological context. How peculiar and difficult this problem is may be judged when we remember that it is precisely in his single, dreading being-unto-death that Da-sein becomes originally manifest to himself in his "owing"—that is, as a not-self-grounded ground. Further, it is the originally revealed nothing of himself that throws Da-sein into a world, refers him to beings as a whole as dependent upon them. Is there, then, any sense in asking whether Da-sein can be "independent," whether he can "stand-in-himself" in a way appropriate to his being? If there is—and Heidegger seems to suggest that there is—then the question can concern only the different ways in which Da-sein is capable of "standing as a self." The authentic way in which he "stands as himself" is in the singleness of a silent, dread-disposed resoluteness. A resolutely owned self does not constantly say "I, I, I . . . ," but "'*is*' in reticence the thrown being that it can authentically be" (SZ, 323). This self provides the "primordial phenomenal basis for the question of the being of the 'I'" (SZ, 323).

What, then, is the decisive result reached in the present elucidation of the self? It has shown that the tentatively raised notion that the "I" "holds" the structural whole of care "together" must be given up once and for all, and that care cannot be stuck together with the glue of an ontic "I" and "self," but on the contrary, the "standingness" of the self can only be explained from the existentiality of care. The full structural content of care must also explain how and why an irresolute falling into a not-self essentially belongs to it.

This means, however, that the problem of the original unity of care still remains unanswered. On the other hand, the full phenomenal content of care has now been laid bare. The investigation can now proceed to the problem of its unity. Its solution lies in the concrete interpretation of the meaning of care.

4. TEMPORALITY AS THE ONTOLOGICAL MEANING OF CARE

"Meaning," according to Heidegger, is that "in which the intelligibility of something keeps itself" (SZ, 324). The unity of the complex structure of care must now be made explicitly understandable from temporality. Up to now the unity of thrownness (facticity), forethrow (existence), and falling has always been asserted, but has not yet been led back to the ground of its possibility. However, if temporality is to be exposed as this "ground," it evidently cannot mean the "being-in-time" of a thing that comes into being, endures and passes away. Da-sein's being cannot grow into a unity "in" time or "with" time, as though there were first thrownness, then forethrow, then falling away to beings within the world. The unity of care can be envisaged only as an interplay in which thrownness, forethrow, and falling mutually affect and illuminate each other. The tendency of the preceding two chapters has unmistakably been to stress that it is the possibility of death which, openly or disguisedly, affects and illuminates the whole of care in a preeminent way. Indubitable as this may be in our ontic experience, its ontological possibility most urgently demands an explanation, because death is incomparably different from our everyday possibilities. The latter—finding a home, a means of livelihood, and so on—are anticipated by us as "realizable," and are thus in advance drawn back into our here-being as things or happenings that will some day become "actual." Death, on the other hand, is in no way "realizable." If care as a being-unto-death had the character of reality, we would have to say: death is "real" only as long as it remains a possibility; its "actuality" is the sheer impossibility of being-here at all. How, then, can precisely *this* possibility affect all that we are and have been in a preeminent way? Only in that we can let it constantly *come toward us*, that is, approach and affect us in its constant coming nearer. We let our extremest possibility come toward us by holding it out before and toward ourselves *as coming*. The coming, in which a factical existence lets-himself-come-to-himself in his ownmost possibility, is the "primordial phenomenon of the *future*" (SZ, 325).

The German word for "future," *Zukunft*, literally means "coming to" or "coming toward." In English, the transition from "coming" to "future" cannot be nearly so effortlessly made, nor can we be constantly reminded by an ambivalent word like *Zukunft* that the familiar concept of a "future-time" originally springs from the "primordial future." How the vulgar concept of time is derived from original time, that is, from the temporality of care, will be shown in the sixth chapter of Division Two. For the present, it is sufficient to note that in the derivative concept of time the future itself is conceived as "coming"—the future as the "now" which has not yet become "real," but which will be when it has arrived into the present now. The "primordial future," on the other hand, is the coming in which Da-sein as care comes-to-himself in the extremest possibility of his existence. The coming is authentic when the possibility is resolutely disclosed in running forward to it.

The forward-running anticipatory resoluteness, however, modifies not only the way in which Da-sein exists, but rebounds back into and affects his thrownness. The authentic disclosure of his utmost possibility *as coming* brings Da-sein understandingly *back to* his hereness as it has always already been. The resolute taking over of his owing-being means: he authentically *is* the thrown ground which he has already been. This, however, is possible only because each factical existence *is* his own "has been."

> Only because Da-sein in general *is* as I *am*-having-been, can it come futurally toward itself in such a way that it comes-*back*. Authentically futural,

Da-sein is authentically *having-been*. Anticipation of the most extreme and ownmost possibility comes back understandingly to one's ownmost *having-been*. Da-sein can *be* authentically having-been only because it is futural. In a way, having-been arises from the future. (SZ, 326)

The difficulty of this passage is unavoidably aggravated by the translation into English. As we have already noted, Heidegger has the advantage of being able to say *Ich bin gewesen*, literally, "I *am* been," instead of "I have been." The German "I am been" expresses concisely and directly that Da-sein is his own "been," whereas in English we have to use the roundabout and confusing phrase "I am-(as)-having-been." *Gewesenheit*, literally, "beenness," will henceforth be used by Heidegger to denote the "primordial past" that belongs to the temporal structure of care, while the usual word *Vergangenheit*, literally "goneness," will be reserved for the past in which things were, or happenings within the world took place. No matter what Da-sein may have forgotten of his "past," his thrownness can never be "gone" from him, for as long as he factually exists, he is always "present" to himself as already having been. Further, he *is* as having-been only as long as he *is* coming, for when he no longer comes-to-himself from his ultimate possibility, he is no longer here at all.

The primordial or original past, the has- or having-been, Heidegger says, springs in a way from the future (coming). Although we are given no explanation in what certain way the past springs from the future, it clearly cannot be in any way "produced" by the future. What Heidegger presumably means is this: were the forethrow of our possibilities infinitely open, we would be constantly streaming away beyond ourselves. It is only because the "forward" movement of care is halted by the impassable possibility of death that its movement is turned back upon itself. This streaming back upon itself of care is the "coming" that illuminates the having-been and first of all opens it up as the dimension to which we can come back. Without the coming of the original future there could be no coming back to the past.

The forward-running resoluteness at the same time discloses Da-sein's *situation*, that is, brings him authentically into his "here." He actively grasps his situation as his own by circumspectly taking care of the things that are handily present within the world. The discovery of the things present (*das Anwesende*) within the world is only possible in a *presenting* of these beings (*Gegenwärtigen*). Only as a *presenting* can resoluteness let the things come undisguisedly face to face with itself which it actively grasps (takes care of) in a factical situation.

In coming-toward and back-to itself, resoluteness brings itself presentingly into the situation. The having-been springs from the coming in such a way that the having-been coming (*gewesende Zukunft*, literally: "beening coming") releases the present from itself. The unity of the having-been-presenting-coming is the phenomenon which Heidegger calls "temporality."

> Only because Da-sein is determined as temporality does it make possible for itself the authentic potentiality-of-being-a-whole of anticipatory resoluteness which we characterized. *Temporality reveals itself as the meaning of authentic care.*
>
> The phenomenal content of this meaning, drawn from the constitution of being of anticipatory resoluteness, fulfills the significance of the term *temporality*. (SZ, 326)

This passage is expressly designed to warn us not to ascribe already familiar concepts of time to the "authentic temporality" of care. Especially the vulgar concepts of a "future," "past," and "present" are to be rigorously kept away. These concepts, although they are genuine time-phenomena, spring from the disowned temporality of care, and will be discussed only when the authentic phenomenon has been further exposed and made more secure than it is as yet. Similarly, all concepts of a "subjective" and "objective," or an "immanent" and "transcendent" time must be put aside, because they are based on an a prior distinction between "being-a-subject" and "being-an-object," a distinction which the existential interpretation of Da-sein's being as care is designed to overcome by leading it back to a more fundamental origin.

But there is a further implication of the above passage, although it is not stressed by Heidegger in the present context. The passage shows a remarkable reciprocity, or perhaps better, an interpenetration between care and temporality. While temporality is to make understandable the articulated unity of care, it is only through and as care that temporality itself becomes accessible and understandable. They mutually illuminate and define each other. This is why even the first definition of care in Division One could not do without the "ahead-of" and the "already," both of which have an evident temporal meaning. The "ahead-of-itself" (*Sich-vorweg*), indicates a "before" (*vor*). The "before" could mean a "not-yet-now, but later," while the "already" could mean a "no(t)-more-now, but earlier." If, however, this were the meaning of the "ahead" (before) and the "already," then care would be conceived as a thing which occurs and has a duration "in time," and which, moreover, is earlier and later, not-more and not-yet at the same time. Since this is impossible, the temporal characters of care must evidently have a different meaning. As Heidegger says:

The "before" [*vor*] and "ahead of" [*vorweg*] indicate the future that first makes possible in general the fact that Da-sein can be in such a way that it is concerned *about* its potentiality-of-being. The self-project grounded in the "for the sake of itself" in the future is an essential quality of *existentiality. Its primary meaning is the future.* (SZ, 327)

This passage is ambiguous and misleading because it could easily be taken to mean that the forethrow (projecting) structure of care is "grounded" in the "coming." This, however, would be possible only if care had, as it were, a ready-made future before itself, into which its forethrow would proceed; but this is precisely the interpretation that Heidegger expressly repudiates. What he attempts to show, on the contrary, is how the concept of a future that we accept "ready-made" originates in Da-sein's coming-to-himself in the possibilities of his being. Those, however, must be *thrown forward* as the being that can *come* to him, otherwise it would be incomprehensible how a dimension could be opened up in which a "coming" could take place. As far as we can see, therefore, the "coming" cannot be envisaged as in any way "prior" to the forethrow. It seems rather that the forward-to and coming-(back)-to are correlative movements that form a single structural whole. On the other hand, it is perfectly well understandable that the "for the sake of itself" character of existentiality is "grounded" in the coming. If we supposed that the forethrow simply ended in the disclosure of possibilities, without their coming nearer to us, touching and affecting us, our here-being could not be a concern for our ability-to-be. Indeed, it would be impossible to distinguish the possibilities of our own being from those of other beings. According to our interpretation, therefore, it is not the forethrow structure of care that is "grounded" in the coming, but only the "for the sake of itself" character of existentiality.

Just as the "ahead-of-itself" does not mean a future in which care is "not-yet" but eventually "will be," so the "already" of "already-being-in" (-the-world) does not mean a past in which care is "no(t)-more." The "already" is the existential-temporal character of a being who, insofar as he *is* at all, *finds himself* already thrown into his being. As long as Da-sein exists, he can never observe himself coming-into-being "in" time or "with" time, in which he is already partially gone; he can only find himself as a thrown fact.

In *attunement* Da-sein is invaded by itself as the being that it still is and already was, that is, that it constantly *is* as having been. The primary existential meaning of facticity lies in the having-been. The formulation of the structure of care indicates the temporal meaning of existentiality and facticity with the expressions "before" and "already." (SZ, 328)

The third constitutive moment of care, the being-together-with or near-to (things within the world), on the other hand, remains without a corresponding indication of its temporal meaning. The reason for this is that in the authentic mode of care the "presenting" remains "enclosed" (*eingeschlossen*) in the coming and having-been, in contrast to the disowned "present" which, as we shall see later, seeks to "run away" from (*entlaufen*) the original coming and having-been of care and seeks to exhaust itself in the presenting of beings within the world. This "run-away" presenting, will turn out to be the primary temporal meaning of falling. A resolutely disclosed existence, on the other hand, brings himself back to himself from his fallenness, "in order to be all the more authentically 'there' for the disclosed situation in the 'Moment' [*Augenblick*]" (SZ, 328).

The authentic "presenting" is called by Heidegger the moment or instant, *Augenblick*. Literally, however, *Augenblick* means a glance of the eye, "the moment of vision," as Macquarrie and Robinson render it. The "instant vision" of what meets us in the situation remains "enclosed" or "held in" the temporality of authentic care. Although Heidegger does not further explain how or why it is so, we may remember that death was shown earlier to be the certain possibility which is indefinite as to its "when"; it is at every instant (*Augenblick*) possible. A resolutely grasped existence does not seek to "run away" from the certain coming of this possibility, but remains open to its possible arrival at any instant. Hence his meeting with the beings "present" in his situation has the character of an instant readiness for them.

> Temporality makes possible the unity of existence, facticity, and falling prey and thus constitutes primordially the totality of the structure of care. The factors of care are not pieced together cumulatively, any more than temporality has first been put together out of future, past, and present "in the course of time." Temporality "is" not in a *being* at all. It is not, but rather *temporalizes* itself. (SZ, 328).

Temporality temporalizes itself (*zeitigt sich*). *Sich zeitigen* means to bring itself to ripeness. We have already come across such tautological expressions as "the world worlds" and "the nothing negates." Such tautologies are not only eminently meaningful, but are perhaps the only precise and appropriate way we have of saying how the "is is." Being evidently cannot "be" in the same way as beings are, but, on the other hand, it is not an absolute nothing. Even the nothing "is" insofar as it negates. Temporality, as the ground-structure of care, "is" not but "temporalizes itself." Why we are nonetheless forced to say, for instance, "temporality is—the meaning of care," or "temporality is—

defined in such and such a way," Heidegger promises to make understandable from "the clarified idea of being and the 'is' as such" (SZ, 328). In the absence of Division Three, this promise is not fulfilled. What the present division will show in detail are the different ways in which temporality can temporalize itself. These make it possible that Da-sein can exist in different ways, above all in the basic modes of owned and disowned existence.

> Future, having-been, and present, show the phenomenal characters of "toward itself," "back to," "letting something be encountered." The phenomena of toward . . . , to . . . , together with . . . reveal temporality as the *ekstatikon par excellence*. *Temporality is the primordial "outside of itself" in and for itself*. Thus we call the phenomenon of future, having-been, and present, the *ecstases* of temporality. Temporality is not, prior to this, a being that first emerges from itself; its essence is temporalization in the unity of the *ecstases*. (SZ, 328–29)

The difficulty of this passage is not to be mitigated, nor can Heidegger be reasonably blamed for what is, after all, the ungraspable nature of time itself. We must await Heidegger's further analyses to make the ecstatic unity of temporality more concretely understandable. One thing, however, is already evident. The three ecstases of temporality correspond to, or are correlative to the different directions in which Da-sein as care transcends himself: in the direction of his being as thrown (that I am), of his being as a possibility (I will be), and of the being of beings within the world. The ecstatic "standing-out-of-itself" of temporality is Da-sein's self-transcendence as it faces and comes back upon itself. The ecstases of temporality thus bring the different modalities of being disclosed in transcendence nearer to each other, let them affect each other. It is only in this turning toward and back upon itself of transcendence that being becomes truly "meaningful," understandable.

One of the reasons why the "outside-itself" character of temporality is so hard to grasp is that in the "vulgar concept" of time it is precisely this ecstatic character of time that is levelled down to a uniformity. This levelling-down process will turn out to be analogous to the modification of the "significant" space of the everyday world, where "space" has the character of a "place for" this or that thing, into a featureless, homogeneous three-dimensional space of nature. Similarly, the "significant" world-time, which essentially belongs to everyday care as a presenting being-near-to things, can be leveled down to the beginningless, endless now-time. If the vulgar concept of time can be demonstrated as nonoriginal and derived from care in the mode of disownment, then the authentic and original temporality of care in the mode of forward-running and resoluteness may be aptly called original or primordial time.

The levelled-down "unecstatic" character of the vulgar concept of time expresses itself in the predominance of the present, the now. The future and the past are understood only as modes of the present; they are, one might say, the "absent" present as the not-more-now and the not-yet-now. Among the two ways in which the present can be "absent," moreover, we would be inclined to give more weight to the past than to the future, for the past seems to be more "real" to us than the future. Heidegger's interpretation of original time differs strikingly from the traditional concept insofar as its *primary mode or ecstasis* is the *future* (SZ, 329). As we can already see, this is not an arbitrary invention of Heidegger's, but arises from the existential interpretation of Da-sein's being as care: it is in the running-forward—the transcending to the utmost, impassable possibility of not-being-here-anymore—that the turning-back upon itself of transcendence first becomes phenomenally accessible.

Once it is firmly grasped that the original "future" is the coming-to-himself of an existence in the possibility of his end, it becomes "obvious" that this future is *finite*. It is the primary ecstasis of a temporality that belongs to care as a thrown being-unto-death. Da-sein does not merely "have" an end at which he ceases to be, but *"exists finitely," "exists endingly"* (SZ, 329). But, Heidegger asks, "'does time not go on?' And can there not be an unlimited number of things that still lie 'in the future' and arrive from it?" (SZ, 330).

These questions, although they are to be answered in the affirmative, do not in the least refute the finiteness of the original coming, for they do not refer to it at all. Heidegger has so far not even raised the question of what can happen "in a time that goes on," or what sort of future and coming may be possible in that time; he has so far restricted himself to showing how the "coming" of this future itself and as such is to be determined.

> Its finitude does not primarily mean a stopping, but is a characteristic of temporalizing itself. The primordial and authentic future is the toward-oneself, toward *oneself*, existing as the possibility of a nullity not-to-be-bypassed. The ecstatic quality of the primordial future lies precisely in the fact that it closes the potentiality-of-being, that is, the future is itself closed and as such makes possible the resolute existentiell understanding of nullity. Primordial and authentic coming-toward-oneself is the meaning of existing in one's ownmost nullity. (SZ, 330)

As we have already pointed out, the derivation of the nonprimordial, endless time from the primordial temporality of care will be explained in the last chapter of this division. It must now be emphasized that the order of explanation cannot be reversed. Primordial time cannot be explained from the derivative time that springs from it. With regard to the former, Heidegger has so far established the following theses:

> Time is primordial as the temporalizing of temporality, and makes possible the constitution of the structure of care. Temporality is essentially ecstatic. Temporality temporalizes itself primordially out of the future. Primordial time is finite. (SZ, 331)

The results so far achieved, however, are only the first steps in the temporal analysis of care. The tasks to be taken in hand in the next three chapters are briefly outlined by Heidegger in the next section.

5. A Primordial Repetition of the Existential Analysis Arising from the Temporality of Here-being [Da-sein]

If temporality is the meaning of care, its "constitutive power" must be confirmed by all the fundamental structures and characters of care that the existential analysis has brought to light. The fundamental character of care central to all Heidegger's analyses is its disclosedness. This is constituted by understanding, attunement, speech, and falling. The temporal structure of these disclosing existentials must now be shown in detail, both in the mode of owned and disowned existence. Their analysis will lead to an understanding of the care-taking being-in-the-world and of the temporal meaning of an average, indifferent everydayness, which formed the starting-point of the Preparatory Fundamental Analysis in Division One.

It is interesting to remind ourselves once again that the order Heidegger follows in the next chapters is almost exactly the *reverse* of the course he has taken in the first division. There he began with the exposition of being-in-the-world followed by the detailed analysis of its constitutive moments, world, self, being-in. The reason for this was that the indivisible unity of being-in-the-world had first to be secured even at the risk of appearing dogmatic or arbitrary. Now, however, the inner possibility of this unity is beginning to come to light. The first task now is to show that the whole of temporality lies in every single structure of care, for instance, that understanding is not grounded purely and solely in the "coming," nor attunement purely and solely in the "having-been," and so forth, but in the whole ecstatic unity of temporality. These detailed analyses will then lead on to the whole of care as a factually existing being-in-the-world.

The interpolation in the previous chapter has shown that being-in-the-world has the basic character of "ground," and that the temporal meaning of ground is constancy and self-standingness. Temporality, on the other hand, is the way in which Da-sein lets the various modes and possibilities of his being approach and affect him*self*. The temporal structure of the "self-standingness" of existence constitutes the steadfastness, continuity, and "span" or "stretchedness" of Da-sein's being. As a not-self-grounded ground, Da-sein stabilizes himself in his factical being-in-the-world on the ground of "tradition"; that is, in disclosing and making his own the possibilities of existences who have-been-here. The temporal "happening" of a self-standing being-in-the-world will prove to be constitutive of Da-sein's historicity (*Geschichtlichkeit*). In contrast to the authentic historicity of a resolute existence, everydayness will turn out to be the inauthentic way in which man is "historical" (*historisch*).

Through the analyses of everydayness and historicity, original time will become graspable as the condition of the possibility and necessity of the everyday experience of time.

> *Da-sein expends itself primarily for itself* as a being that is concerned about its own being, whether explicitly or not. Initially and for the most part, care is circumspect taking care of things. Expending itself for the sake of itself, Da-sein "uses itself up." Using itself up, Da-sein uses itself, that is, its time. Using its time, it reckons with it. Taking care of things, which is circumspect and reckoning, initially discovers time and develops a measurement of time. Measurement of time is constitutive for being-in-the-world. Measuring its time, the discovering of circumspection which takes care of things lets what it discovers at hand and objectively present be encountered in time. Innerwordly beings thus become accessible as "existing in time." We shall call the temporal quality of innerworldly beings "*within-time-ness*." The "time" initially found therein ontically becomes the basis for the development of the vulgar and traditional concept of time. But time as within-time-ness arises from an essential kind of temporalization of primordial temporality. This origin means that the time "in which" objectively present things come into being and pass away is a genuine phenomenon of time; it is not an externalization of a "qualitative time" into space, as Bergson's interpretation of time—which is ontologically completely indeterminate and insufficient—would have it. (SZ, 333)[3]

Since the present section lays down only the program to be worked out in Division Two, we shall not anticipate Heidegger's detailed analyses by commenting on the above paragraph. It is sufficient at this stage to note that the three main themes of the next three chapters will be the temporality of everydayness, of historicity, and intimeness. These will give us an insight into the extraordinary complexities of an original ontology of Da-sein.

> As being-in-the-world, Da-sein exists factically together with beings encountered within the world. Thus the being of Da-sein gets its comprehensive ontological transparency only in the horizon of the clarified being of beings unlike Da-sein; that is, even of what is not at hand and not objectively present, but only "subsists." But if the variations of being are to be interpreted for everything of which we say that it *is*, we need beforehand a sufficiently clarified idea of being in general. As long as we have not reached this, the retrieve of the temporal analysis of Da-sein will remain incomplete and marred by lack of clarity, not to speak extensively of the factual difficulties. The existential-temporal analysis of Da-sein requires in its turn a new retrieve in the context of a fundamental discussion of the concept of being. (SZ, 333)

This last paragraph is especially significant because it no longer deals with Division Two, but gives us a long-term glimpse of the problems that Division Three will have to solve. It seems to hint that the scope of the first two divisions, dealing as they do with the existence of Da-sein and the reality of real beings, does not exhaust the whole range of being, for among the things of which we say "it is," there are such as are neither handy nor substantial but only "subsist" (*besteht*). Unfortunately, Heidegger nowhere gives us a hint of what kind of things he has in mind. Could we say, for instance, that nature in the ontic sense "subsists." Certainly, nature is neither an individual handy or substantial thing, yet the "only subsists" seems inappropriate to it. It is regrettable that Heidegger gives us no guidance on this point that would have shed some light on the scope of Division Three.

XIII

Temporality and Everydayness

Heidegger introduces the present chapter by reminding us of the multiplicity of phenomena the Preparatory Fundamental Analysis has made accessible. Such multiplicity is positlvely demanded by the disclosing character of here-being, for "the ontological origin of the being of Da-sein is not 'less' than that which arises from it, but exceeds it in power from the beginning. Any 'arising' [*Entspringen*] in the field of ontology is degeneration" (SZ, 334). These reflections are not introduced by Heidegger incidentally, but to forestall the erroneous expectation that the temporal analysis is going to reduce the complexity of care to a last, uniform building brick. In its efforts to reach the "ultimate," philosophy has only too often been misled to search for a simple, undifferentiated building block from which the whole of reality could be constructed. The aim of the following analysis is not to dissolve all existential phenomena into temporality, or to "deduce" or "derive" them from time, but to show that their complexity could not be an original whole except on the basis of the ecstatic unity of temporality. The penetration to the ontological "origin" of care, moreover, must not be expected "to arrive at things which are ontically self-evident for the 'common understanding,' but rather it is precisely this that opens up the questionability of everything" (SZ, 334). What could be more obvious, for instance, then the everydayness with which the existential analysis started? It is, however, precisely this obvious phenomenon that will emerge at the end of this chapter as a central and most puzzling problem, which will direct the inquiry to the question of history and historicity.

1. The Temporality of Disclosedness in General

Resoluteness represents the authentic disclosedness of care. Resolutely existing, Da-sein is authentically "here" to himself and to the beings that meet him in his situation. The constitutive moments of disclosedness are attunement, understanding, falling, and speech. The unity of these existentials was stressed already in Division One. Understanding is always attuned; attunement always has its understanding. Attuned understanding articulates itself in speech. The attuned-articulating understanding has the character of "falling," of losing itself to the "world." Da-sein's predominantly falling way of existing has its own characteristic way of understanding, of feeling, of explaining. The explanation of an average being-together-in-the-world is "published" in everday idle talk and hearsay . These complex constituents of the disclosedness (truth) of existence will now be shown to form a structural unity, because each of them leads back to the one temporality.

(a) The Temporality of Understanding

Understanding (*Verstehen*) is first discussed in detail in the fifth chapter of Division One. It is there that Da-sein's being first comes into view as the thrown forethrow. Thrown into his "here," Da-sein essentially throws himself forward to his ability-to-be-here. This forethrowing way of being is what Heidegger calls "existential understanding." Understanding discloses to Da-sein his own being-here as a possibility. The mode (ecstasis) of temporality in which understanding is primarily grounded is the primordial future. Here-being's (Da-sein's) future is its coming-to-itself (advancing-to-itself) in such a way that it holds out its own possible here-being before and toward itself as the end to which its "coming" is in advance directed. The essentially "futural" character of here-being is formally expressed in the first constitutive moment of care, the ahead-of-itself. Care is authentically ahead-of-itself in running forward to the ownmost, utmost, impassable possibility of being-here. The authentic future makes possible a resolute understanding of existence wholly to its end. In the first place and for the most part, however, Da-sein exists "irresolutely"—that is, remains closed to himself in his utmost ability-to-be. This irresolute understanding is grounded in an inauthentic future. How is this to be defined and how does it modify the whole structure of temporality?

The inauthentic future becomes accessible through the everyday, care-taking being-in-the-world. In this way of existing, Da-sein understands himself primarily from *what* he takes care of. The disowned understanding throws itself into the needful and urgent business of everyday occupations. These, however, are undertaken *for the sake of* Da-sein's own ability-to-be-here, so that even in its lostness to the world, here-being is still "futural" in the sense of coming-to-itself. Now, however, "Da-sein does not come-toward-itself primarily in its ownmost, nonrelational potentiality-of-being, but it *awaits this* heedfully *in terms of that which what is taken care of produces or denies*. Da-sein comes toward itself in terms of what is taken care of. The inauthentic future has the character of *awaiting [Gewärtigens]*" (SZ, 337).

The German "gewärtigen," it may be remarked, has a much more positive undertone than the English "awaiting" and "waiting for." It implies readiness and preparedness for something that can be counted upon. Further, It must always be remembered that what this awaiting "comes toward" is not primarily happenings within the world, but here-being itself in its everyday ability-to-be-in-the-world. The inauthentic future is still "my future," although I now approach my possible here-being in a round-about way through the success or failure of my makings and doings. So, for instance, "my future" may be threatened by the possible failure of a business venture in which I have heavily invested, or it may look rosy because I can count upon a steady advancement in my profession, and so on. In all such ontic-existentiell projections of "my future" my own possible here-being is clearly "awaited," although this awaiting may be well-nigh forgotten in a distracted preoccupation with the happenings I hopefully or fearfully await. In the ontological-existential order, however, here-being's "awaiting" or advancing-to-itself has an essential priority, for it first of all forms and holds out to itself a horizon of foreseeability as such, from which something can be counted on to approach at all. Hence Heidegger says: "Awaiting must always already have disclosed the horizon and scope in terms of which something can be expected. *Expecting is a mode of the future founded in awaiting [the future] that temporalizes itself authentically as anticipation*. Thus a more primordial being-toward-death lies in anticipation than in the heedful expecting of it." (SZ, 337).

Let us sum up briefly the results reached so far. Understanding in all its modes is *primarily* grounded in the future. The resolute understanding of owned existence is made possible by here-being's running-foward to its ownmost possibility of not-being-here-anymore. The irresolute understanding of disowned existence is grounded in an awaiting in which here-being comes-to-itself in its worldish possibilities. The awaiting can modify itself further into an expecting.

Both the authentic and inauthentic future are modes (ecstases) of "primordial time," that is, belong to the unity of future, past, and present of the *one* temporality of care.

It follows from this that understanding cannot be purely and simply "futural," but that it must be cooriginally constituted by a past and a present. The inauthentic present will prove to be the primary meaning of the falling way of existing in which Da-sein "irresolutely" loses himself to the beings whose presence within the world is disclosed in and to his "presenting." The inauthentic present will be more fully disclosed in connection with the temporality of falling (see subsection c of this chapter). At this point, it is sufficient to recall that the unity of here-being's past and future (its having-been-coming-to-itself) "lets the present out of itself" (*aus sich entlässt*). The operative words in this phrase are the "aus sich," the "out of itself." They indicate that whereas the original past and future are here-being's removal (ecstasis) *to itself*, its presence as a "presenting of . . . ," is a turning away from itself and a turning to "another" over against itself. In its "presenting of . . . ," here-being brings itself face to face with a vis-à-vis. This is why Heidegger now says that here-being's present is a "Gegen-wart," a looking out for a "gegen," for something opposite to itself. This, however, raises a difficult problem. How can a "presenting" in this sense belong a priori to here-being, when it can neither create the concrete beings it might encounter, nor has it the power to command their presence within the world? This problem is not explicitly resolved in Division Two, but fortunately we can draw on Heidegger's interpretation of Kant to throw a light on it (especially KPM, § 16, § 25 and § 34). According to this interpretation, a "presenting of . . ." can very well belong a priori to the temporality of care, because the "gegen," the vis-à-vis for which it "looks out," is not in the first place any concrete beings at all, but a "nothing," a "nonentity." This "nothing," however, is not an absolute nothing, but a pure horizon formed in the presenting itself as something that faces, that stands over against it. Thus here-being a priori *gives itself* its own "gegen" by forming a horizon that looks back at it, presents itself to it. This horizon of pure presentness anticipatingly awaits the concrete beings which, in reference to it, become recognizable and understandable as independent, self-standing "presences."

In contrast to the inauthentic present of a disowned, self-scattered existence, how is the authentic present to be characterized? This belongs to the forward-running future of a resolutely disclosed existence, which brings itself face to face with its own factical "here." The resolution that discloses here-being's "situation" as its own not only brings it back from its scatteredness among the things taken care of, but its "presenting" is *held* by the authentic future and past; that is, it does not "fall out of" and "run away from" the finite time of care. The authentic present is called by Heidegger "Augenblick," which is ordinarily translated by "moment" or "instant." As already remarked, the literal meaning of "Augenblick" brings us much nearer to what Heidegger intends to say: Augenblick means the "glance of the eye," which instantly discloses here-being's situation; it is an active "ecstasis," that is, removal of here-being to the possibilities and circumstances which face it in its hereness without losing itself to them. The authentic present may be called an "instant attending to . . ." or, briefly, an instant. The original meaning of *in-stare*, standing-in, should remind us that this mode of presenting "stands in," is "held by" the authentic future and past of care. To help keep this in mind we shall therefore use both the term *moment* and the term *instant*.

The *existentiell* phenomenon of the moment or instant, Heidegger points out in a footnote (SZ, 338), was most penetratingly seen by Kierkegaard, without being *existentially* clarified by him. Such clarification is not possible in the horizon of the vulgar concept of time in which Kierkegaard remained caught, so that he attempted to define the *Augenblick* with the help of the "now" and "eternity." The vulgar concept of an infinite now-time, however, is *derived* from the original temporality of care and is incapable of explaining it. Hence, Heidegger says:

> The phenomenon of the Moment (*Augenblick*) can *in principle not* be clarified in terms of the *now*. The now is a temporal phenomenon which belongs to time as within-time-ness: the now "in which" something comes into being, passes away, or is objectively present. "In the Moment" nothing can happen, but as an authentic present it lets us *encounter* [begegnenlassen] *for the first time* what can be "in a time" as something at hand or objectively present. (SZ, 338)

The instant, as the authentic attending to (looking out for) a "gegen," is the condition of the possibility that, within the horizon that it holds out over against itself—within the horizon of presentness—within-worldish beings can come face to face with here-being in their own, bodily "presence." The instant attending to here-being's situation springs from the authentic future. The temporal structure of a resolute understanding is thus an instant running-forward. In constrast to this, the irresolute understanding projects here-being's future (ability-to-be) from what can be taken care-of; that is, here-being comes-to-itself from a falling presenting. The inauthentic understanding has the temporal structure of a presenting awaiting.

What is the corresponding past (beenness) that belongs to these modifications of the future and present? As we have heard in the last chapter, the coming-to-itself of forward-running anticipatory resoluteness at the same time comes-back-to its ownmost self as already thrown. This ecstatic comlng-back-to-itself makes it possible that a factical existence can resolutely take over the being that it is as having-been. "In anticipation, Da-sein *brings* itself *forth again* to its ownmost potentiality-of-being. We call authentic having-*been* [*Gewesen*-sein] retrieve [*Wiederholung*]" (SZ, 339).

The authentic having-been is thus a gathering up of here-being's thrownness and a bringing it forward to the utmost possibility of its self, a "retrieve" or "recollection" or, with something of the sense in which the term is used of music, a "recapitulation."

It is illuminating to glance back from the position we have reached to Heidegger's interpretation of conscience as the call of care. This call is defined as a "forward-calling recall" (see above chap. 11). Care calls *from* the depth of thrownness revealed in dread *forward* to the utmost ability-to-be, *to* the disowned self whom it recalls from his lostness back to his thrown being unto death. It has now become evident that the forward-calling recall reflects the authentic-temporality of care and summons the factical self to take over precisely this temporal being in its fully disclosed finiteness. Further, the "movedness" (*Bewegtheit*) of the "ecstatic unity" of temporality now begins to reveal itself as a kind of circling in itself: on the one hand, here-being must already be thrown to let-itself-come-to-itself, but, on the other hand, only in an authentic coming-to-itself does here-being become fully manifest *as itself*, and only in being thrown back upon itself by the impassable limit of its hereness can this thrown being recollect itself and bring itself forward to its utmost possibility. The recollecting running forward or anticipation at the same time brings itself instantly face to face with its situation.

The full temporal structure of resolute understanding has now been brought into view as a recollecting-instant running-forward. The ecstasis Heidegger mentions in the third place always indicates the mode of time in which an existential phenomenon—in the present instance understanding—is *primarily* grounded.

As against the authentic recollectlon of here-being's thrownness, what is the character of the having-been that belongs to a disowned understanding? Heidegger explains it as follows:

> But when one projects oneself inauthentically upon the possibilities drawn from what is taken care of in making it present, this is possible

only because Da-sein has *forgotten* itself in its ownmost *thrown* potentiality-of-being. This forgetting is not nothing, nor is it just a failure to remember; it is rather a "positive," ecstatic mode of having-been; a mode with a character of its own. The ecstasy (rapture) of forgetting has the character of backing away *from* one's ownmost having-been in a way that is closed off from oneself. This backing away from . . . ecstatically closes off what it is backing away from, and thus closes itself off, too. As inauthentic having-been, forgottenness is thus related to its own thrown *being*. It is the temporal meaning of the kind of being that I initially and for the most part *am* as having-been. And only on the basis of this forgetting can the making present that takes care of and awaits *retain* things, retain beings unlike Da-sein encountered in the surrounding world. To this retention corresponds a nonretention that presents us with a kind of "forgetting" in the derivative sense. (SZ, 339)

The self-forgetful way of having-been hides the "what" before which it retreats (*das Wovor*). This "what," however, is the nothing that negates in Da-sein's thrown being as the not-self-originated ground of its own negativity, that is, of its not-being-able-to-be-here-anymore. At the same time, this forgetting forgets itself, remains hidden to itself as a disownment of here-being's own thrownness. But does this mean that here-being is altogether cut off from a "before" of itself to which it can go back? Evidently not, for the self-forgetful having-been opens up a different kind of "before" into which memory can penetrate. This is further explained by Heidegger as follows:

In the mode of forgottenness, having-been primarily "discloses" the horizon in which Da-sein, lost in the "superficiality" of what is taken care of, can remember. *Awaiting that forgets and makes present* is an ecstatic unity in its own right, in accordance with which inauthentic understanding temporalizes itself with regard to its temporality. (SZ, 339)

The backing away from *before* here-being's ownmost thrownness is in itself a turning to the before of its having-already-taken-care of things within the world. Just as the disowned future is an awaiting of here-being's ability-to-be-in-the-world by way of taking care of things, so the self-forgetful past is a retaining (remembering) of what has happened to "oneself" in "one's" care-taking occupations with things. The horizon of the "before" into which a self-forgetful, inauthentic understanding penetrates in memory is different from the horizon of the "before" in which an authentic understanding "recollects" or "retrieves" its thrownness and brings it forward into the forethrow of the utmost possibility.

For later reference, it will be helpful to summarize the results of the present section in the formulas given in tables 13.1 through 13.4:

TABLE 13.1
The Temporality of Understanding

Inauthentic	Authentic
forgetfully-presenting awaiting	recollecting (or retrieving or recapitulating)-instant anticipatory running-forward

(b) The Temporality of Attunement

It will be remembered that what we translate by the single word *attunement* is the existential character of a feelingly attuned self-findsomeness (*Befindlichkeit*). Understanding is always in some way "tuned" by moods and feelings, just as in our "feeling this way or that" we always in some way understand ourselves. Accordiing to Heidegger, in attunement lies a most original and fundamental disclosure (truth) of here-being, which reaches far beyond our powers of explicit knowing and explaining. But since Da-sein "stands cooriginally in truth and untruth," attunement can not only reveal but also obstinately conceal his thrownness. Whether authentically revealing or inauthentically concealing, the *primary* disclosing function of attunement is to *bring Da-sein before* the "that" of his already-being-here. Even in its inauthentic modes, attunement brings Da-sein to his "that I am and have to be," for the "that" follows him and is revealed even in turning away and fleeing from it.

Da-sein can be brought before his "that" only because he constantly *is* as having-been. Attunement does not "create" the having-been, but, on the contrary, the latter makes it possible that Da-sein can be brought back to himself in such a way that he *finds himself* (*sich findet*) in how he *feels* (*sich befindet*). Conversely, attunement cannot be simply dissolved into temporal phenomena or be "deduced" from temporality. All that the existential interpretation intends to show is that moods and feelings could not be as they are except on the basis of their temporal structure.

If the basic existential meaning of attunement is a bringing-back-to . . . , then, as the "back-to" indicates, it must temporalize itself *primarily* from the "past." This is now to be demonstrated for two exemplary modes of attunement, fear and dread, which have already been analyzed in a preliminary way in Division One (chapters 5 and 6).

Fear is an inauthentic mode of attunement, insofar as it arises from a care-taking being-in-the-world and refers Da-sein to a fearsome thing or event that approaches from the sphere of circumspectly discovered circumstances. As Heidegger rightly insists, only fear can discover something to be feared; the sharpest, most minute "objective observation" could never reveal that something fearsome threatens the factical self. Da-sein discovers a coming threat to his care-taking ability-to-be, because, tuned by fear, his being-in-the-world is a fearfully awaiting looking-out-for the fearsome that may bear down on him from within the world.

But, Heidegger now asks, does this not prove that the primary time-character of fear is the future and not the past? Has fear not been rightly defined as the expectation of a future evil (*malum futurum*)? To be sure, a future must belong to the temporality of fear. The expectancy of a threat to a possible-here-being is, in fact, doubly "futural." First, the oncoming evil is not-now but "in the future," that is, it is "futural" in the sense of the in-timeness of things. Secondly, the fearful expectancy lets here-being come-to-itself in its threatened ability-to-be-in-the-world; it is "futural" in the original sense of belonging to the temporality of care, albeit in the inauthentic mode of expectancy.

This, however, is not enough to constitute the *affective* character that distinguishes fear and attunement in general. The affectivity of fear is constituted by letting the threat *come-back-to* the factical, care-taking self that I already am as having-been. It is in coming-back-to-itself that the fearing self *lets itself be affected* by the approaching threat, so that the fear of something is at the same time the fear for itself. Affectivity is grounded in the streaming-back-upon-itself of temporality. This constitutes the primary disclosing character of attunement: it discloses here-being in the facticity of its having-already-been delivered over to its threatened ability-to-be-in-the-world.

What is the character of the having-already-been which is constitutive of fear? As an inauthentic past, it is a self-forgetting. But has it not just been said that fear brings here-being back to itself? Must the disclosure of its threatened having-been not jolt it out of its self-forgetfulness? These questions are answered by remembering precisely what Heidegger has said about the authentic and inauthentic past. Here-being "forgets" itself in a self-disowning *backing away* or *retreat before* its ownmost thrownness—that is, before the nothing of himself which threatens it not from the "outside," but purely from its own thrown self. But the *retreat before* the threat that is solely and singly here-being's own, is in itself a *turning to*. . . . What is it *to* which here-being turns? What can it turn to? Only to itself, but itself as already thrown into a care-taking being-in-the-world. The concealing retreat before here-being's ownmost having-been does not simply blot out its "past"—this would be impossible—but covers it over by a self-forgetful "remembering" its having already taken care of the world. Just because being-in-the-world is a fundamental structure of care itself, it can screen the authentic having-been by shifting the horizon of the "before" to which care is ecstatically removed.

Since, however, fear is only one among many other modes of attunement, it must affect here-being in a specific way, which distinguishes it from other affections. The specific mood that characterizes fear, as Aristotle already recognized, is a depression or confusion (*Rhetoric*, chap. 5, 1382 a 21).[1] Fear, as a depression, literally presses Da-sein back on to his thrownness, but at the same time covers over his ownmost having-been by the exclusively "worldish" character of the thing that threatens him. The past to which Da-sein is brought back in fear is therefore not authentically his own, but the *self-forgetful* having-already-been-taking-care-of-the-world. The *confusion* that characterizes fear, Heidegger explains, arises from the *forgetting* of here-being's own thrown self.

> When one forgets and backs away from a factical, resolute potentiality-of-being, one keeps to those possibilitiies of self-preservation and evasion that have already been circumspectly discovered beforehand. Taking care of things which fears for itself leaps from one thing to the other, because it forgets itself and thus cannot *grasp* any *definite* possibility. All "possible" possibilities offer themselves, and that means impossible ones, too. He who fears for himself stops at none of these—the "surrounding world" does not disappear—but he encounters it in the mode of no longer knowing his way around in *it*. This *confused making present* of the nearest best thing belongs to forgetting oneself in fear. That, for example, the inhabitants of a burning house often "save" the most unimportant things nearby is known. When one has forgotten oneself and makes present a jumble of unattached possibilities, one thus makes possible the confusion that constitutes the nature of the mood of fear. The forgottenness of confusion also modifies awaiting, and characterizes it as depressed or confused awaiting that is distinguished from pure expectation. (SZ, 342)

The headless running hither and thither, as described by Heidegger, is of course a well-known symptom of fear. But equally well-known is the "paralysis" that can overtake us in an experience of "paralyzing fear." How would Heidegger explain this? Is the "paralysis" due to an extremity of confusion or to a deficiency of coming-back-to-oneself? In this kind of fear, we seem to be caught in a fascinated staring at the fearsome (the whereof of fear). This would suggest a deficiency in the primary existential function of attunement, which is to bring us back to our thrown selves.

The ecstatic unity that makes the full phenomenon of fear possible is a (confusedly) awaitingly presenting forgetting. Except for a change in the primary ecstasis, this corresponds exactly to the temporality of inauthentic understanding, which was shown to be a forgetfully presenting awaiting. Now it might be reasonably assumed that the temporality of the authentic mood of dread will show a similar correspondence to the recollecting, instant running-forward of a resolute understanding. But the temporality of dread will turn out to be not a fully fledged, authentic forward-running, instant recollection, but only the *possibility* of it. How Heidegger works this out must now be considered.

Before proceeding to the temporal analysis, we must briefly recall the phenomenal characteristics of dread. It is similar to fear inasmuch as it also discloses a threat. But whereas fear discovers a definite *something* within the world as the thing to be feared (the what of fear), dread reveals the *nothing* as the threat that lies purely in here-being itself as a thrown (not-self-grounded) being unto death. Dread is thus not only essentially different from fear, nor is it only one authentic mode of attunement among others; it is the most basic mood. Its unique disclosing function is to bring here-being originally before the nothing which negates in the being of beings, and first and foremost in here-being itself.

How does dread reveal the negating of the nothing in the being of beings? In dread, the familiar, reliable things that we usually understand as relevant to our own existence sink into complete *irrelevance* (*Unbewandtnis*). They do not simply disappear, but all weight and hold seems to vanish from them, so that they can give us nothing to which we could cling for support. The world as a whole appears in the character of complete *insignificance*, and in this "negated" mode it can no longer refer us "significantly" to other beings as relevant to our own being. It follows from this that "our heedful awaiting finds nothing in terms of which it could understand itself, it grasps at the nothingness of the world. But, thrust toward the world, understanding is brought by *Angst* to being-in-the-world as such" (SZ, 343).

What does Heidegger mean by the "nothingness of world"? In the first place and most obviously, the world in the "negated" mode of insignificance. But more than that, it is precisely the "nothing of world" that reveals the world *as such* in its "otherness" to the concrete beings that appear within it. As the "other" to beings, the world itself is a "nothing," though not an absolute, negative nothing. That is why it is in the "nothingness of world" that we are first "thrust toward" the world itself: it is now revealed, not as we usually think of it—as the all of beings—but as a pure ontological horizon that belongs to our own being as being-in-the-world.

What dread dreads is being-in-the-world itself. But this "what" of dread is not an expected "approaching evil" that may someday destroy our care-taking ability-to-be. The what of dread is already here: it is here-being itself. Does this mean that dread is not "futural" at all? No, it means only that the dreading here-being does not come-to-itself in an inauthentic expectancy.

When dread overturns our familiar at-homeness in the world, the "nothingness of world" reveals the impossibility of relying primarily on a care-taking occupation with things for our own existence. The revelation of this impossibility, however, lets the possibility of an authentic ability-to-be come to light (*aufleuchten-lassen*). How this revelation is existentially possible is explained by Heidegger in an extremely condensed way. To follow him here, it is well to remember that the primary disclosing function of attunement in general lies in its *affective* character: the attuned self lets itself be affected by what it is attuned to. Now the affectivity of dread is of a preeminent kind, inasmuch as it is the purest self-affection: the dread of here-being is at the same time dread *for* this same, naked here-being-itself as already thrown into an uncanny not-at-homeness. The dreading here-being lets itself be affected purely by the dreadsomeness of itself. This means in terms of temporality: the dreading here-being brings itself *back to* the pure "that" of its own thrownness. This "back-to" cannot have the character of a self-forgetful retreat—that is, of an inauthentic having-been—nor, on the other hand, is it already a fully fledged *recollecting* or retrieve—that is, a gathering-up of the ownmost having-been and bringing it forward into a resolutely taken-over existence. The latter can become a fact only through the decision of a concrete self who resolutely answers the call of conscience by an anticipatory forward-running recollection of his thrown being unto death. This *answer* cannot be enforced by dread. Dread can only bring a factical here-being back to its thrownness *as possibily recollectable* (*als mögliche wiederholbare*). Thus reduced wholly and singly to its own thrownness, the possibilities of here-being that can be thrown forward can be drawn solely from this same thrownness itself. Hence the dreading here-being can come-to-itself only in its ownmost ability-to-be as a thrown being-unto-death. In bringing here-being before the recollectability of its ownmost having-been, dread at the same time reveals the possibility of its utmost ability-to-be. An authentic forward-running recollection, however, remains only an *existential possibility of care*, unless it is resolutely taken over by a factical self. Failing this, the choicelessly thrown self remains in the inauthentic mode of his being.

It will now be easily understood that the *present* that belongs to the ecstatic unity of dread is neither the confused presenting of fear, which loses itself among ungrasped possibilities, nor, on the other hand, the fully fledged *Augenblick*, the instant attending to here-being's situation. The instant arises only from a concrete resolution. Dread, however, brings the factical self into the mood for a possible resolution. The presence of dread holds the instant, as Heidegger vividly says, "on the jump" or, less literally, in readiness (SZ, 344).

The full temporal meaning of dread may thus be defined as a bringing before a possible forward-running-instant recollectability. Its peculiarity is that it is originally grounded in here-being's having-been, which brings forth the corresponding coming-to and presenting. In this peculiar temporality "the possibility was shown of the powerfulness that distinguishes the mood of *Angst*" (SZ, 344). Dread (*Angst*) is a "powerful" mood, for in it here-being confronts and is held fast solely by itself; hence in it lies the possibility of the most original disclosure and experience of being. But this possibility is not fully explained at this point; the temporal analysis does not go beyond the limits reached in the preparatory analysis. The negating of the nothing is shown in the not-at-homeness of a thrown being-in-the-world, in the possibility of not-being-in-the-world. But what of the nothing of the ownmost, single self? How does being become understandable from this nothing, how must it already be articulated in this original disclosure? What is the temporal meaning of the nothing itself, assuming that it must have a temporal meaning in a preeminent sense? None of these questions is raised, let alone answered, at the present stage.

On the contrary, Heidegger's final remarks seem to suggest that the present analysis, while indispensable, is to some extent artificial, because it must consider the constitutive moments of care in isolation; whereas, they are as they are only in the interplay of the whole of care. So, for instance, fear and dread never occur as isolated phenomena in a "stream of experience," but attuningly determine (*be-stimmen*) an understanding and are in turn determined by it. That is why, although both moods are primarily grounded in a mode of having-been, when they are considered in the whole of care, their origin proves to differ in each case. "*Angst* arises from the *future* of resoluteness, while fear arises from the lost present of which fear is fearfully apprehensive, thus falling prey to it more than ever" (SZ, 344–45).

This closes the temporal analysis of the two exemplary moods. But now the question arises whether they really represent attunement in general. What kind of temporal meaning can be found in the dull lack of tone that characterizes our everyday existence? And what of moods like hope, joy, and enthusiasm? Heidegger's answer to these misgivings may be briefly summed up as follows.

That attunement in general is primarily founded in having-been, may be most easily seen in the "depressive" moods like sorrow, despair, melancholy, and the like. These moods obviously press here-being down into the heaviness of the thrown ground of itself. But even those moods that "lighten" or "uplift" us arise from the burden of thrownness, and that is precisely why we experience them as "making our hearts lighter" and "raising our spirits." Why, then, are such moods—hope especially—thought to have a primarily futural character? Hope, as the counterpart to fear, has been defined as the expectation of a coming good (*bonum futurum*). This definition betrays the essential tendency of a falling being-in-the-world to explain existential phenomena primarily from *what* they relate themselves to within the world—so, in the present instance, from the what of hope, the future good. Heidegger, on the other hand, rightly insists that the true weight and meaning of all moods and feelings lie in their *affective* character. In the case of hope, also, "the mood-character lies primarily in hoping as *hoping something for oneself*. He who hopes takes himself, so to speak, *along* in the hope and brings himself toward what is hoped for. But that presupposes having-gained-oneself" (SZ, 345). The self must already have "gained himself," that is, gained a stand, won ground in his thrownness among beings as a whole as a self. Otherwise he could not hope for anything *for himself*.

As for the toneless indifference of a gray everydayness, which drifts along with what the day brings, it "demonstrates in the *most penetrating* fashion the power of *forgetting* in the everyday moods of taking care of what is nearby" (SZ, 345). The mere, indifferent carrying on from day to day is grounded in a forgetting self-abandonment to thrownness (see the next section for more on "self-abandonment"). Its temporal meaning is an inauthentic having-been. A mood of "could not care less" indicates an extreme self-loss, even though it may go hand in hand with an extreme activity. The authentic counterpart to indifference is equanimity (*Gleichmut*), the mood in which a resolutely forward-running existence is *instantly* here to its possible situations.

TABLE 13.2
The Temporality of Attunement

Inauthentic	Authentic
fear	dread
a confused	bringing before a possible
awaiting-presenting	anticipatory forward-running-instant
forgetting	recollectability (or retrievability or recapitulation)

(c) The Temporality of Falling

We must remind ourselves again and again that falling is a movement *within* here-being itself: a movement *away from* a resolutely grasped, authentic self *to* an absorption in the world as one-of-them with whom together one takes care of things (*das Man*). The everyday being-together in a mutually shared world has the tendency to develop and increase the momentum of the fall. It develops its own kind of communicating talk, the hearsaying idle chatter (*Gerede*); it has its own way of "seeing," curiosity (*Neugier,* literally greed for the new); and it spreads an ambiguity (*Zweideutigkeit*) over the meaning of here-being. The ambiguously curious hearsaying idle talk publishes an average explanation of self, world, and beings within the world, which is accessible to everyone and so relieves one of the burden of an immediate, genuine contact with beings and of an original disclosure of being. In everyday being-together, one constantly seduces oneself from a genuinely understood, resolutely grasped ability-to-be, leading to an increasing uprootedness in one's relations to other beings and to the loss of a firmly grounded dwelling in the world.

The present analysis is restricted to the phenomenon of curiosity, in which the temporal structure of falling is most easily seen. Heidegger treats curiosity not merely as a psychological trait that distinguishes only certain individuals, but as "an eminent tendency of Dasein in accordance with which it takes care of a potentiality of seeing" (SZ, 346). What is the specific kind of "sight" (*Sicht*) of which curiosity takes care and how does it differ from other kinds? Here it must be remembered that Heidegger uses the terms *seeing* and *sight* in an extremely formalized sense. They denote quite generally any kind of *access* we have to being and beings (SZ, 147). All "seeing" is primarily grounded in the disclosing forethrow of understanding, which makes transparent (*durchsichtig*) here-being as a whole through all its constituent moments (SZ, 146). This original "foreseeing" of our own existence, however, is by no means the only one appropriate to our disclosing way of being. Our caring-for being-with-others, for instance, has its own specific "sight" that discloses the other as the other: *Rücksicht,* a considerate regard (for the other in his thrown dependence upon a world), and *Nachsicht* a forbearing looking to (the other in his ownmost self). Everyday care has again its own proper access to things in a circumspect "for-sight" (*Umsicht*), which discovers the things at hand as utensils, that is, in what they are *for.*

The practical circumspection of everyday care can modify itself in various ways. It can become a theoretical only-looking-at things, which discovers things not as utensils for doing something with, but as pure substances. Curiosity also springs from everyday circumspection, but while normally we would speak of a "scientific curiosity" as well as of curiosity in the sense of undue inquisitiveness, Heidegger restricts its meaning to a greed for seeing always something new.

Curiosity arises when everyday circumspection "sees" nothing more at hand that needs to be done. The care of making, improving, finishing something comes to a rest; circumspection, whose proper function is to bring things near (*ent-fernen*) so that they can be taken care of, becomes liberated from the workaday world to which it has been bound. The unoccupied care, however, does not thereby disappear, but gathers itself in the liberated circumspection. Since its very essence is to bring something near, yet there is nothing at hand that has to be done, circumspection creates new possibilities for seeing itself:

> It tends to leave the things nearest at hand for a distant and strange world. Care turns into taking-care of possibilities, resting and staying to see the "world" only in its *outward appearance* [*Aussehen*]. Da-sein seeks distance solely to bring it near in its outward appearance. Da-sein lets itself be intrigued just by the outward appearance of the world, a kind of being in which it makes sure that it gets rid of itself as being-in-the-world, gets rid of being with the nearest everyday things at hand. (SZ, 172)

But, it may be asked, is the specific way in which curiosity "sees" things not the same, after all, as the theoretical only-looking? Certainly, there is a resemblance between the two: both are modifications of everyday circumspection, both are liberated from their boundedness in the nearest workaday world and in the utensil-character of things; both arise from an "unoccupied" care. But there is an essential difference between them. The leisurely only-looking of theory is a dwelling upon things, a staying with them (*Verweilen*) in order to understand them and so to "stand in their truth," whereas curiosity is not concerned with understanding, but merely with the "looking" itself; hence its distinguishing character is that it does not stay with anything, but as soon as it has seen something new, it jumps away to the still newer. Curiosity is a mode of care that cares only for finding always new opportunities for "abandoning itself to the world" (SZ, 172).

Although the difference between these two ways of "looking" has now become sufficiently clear, it will greatly help us to understand the temporal structure of curiosity if we make the implications of this difference more explicit than Heidegger does. What is implied by a "staying with things"? It implies that a theoretical approach to things, although it has liberated itself from its original groundedness in the nearest handy things, *gains a new ground* by binding itself to things as pure substances. The theoretical only-looking finds a stand and stability (i.e., ground) in the substantial presence of things. The wondering contemplation of things is furthermore guided and stabilized by a desire for understanding, for coming to "stand in the truth," that is, it grounds itself in the most fundamental possibilility of existence of being-in-the-truth; and finally, it grows roots in binding itself to the "facts," which is possible only on the basis of here-being's own thrownness among beings as a whole. In a word, the theoretical only-looking, while it breaks through the boundaries of the nearest world, conquers a new ground for itself in staying near to things, which is itself "grounded" in an authentic being-in-the-world.

A roaming curiosity, on the other hand, completely fails to gain a ground for itself. It hovers merely on the public surface of things. Hence the well-known rootlessness and inconstancy of curiosity that increasingly uproots here-being from any stable hold on anything. Even the "new things" that curiosity desires to see are not chosen and decided upon by itself, but by "them," who prescribe what it is that one must see if one is to be "with it."

What, then, is the temporal unity that makes this uprooted curiosity possible? All "seeing," "apprehending," "perceiving," of beings in their "bodily presence" is primarily grounded in a presenting, which "provides the ecstatic horizon in general within which beings can be bodily *present*" (SZ, 346). But the curious presenting of things does not dwell admiringly even upon their "looks," but "seeks to see *only* in order to see and have seen" (SZ, 346). The presenting thus becomes completely tangled up (*verfangen*) in itself. What does Heidegger mean by this entanglement in itself? He means that the presenting cannot fulfil its genuine function as a presenting-of-something; the ecstatic removal to . . . cannot come to a stand and find a hold in the beings it discovers in their presence, for no sooner has it looked on a new "sight" than it is already off to something else to see. Thus the presenting casts itself loose from its proper anchorage in things and becomes entangled in itself—that is, presents merely for the sake of presenting.

> As this making present that gets tangled up in itself, curiosity has an ecstatic unity with a corresponding future and having-been. Greed for the new indeed penetrates to something not yet seen, but in such a way that making present attempts to withdraw from awaiting. Curiosity is altogether inauthentically futural, in such a way that it does not await a *possibility*, but in its greed only desires possibility as something real. Curiosity is constituted by a dispersed making present that, only mak-

ing present, thus constantly tries to run away from the awaiting in which it is nevertheless "held," ["*gehalten*"] although in a dispersed [*ungehalten*] way. (SZ, 346–47)

Even a superficial reading of this passage shows that the key to its understanding lies in the meaning of "held" and "unheld." Their meaning, however, is left obscure by Heidegger, not only here but throughout Division Two. All that we know so far is that the authentic instant is *held* in the forward-running recollection of a resolute existence and is clearly the extreme opposite of the *unheld* presenting of curiosity, which seeks to run away from even an inauthentic awaiting. How can we grasp more precisely what Heidegger intends to say with the "held" and "unheld" presenting? By remembering that what the analysis seeks to show is the temporal structure of an uprooting curiosity that leads to an increasing groundlessness of a falling here-being. The held and unheld presenting must therefore belong to the temporality of a *firmly grounded* and an *ungrounded* here-being respectively. Once this connection is seen, the meaning of the present analysis can be clearly grasped and even the reason for Heidegger's obscurity becomes understandable. Heidegger cannot give an explicit explanation at this point because the ground-character of here-being is left entirely in the preliminary state in which it is discussed in the second chapter of Division Two. It was only two years after the publication of *Being and Time* that the essay "On the Essence of Ground" was published, in which the problem of "ground" was carried a step further.

This essay tells us of the three ways in which a factical here-being grounds itself, that is, stabilizes itself, gains a stand and constancy in itself as a thrown being-in-the-world. The self-grounding character of Da-sein is, in turn, "grounded" in the temporality of care, which holds the present in an ecstatic unity with the future and past. In resolutely running-forward to its utmost possibility, here-being comes wholly to itself as a self; it "identifies" itself as the presenting being-in-the-world it already is. Here-being's future holds the instant to itself as the end by which all presenting is in advance guided. That is why a resolute existence does not vacillatingly lose itself among the "sights" offered by the world, but "instantly" grasps what is relevant to its own possibilities and lets go what is irrelevant.

The resolutely forward-running existence, however, must recollectingly come-back-to its ownmost having-been. The recollection nakedly reveals here-being's thrownness which has already delivered it over to itself in its dependence upon a world. The not-self-original throw into a world is the reason why the hereness of a thrown existence must be a presenting of those beings it needs for its own ability-to-be. The authentic recollection thus holds the instant in itself as the "ground of" its attending to the beings to be met within the world.

In contrast to the steadfastly held instant, the unheld presenting of an uprooted curiosity becomes more easily understandable. As we have already seen above, this presenting seeks to escape from the hold given to it by even an inauthentic waiting for a possibility. The unheld presenting arises or springs from (*entspringen*) the inauthentic future in such a way that it seeks to "spring away" or "run away" from it (*ent-springen*, literally, to leap away).

But in so losing its steadying hold on its own future, curiosity cannot gain a lasting hold in the things it desires merely to see; as soon as it has caught sight of something, it is "already looking for the next thing. The making present that "arises" from the awaiting of a definite, grasped possibility makes possible ontologically *the not-staying* that is distinctive of curiosity" (SZ, 347).

The graphic terms in which Heidegger describes the "running away" of the present may easily mislead us into envisaging it as an ontic happening in which one thing breaks loose from another thing. But the presenting is not any thing; it cannot "stand" in and by itself at all but can only bring itself forth (temporalize itself) in the unity of time. Even the unheld presenting is still in some way "held" in here-being's coming-to-itself awaitingly. How, then, is the running-away to be understood in an existential-temporal sense? It *modifies* the awaiting in such a way that the awaiting "runs after" (*nachspringen*) the presenting. The awaiting can no longer fulfil its proper function of "running ahead" and holding out possibilities before and toward the presenting; it "gives itself up," it abdicates its role of leading and guiding the thrown self in its choice of "present" opportunities. The awaiting cannot let even inauthentic possibilities come to a care-taking presenting, but must "run after" the insatiable demands of curiosity by discovering possibilities for a mere, fleeting looking-at. By taking over the lead, the presenting modifies the inauthentic future into an awaiting that runs after. It is this ecstatic modification that makes possible the *dispersion* or *distraction* or *scatteredness* (*Zerstreuung*) which is a constitutive character of falling.

The modified awaiting, in turn, reacts back on the presenting. It is now that the *movement* of falling first comes into view.

> Making present is left more and more to itself as it is modified by the awaiting that pursues. It makes present for the sake of the present. Thus tangled up in itself, the dispersed not-staying turns into *the inability to stay at all*. This mode of the present is the most extreme opposite phenome-

non to the Moment. In this inability Da-sein is everywhere and nowhere. *The Moment* brings existence to the situation and discloses the authentic "There." (SZ, 347)

The growing momentum of the fall is made possible by the interacting modifiability of the whole temporal structure. The more fleeting the presenting, the more "flightily" it conceals a definite ability-to-be, the less able is the futural here-being to come back to its thrown self. "In the 'arising' of the present, one also forgets increasingly. The fact that curiosity always already keeps to what is nearest by, and has forgotten what went before, is not something resulting *from* curiosity, but the ontological condition of curiosity itself" (SZ, 347).

In Division One (chapter 5, B), falling was defined as a seductively reassuring, estrangingly entangling way of being-in-the-world. Da-sein "seduces itself" in the literal sense of leading itself away from its ownmost ability-to-be by throwing itself primarily into its worldish possibilities of being-with-others in a mutual taking-care of things. The "self-seduction" estranges here-being from its own genuinely understood possibilities, which are primarily grounded in an authentic future and past. The growing self-estrangement culminates in the "runaway" presenting of curiosity, which seeks to temporalize itself from itself. Unable to find a firm foothold even in the things it presents, it becomes completely entangled in itself. "But since making present always offers something 'new,' it does not let Da-sein come back to itself and constantly tranquillizes it anew" (SZ, 348). The tranquillizing reassurance arises from the looking at an endless variety of sights that prevent here-being from coming back to the being it is: a being that exists *endingly*. It is here that the true origin of the running-away presenting reveals itself: it is nothing else than "the essence of temporality, which is *finite*." It is because the factical self is choicelessly thrown into its being unto death that "the present arises from its own future and having-been, so that it lets Da-sein come to authentic existence only by taking a detour through that present" (SZ, 348). The way to a resolutely grasped existence is a roundabout way, leading through the self-forgetful presenting of an already fallen being. In the next two paragraphs, Heidegger goes on to elaborate how and why the throw of thrownness in itself leads to the falling mode of being. These paragraphs only recapitulate what is already familiar to us, but they do so in a way so obscure that the unsuspecting reader is apt to be startled into thinking them something new. A close analysis is certainly needed to disentangle their meaning, especially of the one we are now going to consider.

> The thrownness *before* which Da-sein can indeed be brought *authentically* and in which it can authentically understand itself yet remains closed off from it with regard to where it comes from and how it comes ontically. But this closed-off-ness is by no means only a factually existent lack of knowledge, but constitutes the facticity of Da-sein. (SZ, 348)

In the first sentence of the paragraph Heidegger follows his usual practice of italicizing the *before* (*vor*) when the word occurs in this particular context. In so drawing our attention to the *before*, Heidegger reminds us that while we can be *confronted with* our thrownness, we can never go beyond or behind the limit it sets us; that is, we can never find ourselves already here previous to it as the ground and origin of ourselves. Hence the where it comes from and where it goes remain ontically closed off. What is nakedly *disclosed* is *that* I am already here, not originated by myself. This *not* of myself, which hides and denies me to myself as my own origin at the same time *reveals* my already being-here. Hence the closedness of the ontic where and how it comes cannot be compared with any other not-knowing, for it makes possible all other kinds of knowing by revealing to me my facticity, that is, the *that I am*.

This same closedness, furthermore, "also determines the *ecstatic* nature of existence, left to the null ground of itself." It *also* determines; it codetermines (*bestimmt mit*); it is not the sole determinant, but one in a complex interplay with others. What it helps to determine is existence, i.e. the understanding forethrow of here-being's ability-to-be. But, more precisely, it determines existence in a specific respect, namely in its being "left to the null ground (*an den nichtigen Grund*) of itself (*Überlassenheit*)." The *null-* or *not*-determined ground is the thrown being which I already am, revealed to myself from a nothing of myself that dominates me as long as I am. How, then, is my own ability-to-be left or delivered over to me? Heidegger's word *Überlassenheit* is often translated "abandonment." The concept of abandonment has indeed become central in much existentialist philosophy and is often referred back to Heidegger as its originator. But if "abandoning" means letting something go, having nothing more to do with it, then our passage suggests that Heidegger has just the opposite in mind. The closedness, the not-self-originated throw that throws each factical self into his "here," certainly *leaves it* to him (*überlassen*) to throw himself forward into his possibilities, but in such a way that it keeps the "handed over" existence in its own hand. But how or where does our passage tell us this? It tells us by specifying that it is the *ecstatic* character of the deliveredness that the closedness of here-being helps to determine.

What is the *ecstatic* character of the delivered-over existences? It is the removal of here-being to itself, the resolute running forward to or the irresolute waiting for the possibility of being-here. The closedness of the where-from and how not only reveals the *that* I am, but throws this factical self into his forethrowing way of existing and helps to determine the how of the forethrow. It hands out his ability-to-be to the thrown being, but does not abandon it in the sense of letting it go. On the contrary, it determines and directs the whole of here-being to its end.

How precisely the forward movement of a being-unto-death originates in the "throw" is not explained in the two divisions we have of *Being and Time*. We have already remarked on the astonishing circumstance that in the considerable body of Heidegger's works of this period it is left to one short paragraph to explain this vital point (WM, 34, W, 11, G9, 114, P, 90, BW, 105, EB, 369). This paragraph tells us that the movement takes its start from the dreadingly revealed nothing, which repels us, refuses us admittance to itself. In repulsing us, it refers us to the "other" of itself, to the not nothing, to beings as a whole. Our recoil from the nothing, our turning away from it, is therefore "within certain limits according to its inmost meaning (intention). It—the nothing in its negating—itself refers us to beings" (WM, 36, W, 13, G9, 116, P, 92, BW, 106-107. EB, 371). The nothing reveals itself solely in its negating, in its denying us any admittance to a nothing of ourselves. This repulsion by the nothing is the "throw" that originates the forward movement in which here-being comes-to-itself in its possibilities—that is, exists. The throw by the nothing not only delivers over an existence to its not-determined ground, but refers it to beings as a whole—throws it into a world. Only when this is explicitly kept in mind can the connection between the last two paragraphs of the analysis of curiosity be grasped. We can now turn to the last paragraph, which follows immediately on the sentence "It also determines the *ecstatic* nature of existence, left to the null ground of itself."

> Initially, the throw of being-thrown-into-the-world does not authentically get caught by Da-sein. The "movement" in it does not already come to a "stand" because Da-sein "is there." Da-sein is swept along in thrownness, that is, as something thrown into the world, it loses itself in the "world" in its being factically dependent on what is to be taken care of. The present, which constitutes the existential meaning of being swept along, never acquires another ecstatic horizon of its own accord, unless it is brought back from its lostness by a resolution so that both the actual situation and thus the primordial "boundary situation" of being-toward-death are disclosed as the held Moment. (SZ, 348-49)

In the first sentence Heidegger tells us that the "being thrown" is not properly "caught" by a factical here-being, conjuring up the picture of a fielder fumbling the catch of a cricket ball. The picture is of course misleading as well as illuminating, because what we have to catch and so bring to a stand is not the motion of a flying object but the movedness of our thrown coming-into-being. Now the coming-into-being of a thing is thought to come to a stand in the unchanging, durable presentness ascribed to a substance. But in the case of here-being, the authentic way to bring its thrownness to a stand is to gather up its movedness into a self who steadfastly holds himself in his being-here-to-the-end. In the first place, however, the throw is not properly caught and gathered up, because the throw itself, in repulsingly relegating the concrete self to beings as a whole, lets them become his primary and all-absorbing care. The lost presenting of these beings, as we have seen, tries to run away from the hold of its own finite future, modifying it in turn to a running-after awaiting. It is in this way that the closedness of here-being's "where and how it comes" helps to determine the ecstatic character of the deliveredness over of existence to the *not*-determined or null ground of itself.

A close analysis of the last two paragraphs of the present section has brought to light that what Heidegger has really in mind all along is the "owing" character of care and how this is rooted in or uprooted from the hold of a finite time. It will be remembered that "owing" (*Schuldigsein*) was defined in the chapter on conscience as "being-the-ground of a being which is determined by a not" (SZ, 283). The concept of a being that is determined by a not was further compressed into the single term *nullity* or *negativity* (*Nichtigkeit*). But here-being, as the ground of a negativity, already owes itself to not-itself. Hence the owing-character of care must be fully defined as the not-determined ground of a negativity. How this is made possible by the temporality of care is the real theme of the analysis of curiosity, but this theme remains implicit and obscured by hints that are impossible to understand from the fragment of *Being and Time* alone. Hence even the most attentive reader of *Being and Time* is apt to miss the importance of this analysis and to pass over its difficulties without the attention they deserve.

One difficulty that the preceding interpretation has not been able to remove lies in the onesidedness and incompleteness of the investigations that Heidegger has carried out so far. This becomes strikingly obvious when, in table 13.3, we try to bring the results of the present section into the same schematic form as we have done with the temporal analysis of understanding and attunement.

TABLE 13.3
The Temporality of Falling

Inauthentic	Authentic
curiosity awaiting-forgetting-(running after, running away)-making present	

Why is it that the "authentic" mode of falling remains a complete blank? Is it because Heidegger has so far not dealt with it, or is it because there can be no such thing as an authentic falling? If falling, as Heidegger has explained it, is the very movement of disownment to the world, then indeed an "authentic falling" is a contradiction in terms. Nonetheless, if man's being as care is essentially a being-in-the-world, then there must be an authentic way in which a concrete self can exist with others and take care of the things on which he is dependent. Heidegger himself repeatedly assures us that the radical singleness of a resolute self does not mean a withdrawal from the world; on the contrary, he alone can "instantly" face and grasp his situation.

Beyond such general assertions, however, we are left completely in the dark about the concrete details of this authentic being-in-the-world. The most exhaustive analyses have been devoted to the circumspect using and handling of things as utensils, in order to show the reference-structure of the everyday world. But how does an instant attending to the situation discover the things within it? Do these things reveal themselves in a different possibility of their being from the handy-being of utensils? Judging from Heidegger's later works, they do. At present, however, the authentic way of being-in-the-world lacks all concreteness. The question must be left open whether and in how far these deficiencies will be made good by the end of Division Two.

(d) The Temporality of Discourse

One of the tasks of the preceding sections has been to demonstrate concretely how temporality *unifyingly differentiates* the whole existential structure of care. This belongs to temporality only because it itself is the differentiated unity of its three ecstases. It follows from this that the being constituted by temporality and disclosed in its hereness by an attunedly falling understanding is never a featureless, uniform whole, but is already in itself "jointed" (*gegliedert*, literally: limbed; so, for instance, being-in-the-world is a jointed structural whole). The disclosedness of an already jointed here-being can be expressly articulated in discourse or speech (*Rede*). Discourse is an existential character of Da-sein's being as an attunedly falling, understandingly articulating (discursive) being-in-the-world. It is because Da-sein factually exists in a world with others that the articulated understandability of his hereness comes to word and concretely voices itself (utters itself) in language. The existentiell-ontic phenomenon of language is therefore not a manmade tool consisting of words into which mutually agreed meanings have been infused, but is the signifying voicing of the already disclosed and articulated meaning of man's hereness. Where language is a communicating talk, what is communicated, shared, is not the inner experience of an isolated subject with another isolated subject but the mutually understandable hereness in a mutually shared world. A verbal expression, however, is not always indispensable to discourse, as the silent, wordless call of care has strikingly shown.

The distinctive function of discourse helps to explain why its temporality is different from that of the other disclosing characters of here-being. While understanding, attunement, and falling are primarily constituted by one ecstasis in the unity of time, there is no definite ecstasis that has a similar constitutive function for discourse. Speech articulates the *whole* dislosedness of here-being; so that in principle neither the futural character of existence, nor the having-been of thrownness, nor the presenting of falling can have a preponderant weight. In fact, however, discourse usually expresses itself in concrete language and speaks primarily in the mode of care-taking talking-over of the world roundabout us—hence the *presenting* has a "*privileged* constitutive function" (SZ, 349).

For the reason just stated, this analysis must clearly be different from the preceding ones. There is no immediately obvious reason, however, why it must be so disappointingly short, occupying barely a page. It confines itself mainly to stating the temporal problems that will have to be dealt with, such as the tenses of verbs, the gradations in time (*Zeitstufen*), and the kinds of action (*Aktionsarten*) distinguished by language. These temporal characteristics do not arise from the fact that language expresses, among other things, processes that happen in time, nor from the fact that speaking takes place in a "psychological time," but discourse is *in itself* temporal, insofar as all speaking of . . . , about . . . , and to . . . , is grounded in the ecstatic unity of temporality (SZ, 349). With the help of the traditional and vulgar concept of time,

Heidegger maintains, the temporal problems of language cannot be even properly formulated, and the science of language (*Sprachwissenschaft*) has been in the invidious position of having nothing else but that wholly insufficient concept to lean upon.

After this repudiation Heidegger might well be expected to proceed to a positive interpretation of the problems of language. But the analysis of temporality, it now appears, has not yet been carried far enough to make their solution possible. All further discussion is deferred to Division Three, with the following rather curious justification.

> But because discourse is always talking about beings, although not primarily and predominantly in the sense of theoretical statements, our analysis of the temporal constitution of discourse and the explication of the temporal characteristics of language patterns can be tackled only if the problem of the fundamental connection between being and truth has been unfolded in terms of the problematic of temporality. (SZ, 349)

The first clause of this sentence tells us categorically that discourse is in effect always a "talking about beings." This statement, made in the form of an unqualified and unrestricted assertion, strikes a strange note in the middle of a book that is directly and explicitly concerned with being as such. Taking Heidegger strictly at his word, we would have to conclude that it is only the discoveredness (truth) of beings that is expressly articulable in language, while the disclosedness (truth) of being remains "unsayable," and a genuinely philosophical speaking would have to be, like the call of care, a wordless silence. Attractive as this idea may be in many ways, and certainly not lightly to be dismissed, it is incompatible with Heidegger's own interpretation of discourse and, above all, with his lifelong search for a language appropriate to the "saying of being" (*das Sagen des Seins*).

Leaving this puzzle aside without any pretense at having solved it, and examining what is involved in a "talking about beings," we shall put ourselves in a position to appreciate why the connection between being and truth has to be established before the temporal problems of language can be tackled. In the first place, the beings we talk about must already be manifest *as beings*; they must be already understandable in what they are and how they are. In all our talk about beings, therefore, being must in some way have a say.

For instance, in an ordinary everyday sentence, like "that apple tree is too old," being speaks in its most common form, the "is." But in all such everyday is-saying, being is not directly and thematically in view; on the contrary, the "is" withdraws itself, it claims no attention for itself, but turns the light entirely on the manifest (true) beings—for example, the apple tree, which it expressly presents in a definite mode of its discoveredness (truth), as too old.

Our habitual is-saying has long ago lost the power of invoking being and has sunk down to connecting a subject with a predicate. In proposing to define the ontological meaning of the "is" Heidegger promises to give a radical solution to a problem which became central to Aristotle's thought. Although in the absence of Division Three the promise is not fulfilled, there is at least one thing that the temporal analysis so far carried out makes unmistakably clear: the "is" originates in the *making present of*. . . . As the preceding interpretation has shown, the *making present of* . . . forms the horizon of a face-to-faceness with itself, that is, of presentness, which is anticipatingly held out before the beings which are there of themselves and which, from and within this horizon of presentness can manifest themselves in their own bodily presence. It is their disclosed (true) presence that comes to word in the "is," so that in all our talking about beings it expressly presents the beings talked about (e.g., the apple tree) in a definite mode of their discoveredness (e.g., as too old).

A further important task that Heidegger defers to Division Three is summed up by saying that "the 'origination' of 'significance' can be clarified and the possibility of the formulation of concepts can be made ontologically intelligible only in terms of the temporality of discourse, that is, of Da-sein in general" (SZ, 349)

In a general way, we can already see why and how language must in itself be "significant." The temporality of here-being is the threefold removal *to*. . . . The ecstatic removal *to* . . . in-itself refers *to* something, signifies something. Meanings or significances are not something which we, by mutual agreement, hang on to word-signs, nor does language reflect or mirror an "external reality" with which it happens in some way to come into contact, but as the express articulation of the disclosedness (truth) of the "here," language is grounded in the "signifying" removal *to* something.

The fact that the general outline of Heidegger's promised solution of the problems of language is visible already, does not of course make up for the absence of a fully worked-out solution in a sphere where precision and detail are all-important. Although in Heidegger's later works language comes more and more importantly to the fore, the precise and detailed explanations promised here are never given and cannot be given because the final clarification of temporality itself is missing.

2. The Temporality of Being-in-the-World and the Problem of the Transcendence of the World

The inquiry now comes back to the point from which Division One started, to being-in-the-world as a fundamental constituent of care. Heidegger's first task in *Being and Time* was to show that Da-sein is never merely "here" as an isolated, relationless subject, but with his disclosed hereness the whole complex of interlinked relations (world) from which he refers himself to other beings is cooriginally disclosed. Being-here is therefore in itself a being-in-relation-to . . . , a being-in-a-world.

The fundamental constitution of being-in-the-world carries and makes possible Da-sein's being-together-with things within the world, whether in the mode of a circumspect having-to-do-with-them, or in the mode of a theoretical-scientific observation of them. Both these ways of taking care of things are grounded in Da-sein's being as care. The ecstatic temporality of care lies already in all Da-sein's relations to things and makes them first of all possible. To show this in detail will be the task of the first two subdivisions (a and b) of the present section. In the third subdivision (c) the temporal analysis of being-in-the-world will lead to the following questions:

> How is something like world possible at all, in what sense *is* world, what and how does the world transcend, how are "independent" innerworldly beings "connected" with the transcending world? The *ontological exposition* of these questions does not already entail their answer. On the other hand, they do bring about the clarification, previously necessary, of *the* structures with reference to which the problem of transcendence is to be interrogated. (SZ, 351)

In subdivision c transcendence becomes *explicitly* a central theme for the first time. Tho importance of this development can be fully evaluated only in the light of Heidegger's thesis, stated at the beginning of *Being and Time*, that

> as the fundamental theme of philosophy, being is not a genus of beings; yet it pertains to every being. Its "universality" must be sought in a higher sphere. Being and its structure transcend every being and every possible existent determination of a being. *Being is the transcendens pure and simple.* The transcendence of the being of Da-sein is a distinctive one since in it lies the possibility and necessity of the most radical *individuation*. Every disclosure of being as the *transcendens* is *transcendental* knowledge. *Phenomenological truth (disclosedness of being) is veritas transcendentalis.* (SZ, 38)

Temporality and Everydayness 257

How this *veritas transcendentalis* is at all possible in a factical herebeing, how disclosing understanding of being is grounded in the ecstatic temporality of here-being is the central question of *Being and Time*. In taking the transcendence of world for its theme, the present section is visibly moving toward the very center of the problem of *Being and Time*. Although it will not give us any final answers, we can expect it to give us at least a hint of where the answers might eventually be found.

(a) The Temporality of Circumspect Taking Care

A practical occupation with utensils is the primary way in which everyday existence takes care of things, that is, reckons with them, takes account of them. Even the most resolutely owned existence necessarily engages in the acquisition, production, alteration, and use of the things he needs to be able to exist. The concrete way in which Da-sein is near to things raises the decisive philosophical question, How does Da-sein's care-taking being-in-the-world hang together with the things that are handily there within the world? The things obviously cannot cause the care-taking as Da-sein's way of existing, nor, on the other hand, can their bodily presence be deduced from the care-taking. Nonetheless, the two do not simply occur side by side; they have an essential bearing on each other. To determine the connection between them, Heidegger's first step is to elucidate the phenomenal character of the things with which we are busy, the things we use as the means to achieve our practical ends. The decisive feature of Heidegger's phenomenological analysis of utensils in Division One (chapter 3) is not that it concentrates on the handy things in daily use, in contrast to indifferent substances, but that it fixes from the start the *within-worldish* character of things. Although in our daily dealings with things their world-character is not explicitly grasped, it is implicitly understood. The whole work-world is already "there" (disclosed) when, for instance, we are searching for a mislaid tool. A single, isolated tool—such as a hammer—is impossible. The hammer is in advance referred to hammering something, the hammering to fixing things together, the fixing to putting a roof on a house, and so forth. The hammer can show itself for what it is only from and within the equipment- (utensil-) whole, which belongs to the work-world of a builder or carpenter. The utensil-being of the hammer is constituted by its being referred to something beyond itself. The reference structure from which utensils show themselves in their handy being within the world is called by Heidegger *Bewandtnis mit . . . bei . . .* , the relevance *of* something *to* something, or the relevance *of* something *at* some occasion, for example, the relevance of the hammer *to* hammering. The being of a utensil lies in its being destined for a purpose. The purpose is the specific task to be accomplished, for example, the house to be built. This carries and unifies the whole complex of references from which and within which each utensil can be what it is, a tool relevant to a particular task (destined for a particular purpose) within the whole. The accomplished task—the house—has in turn a utensil-character; it is relevant to (destined for) living in.[2] With this, however, the reference structure terminates. The house is destined for sheltering a factical existence, whose "destiny" it is to be the care of being-here. As the temporal analysis has now made clear, here-being is constituted by its coming-to-itself in its utmost, impassable possibility, and cannot therefore refer itself to something beyond itself as the means to an end. On the ground of its own temporal structure, here-being is its own end. From the predisclosed "for the sake of" his own ability-to-be-here a factical Da-sein *signifies* to himself how he can be toward other beings; that is, how he can refer himself to them and, conversely, how they can bear upon—be referred to—his own ability to exist. The whole complex of predisclosed references, the of . . . to (at) . . . for . . . constitutes the ontological structure of the everyday world, which, in turn, makes it possible for the things within it to manifest themselves as relevant to (at) some task to be achieved (or, to say the same thing in another way, as destined for a purpose). A care-taking being-together-with things, therefore, *lets things be relevant* (*Bewendenlassen*). This, however, is an essential constituent of Da-sein's being as care, whose unity is grounded in temporality. What is the specific mode of temporality that makes a care-taking occupation with things possible?

> Letting something be relevant lies in the simplest handling of a useful thing. Relevance has an intentional character with reference to which the thing is useable or in use. Understanding the intention and context of relevance has the temporal structure of awaiting. Awaiting the intention, taking care can at the same time come back to something like relevance.[3] *Awaiting* the context and retaining the means of relevance make possible in its ecstatic unity the specifically handy way on which the useful thing is made present. (SZ, 353)

The ecstatic unity of an awaiting-retaining making present is thus the condition of the possibility of a practical having-to-do-with-things. The retaining was mentioned briefly in connection with inauthentic understanding. It must be noted that the retaining (remembering) refers to beings within the world which do not have the character of here-being. The retaining is founded upon a *forgetting* of the thrown self, which first of all opens up the horizon of a "before" into which the self-forgetful here-being can remember the relevant utensils. The everyday retaining, however, is not an explicit "fixing" of a utensil-whole, just as the awaiting is not an explicit, theoretical contemplation of an end; it is rather the making present that springs from the unity of an awaiting-retaining that makes "the characteristic absorption in taking care in the world of its useful things possible" (SZ, 354).

The awaiting-retaining making present unifies the implicitly understood references within which everyday care circumspectly moves without any explicit, theoretical grasp of them. The smooth, matter-of course movement within these familiar references, however, can be interrupted. As Division One has explained in some detail (chap. 3, § 16), it is on the occasion of such breaks that the utensil-world as a whole may first come into view, and the hitherto taken-for-granted, inconspicuous utensils may suddenly arrest our attention by showing themselves in the unfamiliar mode of mere substances.

What is the ontological-temporal condition of the possibility that something unusable—for example, a tool which fails to do its job—can arrest our attention? In the following analysis, Heidegger proceeds to show the inadequacy of a "theory of association" to explain even our simplest dealings with things. First, "association" takes account only of the connection between "past experience" and "present experiences." Further, as a psychological theory, it lacks an adequate-ontological foundation. In such a seemingly simple experience as, for instance, our attention being caught by a damaged tool, lies already the whole of temporality. The awaiting-retaining making present is "caught," "held up" in its absorption in the relevance-relations, by what turns out to be, on inspection, damage to the tool. The making present is held fast by the unfitness of the tool for the work in hand, so that it is only now that the implicit awaited what-for, together with the presently manipulated tool, become explicit. The making present, on the other hand,

> can meet up with something unsuited for . . . because it is already moving in an awaiting retention of what is in relevance. Making present is "held up," that is, in the unity of the awaiting that retains, it shifts more to itself and thus constitutes the "inspection," checking, and removal of the disturbance. If heedful association were simply a succession of "experiences" occurring "in time" and if these experiences "associated" with each other as intimately as possible, letting a conspicuous, unusable tool be encountered would be ontologically impossible. Whatever we have made accessible in contexts of useful things, letting things be in relevance as such must be grounded in the ecstatic unity of the making present that awaits and retains. (SZ, 355)

But the unusability of a utensil is not the only way in which the smooth flow of having-to-do-with-things may be broken. We may find, for instance, that something we were looking forward to finding at hand is not there at all. This discovery is made by our missing the utensil. Missing something is not merely a not-making-present (*Ungegenwärtigen*) of the utensil in question, but rather a "not-making-present" as "a deficient mode of the present in the sense of the not-making-present of something expected or always already available." Though deficient, this mode is positive. Missing something necessarily stands in an ecstatic unity with awaiting, since we could never miss something unless we were already awaiting it.

We can be taken by surprise, on the other hand, only by something not awaited. Just as the "not-making-present" is not a sheer absence of awaiting, nor is the "not awaiting"; it is rather a positive, though deficient, mode of it. Otherwise, it would be wholly inexplicable why Heidegger says that "The not awaiting of the making present that is lost first discloses the 'horizonal' realm in which something surprising can overcome Da-sein" (SZ, 355).

Obscure as this sentence is in many respects, one thing at least is clear: unless the not awaiting were a positive ecstasis of temporality, it could not possibly disclose a horizonal realm within which a surprise can overtake a falling here-being. As we have heard earlier, the momentum of the fall constricts the falling here-being more and more in a making present that seeks to uproot itself from the hold and guidance of a genuine awaiting.

Finally, a most important way in which a circumspect taking-care of things can be interrupted is by knocking up against those things it can neither produce, procure, nor guard against, avoid, or eliminate. These insuperable obstacles are coped with or put up with by a caretaking here-being. The "coping with . . ." (*Sichabfinden mit* . . .) is not a merely negative acquiescing in or ignoring of things, but a specific mode of discovering them in the character of the inopportune, hindering, troubling, and endangering. Generally speaking, these things encounter us in the mode of *resistance* (*Widerständigkeit*).

> The temporal structure of accepting something lies in a *nonretention* that awaits and makes present. The making present that awaits does not, for example, count "on" something that is unsuitable, but yet available. Not counting on . . . is a mode of taking into account what one cannot hold on to. It is not forgotten, but retained so that it remains at hand precisely in its *unsuitability*. Things at hand like this belong to the everyday content of the factically disclosed surrounding world. (SZ, 356)

The present passage completes the analysis of the modifications of an awaiting-retaining making present. Further, it elucidates and justifies Heidegger's earlier comment on certain phenomenological interpretations—notably those of Dilthey and Scheler—which ascribe the discovery of the reality of the "external world" primarily to the experience of resistance (SZ, 205, 209ff.). Heidegger in no way denies the resistant character of things and its importance for the discovery of their "reality," but points out the insufficiency of this explanation. For one thing, resistance is only *one* character of reality. For another thing, it characterizes beings *within the world*, and by no means explains the phenomenon of the world itself. Our last passage has shown the existential-temporal conditions that make the discovery of resistance first of all possible. Once these foundations are laid bare, the importance of experiencing the resistant character of things can be fully conceded: it gives a factical existence to understand his exposedness to and dependence upon a "world of things" which, in spite of all technical progress, he can never master.

Before proceeding to the next subsection, let us briefly summarize the main conclusions reached.

1. The temporal structure of letting-things-be-relevant is an awaiting-retaining making present. This constitutes the familiarity of here-being's nearest world, by virtue of which even a "strange world" is not totally strange to us but to a certain extent we find our way about in it.
2. Modifications of the basic ecstatic unity:
    (i) An "arrested" awaiting-retaining making-present (e.g., on the occasion of being held up by a damaged tool).
    (ii) An awaiting-retaining not-making-present (on the occasion of missing something).
    (iii) An unawaiting-retaining making-present (being taken by surprise).
    (iv) An awaiting-unretaining making-present (resistance of the unfit things at hand).

With regard to ii and iii, it should be noted that Heidegger himself does not give the full temporal structures, but the above formulations are well supported by what he says.

(b) The Temporal Meaning of the Way in Which Circumspect Taking Care Becomes Modified into the Theoretical Discovery of Things Objectively Present in the World

Heidegger now takes up the problem of the *ontological genesis* of a theoretical-scientific approach to things, which, in losing the character of handiness, reveal themselves as mere substances (*Vorhandenes*). It is not the chronological-historical development of the sciences from everyday practice that is in question, but the ontological constitution which makes it possible for a factical here-being to exist in the way of scientific research. The existential concept of science differs fundamentally from its logical concept. The latter defines the results of science as a systematic nexus of proof (*Begründungszusammenhang*) of true, valid propositions. The existential concept, on the other hand,

> understands science as a mode of existing and thus as a mode of being-in-the-world which discovers or discloses beings or being. However, a completely adequate existential interpretation of science cannot be carried out until the *meaning of being and the "connection" between being and truth* have been clarified in terms of the temporality of existence. The following considerations are to prepare the understanding of *this central problematic* within which the idea of phenomenology can first be developed, as opposed to the preconception indicted in an introductory fashion. (SZ, 357)[4]

Once more, Heidegger draws our attention to the ultimate aim of *Being and Time* and to the importance of the connection between being and truth. His immediate aim, however, is a restricted one. It is to examine the *change* from the circumspect discovery of handy things in everyday practice to the pure looking at things (*Hinsehen*) that is characteristic of the theoretical-scientific discovery of them as mere substances. To make Heidegger's elucidations easier to follow, let us recall the following points. First, all ways of "seeing," intuiting, apprehending—that is, of gaining access to being and beings—are primarily grounded in the forethrow of understanding. This constitutes here-being's own ability-to-be *for the sake of which* he refers himself to beings as relevant to (handy *for*) this or that provisional purpose, and ultimately to his own existence. Secondly, this primary understanding of existence and world takes *explicit* possession of itself in *interpretation* (*Auslegung*). In interpreting something, "understanding appropriates what it has understood in an understanding" (SZ, 148). So, for instance, a circumspectly discovered handy thing becomes explicitly understood by being *aus-gelegt*, "laid out," exhibited, together with its what-for. The everyday question "What is this thing?" receives the answer "It is a knife," where a knife is already known as a utensil for cutting. Further, the explanation need not necessarily be expressed in a proposition. We might just as well take up the thing in question and, without saying a word, demonstrate what and how it cuts.

Keeping these matters in mind, we now examine in detail Heidegger's renewed analysis of everyday circumspection. The explanation already given of this phenomenon in Division One turns out to have been incomplete. It now appears that circumspection is itself subject to the guidance of an "overall view" (*Übersicht*), which *surveys* the utensil-world as a whole together with the public world that belongs to it. This overall view or survey over things as a whole illumines everyday care-taking and, in turn, "gets its own 'light' from the potentiality-of-being of Da-sein *for the sake of which* taking care exists as care" (SZ, 359).

In what way does the surveying-circumspection "illumine" our everyday practice? It *brings* the already discovered handy things closer by way of interpreting them; that is, it makes them clearer and more explicit to our understanding. The circumspectly interpreting bringing-closer of handy things is called by Heidegger "deliberation" (*Überlegung*). In what connection it stands with interpreting something *as* something will be discussed later. The first task is to elucidate the structure or what Heidegger now calls the "schema" of deliberation.

> The schema peculiar to it is the "if-then": If this or that is to be produced, put into use, or prevented, for example, then we need these or those means, ways, circumstances, or opportunities. Circumspect deliberation throws light on the actual factical position of Da-sein in the surrounding world taken care of. Thus it never simply "confirms" the objective presence of a being or of its qualities. Deliberation can also come about without what is circumspectly approached itself being concretely at hand or present within the nearest range. Bringing the surrounding world near in circumspect deliberation has the existential meaning of *making present* [*Gegenwärtigung*]. For *re*presenting [*Vergegenwärtigung*] is only a mode of making present. In it, deliberation catches sight directly of what is needed, but not at hand. Representing circumspection does not relate itself to "mere ideas." (SZ, 359)

Every point made in this passage is important. In the first place, the deliberating interpretation is anticipatingly contrasted with the scientific explanation; the former brings closer, makes clearer, here-being's own situation in a world that concerns him, while the latter makes explicit the actual occurrence of indifferent substances and their properties. A handy thing has no properties; it reveals what it is in itself by its *fitness for* the job for which it is destined, or by its unfitness for it.

A circumspect deliberating, then, explicitly brings together the awaitedly desired or feared thing with the ways and means of achieving or avoiding it. This "bringing together" (in Kantian terms, synthesizing) moves in the scheme of "if-then." The primary temporal meaning of deliberating is a making present, even though the things we deliberate about may not be, and in fact usually are not, visibly present. Heidegger now introduces a mode of presentation for which German has the excellent word *Vergegenwärtigung*: making something present to ourselves, bringing it face to face with ourselves in thought, literally envisaging it. A cardinal point with Heidegger is that this mode of presentation refers no less directly to *things themselves* than to an immediate perception of them in their "bodily presence." In thinking, for instance, of something far away from us, we are not merely occupied with "immanent" processes in our minds; we are *out in the world* with and at the thing we are thinking of. Just because thinking is a way of being-in-the-world, it is essential to it, so to speak, to extend itself, to straddle the distance from us to the things to which we remove ourselves in thought (see "Bauen Wohnen Denken," VA, 157, "Building Dwelling Thinking," PLT, 156–57).

Heidegger's next step is to give a fuller analysis of circumspect making present, which is by no means a simple phenomenon, but has complex existential-temporal foundations. In the first place,

> it belongs to the full ecstatic unity of temporality. It is grounded in a *retention* of the context of useful things that Da-sein takes care of in *awaiting* a possibility. What has already been disclosed in awaiting retention is brought nearer by one's deliberative making present or representing. (SZ, 359)

So far, the analysis is easily followed. Indeed, we become aware at this point how firmly Heidegger has succeeded in establishing his temporal interpretation. Already we take it for granted that the presenting must belong to an ecstatic unity with a "coming to" and a "having been." Heidegger's further elucidations, on the other hand, are extremely difficult and confusing. Let us follow them step by step.

> But if deliberatrion is to be able to move in the scheme of "if-then," taking care must already understand a context of relevance in an "overview." What is addressed with the "if" must already be understood *as this and that*. For this, it is not necessary that the understanding of useful things be expressed predicatively. The scheme "something as something" is already prefigured in the structure of prepredicative understanding. The as-structure is ontologically grounded in the temporality of understanding. (SZ, 359)

What is addressed with the "if" is the awaitedly forethrown possibility of something desired or feared. Awaiting, we remember, is that mode of the future in which here-being inauthentically comes-to-itself. It is the primary temporal constituent of inauthentic understanding, and so makes possible the everyday understanding of something as something. This as-structure, however, already lies in the schema of "if-then." In deliberating, for instance, about building a house (*if* I am to have a house built), the house must already be understood from its relevance to dwelling, that is, as a dwelling-place; the dwelling, in turn, is a disclosed possibility of my own existence, for the sake of which the house is to be built. So far, all is clear. The real difficulties are only just beginning.

> Only because Da-sein, awaiting a possibility (that is, here a what-for), has come back to a for-this (that is, retains a thing at hand), can *conversely* the making present that belongs to this awaiting retention start with this retention *and bring it explicitly nearer* in its reference to the what-for. The deliberation that brings near must in the scheme of making present adapt itself to the kind of being of what is to be brought near. The character of relevance of what is at hand is not first discovered by deliberation, but only gets brought near by it in such a way that it circumspectly lets what is in relevance be seen *as* this. (SZ, 359–60)

The first sentence tells us that the explicit interpretation of things can take the *reverse direction* to the originally disclosing understanding of them. While the latter starts from the "futural" forethrow of possibilities and rebounds back to what already is, the former can start from the already "retained" things and go forward to the relevant possibilities. In every case, Heidegger stresses, the future preserves its primacy, its leading role: only because and on the ground of it can the presenting explanation take the reverse direction.

The first sentence of our passage, in spite of its difficult construction, is really quite clear. What is puzzling is why it should be there at all. Deliberation starts with the awaited possibility addressed with the "if." To introduce the possible reversal of the process of interpretation seems not only unnecessary at this juncture, but positively confusing. We simply do not see what Heidegger is aiming at. On further reflection, however, several reasons suggest themselves. First, our interpretations do in fact usually start from what is already "there." Second, Heidegger may want to say, though does not explicitly do so, that deliberation is in fact a going back and forward within the "if-then" schema. Its movement traverses the schema in *both* directions. Third, there may be a more distant aim in Heidegger's mind. He may be thinking forward to a fundamental modification of the "if-then" schema: if (because) such and such a thing has happened, then (therefore) such and such a thing must follow. The circumspectly deliberating "if-then" can change into the schema of causality, within which the scientific explanation of the connection between substantial things moves (FD, 109, WT, 139–40). The double movement of thought is especially evident here. It goes back from effects to causes and goes forward from causes to their already discovered or awaitedly "forethrown" effects. The curious thing is that when he comes to examine the theoretical-scientific way of purely "looking at" things, Heidegger makes no mention at all of the possible modification of the deliberating "if-then" to the schema of causality, which, in view of his careful analysis of the "if-then," he might well be expected to do.

Let us now consider the last two sentences of our passage. They tell us that in order to bring something nearer to a care-taking here-being, deliberating must "conform to" (*sich anmessen*) the manner of being of what is to be brought closer. The expression "sich anmessen" (literally: "to measure itself to . . . ," "to fit itself to . . . ," "adapt itself to") has the sense of "be adequate to" or "conform to" or "correspond with" in the sense of the traditional theory of truth as adequacy, conformity, or correspondence. A judgment is true when it corresponds with the judged object. But in order that a judgment can correspond, that is, measure and bind itself to and by an object, a whole series of preconditions must already be fulfilled. One of these is that the object must already be discovered (true) and understood not only in *that* it *is* but in *how* it *is*, that is, in the specific manner of its being.[5] The specific manner (the "how") in which things within the world meet a care-taking being-in-the-world is in their handy-being. The handy-being of a utensil is disclosed from the ecstatic unity of an awaiting-retaining which in advance understands it in its belonging to the whole of a relevance-complex. Deliberation *corresponds with* the handy-being of utensils by presenting them precisely *such* (in the selfsame manner) as they show themselves in and from their relevance-relations. More concretely expressed, deliberation brings the handy things "truly" closer by explicitly making present the for-what of relevance together with its with-what (the means) *as* such, that is, *as* this relevance-complex from which and in which the utensils in question present themselves. The "schema of presenting" is the "as." The "as" expresses the correspondence or conformity of the presenting with the "how" of the utensil's being; it brings the utensil closer precisely *as* it shows itself in its "relevant" handy-being.[6] The interpretative presenting of something *as* something may be simple or complex. In any case, it is possible only in the ecstatic unity of the whole temporality.

> The way the present is rooted in the future and in the having-been is the existential and temporal condition of the possibility that what is projected in circumspect understanding can be brought nearer in a making present in such a way that the present must adapt itself to what is encountered in the horizon of an awaiting retention, that is, it must interpret itself in the schema of the as-structure. This gives us the answer to our question whether the as-structure is existentially and ontologically connected with the phenomenon of the projecting [SZ, 151]. *Like understanding and interpretation in general, the "as" is grounded in the ecstatic and horizonal unity of temporality.* (SZ, 360)

This passage only sums up what has already been discussed above, making its connection with a problem formulated on page 151 explicit. We notice, further, that Heidegger once more recurs to the still unexplained phenomenon of the "ecstatic and horizonal unity of temporality," thereby referring us forward to the next subsection, where the temporal constitution of world and its "horizonal schema" will become the theme. But even there the final interpretation of "schema"—a concept whose importance is becoming more and more evident—will not yet be given. This is explicitly deferred by Heidegger to the "fundamental analysis of being," which was to have been carried out in Division Three. There, Heidegger promises us—and more precisely "in connection with the interpretation of the 'is' (which as a copula 'expresses' the addressing of something as something)"—that "we must again make the as-phenomenon thematic and define the concept of the 'schema' existentially" (SZ, 360).

That this promise remains unfulfilled is all the more regrettable because there is good reason to think that Heidegger intends the existential-temporal interpretation or the "schema" to cast light on "the obscurity of his [Kant's] doctrine of the schematism" (SZ, 23; and see KPM, especially §§19-23, for fuller explanation of these connections). The preceding discussion, it is true, has cast some light on the meaning of the circumspectly deliberating "if-then" and of the "as." But this obviously cannot exhaust their meaning, for the "schema of making present" must conform to the manner of being in which the beings to be explained encounter us. Our understanding of being is capable of a wide range of modifications. If, for instance, the being of within-worldish beings is called "reality," then handy-being (handy reality) is only one manner of it, substantial reality another manner, and, as Heidegger occasionally hints, there may be still further modifications of it. It follows that even if the form of the schemata in which our explanations move should remain the same, their meaning must be modifiable. The same considerations lead to the conclusion that the "is," which gives expression as the copula to "something *as* something," will have a different meaning in, say, an everyday pronouncement compared with a scientific proposition.

This brings us to the change from a circumspect taking care to a theoretical discovery, a change so abrupt and far-reaching that Heidegger calls it an *Umschlag*, an overturning. Its analysis is introduced by taking as a lead "an elemental statement of circumspect deliberation and its possible modifications" (SZ, 360). The actual pronouncement "The hammer is too heavy (too light)" has already been discussed by Heidegger earlier (SZ, 157–58), so that he can forego a further discussion at this point. For us, on the other hand, it will be helpful to consider the sentence briefly, and especially to follow up Heidegger's hint that the "is" gives expression to "something *as* something."

In the pronouncement "The hammer is too heavy (too light)," the "is" expressly presents this particular tool, the hammer, *as* too heavy (too light), that is, *as* unfit for the job in a definite way. Although the "too heavy" may make the tool's unfitness explicit only for the job immediately in hand, implicitly it reaches out into a whole relevance-complex, into the whole workworld, and further into the care of an everyday existence to earn his daily bread. Now, it may be thought that the power of reaching out beyond its immediate application is conferred on this pronouncement by qualifying the "heavy" by the "too." (It might be interesting to compare here Plato's reflections in *The Statesman* 283ff. on the difference between the "more" and the "too much.") But this is not at all the case, as Heidegger points out. When we simply say "The hammer is heavy," we may be deliberating about our work being made "heavier," "more difficult," by the hammer or about the strength it will require to use it. On the other hand, the sentence *can* also mean

> the being before us, with which we are circumspectly familiar as a hammer, has a weight, that is, the "property" of heaviness. It exerts a pressure on what lies beneath it, and when that is removed, it falls. The discourse understood in this way is no longer in the horizon of the awaiting retention of a totality of useful things and its relations of relevance. What is said has been drawn from looking at what is appropriate for a being with "mass." What is now in view is appropriate for the hammer, not as a tool, but as a corporeal thing that is subject to the law of gravity. Circumspect talk about being "too heavy" or "too light" no longer has any "meaning"; that is, the thing now encountered of itself provides us with nothing in relation to which it could be "found" too heavy or too light. (SZ, 360–61)

What the thing no longer "provides" is nothing less than its within-worldish character. As Heidegger said earlier, the thing "falls out of the world," it succumbs to an "unworlding" (*Entweltlichung*) (SZ, 75). This radical change has certainly not come about through the way we talk about things, for we see that exactly the same sentence can be understood in vastly different ways. What, then, is the reason for this modification? Not that we simply abstain from a practical having-to-do-with-things, nor that we simply disregard their utensil-character, but that we look at the thing in a *new way*, namely as a substantial thing. "*The understanding of being* guiding the heedful association with inner-worldy beings *has been transformed*" (SZ, 361).

Before considering how the things that have "fallen out" of the world round about us reveal themselves to a theoretical approach, we have to take special note of a point made in the paragraph that immediately follows the one quoted above.

> In our first characterization of the genesis of the theoretical mode of behaviour from circumspection, we have made basic a kind of theoretical grasping of innerworldly beings, of physical nature, in which the modification of our understanding of being amounts to a transformation. (SZ, 361)

The point to be noted here is that it is not the world that is modified into a "physical nature," but that nature itself, according to Heidegger, is a concrete "within-worldish being" which is discoverable only within and in transit through (*im Durchgang*) a predisclosed world. Now, taking the sentence "The hammer is heavy" to assert a "physical" proposition—though, strictly speaking, there are no such things as hammers in physics—Heidegger goes on to analyze how it now presents the former utensil:

> We *overlook* not only the tool-character of the being encountered, but thus also that which belongs to every useful thing at hand: its place. The place becomes indifferent. This does not mean that the objectively present thing loses its "location" altogether. Its place becomes a position in space and time, a "world-point," which is in no way distinguished from any other. This means that the multiplicity of places of useful things at hand defined in the surrounding world is not just modified to a sheer multiplicity of positions, but the beings of the surrounding world are *released [entschränkt]*. The totality of what is objectively present becomes thematic. (SZ, 362)

Although no explicit mention was made in the sentence "The hammer is heavy" of either place or space, Heidegger evidently considers that a definite conception of space belongs to each definite mode or manner of being in which beings are understandable to us. The theoretical understanding levels down the "significant" places, the places *for* this and that thing of the everyday world, to a featureless, indifferent, uniformity. In a later lecture, however, Heidegger remarks that "even modern physics has been forced by the facts themselves to conceive the spatial medium of cosmic space as a field-unity which is determined by the body as a dynamic center . . ." ("Bauen Wohnen Denken," VA 156-57, "Building Dwelling Thinking," PLT,156). Whether Heidegger sees in this development a vindication of our primary experience of space is unfortunately not further elaborated.

However that may be, the expansion of the significant place-manifold into something like a universal space must clearly go hand in hand with the "theoretical" breaking down of the boundedness of the everyday world. But this breaking down is at the same time a new and positive delimitation of the "region" of substantial beings, a delimitation led by the dominant understanding of being as objective, substantial reality. This is the "manner of being" to which the theoretical-scientific investigation and explanation of beings must conform, to which and by which it must measure and bind itself.

> The more appropriately the being of the beings to be investigated is understood in the guiding understanding of being and the more the totality of beings is articulated in its fundamental determinations as a possible area of subject-matter for a science, the more assured will be the actual perspective of methodical questioning. (SZ, 362)

What Heidegger has in mind here is obviously not the positive work of a science and its results, but rather the first encirclement of its field, the laying down of its fundamental principles and the definition of its basic concepts, such as we find for instance in Newton's *Principia* or in Galileo's *Discorsi*. It is with these works of "natural philosophy" that Heidegger compares Aristotle's *Physics*, setting off the Greek experience of the *phusis*, movement and place against the modern experience of "nature" and the conception of its constitutive moments (FD, 59-73, G41, 77-95, WT, 76-95). But although such comparisons of detail are highly interesting and no doubt valid, it is at least open to question whether the intention of these works as a whole can show a one-to-one correspondence. It can hardly be doubted that Aristotle's *Physics* is, in phenomenological language, a "regional ontology" or an "ontology of nature," whose intention is primarily philosophical and whose connection with "first philosophy" is clearly laid down by Aristotle himself. But could the same be said without qualification of a modern theoretical work on physics, fundamental though it may be?

How Heidegger would answer this question is not quite clear, because he does not seem to be concerned with the exact demarcation of a "regional ontology" against the theoretical groundwork of an experimental science.[7] Why and in what precise sense he thinks it proper to call the latter "philosophy" (ontology) will become clear as we follow up our passage in *Being and Time*.

Here the rise of mathematical physics is cited as the classical example of both the historical development and the ontological genesis of a science. What Heidegger considers to be decisive for this development is neither the greater stress laid on observation of facts nor the actual application of mathematics, "*but the mathematical project of nature itself*" (SZ, 362). We must note especially that the word Heidegger uses is *Entwurf* (forethrow), where we have to resort to a "plan" or "design" or, as translated here, "project." At any rate, it is certain that Heidegger means a "forethrown" plan, a previously drawn-up blueprint of nature, which, however, is by no means arbitrarily invented, but is drawn from conformity to the dominant character of being a substantiality.

> This project discovers in advance something constantly objectively present (matter) and opens the horizon for the guiding perspective on its quantitatively definable constitutive moments (motion, force, location, and time). Only "in the light of" a nature thus projected can something like a "fact" be found and be taken in as a point of departure for an experiment defined and regulated in terms of this project. The "founding" of "factual science" was possible only because the researchers understood that there are in principle no "bare facts." (SZ, 362)

The irony of the last sentence is directed against that trend in scientific thinking which may be generally entitled "positivism." The hallmark of positivism is its belief that it can "manage with facts or with more and newer facts, while concepts are merely expedients which one for some reason needs, but with which one must not get too deeply involved—for that would be philosophy" (FD, 51, G41, 67, WT, 67). The tragic irony of this situation is that it means to overcome positivism by positivism. On the other hand, Heidegger reflects, it is only the second-line scientists who cling to such views; the leading minds who create new positions and new ways of questioning always "think philosophically through and through" (FD, 51, 941, 67, WT, 67).

Why and in what precise sense such "ground-laying" scientific thinking must be called "philosophical" is indicated in the following passage.

What is decisive about the mathematical project of nature is again not primarily the mathematical element as such, but the fact that this project *discloses* a priori. And thus the paradigm of the mathematical natural sciences does not consist in its specific exactitude and binding character for "everyone," but in the fact that in it the thematic beings are discovered in *the* only way that beings can be discovered: in the prior project of their constitution of being. When the basic concepts of the understanding of being by which we are guided have been worked out, the methods, the structure of conceptuality, the relevant possibility of truth and certainty, the kind of grounding and proof, the mode of being binding and the kind of communication—all these will be determined. The totality of these moments constitutes the complete existential concept of science. (SZ, 362-63)

In what sense, then, is the theoretically forethrown or projected plan of nature "philosophical"? First of all, it "discloses an a priori," that is, it brings explicitly into view the vaguely and implicitly understood being that already lies in and makes possible all our discovery of beings. In the opening pages of *Being and Time* (SZ, 12) Heidegger calls this implicit understanding of being *preontological* (prephilosophical). In the same paragraph he defines *ontology* in a very wide sense as the explicit theoretical inquiry into the *meaning of beings* (*Sinn des Seienden*). What phenomenology understands by the *meaning of beings* (not of being) is nothing other than *what* these beings are, their essence. It is the whole structure of the whatness, the essence of beings in all its constitutive moments, that is called "ontological constitution." It is, therefore, the essence of the "physical beings," the things of nature, which the mathematical plan in advance has in view. But this essence (the ontological constitution) is no longer understood from the handy-being (handy reality) of things within a world; the *essential* character of things as handiness *for* something has been covered over. The essence of "physical beings" is drawn from the now leading understanding of being as substantial reality. The essence (ontological constitution) that the mathematical design of nature anticipatingly brings into view is the substantiality of substances.

But if this new way of discovering beings is to deserve the title of philosophy (ontology) in the widest sense, it must, according to Heidegger's definition, be explicitly theoretical. In other words, it must not only implicitly conform to the manner of being in which the discoverable beings show themselves, but must explicitly explain and articulate their being. Now, if we look back to the passage quoted above, we read there that the "basic concepts of the understanding of being by which we are guided have been worked out [*Ausarbeitung*]." In § 32 of

Division One, Heidegger expressly defines "interpretation" as "the development [or working out (*Ausarbeitung*)] of possibilities projected in understanding" (SZ, 148). Substantiality is *one* possible way in which the essence of beings can be disclosed by understanding—*one* possible way, for, as we have seen, there are other ways. The explicit-theoretical working-out, the interpretation of substantiality, is concretely carried out in the articulation and conceptual definition of its constitutive moments (location, time, motion, etc.), in other words, in the definition of the basic concepts of the science. This interpretation is mathematical in character insofar as it fixes the constitutive moments of substantiality as quantitatively definable. It is these "ground-laying" definitions, Heidegger says, which further determine all that belongs to the structure of the science: its methods, its truth and certainty, the kind of evidence and proof it admits and seeks, and so on.

No detailed comparisons are needed to show how vastly different is the theoretical mode of explanation from a circumspectly deliberating bringing closer of handy things. To mention only one of its features, the explicitness and rigor of scientific method, which guides and regulates all approach and access to things within its field, would be quite out of place in a circumspect taking care, not because the latter is unmethodical, but because it is guided and stabilized by the care of his own ability-to-be-here of a factical existence. In the scientific investigation of substantial beings, on the other hand, this guidance is lost and must be replaced by the strictness and appropriateness of method.

Up to now, Heidegger has dealt primarily with the ontological-theoretical side of science, so much so that he might easily be accused of being a pure theorist, just as onesided in his own way as the extremest positivist. But the accusation would be quite misplaced; Heidegger is well aware of the constant interplay between working experience and theory and their mutual influence on each other. Moreover, we must not forget that Heidegger is not speaking of being "in itself," as though being were a substance, a thing which existed somewhere "in and by itself." What he has constantly in view is the ontological difference *as a whole*, in which and from which being is manifest as the being *of* beings, and conversely, beings show themselves only in their being. As far as the sciences are concerned, their theoretical work has the sole aim of making the beings, which we have already encountered and which are known to us in a prescientific way, accessible in distinctively new ways.

> The scientific project of the beings somehow already encountered lets their kind of being be explicitly understood in such a way that the pos-

sible ways of purely discovering innerworldly beings thus become evident. The articulation of the understanding of being, the definition of the subject-matter defined by that understanding, and the prefiguration of the concepts suitable to these beings, all belong to the totality of this projecting that we call *thematization*. It aims at freeing beings encountered within the world in such a way that they can "project" themselves back upon pure discovery, that is, they can become objects. Thematization objectifies. It does not first "posit" beings, but frees them in such a way that they become "objectively" subject to questioning and definition. (SZ, 363)

The scientific thematization does not originally "posit" beings, that is, does not originally discover them in their being. Heidegger says "posit" in quotation marks, alluding perhaps to being, *Dasein*, in Kant's sense of *existentia* and its modalities, possibility and necessity, as different ways of "positing."[8] The thematization "sets them free" (*freigeben*)—lets beings show themselves in a new way, namely as objects of a pure "looking at." But, it is important to remember, the "looking at" is a mode of a care-taking being-near-to things. Its primary temporal character is a making present, but one Heidegger calls an "ausgezeichnete Gegenwärtigung," a distinguished, preeminent presenting. It is distinguished from a circumspect making present principally by its awaiting purely and solely the discoveredness (truth) of the substantially present being.

> This awaiting of discoveredness is grounded existentielly in a resoluteness of Da-sein by means of which it projects itself upon its potentiality-of-being-in-the-"truth." This project is possible because being-in-the-truth constitutes a determination of the existence of Da-sein. How science has its origin in authentic existence is not to be pursued here. (SZ, 363)

Heidegger's last remark comes as a surprise, even when we read it for the first time in the context of *Being and Time*, but especially when we come back to it from his later works. There the stress is usually on how far science has fallen away from its "origin," rather than on the origin in a resolutely disclosed existence. But even in *Being and Time* Heidegger always stresses the primariness of the circumspect discovery of handy things, compared to which the objectifying presentation of mere substances appears secondary, derivative, and therefore degenerate ("Any 'arising' [derivation, deduction ('*Entspringen*')] in the field of ontology is degeneration" (SZ, 334)). It is surprising, but nonetheless illuminating, that in its pure waiting upon truth, science springs from owned existence, and is in that respect distinguished "above" a circumspect discovery springing from the disownment of a falling being-in-the-world.

The text does not mention the specific character of having-been that belongs to the ecstatic unity of a "distinguished" awaiting making present. We may, however, assume it to be a *retaining*, since it helps to constitute a definite mode—the objectifying mode—of *being-near-to* things. This structure, in turn, belongs to the fundamental constitution of here-being as being-in-the-world.

It is at this point that the inquiry turns back to its own central concern, and seems indeed to come to a decisive stage, which announces itself in the word *transcendence*. If "being is the *transcendens* pure and simple," (SZ, 38)—that which sheerly transcends *beings* as such—and if this *transcendens* is disclosed in here-being, then here-being must always transcend (go out, stand out beyond) beings as such and as a whole. "If the thematization of what is objectively present—the scientific project of nature—is to become possible, *Da-sein must transcend* the beings thematized. Transcendence does not consist in objectivation, but is rather presupposed by it" (SZ, 363). Those theories of knowledge, on the other hand, which take their start from the subject-object relation as the supposed "ultimate" that cannot or need not be further explained, see in this relation itself the "transcendence" whereby a "worldless subject" goes out from his "immanent sphere" to an object outside himself. To expose the inadequacy of such theories and of the wholly insufficient conception of here-being as a "subject," is of course only a negative, but by no means negligible, aim of *Being and Time*, considering the stranglehold of such conceptions on our whole way of thinking.

In raising the question of transcendence, the inquiry brings itself face to face with the central problem of how being as the *transcendens* can be disclosed by the transcending here-being. The problem has been brought to the foreground by the *modification* of the implicit, everyday understanding of being into the theoretical understanding of being as substantial reality and its explicit articulation in a predesigned plan of nature.

Whether explicit or implicit, an understanding of being, and therefore a transcendence of here-being must already underlie the discovery of beings, whether in the mode of a circumspect care-taking or of a theoretical observation. Heidegger explicitly identifies transcendence with being-in-the-world, as we now know from *Vom Wesen des Grundes* (WG, 37ff., W, 53ff., G9, 156ff., P, 121ff.). On the ground of this fundamental structure, the factical here-being transcends beings as such and as a whole, among them first and foremost his own thrown self. This transcendence, however, is ultimately made possible by the primordial transcendental (ecstatic) structure of here-being as temporality. In the ecstatic removal of here-being to itself, in its coming-to- and back-to-itself here-being transcends itself to its own possibility and its own having been. It is from this primordial self-transcendence that the ecstatic removal *to* a vis-à-vis springs. In forming the horizon of a face-to-faceness with itself, here-being in advance transcends the beings as such that can show their presence within that horizon.This brings the inquiry back to the problem of world, its temporal constitution and transcendence.

(c) The Temporal Problem of the Transcendence of the World

The question to be raised now is different from the one asked and answered in Division One (chap. 3). There it was the worldishness of world, its ontological structure, that was to be laid bare. This was found to lie in *significance,* which constitutes the coherent unity of world. A *significant* coherence might be called the "essence" of world, were the word *essence* not so misleading in its usual meaning of the whatness or the inner possibility of beings. The world is not a concrete being, nor the totality beings, but rather the significant way in which they bear on each other and on here-being's existence as a whole. To call this the "essence" of world would therefore be misleading. But the predicament into which Heidegger's present question puts us is even worse, for now he asks in what way world must *be,* how its "being" is ontologically possible. The "being" of world obviously cannot mean *existentia,* "reality," or by whatever name we call the actual thereness of beings.

The cardinal point to be noted is that the "being" of world is not a problem about a world "in and by itself," as though the world were the all of substantial beings that can be there in and by themselves. The question of how these substantial beings were there and what real connections there are between them before and without a disclosure of being, is not a question for a fundamental ontology. This takes its departure from the "ontological difference," the basic "fact" that from this differentiation beings show themselves as the beings they are only in the light of being and, conversely, being shows itself (in a totally different way) as the being *of* beings. Since world "is" only as an irreducible and unique character of being, and since being only "is" in its disclosedness in a factical here-being (Da-sein), the possibility of the being of world can lie only in its *unity* with here-being as a being-in-the-world.

A minor, but not quite negligible point to be noted is that Heidegger now takes the "for-the-sake-of-which" into the unity of "significance," whereas in Division One he spoke of "the for-the-sake-of-which *and* of significance" (SZ, 143, emphasis added). This gave rise to the misleading impression that the everyday world was, after all, the utensil-world.

Here-being's understanding of *himself in connection with* other beings, that is, in a world, is an existential constituent of care. Only when and as long as beings of the character of here-being "are here," is a world "here" also. Heidegger does not merely say that here-being "has" a world, that the world is his world. He says more than that; namely, that in existing, here-being *is* his world, that is, it is disclosed in and with his existence. The solipsist, on the other hand, believes that the world is "his world" in the sense that all the other beings he experiences exist only in his consciousness, only as his representations or perceptions (*Vorstellungen*). Heidegger's interpretation of world as an ontological character of here-being exposes not only the fallaciousness of this reasoning, but also that it has arisen from a thoroughgoing confusion of being with beings. *Reality* is confused with the *real things*, their real connections and properties. The whole of reality is identified with the totality of real beings, and this is what is usually called "the world." Reality, however, is a mode of being which only "is" in its disclosedness. When this disclosure no longer happens, when, for instance, through a catastrophe beings like ourselves no longer factually exist, then there will be no "reality." But this does not in the least mean that *real beings*—the earth, the seas, the stars—will suddenly dissolve into nothing. It means only that they would no longer be manifest as the beings they are, they would be neither discovered nor hidden (SZ, 212), and would, in *that* sense, remain beingless and nameless, for only as long as there is disclosure and discovery (truth), can beings be called by a name.

The disclosedness of the "here," as the preceding analyses of this chapter have shown in detail, is grounded in temporality. This must also make possible the significance which is the ontological structure of world.

> *The existential and temporal condition of the possibility of world lies in the fact that temporality, as an ecstatic unity, has something like a horizon.* The ecstases are not simply raptures toward. . . . Rather, a "whereto" of raptness belongs to the ecstasy. We call this whereto of the ecstasy the horizonal schema. (SZ, 365)

The "horizon of temporality" that has been anticipatingly mentioned in the previous subsection now moves into the center of the investigation. The "whereto" of the ecstasis is the horizon formed in the rapture or removal itself; it is the limit in which the removal ends itself. This pure existential-temporal horizon, however, is not an undifferentiated uniformity, not a mere characterless boundary, but is defined by the "horizonal schema."

> The ecstatical horizon is different in each of the three ecstases. The schema in which Da-sein comes back to itself *futurally*, whether authentically or inauthentically, is the *for-the-sake-of-itself*. We call the schema in which Da-sein is disclosed to itself in attunement as thrown, *that in the face of which* it has been thrown and that to which it has been delivered over. It characterizes the horizonal structure of the *having-been*. Existing for the sake of itself in being delivered over to itself as thrown, Da-sein is at the same time making present as being together with. . . . That horizonal schema of the present is defined by the *in-order-to*. (SZ, 365)

The horizonal schemata thus turn out to be, somewhat surprisingly, nothing but the already familiar references that articulate the significance of world. Among them, only the schema of the having-been needs further clarification. Heidegger speaks of the *Wovor der Geworfenheit*. The preposition "vor" has many meanings, predominant among which is "before"—already in itself a polyvalent expression. We have to recur, therefore, to the most significant ways in which Heidegger uses the *Wovor*. One of those is the *Wovor der Angst*—that in the face of which, or of which, we are in dread. This "whereof of dread," however, is disclosed by dread itself, which brings us nakedly before (face to face with) our already-being-here as *not* originated by ourselves; that is, as an accomplished fact elementally revealed from a nothing of ourselves. Heidegger's *Wovor*, it may seem, is a complexly jointed unity, which can be only approximately expressed by the "whereof." The "whereto" (*Woran*), the "to which it has been delivered over," is also complex, since the self *to* which thrownness delivers the factical here-being is disclosed *in connection with* . . . ; that is, the deliveredness to the thrown self is in itself deliveredness to a world.

Since Heidegger's own explicit and final explanation of the concept of "schema" has been deferred to Division Three and so remains inaccessible to us, it is important to note the precise terms in which Heidegger speaks of it here. In connection with the "whereof" and "whereto" he says: "Es kennzeichnet die horizontale Struktur der Gewesenheit." "Kennzeichnen" means to make something distinctively knowable by a mark or a sign. The having-been to which here-being removes itself is made distinctively knowable by its characteristic schema. On the other hand, the schema of presenting is formulated in a very misleading way: "Das horizontale Schema der Gegenwart wird bestimmt durch das Um-zu." This seems to suggest that first there was a horizonal schema, which is then defined by the "for"; whereas, the meaning is surely that the horizon of presenting is schematically defined by the "for."

From all this it emerges that the function of the schema is to give a distinctive and unifying character to the horizon to which the three differently directed ecstases remove themselves. The thus differentiated and defined horizon, however, belongs to the unity of the whole temporality. It

> determines *whereupon* the being factically existing is esentially *disclosed*. With factical Da-sein, a potentiality-of-being is always projected in the horizon of the future, "already being" is disclosed in the horizon of the having-been, and what is taken care of is discovered in the horizon of the present. (SZ, 365)

This paragraph, we notice, does not speak of the horizonal *schema*, but of the horizon itself. What becomes understandable from it is the being of beings, in the mode of future-being, past-being, and present-being. Now the question that usually arises with regard to a "limit" is that it already implies another "side" from which alone it can be understood as a limit at all. Heidegger's answer to this question, as we have seen before, is not fully worked out, but we can infer it in the main both from passages in *Being and Time* and in "What Is Metaphysics?" Accordingly, it is the confrontation with the nothing, both in the sense of the "other" to beings (not-beings) and of the "other" to being (not-being) which makes manifest to the factical here-being the impossibility of any further coming-to-himself beyond the impassable limit of death, and of coming-back-to-himself as having-been-here *before* his thrownness. The temporality of here-being must end itself in a horizon of its removals to . . . because the manifestness of the nothing in advance *closes* them and so gives the factical existence a constant limit which, as the original "image" of a "standing something," makes the being of beings (the standingness of something) first of all "apprehensible."

Even if these inferences from what Heidegger explicitly says should prove to be untenable, or could be improved upon by further attempts to work out the details left unfinished in *Being and Time*, it is at any rate clear that Heidegger's existential-temporal analysis of here-being goes radically beyond the solutions offered in, say, Kant's *Critique of Pure Reason*. Kant's attempt to "lay the ground of metaphysics" was concretely carried out by an analysis of "our inner nature." So it resulted that our "highest faculty," "pure reason," could not be further explained by Kant. It is the "nature" of pure reason to bring the concepts of pure understanding to completeness, to conclude a series of conditions by seeking, for instance, an absolute beginning of the world. Heidegger, on the other hand, shows that all understanding, both the originally disclosing and the explaining, inferring, and "concluding" that may be derived from it, is grounded in the finiteness of temporality, which in advance "concludes" the ecstatic forethrow of existence, bringing being to a "stand" by the disclosed possibility of not-being, and it is from this horizon formed by the "other" to being that being itself becomes in the first place fully understandable.

It may be easily seen that the horizonal character of a finite temporality can also explain—and explain perhaps for the first time in a satisfactory way—how we can experience ourselves together with other beings in the *wholeness* of a world. As long as the world is conceived as a *totality of beings*—whether these beings are interpreted as things or facts, makes no difference—it remains a mystery how we can experience such a totality. Kant held that the idea of the totality of world, although a necessary idea, lay beyond a possible experience, meaning by "experience" the empirical intuition of "what is," that is, of the substantial things of nature, unified by the a priori synthesis of the categories with the pure intuition of time and space. Heidegger also maintains that the totality of beings can never be grasped by us, but at the same time explains why we nonetheless experience these beings in the whole of a world: the prior disclosure of the nothing in advance gathers all beings *into a whole* by making them manifest as *not nothing*, as things that are. But since the "nothing" does not "exist" at all, it can reveal itself only to concrete beings like ourselves as a *negating*, as a denying or withdrawing: it denies us to ourselves as our own ground and withdraws from us the possibility of being-here-anymore. Hence the disclosure of being that happens with the disclosure of nothing cannot be an indifferent happening, but is a *throw* which hands us out to our factual selves and directs us to the *beings* upon which we are dependent. Heidegger thus succeeds in giving an explanation not only of how we can experience the world as a whole, but why this world-horizon must refer us to the beings discoverable within it. It may be added that Heidegger's explanation has a compellingness which Kant's arguments about the applicability of the categories solely to the a priori forms of intuition, and mediately to a possible empirical intuition of objects, never achieve.

Since the world is grounded in the horizon of an ecstatic temporality, it must necessarily be "transcendent"; that is, it must be "further out" than any beings that can be discovered within it. Heidegger's elucidations of the "transcendence of world" will bring strikingly into view a characteristic of his thinking: it always seems to start, so to speak, from the outmost circumference and work inward; whereas, our usual thinking works in exactly the opposite way. For instance, we are apt to think of the past as stretching out behind us from our "here and now," and the future as stretching out in front of us from "here and now." Similarly, we envisage space as radiating out in all directions, with ourselves as a center. Heidegger, on the contrary, starts from the furthest distance and comes back to the "here and now." So, for instance, he finds the first constituent of an existential spaceishness in "un-distancing" (*Ent-fernung*), a diminishing of distance. This peculiarity of Heidegger's thought has been noted already, but it is only now, with the exposition of the ecstatic horizon of temporality, that its full force can strike us:

> Temporality already holds itself ecstatically in the horizons of its ecstasies and, temporalizing itself, comes back to the beings encountered in the There. (SZ, 366)

> factical Da-sein, ecstatically understanding itself and its world in the unity of the There, comes back from these horizons to the beings encountered in them. Coming back to these beings understandingly is the existential meaning of a letting them be encountered in making them present; for this reason they are called innerworldly. (SZ, 366)

Both of these passages evidently say the same thing, the only difference being that in the first Heidegger is thinking purely of the structure of temporality, while in the second he thinks of the factical here-being as temporality become existent. Incidentally, the language of the first passage comes dangerously near to suggesting that temporality is something existing in and by itself, a possibility that Heidegger has decisively ruled out and any suggestion of which must be strenuously resisted. What Heidegger's language reveals is rather the concrete way in which he "sees" those phenomenal structures which to us only too often remain vague abstractions.

The main point of our passages is the *constancy* of the ecstatic removals to a corresponding horizon. Temporality "holds itself . . . in the horizons of its ecstasies. . . ." It constantly *stands out* beyond itself and *stays* in its distant horizons. All movement originates from and takes place within them, as the *throw forward* from thrownness to the impassable possibility of not-being-here and the *throw back* from the impassable not-being-here to the factical self, already on the "look out" for a possible vis-à-vis. The horizon of the present temporalizes itself cooriginally with those of the future and the having-been. As an anticipating removal to a wholly insubstantial "something" facing the presenting here-being, the horizon of presentness is necessarily "further out" than any beings whose bodily presence becomes discoverable and understandable from and within it.

According to Heidegger, then, our knowledge of beings does not start from an immediate perception of them "here and now," but rather the area of openness in which we move must be much wider than the pin-point of "here and now."[9] It is only in *coming back from* the distance opened up primarily by an ecstatic temporality that a concrete being can meet us "in the There"—or "in the Here," as we prefer to say in discussing Division Two. (See above, our section entitled "The Language of Division Two.")

But perhaps we should also prefer to say "*into* the Here," for Heidegger's words are "in das Da begegnende Seiende." Compare his phrase "in die Zeit begegnen" in the later discussion of "world-time." The use of the accusative suggests that Heidegger really intends to say "into" and not "in." This is his way of expressing that the "here" and the "now" are not self-subsistent media *in* which our encounters with other beings take place, but are "here" only with the disclosed hereness of being. Only when and as long as a world is opened up with a factically existing being-in-the-world can beings enter into its openness and reveal themselves as the beings they are. That these beings become discoverable within the world is, of course, in no way in the power of here-being. They must in some way be "there" of themselves, otherwise we could not discover them.

With the ecstatic-horizonal unity of temporality, the problem of the transcendence of world has been satisfactorily solved. Since the world is grounded in the schematically defined horizon of the whole temporality, it is necessarily transcendent: it is always "further out" than any "objects" can possibly be. But, it may be asked, does Heidegger not interpret the world entirely subjectively? Indeed, Heidegger says that "if the 'subject' is conceived ontologically as existing Da-sein, whose being is grounded in temporality, we must say then that the world is 'subjective.' But this 'subjective' world, as one that is temporally transcendent, is then more 'objective' than any possible 'object'" (SZ, 366).

A hurried reading of this passage could easily mislead the reader into thinking that Heidegger is, after all, slipping back into the much-maligned subject-object relation. But, in fact, Heidegger is doing the opposite. He is restating once more that the first requisite for a fundamental ontology is to overcome the conception of man's essence as subjectivity. Not only is the subjectivity of the subject a wholly inadequate foundation on which to answer the questions, How is a disclosing understanding of being at all possible to a finite existence? and, What does being mean? It only too readily gives rise to the impression that the self-glorifying subject, solely by his own power, imposes his own law and order on an objective nature ("world") which he has not created, which he can never master, and on which he himself is dependent. The existential-temporal interpretation of a finite here-being, on the other hand, in advance conceives Da-sein as belonging to a disclosure (truth) of being which is not of his own making, but into which he has been "thrown." It is its "power" that confers on Da-sein the unique task of discovering beings and so bringing them into the truth that is appropriate to their specific ways of being. The horizonal schema, Heidegger claims, which defines the being of things within the world by a "for," and reveals their referredness to a for-the-sake-of-itself, is not an arbitrary "network of forms that is imposed upon some material by a worldless subject," but rather here-being's original understanding of himself *and* his world in the ecstatic-horizonal unity of his "here." The coming-back-from these horizons to the concrete beings discoverable within them, and understanding them in their "significant" bearings on a finite existence, reveals the connection between Da-sein and things far more elementally than a theoretical observation of mere substantial objects can ever do.

Before we leave the fascinating subject of Heidegger's conception of world, we must briefly recur to the concept of "schema," which first became thematic in the previous subsection. What Heidegger discussed there under the title of "schema" seemed to be only tenuously, if at all, connected with Kant's schematized categories. The exposition of the "horizonal schema," however, puts the whole matter into a different light. We can now see that the theme of Heidegger's previous discussion (the "if-then" and the "as") was only the schema of *interpretation*, and therefore not at all on a par with Kant's transcendental schema. The latter can be compared only with Heidegger's horizonal schema, for this belongs to the original existential understanding of being, and defines the being (makes it "apprehensible") that is disclosed in the ecstatic horizon of temporality. However, when we try to compare them we are struck by the differences rather than by any resemblance. In the first place, Heidegger gives us only three schemata. (It is doubtful whether the "whereto," the schema of facticity, could be counted as a fourth.) Kant's transcendental schema, on the other hand, "sensifies" the categories, of which there are four groups, each subdivided into three concepts that Kant regards as indispensable. But the greatest contrast is that two of Heidegger's three schemata define here-being's ecstatic removal to himself—that is, are existential schemata—and only the "for" defines the being of within-worldish beings, so that it alone can be called a "categorial schema" at all. Kant's schematized categories, on the other hand, all define being as *substantial reality*. This, however, is the mode of being of things as mere substances. The task would be to see whether the for-whatness of handy things could be so modified into the mere-whatness of substantial things as to yield all the categories Kant regarded as primordial concepts, and whether the schematization of these categories into the pure image of time could be really adequately explained from the derivative concepts of time as a pure succession of nows.

It is very likely that Heidegger intended to carry out this task in the first division of Part II of *Being and Time*. It would undoubtedly have thrown a light into the "obscurity" of Kant 's teaching of schematism, and especially, perhaps, upon the much-debated and highly doubtful source and origin of the Kantian categories. Unfortunately, the whole of Part II of *Being and Time* remains unwritten in the way it was originally planned, because it required Division Three of Part l as its indispensable basis.

3. THE TEMPORALITY OF THE ROOMINESS CHARACTERISTIC OF HERE-BEING

Heidegger gives an entire section to his present theme, instead of integrating it into the series of expositions which have dealt with the temporality of being-in-the-world. Since space was shown in Division One to be discoverable only within the world and to be constitutive of it, it is surprising that Heidegger should now single it out for a separate discussion. His reason for doing so is suggested rather than explicitly stated at the beginning of the present section. It would appear that the roominess constitutive of being-in-the-world is so fundamental that it might have to be coordinated with temporality. Must "time and space" be set side by side as of equal rank, or does the "original time" of care retain its priority as the existential foundation for all ways of existing?

While there can be little doubt at this stage that temporality "encompasses" (*umgreift*) all possible spatial relations, an important qualification must be added. Heidegger emphasizes that space cannot be dissolved into time or deduced from it. Whether he has in view an oblique criticism of Hegel's attempt to deduce all categories from each other is not certain, but at any rate, Heidegger's own position is clear: space is an irreducible phenomenon that cannot be deduced from or explained by anything other than itself. This is perfectly compatible with a certain precedence of temporality, but a sounder explanation must be demanded than that given by Kant for the preeminence of time before space. In Kant's thought the representations of objects in space are regarded as psychical occurrences that take place in time, and therefore the "physical" is in an indirect way also "in time." This purely ontic (empirical) explanation is rejected by Heidegger on the ground that it is completely inadequate to explain the relation between space and time as a priori forms of intuition. If a properly ontological reason can be given at all for the universality of time, then it must show that "although space and time as pure intuitions both belong 'to the subject,' time dwells more originally in the subject than space. But then the time limited to what is immediately given in the inner sense is at the same time ontologically more universal only if the subjectivity of the subject consists in an openness to beings" (KPM, 52, G3, 50, KPM(E), 33).

Now Heidegger does not make idle demands on Kant without being confident that he himself can satisfy them. The existential-ontological reason for the preeminence of time has in fact been amply demonstrated in the preceding chapters. Not only does temporality constitute the being of a finite self, but it originally opens up the removedness (distance) of this self to itself and to other beings. In a general way, we can already see that this "distance" must be the condition of the possibility of any "spatial" bringing-near (undistancing) of things to the factical here-being. The task of the present section is to show the specific way in which the temporality of an everyday being-in-the-world makes the discovery of the significant within-worldish space and place possible.

Heidegger begins his exposition, as usual, with a short summary of what has already been established in Division One. He reminds us that "Da-sein can be spatial only as care, in the sense of a factically entangled existing" (SZ, 367). Beings like ourselves are not "in space" like a thing that fills out a part of space, "so that the boundaries dividing it from the surrounding space would themselves just define that space spatially" (SZ, 368). Here-being literally "occupies space," where "occupying" must be understood in the pregnant sense in which we say that troops occupy a town. Without any conquest of "outer space," here-being has already existentially "conquered" space for himself by opening up a "Spielraum," a room for movement and action as a self-allocated area for his care-taking comings and goings among things. It is from this self-allocated space that here-being comes back to the "place" which he already keeps occupied. It is no argument against the existential interpretation to say that we *can* determine the size and location of a human being in just the same way as we can of a thing, because to do so we have to reduce him to the ontological status of a material body, which is a glaring anomaly. Here-being is incomparably "roomier" than any material body can possibly be, just because his spatial limits are not the limits of his own body, but the nearer or farther distances which he has allocated to himself as his existential room for movement. This is why Heidegger decisively rejects the often-held view that here-being's roominess (spatiality) is the fatal result of "binding a spirit to a body." On the contrary, "Da-sein is 'spiritual,' *and only because it is spiritual*, it can be spatial in a way that essentially remains impossible for an extended corporeal thing" (SZ, 368).

The opening up of an existential space is constituted by the irreducible constitutive moments of directing (orientating) and undistancing (diminishing distance, bringing-near). Further, the discovery of region (*Gegend*) as the "whereto of the possible belonging somewhere of useful things at hand in the surrounding world" is essential to the roominess of a care-taking being-in-the-world. The discovery of locality is ontologically prior to any actual arranging and directing things to their place, determining *where* they are *to go*. For instance, in choosing a building site for a house, we must already understand a where to which something can belong, otherwise we could never fix on a particular site where a particular house is to go. In the everyday world, locality has an essential bearing on the relevance-whole of handy things. "The relevant relations are intelligible only in the horizon of a disclosed world. Their horizonal nature also first makes possible the specific horizon of the whereto of regional belonging" (SZ, 368). In other words, the horizon-forming structure of ecstatic temporality already underlies the discovery of within-worldish space, and the horizonal schema in advance defines the significance-character of the thus discovered space. Now Heidegger goes on to show more specifically that it is the temporality of circumspect care-taking that is the foundation of the roominess of everyday here-being.

> The self-directive discovering of a region is grounded in an ecstatically retentive awaiting of the possible hither and whither. As a directed awaiting of region, making room is equiprimordially a bringing-near (or de-distancing) of things at hand and objectively present. De-distancing, taking care comes back out of the previously discovered region to what is nearest. Bringing-near and the estimating and measurement of distances within what is objectively present within the de-distanced world are grounded in a making-present that belongs to the unity of temporality in which directionality is possible, too. (SZ, 368–69)

An awaiting-retaining making present was previously shown to be the specific temporal unity of a circumspect taking care of things. It is not clear whether this is the specific "unity of temporality" to which

Heidegger refers above, or whether he has some possible modification of it in mind. A retaining awaiting certainly seems to have a primary constitutive function for the discovery of region, from which the presenting undistancing (bringing-near) of something *comes back* to the here. On the other hand, the succeeding passage indicates that the presenting can gain *predominance* in a falling bringing-near of things.

> In the bringing-close that makes the handling and being occupied that is "absorbed in the matter," the essential structure of care—falling prey—makes itself known. Its existential and temporal constitution is distinguished by the fact that in falling prey, and thus also in the bringing near which is founded in "making present," the forgetting that awaits pursues the present. In the making present that brings something near from its wherefrom, making present loses itself in itself, and forgets the over there. For this reason if the "observation" of innerwordly beings starts in such a making present, the illusion arises that "initially" only a thing is objectively present, here indeed, but indeterminately, in a space in general. (SZ, 369)

This passage suggests that even the everyday discovery of space can be modified with the corresponding modifications of the temporality of care. It is not the explanation of such possible modifications, however, that seems to be Heidegger's main concern, but the demonstration why the ecstatic-temporal constitution of space is easily overlooked or forgotten. The self-constricted presenting of a falling being-in-the-world, from which the observation and contemplation of things usually starts, is the reason for this.

From this situation Heidegger proceeds to draw another highly interesting conclusion. It is well known that here-being's self-interpretations and language in general are far-reachingly dominated by spatial imagery and conceptions. According to Heidegger:

> The priority of the spatial in the articulation of significations and concepts has its ground, not in some specific power of space, but rather in the kind of being of Da-sein. Essentially entangled, temporality loses itself in making present, and understands itself not only circumspectly in terms of the things at hand taken care of, but from those spatial relations that making present constantly meets up with in what is at hand as present, it takes its guidelines for articulating what is understood and can be interpreted in understanding in general. (SZ, 369)

Even in the prevalence of spatial imagery in language, Heidegger finds a document not of the "power" of space, but of the power of time. Time as the ecstatic-horizonal unity of the three ecstases indeed dwells in the subject more originally than space, for the "subject" is the factical here-being who is temporality become existent; whereas, only on the ground of this temporality can here-being "break into space," "occupy space." Heidegger has not only demonstrated the existential-ontological priority of "original time," but from his interpretation of space a sudden light is thrown back onto the structure of temporality. If we reflect, for instance, how an experience of *movement in space* is possible, we find that unless we could *await* the whither to which the movement proceeds and *retain* the where from which the movement proceeds, we could not experience spatial movement at all. A presenting alone would certainly not be sufficient, because if we could experience something only "here and now," without *simultaneously* awaiting its whither and retaining its wherefrom, we could never know that it is moving. Heidegger's difficult and even seemingly paradoxical doctrine that the "future-present-past" of the temporality of care do not occur in succession, but are "simultaneous," thus receives fresh illumination. It might be argued, of course, that in order to see something actually move, we must see the change of its position relative to other things; that is, the whither and the wherefrom cannot be a mere emptiness, but must be marked by something other than the moving thing. This argument in no way destroys Heidegger's thesis that temporality temporalizes itself in the unity of its three ecstases. If our seeing were purely and solely a presenting, so that we could perceive things only "here and now," we could never judge that they had changed their relative positions, and an experience of movement would still be impossible.

The present section brings the long chapter "Temporality and Everydayness" almost to an end. It is followed by only one more section, which deals with the temporal meaning of everydayness. The discussion of this topic is condensed into only two pages, but their importance is out of proportion to their brevity, for reasons that will emerge in the course of examining their content. A summary of the principal results of this chapter will be given by setting out the various modifications of temporality in table 13.4.

TABLE 13.4
The Temporality of Care
Its General Structure: Having-Been Making-Present Coming-to-Itself

Inauthentic	*The Temporality*	*Authentic*
forgetfully presenting awaiting	of understanding	recollecting (or retrieving or recapitulating)-instant anticipatory running-forward

(continued on next page)

TABLE 13.4 *(continued)*

Inauthentic	The Temporality	Authentic
fear awaiting-presenting forgetting	of attunement	dread bringing before a possible forward- running-instant recollectability (or retrieval or recapitulation)
curiosity awaiting-forgetting (running-after, running-away)- making present	of falling	—
	of discourse no specific primary ecstasis	
circumspect taking care awaiting-retaining making present	of being-in-the-world	

possible modifications:
(i) an "arrested" awaiting-retaining making present
(ii) awaiting-retaining not-making-present
(iii) unawaiting-retaining making-present
(iv) awaiting-unretaining making-present

Theoretical thematization:
a preeminent awaiting-
retaining making present

of world
horizon of the ecstatic unity of
future, having-been, present

Horizontal schema:
future: for-the-sake-of-itself
having-been: whereof of thrownness
present: for

of space
ecstatic retaining-awaiting (of possible thither and
hither)
making present (undistancing)

4. THE TEMPORAL MEANING OF THE EVERYDAYNESS OF HERE-BEING

Although the everydayness of being-in-the-world was the central theme of Division One, and although it remained the basis from which the interpretation of authentic existence took off in Division Two, we are still far from having grasped this phenomenon ontologically. Moreover, as Heidegger points out, "It even remains questionable whether the explication of temporality carried out up to now is adequate to explain the existential meaning of everydayness" (SZ, 370).

This unobtrusive remark gives us the first hint that the inquiry is about to take an important step that will lead into a new dimension of temporality constitutive of the *historical* character of here-being (*Geschichtlichkeit*). This dimension of temporality has so far been left out of account, or more precisely, it has been lying latent in the previous analyses, for it will turn out later that everydayness itself is the inauthentic way in which here-being is *historical*. That is why the problem of historicity is forced to the surface precisely by the obscurity of everydayness as an existential phenomenon. Its obscurity is itself strange, because nothing could be more familiar to us than the way we exist "each day." On the other hand, the meaning of "each day" is not transparent. This cannot mean simply the *sum* of all the days in our lifetime, but yet the phrase does carry a suggestion of ticking days off on a calendar. The primary meaning of everydayness, however,

> is a certain *How* of existence that prevails in Da-sein "as long as it lives." In our earlier analyses we often used the expression "initially and for the most part." "Initially" means the way in which Da-sein is "manifest" in the being-with-one-another of publicness, even if it has "basically" precisely "overcome" everydayness existentielly. "For the most part" signifies the way in which Da-sein shows itself for everyone "as a rule," but not always. (SZ, 370)

The last two sentences explain not only the expressions Heidegger mentions, but, at the same time, what he means by calling everydayness the *indifferent* and *average* way of existing. In what way does here-being "manifest" itself in the first place? It "manifests" itself, Heidegger says ironically, in a public being-together-with that covers over the singleness of a finite self, levels it down to the uniformity of "what one does," so that everyone becomes interchangeable with and replaceable by every other one.

This way of being-here is "indifferent," insofar as one is not differentiated from any other one. The inauthentic and authentic self appears equally as one, even if the latter has just "overcome" everydayness. The "overcome" has again an ironical tone. Heidegger may be thinking of an all too facile assumption that everydayness can be once and for all "overcome," when in fact it is so deeply embedded in care that it can never be wholly eliminated.

In the first place, that is, in the publicity of the everyday world, unique existence appears as an indifferent "one." This is at the same time the *average* way in which here-being is manifest to everyman. The average is not what is always and necessarily so, but what is so "for the most part," "usually," "as a rule." What begins to appear with the "usual," the "as a rule," is something like a span or stretch of time, for all usage and habit imply a long period of practice. This becomes explicit in the next paragraph, where Heidegger describes the way (the how) in which here-being "lives unto the day," drifting along from day to day, whether in all respects or only in those which are prescribed by "them."

> Being comfortable belongs to this How, even if habit forces us to what is burdensome and "repulsive." The tomorrow that everyday taking care waits for is the "eternal yesterday." The monotony of everydayness takes whatever the day happens to bring as a change. Everydayness determines Da-sein even when it has not chosen the they as its "hero." (SZ, 370–71)

The uniformity characteristic of everydayness is well called "monotony," for it reveals itself to the "individual" here-being in the attunement of a "dull untunedness" (*fahle Ungestimmtheit*), in a "lack of tone" that is familiar to all of us. Indeed, all the varied characteristics of everyday existence are *ontically* so well known that they are hardly noticed, but for the *existential-ontological* investigation they harbor "enigma upon enigma." It is the baffling character of everydayness that reveals the insufficiency of the preceding explanations of temporality. They have brought here-being to a standstill in a certain situation—that is, they have analyzed only the *structure* of temporality itself, while completely disregarding that here-being *stretches itself* "temporally" in the succession of its days. "The monotony, the habit, the 'like yesterday, so today and tomorrow,' and the 'for the most part,' cannot be grasped without recourse to the 'temporal' stretching along of Da-sein" (SZ, 371).

These sentences announce the principal theme—namely, the stretchedness of here-being through time—of the next chapter, but without mentioning that this is basically the problem of historicity. It seems at first sight to have little to do with what we usually mean by history. On second thought, however, a connection begins to emerge. When we ask someone, for instance, to tell us his friend's history, we are in fact asking about what Heidegger calls the stretchedness of here-being through his days, about the events which have happened in the course of them, not as disconnected episodes, but in the meaningful unity and coherence of a single "fate" or "destiny." There is, therefore, at least a rough connection between the popular sense of "someone's history" and the existential concept of it, although the two are by no means identical, and the latter will turn out to include the history of the "past," which is the primary meaning we usually attach to the word.

The first hint of the problem of historicity already raises the problem of the "time" through which here-being stretches itself. This is the time which here-being counts upon and takes account of, which "accounting" is astronomically regulated and published in calendars. The everyday "happening" of here-being and his care-taking counting with time must be drawn into the interpretation of temporality before the ontological meaning of everydayness can be made even a problem. Division Two aims at a full working out of the problem, but the adequate conceptual definition of everydayness, Heidegger announces in the by now familiar formula, "can succeed only in the framework of a fundamental discussion of the meaning of being in general and its possible variations" (SZ, 371–72).

The importance of the present short section is easily overlooked, because the preparatory steps it takes toward the existential problem of history remain implicit, while in following up the complex thought of the next chapter the reader may fail to connect it up in retrospect with what has already been said here. That is why in this interpretation I have made quite explicit what Heidegger only hints at.

An important, perhaps the most important, implication of this section still remains to be mentioned. The time through which here-being stretches itself, as we have heard, is the time that is regulated by astronomical measurements and is kept count of by calendars. But this is also the time *in* which within-worldish beings arise, have a duration and pass away, and *in* which all kinds of events within the world take place. How this world-time belongs to and springs from the original time of care will be elucidated in detail in the last chapter of Division Two. What interests us now is that here-being himself must necessarily enter into the time which determines the in-timeness (*Innerzeitigkeit*) of within-worldish beings and which originates in his own temporality. His own being-in-time essentially belongs to the factical here-being, in contrast to his being-in-space like a within-worldish thing, which Heidegger rejected as inappropriate. To put the point in another way: while it is perfectly well possible for us to conceive our "spatial properties" as though we were merely extended bodies in space, and for certain purposes it may even be extremely useful to do so (for instance, in being measured for clothes), this is in no way an *essential* constituent of our being-here. Heidegger is therefore justified in pointing out its *ontological* inappropriateness and in dismissing it in a sentence. But our being-in-time along with things within the world, if not in the same, at least in an analogous way, is *essentially* constitutive of our being-here, and far from being able to dismiss it, the temporal analysis must make it its task to inquire into this being-in-time. Once more, it seems, the predominance of time over space asserts itself. It is not only that time dwells in the subject more originally than space, but it would appear that the factical here-being as temporality becomes existent, dwells in time, more originally than in space.

The fact that Heidegger devotes a long discussion to our "being-in-time" once more testifies to the predominance of time over space. For undoubtedly we can regard ourselves as "being-in-space" just like other bodies—as when we get measured for a suit of clothes or when we determine our position in relation to something else, we treat ourselves as purely extended things—but the problems arising from this are not dealt with by Heidegger in any detail. This does not mean that he considers our embodiment in space as a negligible accident, but only that the specific problems connected with it need not be discussed in a fundamental ontology (SZ, 108). The problem of history, on the other hand, pinpoints that the "public time," in which we exist and in which historical events as well as the processes of nature take place, is central to a fundamental ontology. It would appear therefore not only that "time dwells in the subject more originally than space," but that the "subject," as a factually existing being-in-the-world, dwells more originally in time than in space.

XIV

Temporality and Historicity

The introductory section to this chapter defines the problems that have arisen from the incompleteness of the preceding interpretation of here-being. The elucidation of the whole of here-being is the necessary precondition for explaining how an understanding of being is at all possible and for interpreting the meaning of the thus understood being. The problem of how here-being can be a whole was raised in chapter 1 of Division Two, but the solution has so far been exclusively gained from the end in death that closes the possibility of a factical existence. The other "end," the beginning in birth, has been neglected, so that in spite of a genuine explanation of an authentic and inauthentic being unto death the analysis has only onesidedly considered here-being, as it exists "forward," advancing to its impassable possibility. This onesidedness must now be corrected. Further and most importantly, here-being stretches itself out between its beginning in birth and its end in death; surely it is this stretch or span of a life that constitutes the whole of here-being, and this is just what has so far been overlooked. The coherence or connection of a life (*Lebenszusammenhang*), that is, its unity and continuity, the "standing and staying" of a self in constant change and movement, are the problems that now come to the forefront of the inquiry. The solution of these problems must explain how a factical here-being can have its own history as well as take root in and stabilize itself (ground itself) in its historical heritage taken over from other existences.

In the fifth paragraph of § 72 Heidegger discusses the views on the coherence or connection of life that were current before and at the time of writing of *Being and Time*.[1] According to them, the coherence of life between birth and death is supposed to consist of a succession of experiences (*Erlebnisse*) in time. The peculiarity of this explanation, Heidegger says, is that only the experience in the "present now" is "real," while those nows that are past or are still to come are no longer or not yet "real."

> Da-sein traverses the time-span allotted to it between the two boundaries in such a way that it is "real" only in the now and hops, so to speak, through the succession of nows of its "time." For this reason one says that Da-sein is "temporal." The self maintains itself in a certain sameness throughout the constant change of experience. (SZ, 373)

A closer examination of Heidegger's account of the current theory reveals a step in his reasoning that at first appears to be logically invalid. For even if he rightly asserts that only each present experience is generally held to be "real," it by no means follows that the experiencing self is also "real" only in each present now. It is precisely by the permanence of a self-same self through changing experiences that the current theory explains the "connection of life." Moreover, it insists on the "insubstantiality" of the self. What justification, if any, does Heidegger's rejection of this theory have? Its justification is that the permanence (*Beharrlichkeit*) of an identical self through a succession of nows is the ontological-temporal character of the reality of a substance, but not of the self-standingness of an existing here-being. Its stretchedness between birth and death cannot be explained by the popular conception of time and the enduringness of a thing in this time, but only from the temporal structure of care. It is not a course and stretch of "life" that is gradually filled up by the "momentary realities" of here-being, but

> Da-sein [. . .] stretches *itself* along in such a way that its own being is constituted beforehand as this stretching along. The "between" of birth and death already lies *in the being* of Da-sein [. . .]. Understood existentially, birth is never something past in the sense of what is no longer objectively present, and death is just as far from being the kind of being of something outstanding that is not yet objectively present but will come. Factical Da-sein exists as born, and, born, it is already dying in the sense of being-toward-death. Both "ends" and their "between" *are* as long as Da-sein factically exists, and they *are* in the sole way possible on the basis of Da-sein as *care*. In the unity of thrownness and the flee-

ing or else anticipatory being-toward-death, birth and death "are connected" in the way appropriate to Da-sein. As care, Da-sein *is* the "Between." (SZ, 374)[2]

The above-mentioned apparently invalid step in Heidegger's argument now turns out to be not illogical but elliptical. Heidegger thinks himself entitled to omit several steps in the argument because he is not telling us anything new: the enduringly self-same presence *in time* that constitutes the identity of a thing has been repeatedly criticized as insufficient to explain the self-standingness (steadfast endurance) of here-being. The latter is grounded in the ecstatic unity of the temporality that determines the whole of care.

> The ontological clarification of the "connectedness of life," that is, of the specific way of stretching along, movement, and persistence of Da-sein, must accordingly be approached in the horizon of the temporal constitution of this being. The movement of existence is not the motion of something objectively present. It is determined from the stretching along of Da-sein. (SZ, 374–75)

The "movement" or "movedness" (*Bewegtheit*) of a "stretched out stretching itself along" is implied already in that early definition Heidegger gives of Da-sein as thrown forethrow. It comes more fully to light in the "owing" character of care, which was expressed in the formula "the not-[or null-]determined ground-being of a negativity." At first sight, it is true, this formula seems to present us with a rigidly static structure, but on closer view it reveals how here-being *stretches itself* from its beginning to its end. The movement of this stretched self-stretching originates in the nothing that negates (denies) each factical self to himself as his own ground, and throws him forward to the nothing of his own possible not-being. But although this forward-stretching of here-being ends itself in the ultimate possibility of not-being-here, this nothing (not-being) does not bring here-being to a standstill, but throws it *back to* its ownmost thrownness. In the movement of this stretching *back to* the not-self-grounded "origin" of here-being its dependence upon other beings, among which it must ground itself, becomes wholly transparent. The moved self-stretching of here-being forward and back was first revealed by the call of care as a "forward-calling recall." The task of the present chapter is to elucidate the full content and structure of the being which discloses itself in that call.

> The specific movement of the *stretched out stretching itself along*, we call the *occurrence* of Da-sein. The question of the "connectedness" of Da-sein

is the ontological problem of its occurrence. To expose the *structure of occurrence* and the existential and temporal conditions of its possibility means to gain an *ontological* understanding of *historicity*. (SZ, 375)

This paragraph prohibits us from taking the "occurrence" or "happening" of here-being for an ontic event, such as the biological birth of a human being. The "occurrence" or "happening" (*Geschehen*) is that movement in which the temporality of care accomplishes itself, that is, brings itself to ripeness, temporalizes itself. The "happening" is not the coming to birth of a here-being, but constitutes the way in which a factically existing being-in-the-world *is here*. The "I am" is never the static presence "here and now" of a thing, but constantly stretches itself forward and back. In this "stretched stretching" lies the steadfast constancy and continuity of the "I," the "self," and not in a lasting presentness from now to now.

But if here-being is that unique way of being that brings *itself to light*, then its "happening" is in itself the happening of the *self-disclosure of being*. This self-disclosure happens in the accomplished temporality of care. Now, as we are about to learn, being discloses itself historically, or, to say the same thing in another way, historicity is an essential character of being. To put the matter in still another way, here-being is essentially historical-being. What the happening (*Geschehen*) of here-being and its historical constitution (*Geschichtlichkeit*) have to do with history (*Geschichte*) as we usually understand the word will be explained in the following sections.

What is important to us to note here is that here-being *can* be historical in two different ways. In his everyday disownment of himself to the world, here-being is inauthentically historical. Heidegger's principal aim, however, is to explain *first* the historicity of a resolutely "owned" existence. This is done in the third section (§ 74) of the present chapter of *Being and Time*. Undoubtedly, this section is the heart of Heidegger's interpretation of historicity, although he discusses also the historical character of everydayness, as well as the popular-ontic concepts of history. The latter indicate the starting points from which a "phenomenological construction" of authentic historicity will have to take off. The ontic concepts of history as a series of happenings "in time" have moreover a certain justification, because the factical here-being is indeed temporal not only in Heidegger's original sense, but also in the popular sense of "being-in-time" (within-timeness). The within-timeness of here-being must be duly considered, all the more so because the processes of nature also take place in the same *time*. Historicity and within-timeness are cooriginally grounded in the temporality of care. The origin of the time *in which* both history *and* the processes of nature take place and by which they are measured will be exhaustively analyzed in his next chapter, chapter 6 of Division Two.

The introductory section to the present chapter ends with a reference to Dilthey, whose researches into the problem of historicity have inspired Heidegger's own inquiries. Heidegger acknowledges his indebtedness in a somewhat startling way: "Basically, the following analysis is solely concerned with furthering the investigations of Dilthey in a preparatory way" (SZ, 377). The word *solely* in this sentence is as exaggerated as it is misleading. In all soberness, we can say that this fifth chapter of Divison Two takes an important step toward the central aim of elucidating the *meaning of being*, and solely by virtue of doing so does it further an assimilation of Dilthey's investigations. This becomes clear from the key passage of the correspondence of Count Yorck von Wartenburg with Dilthey, quoted in the last section of this chapter.[3] In this passage Count Yorck envisages the task of working out "the generic difference between the ontic and the historical" (SZ, 403). "Ontic" and "historical," we must note, are used here in Count Yorck's and not in Heidegger's sense. "Ontic" means the visible and tangible, the substantial, in sharp contrast to the "historical," the spiritual, the self-consciously living. The task outlined by Count Yorck, Heidegger remarks, is the fundamental aim of all "philosophy of life." This aim, however, is not formulated radically enough, as the following key-passage shows.

> How else is historicity to be philosophically grasped and "categorially" conceived in its difference from the ontic than by bringing the "ontic" and the "historiographical" into a *more primordial unity* so that they can be compared and distinguished? But that is possible only if we attain the following insights:
>
> 1. The question of historicity is an *ontological* question about the constitution of historical beings.
> 2. The question of the ontic is the *ontological* question of the being of beings unlike Da-sein, of what is objectively present in the broadest sense.
> 3. The ontic is only *one* area of beings.
>
> The idea of being encompasses the "ontic" and the "historiographical." *This idea* is what must be "generically differentiated." (SZ, 403)

Heidegger's own comments prove that he does not lose sight of the tasks of *Being and Time* even for a moment. It is just by carrying *them* out that his present chapter can prepare the ground for an understanding of Dilthey's aim.

1. The Vulgar Understanding of History and the Occurrence of Here-Being

Even in the popular understanding of history there must be indications of what is originally historical. Heidegger therefore first examines the varied meanings of "history."

An ambiguity in the expression shows itself immediately in the fact that history means the "historical reality" as well as the science of history. The latter meaning, as well as that of a "historical reality" that has already been thematized as the object of scientific research, are for the moment left out of account. Heidegger concentrates solely on the so-called historical reality itself, or more precisely, on the real happenings, changes, destinies, and so forth, which are usually called history. In other words, history is used here in an ontic sense. It is something that is, with a stress on past things and events. The past is understood in a positive and privative way from the present, the today. In a positive way the past still affects and determines the present, or in a privative way it is understood as something gone and no longer effective today, although some pieces that belonged to these earlier times, like a Greek temple or antiquities preserved in a museum, may still be present.

A second meaning of history is not so much the past things and events, but rather the origin or emergence from them. History means the coherence and continuity of a becoming. Something that has a history stands in a causal connection with the past that determines its present and will still have an effect in the future. As a causal nexus of events stretching through the past, present, and future, history does not bear exclusively upon the past.

Thirdly, history can mean the whole of beings that wanders and changes "through time," in contradistinction to nature, which also moves "in time." This juxtaposition is perhaps not so common in English as it is in German. It appears in Count Yorck's concepts of the "ontic" and the "historical." In this meaning, history does not denote the way in which events happen, but rather the region of beings—mankind—which is essentially determined by "spirit" and "culture" in distinction from the things and processes of nature, although the latter also, in a certain way, belong to history. We need only remember, for instance, the natural waterways, the passes, the natural defenses of mountain ranges, the climates, and so on, that have played so large a part in the history strictly understood as the destinies of mankind.

Fourthly, history means what has been handed over and handed down in a tradition; it means the tradition as such, regardless of whether it is "historiographically" recognized as tradition or whether it remains hidden in its origins.

Heidegger now sums up these four meanings of history in the following masterly way:

> If we consider the four meanings together, we find that history is the specific occurrence of existing Da-sein happening in time, in such a way that the occurrence in being-with-one-another that is "past" and at the same time "handed down" and still having its effect is taken to be history in the sense emphasized. (SZ, 379)

No sooner is this popular notion of history formulated than questions and misgivings arise. To be sure, all the various meanings of history are connected by a common reference to Da-sein as the "subject" of historical events. Nonetheless, ontologically it is far from clear how the "happening" of these events is to be defined, and especially how they belong to the history of here-being. Does here-being first become historical through an intertwining with circumstances and incidents that succeed each other in time? Or is there a happening (coming-to-pass) that constitutes the being of here-being, as historical, so that, on the ground of it, circumstances, events, and destinies become ontologically possible? And finally, why does the "past" have such a weight in the popular notion of history? Why is the past the preeminent temporal character of a historical here-being that comes to pass "in time"?

Since the historical character of here-being is to be explained from the temporality of care, the past as the predominantly temporal meaning of the popular notion of history offers a foothold from which the existential explanation of history from the temporality of care can best be approached. Just as in his world-analysis Heidegger starts with the innerworldly utensils, leading up to the world as an existential character of here-being, so now he starts with the "world-historical" utensils and things leading up to what is primarily historical: the factical here-being as a being-in-the-world.

The utensils that Heidegger first gets into focus are those that belong to antiquity and are now preserved in a museum. Why are these utensils historical when they are still substantially present? The suggestion that they are "objects" of a historical interest and knowledge is immediately rejected by Heidegger. These things must in some way be historical in themselves in order to be possible objects of a historical science. With what right are these things called "historical" when they are not yet gone but are still present? Or do they in some way belong to the past although they are still substantially present?

It might be said that the things in a museum are no longer the utensils they once were because they are no longer in use. True, but this does not explain their historical character, for there may be many heirlooms in a household—an old clock, furniture, and the like—which are still in daily use and yet belong to the "past." What is it in them that has "passed"? Nothing less than the *world* within which they were once handily encountered by a here-being and were used by him in his caretaking being-in-the-world. It is the *world* that no longer exists, whereas the utensil that formerly belonged to that world can still be substantially present. But what does the no-longer-being of world mean? There is world only as an existential-ontological constituent of here-being. Strictly speaking, therefore, we should not speak of a "past" world, since Heidegger reserves the word *past* (*vergangen*) for things. We should speak rather of a world that has been (*gewesen*). Similarly, a here-being who no longer exists is not "past," but has-been-here (*dagewesen*). The still present antiquities owe their historical character to their belonging to and descent from the world of here-being who has been here. It is he who is *primarily* historical. *Secondarily* historical are the things in the widest sense—not only utensils but also events and nature in the sense of "historical ground"—which belong to a world, and are called by Heidegger the "world-historical."

With this, however, the problem of historical-being is not yet properly formulated. Indeed, we might be misled into thinking that only the here-being who has-been-here is historical; whereas, Heidegger intends to show that it is precisely the factually existing here-being who is primarily and originally historical. It is in the temporality of his being that the has-been temporalizes itself cooriginally with a making-present-coming. The problem now becomes acute: why should the has- or having-been determine the historical when it belongs to the temporal unity of care as a making-present-coming?

The vulgar ontic notion of history is predominantly drawn from the "world-historical." Although it also understands Da-sein as the primary "subject" of history, it cannot sufficiently distinguish the temporality of the "subject" from the being-in-time of things. Heidegger's positive task now is to show the temporal-ontological conditions on the basis of which the "subjectivity of the subject" is essentially historical.

2. The Essential Constitution of Historicity

The authentic "happening" or "coming-to-pass" (*Geschehen*) of here-being is to be explained from the authentic temporality of care. The latter, as Heidegger reminds us, first came into view from an anticipatory forward-running resoluteness. In this way of existing here-being resolutely brings himself face to face with death as his ownmost, utmost possibility. This impassable limit of his existence turns him back to his own thrownness. In taking over his whole being as his own he is at the same time "instantly" here for his "situation," in which and from which he resolutely grasps the *factical possibilities* he chooses for his own. It is these *factical possibilities* which now give Heidegger a lead into the problem of historicity. The important transitional passage that leads from the first to the second is unfortunately so condensed that the coherence of Heidegger's argument becomes almost invisible. The following exposition will make the steps of the argument much more explicit than they are in *Being and Time* (SZ, 383).

The first step is taken by formulating the hitherto unconsidered question, From where, in principle, can the factical possibilities of existence be drawn? They obviously cannot be derived from the ultimate possibility that closes an existence, especially since the authentic running-forward to it does not mean a contemplative dwelling upon death, but means the resolute coming-back-to the factical "here." Could it be then, Heidegger asks, that the thrownness of the self into a world discloses a horizon from which an existence wrests his factical possibilities?

If it should indeed be our thrownness from which we draw our factical possibilities, then their historical character becomes immediately evident, for the temporal meaning of thrownness is the having-been, the "past." The having-been, in turn, predominantly determines the historical. It is an obvious ontic *fact* that no generation creates its tasks and opportunities from nothing, but inherits them from preceding generations, so that even the new departures from and breaks with tradition are grounded in the "past." Heidegger's problem is to explain how the existential-temporal constitution of care makes this obvious fact possible. How can a factical here-being disclose not only his own having-been in his own world, but go back to other existences who have-been-here before him in *their* world? The coming-back-to himself in his thrownness discloses only the finite having-been of a single existence. Now the problem is how a wider horizon of the having-been can be opened up, a horizon that reaches back behind and before a finite existence, so that a continuity with the past and a handing down of tasks and achievements becomes possible.

No sooner is this problem explicitly formulated than a difficulty becomes evident. As Heidegger has shown earlier, our thrownness is manifest to us from an untransgressable limit that closes our own having-been-already-here as decisively as death closes our possibility of being-here-any-more. The "nothing of myself" is revealed in a negation that becomes explicit in the structure of care as a *not*-determined ground-being of a negativity (Div. Two, chap. 2). Heidegger refers us back to this negation in a single sentence: "Did we not moreover say [at SZ, 284] that Da-sein never gets behind its thrownness?" (SZ, 383). *Never* to come back to myself as my own ground—this is the impotence in which the closedness (finiteness) of my own having-been stares me in the face. The "never" seems to plunge my origins into complete hiddenness. How, then, can that farther horizon of having-been become accessible on the ground of which I exist historically?

Clearly, if the singleness of a finite existence were synonymous with isolation, and if our understanding of being reached no further than our own being, anything like history would be impossible. But the same "not" that reveals my own "that I already am" and delivers me over to my own ability-to-be, at the same time reveals the being of other beings and refers me to them in my impotence to be my own ground, that is, it throws me into a world. Only in a not-self-grounded being-with-others-in-the-world can that wider horizon of having-been be opened up in which a finite existence "grounds himself," that is, comes to stand as himself among beings that have-been-here before him and hand down to him his own factical possibilities. It is to be noted that for an authentic historical being a *being-with-others* in the same world is primarily constitutive. It is indeed self-evident that without an understanding of other existences and a communicating discourse with them, no tradition could be formed, and even our most immediate "history" would remain inaccessible. Even in the authentic history of an everyday being-in-the-world, it is the ambiguous hearsaying idle talk of being-with-others that transmits tradition. But whereas the disowned oneself understands himself among the others from a common preoccupation with things and from what is done and what happens within the world, the resolutely owned self understands himself from the fully disclosed finiteness of his own existence. This discloses other existences in their finite being, and makes authentic being-with-others possible.

We have now come to the end of the *transitional* passage that introduces Heidegger's elucidation of historical-being. Before going any further, it should be remarked that a vital point remains unclarified in Heidegger's argument, namely, the connection between self, ground, and world. It is only from the essay "On the Essence of Ground" that we learn that being-in-the-world is essentially a "grounding," and that one mode of grounding is "having gained ground" among beings, having gained a firm stand in the soil (*Boden*) in which all beings are rooted. All ways of grounding, as Heidegger briefly indicates in the same essay, spring from the care of standingness and constancy, belong to the ecstatic unity of temporality insofar as an enduring self-sameness (self-standingness) and continuity are constitutive of it. Coming back from "On the Essence of Ground" to the present chapter, we shall be able to see that an authentic historicity is nothing other than the concrete unfolding of authentic care as the not-determined ground-being of a negativity. Up to the end of Division Two, on the other hand, this vital connection is merely hinted at, but not made explicit. Why not? Very probably the elucidation of this matter was to have provided the transition from Division Two to Division Three, the turning point between Being and Time and Time and Being.

Keeping these connections in mind, we will be able to understand the tacit implications of the following interpretation. In the first place, Heidegger reminds us briefly of what has already been said in Division One about the everyday being-with-others-in-a-world. The disowned oneself-among-others, it now begins to appear, is inauthentically historical insofar as he understands himself primarily from his worldish possibilities. These are made public by "them," the "others," in the average interpretations of here-being that are current in everyday being-together. Its ambiguous hearsaying idle talk forms and transmits the "tradition" that prescribes to oneself what one can be and do.

The authentic existence does not simply reject and rebel against this tradition, but "from it and against it and yet again for it" *delivers over to himself* the factually given possibilities of his own existence. These are authentically disclosed from *the heritage* which a resolute coming-back-to here-being's thrownness makes its own. It is not an explicit, theoretical knowledge of tradition that distinguishes the authentic taking-over of a heritage, but the undisguised disclosure of a not-self-grounded thrownness that must ground itself in other beings. This illumination of the full meaning of thrownness can only happen in an understanding coming-back *from* the end of being-here. The more undisguisedly a here-being understands himself in and from his ownmost, utmost possibility, the more surely and the less accidentally he can find and choose the inherited possibilities of his existence.

> Only the anticipation of death drives every chance and "preliminary" possibility out. Only being free *for* death gives Da-sein its absolute goal and pushes existence into its finitude. The finitude of existence thus seized upon tears one back out of endless multiplicity of possibilities offering themselves nearest by—those of comfort, shirking and taking things easy—and brings Da-sein to the simplicity of its *fate*. This is how we designate the primordial occurrence of Da-sein that lies in authentic resoluteness in which it hands itself down to itself, free for death, in a possibility that it inherited and yet has chosen. (SZ, 384)

By "fate" [*Schicksal*], then, Heidegger means the authentic way in which a factically existing being-in-the-world "occurs," "happens," or "comes-to-pass"—*is* here in an inherited but nonetheless resolutely chosen situation. But, we are inclined to ask, by what right does Heidegger give such an unusual meaning to fate? Is this meaning completely arbitrary, or does it in some way connect up with what we would usually understand by "man's fate"? Indeed it does. Da-sein's fate, according to Heidegger, is to be the illuminated place, the "here" of the self-disclosure (truth) of being. The authentic happening of here-being is in itself the happening in which *being brings itself to light* in the fullest and widest way possible, namely *historically*. The existentially understood "fate" *accomplishes* "Da-sein's fate" in the usual sense, or, to be more precise, what Heidegger considers to be his fate. But more than that, Heidegger's conception of fate fulfils our obscurely or clearly felt need for a fate that Da-sein cannot himself make or confer on himself. The authentic happening of here-being clearly cannot be man-made, for ontically he is powerless to bring himself into being, and ontologically he cannot possibly confer on himself the disclosing way of being that first of all enables him to exist as Da-sein. On the other hand, according to Heidegger, our not-self-given fate is not imposed on us by a power, be it divine or natural, which exists in and by itself apart from here-being. Since being is nothing like a self-subsistent entity, its self-disclosure needs the being of concrete beings like ourselves. How and why being can bring itself to light (come into its truth) only in and as a *finite* existence, has already been repeatedly discussed. Fate, then, in Heidegger's interpretation, is neither man-made nor imposed by an external power, but is the unique happening of the self-disclosure of being in and as a finite here-being.

Furthermore, we usually think that in his finite freedom man cannot be merely a passive tool in the "hand of fate," but must himself be able to take a hand in fulfilling his fate. Now, we must note, that it is only the coming-to-pass of a resolutely disclosed existence that Heidegger calls fate. Resoluteness, as he has told us in chapter 2, is that free response that only a factical self *can* make, but need not necessarily make, to the call of care. Fate, in Heidegger's strictly defined sense, already comprehends in itself the free choice and willing response on the part of a resolutely "owned" self. A disowned self, on the other hand, exists in the "unfreedom" of not-having-chosen the utmost truth of which his factical being-here is capable.

The free choice that lies in the properly understood fate concerns not only the truth (disclosedness) of our own single existence. It concerns also the factical possibilities of our situation that we inherit but nonetheless take over as our own. To a resolutely disclosed here-being the particular circumstances, opportunities, chances, and accidents (*Zufälle*) that fall to his share (*zu-fallen*) from his world reveal themselves as fortunate or unfortunate, favorable or unfavourable, lucky or unlucky. Heidegger thus gives us a perfectly lucid explanation of how we can legitimately understand such notions as fortune and misfortune or good and bad luck—notions that are often held to be philosophically obscure, if not meaningless. Kant goes as far as to call luck, fortune, and fate "usurped concepts," whose use has no clearly justifiable ground either in experience or in reason (*Critique of Pure Reason*, B 117). In Heidegger's words,

> Da-sein can only be reached by the blows of fate because in the basis of its being it *is* fate in the sense described. Existing fatefully in resoluteness handing itself down, Da-sein is disclosed as being-in-the-world for the "coming" of "fortunate" circumstances and for the cruelty of chance. Fate does not first originate with the collision of circumstances and events. Even an irresolute person is driven by them, more so than someone who has chosen, and yet he can "have" no fate. (SZ, 384)

If, however, a freely willing choice is an essential constitutive moment of fate, then it becomes urgently necessary to define how far and in what way a finite being is free. This is what Heidegger now all too briefly proceeds to do by introducing the existential concepts of *Ohnmacht* and *Übermacht*. The first means literally "without power" and can be easily recognized as our powerlessness in the face of our being *already* here, delivered over to ourselves in a dependence upon other beings. *Übermacht* is more difficult to translate. "Über" means over, beyond, above. At first sight an analogy with Nietzsche's so-called superman (*Übermensch*) suggests itself, but must be quickly rejected.[4] The "Über" in "Übermacht" means exactly the "trans" of "transcendence" which Heidegger explicitly identifies with freedom (WG, 43ff., W, 59ff., G9, 163ff., 125ff., P, 125ff., ER, 101ff.). *Übermacht* is the power of transcending beings as a whole, among them first and foremost our own factical selves. This power of overstepping *beings* "goes over" to and ends itself in the (forethrown) possibilities of *being*. On no account must we conceive this "over-going power" as a superpower that overcomes and annuls the powerlessness of facticity. On the contrary, we must already find ourselves thrown among beings in order to be able to transcend them to being. Powerlessness and over-going power *together* characterize the finite freedom of transcendence. All this is condensed by Heidegger into a single sentence which would be barely understandable without "On the Essence of Ground."

> When Da-sein, anticipating, lets death become powerful in itself, as free for death it understands itself in its own *higher power*, the power of its finite freedom, and takes over the *powerlessness* of being abandoned to itself in that freedom, which always only *is* in having chosen the choice, and becomes clear about the chance elements in the situation disclosed. (SZ, 384)

One point in this sentence remains to be explained. While in the essay "On the Essence of Ground" Heidegger elucidates freedom (transcendence) as the *existential-ontological* character of here-being *as such*, in the present passage he speaks only of the authentic, "positive" freedom of a resolute self. This freedom in fact "exists" only in "having chosen the choice," it is the factical (existentiell-ontic) freedom that can belong only to the concrete self who has willingly responded to the "call of care." In contrast to this, the "unfreedom" of the lost self, while also a mode of factical freedom, is a negative mode insofar as it is an evasion of the most essential choice a free existence can make.

Whereas the disowned self is blindly driven round by the accidents (*Zufälle*) of his everyday being-in-the-world, the resolute self becomes clear-sighted for the accidents that fall to his share (*zu-fallen*) from his world. His world, however, is essentially a "with-world," which he shares with others. The happening of here-being is therefore essentially a happening-with-others in the same world, and is defined by Heidegger as "common destiny" (*Geschick*).

> With this term we designate the occurrence of the community, of a people. Destiny is not composed of individual fates, nor can being-with-one-another be conceived of as the mutual occurrence of several subjects [§ 26, 117f.]. These fates are already guided beforehand in being-with-one-another in the same world and in the resoluteness for definite possibilities. In communication and in battle the power of destiny first becomes free. The fateful destiny [*schicksalhaftes Geschick*] of Da-sein in and with its "generation" constitutes the complete, authentic occurrence of Da-sein. (SZ, 384–85)

Once we have understood what Heidegger means by "fate," the meaning of "common destiny" seems to be easy to grasp. But this apparent ease only hides the difficulties implicit in the above passage. In the first place, we notice with astonishment that what Heidegger defines there in a few sentences is nothing less than an *authentic* being-with-others. The "communication," we must presume, is the *authentic* way of speaking-together in contrast to the uprooted hearsaying idle talk of everydayness, and the "battle," the authentic way of taking care of a mutually shared world, in contrast to a mutual lostness in "what one does." But why, we ask, does Heidegger treat this important theme with such reticence? Why the disproportionately more careful and detailed analyses devoted to an everyday being-together? If the latter is more familiar and common, it requires less explanation than the unfamiliar phenomenon of an *authentic* "common destiny." And further, what criteria do we or can we have for distinguishing the authentic happening of a community, a people, from an inauthentic one? The historical examples of communities most conscious of their "common destiny"—for example, in the fanaticism of religious or ideological or racial wars, when one community feels itself appointed to the "mission" of destroying others—make us extremely doubtful whether such "common destinies" do not arise from an extreme self-loss rather than from the resolute grasp of the *finitude* of all being-with-others and its inherited tasks. It may well be, of course, that ontic criteria for judging in what particular instance we are facing an authentic or an inauthentic happening are in principle impossible to give. So, for instance, a Christian may be convinced that salvation is possible for each human being but may not presume to know whether this or that particular human being has been saved. Or, to take another example, "moral action" in the strictly Kantian sense is possible to every man as a free moral being, but it is impossible to judge whether this or that action is "moral" as Kant understood the term. Similarly, it is possible that an authentic "common destiny" is a factical-existentiell possibility of herebeing as being-with-others and yet we may lack, for essential reasons, the criteria for judgment in any specific instance. But if this is so, we can rightly demand from Heidegger an explanation that—and why—this should be so. The doubts and dissatisfactions that many thoughtful readers of *Being and Time* feel in the face of "authentic existence" and "common destiny"—whether these are mere "phenomenological constructions" without any relevance to our factical existence—are only strengthened by Heidegger's inadequate treatment of this theme.

On the other hand, the *ontological* conditions of the possibility of historical-being are worked out by Heidegger in a highly original and impressive way. These conditions lie in the ontological constitution of care, that is, in its temporal constitution. "Only if death, guilt, conscience, freedom, and finitude live together equiprimordially in the being of a being as they do in care, can that being exist in the mode of fate, that is, be historical in the ground of its existence. (SZ, 385).

The enumeration of death, owing, condolence, freedom, and finiteness gives us, as it were, the full ontological content of care as the not- or null-determined ground-being of a negativity. That these manifold constituents of care can "cooriginally dwell together" is, however, made possible by temporality. The following paragraph (almost the whole of which is printed in italics) is undoubtedly the core of Heidegger's interpretation of historical-being.

> *Only a being that is essentially futural in its being so that it can let itself be thrown back upon its factical There, free for its death and shattering itself on it, that is, only a being that, as futural, is equiprimordially* having-been, *can hand down to itself its inherited possibility, take over its own thrownness and be in the Moment for "its time." Only authentic temporality that is at the same time finite makes something like fate, that is, authentic historicity, possible.* (SZ, 385)

Of all statements in *Being and Time* this one brings most sharply into focus the whole movement in which temporality temporalizes (accomplishes) itself. For the constitution of historical-being, the throw-back from the nothing manifest in death is undoubtedly decisive, since its violence carries us behind our own having-been and makes the inherited character of our world fully understandable.

But, it may be asked, is the back-to-itself movement of temporality not the same as the "reflexivity," the "bending-back-upon-itself" of self-consciousness and thinking? Or if the two are not the same, how are they related? This question is relevant to all modern transcendental philosophy whose essential dimension is undoubtedly a "transcendental self-consciousness" (Kant's pure apperception). Husserl's phenomenology, for instance, is a method of peculiar reflection that aims at penetrating to that transcendental self-consciousness whose function is to "constitute being." According to Heidegger, on the other hand, self-consciousness is only a character of a distinctive *way of being*, namely of self-conscious-being (*Selbst-bewusst-sein*). The attempt to explain being from one of its characters, Heidegger maintains, tackles the problem from the wrong end. The task is rather to explain the temporal structure of this being by virtue of which it can *bring itself to light*, so that it can be "conscious-of-itself." This is a decisive turning *away* from Husserl and from all previous transcendental philosophy.[5] Self-consciousness (thinking) and its reflexivity are, for Heidegger, not primary and ultimate, but derivative phenomena that owe their possibility to the temporality of care.

Nevertheless, the new departure made in *Being and Time* has its immediate historical roots in transcendental philosophy. One of Heidegger's early acknowledgments of this philosophical "heritage" is made in his so-called Kant-book, first published in 1929, where *Being and Time* is called a *Wiederholung*, a bringing-forward-again (recollection, recapitulation, retrieval) of Kant's attempt to lay the ground of metaphysics. *Being and Time*, then, is a specific and concrete example of a historical "recollection," whose general meaning is expounded by Heidegger in a long paragraph that we shall now consider in detail.

> It is not necessary that resoluteness *explicitly* know of the provenance of its possibilities upon which it projects itself. However, in the temporality of Da-sein, and only in it, lies the possibility of fetching the existentiell potentiality-of-being upon which it projects itself *explicitly* from the traditional understanding of Da-sein. Resoluteness that comes back to itself and hands itself down then becomes the retrieve of a possibility of experience that has been handed down. *Retrieve is explicit handing down*, that is, going back to the possibilities of the Da-sein that has been there. The authentic retrieve of a possibility of existence that has been—the possibility that Da-sein may choose its heroes—is existentially grounded in anticipatory resoluteness; for in resoluteness the choice is first chosen that makes one free for the struggle to come, and the loyalty to what can be retrieved. (SZ, 385)

The first thing that strikes us in this passage is that the technical term *Wiederholung*, bringing-again or recollection or retrieve or repetition or recapitulation, is now used in a different sense from its earlier use. Let us glance back to the passage where Heidegger first defined the strictly technical meaning of *Wiederholung*.

> The authentic coming-toward-itself of anticipatory resoluteness is at the same time a coming back to the ownmost self thrown into its individuation. This ecstasy makes it possible for Da-sein to be able to take over resolutely the being that it already is. In anticipation, Da-sein *brings* itself *forth again* to its ownmost potentiality-of-being. We call authentic having-been retrieve. (SZ, 339)

We see that this passage elucidates *Wiederholung* solely with respect to here-being's ownmost, single self. Since, however, this self is not an isolated worldless subject, but is already thrown into a world, and exists historically, the first definition of recollection evidently does not exhaust the range and depth of its meaning. It must already implicitly include the bringing-again into here-being's own existence of those inherited possibilities that have been handed down to him by preceding existences. The new meaning of recollection or retrieve, it might be said, explicitly completes the old.

This explanation, however, is unsatisfactory, because it ignores the repeatedly stressed character of "explicitness" (*Ausdrücklichkeit*) that belongs to a historical recollection. Although an "explicit knowledge" of the origins of our possibilities is not absolutely necessary, some kind of *explicit* acknowledgment is required if we are to make our inheritance fully our own *as inherited*. The recollecting forethrow of our chosen possibility must make it *explicitly* manifest that we are taking it over from existences who have-been-here before us. Why does this "explicitness" or "expressness" belong to a historical recollection? Because the proper understanding of a historical being-in-the-world must articulate itself in communicating discourse (expression). This already underlies and makes possible all explicit interpretation (*Auslegung*) and transmission of those "recollectable" possibilities of existence that each generation must grasp anew and take over for itself.

It seems, therefore, that the moment of "explicitness" does introduce an element into the concept of recollection that was entirely absent from its first definition. Or is this impression to some extent deceptive? We must remember that the resolute recollection of my ownmost, single self is the *willing understanding* of the call of care. This call, in which care makes itself known, is also a mode of discourse. It speaks in the uncanny mode of silence, because it calls myself alone in my own finite being. Hence I properly hear, i.e. understand the call in a reticent silence (*Verschwiegenheit*). Sound and word are not needed to articulate the recollection of my own single self. When, on the other hand, the recollection concerns my thrownness into a world, then a communicating speech (expression) is necessary to make concretely manifest the inherited possibility that I bring-again into my own existence.

Recollection or retrieve is therefore a single, existential-temporal concept. It denotes here-being's understanding of his own thrownness (having-been), but in two different relations: once in relation to his own finite being, and once in relation to his being-with-others in the same world. Hence the two different modes of discourse that articulate the authentic disclosure of thrownness.[6]

Furthermore, just as the silent understanding of the call of care does not lead to a theoretical self-examination, but to the instant resolution for a factical situation, so the express understanding of transmitted possibilities does not primarily consist in a theoretical-objective study of historical personages, but in the choice of a "hero" to be emulated in struggle.

But what does the "emulation of a hero" concretely mean? Does it mean merely the imitation of an admired pattern, or the present accomplishment of possibilities that could not, perhaps, be fully realized when they were first conceived? On these points, Heidegger remarks:

The retrieve of what is possible neither brings back "what is past," nor does it bind the "present" back in what is "outdated." Arising from a resolute self-projection, retrieve is not convinced by "something past," in just letting it come back as what was once real. Rather, retrieve *responds* to the possibility of existence that has-been-there. But responding to the possibility in a resolution is at the same time, *as in the Moment, the disavowal* of what is working itself out today as the "past." (SZ, 385–86)

We notice that this passage is mainly negative. It repudiates inappropriate notions of history drawn from an inauthentic understanding of here-being. The "past" and the "present," for instance, characterize the within-timeness of things and not the temporality of care. Nor can an existential possibility "recur as the formerly real," because it never has had the character of "reality," and its facticity is never a mere occurrence or recurrence. The continuity of a historical tradition is not the continuity of things that stand in a cause and effect relation, but is accomplished in the free response of a factically existing being-in-the-world to a being-in-the-world who has-been-here. This response, as the *instant presentation* of a factual situation, "revokes" a petrified tradition as the effect of the past on the present, revealing that the bindingness of a historical "past" on the today is fundamentally different from a causal necessitation.

The positive definition of recollection as a *response*, while beautifully apt and illuminating, still leaves us in doubt how precisely the emulation of a hero is to be understood. For a more concrete answer we must turn to the Kant-book, where Heidegger expounds how *Being and Time* is a recollection of a fundamental philosophical problem that was brought to light in a specific way in Kant's *Critique of Pure Reason*. The original formulation of the problem was the possibility of philosophical existence as construed by Kant, to which *Being and Time* is a reply. "By the recollection of a fundamental problem we understand the disclosure of its original, hitherto hidden possibilities. In working them out the problem is transformed and so first of all preserved in its problematic content" (KPM, 185, G3, 204, KPM(E), 139).

These few words give us the aptest description of how a specific kind of recollection can be concretely accomplished. *Being and Time* is indeed not a mechanical repetition of the *Critique of Pure Reason*; it does not ask the same questions as its great predecessor; but it seizes upon a possible interpretation of being *from time*, toward which Kant took the first steps. In penetrating more deeply into this possibility *Being and Time* transforms the problem into that of the meaning of being in general.

The principle embodied in a specifically philosophical recollection, repetition, or retrieve must be applicable to other spheres, be our hero a statesman, a scientist, or a saint. An emulating struggle cannot be merely a slavish imitation, nor an impossible return to what has been, but a transformation of a possibility which was perhaps first shown, or outstandingly exemplified, in an earlier existence. The transformation keeps it alive *as the possibility* which I throw forward again in my own particular situation, which can never be identical with what has been.

The more we think about recollection or retrieval, the more we become aware of a distinctive, perhaps unique feature of Heidegger's interpretation. It is not the having-been that is primarily constitutive of historical-being, but the coming-to-itself, the "futural" character of the temporality of care. This is explicitly stated by Heidegger in the following important paragraph.

> We characterize retrieve as the mode of resolution handing itself down, by which Da-sein exists explicitly as fate. But if fate constitutes the primordial historicity of Da-sein, history has its essential weight neither in what is past nor in the today and its "connection" with what is past, but in the authentic occurrence of existence that arises from the future of Da-sein. As a mode of being of Da-sein, history has its roots so essentially in the future that death, as the possibility of Da-sein we characterized, throws anticipatory existence back upon its factical thrownness and this first gives to the *having-been* its unique priority in what is historical. *Authentic being-toward-death, that is, the finitude of temporality, is the concealed ground of the historicity of Da-sein.* Da-sein does not first become historical in retrieve, but rather because as temporal it is historical, it can take itself over in its history, retrieving itself. Here no historiography is needed as yet. (SZ, 386)

It is the throw-back from the impassable possibility of death which makes here-being "ecstatically open" to the having-been. This ecstatic openness is the indispensable and ultimate condition for any going back to the "past." Retrieve makes here-being's own history expressly manifest, but not necessarily in a scientific-objective way. The "hero," for instance, may be transmitted from generation to generation in legend and song. *Existentially* this may be a more original way of opening up our history than a scientific explanation, just as the everyday explanation of handy things is more original than a theoretical-scientific thematization of the substances of nature. But whether our explanations be scientific or prescientific, they are always grounded in the disclosedness of the happening of here-being, and this, in turn, is made possible by the temporality of care.

But how does this happening as fate constitute the "connection" of here-being from birth to death? Not a word has been said so far on the "connection of life," in spite of the fact that this theme has been announced in the introductory section as one of the most important to be discussed. Heidegger now leads us over to this theme in a surprising way. It is not the rightness or wrongness of the usual answers that must be examined in the first place, but the appropriateness of the question itself. In what ontological horizon does this "self-evident" question about the "connection of life" move? Does it not originate in an authentic historical-being? And if so, does an inauthentic understanding of this being not misdirect the approach to its "connection"? These questions will be discussed in the following section.

3. The Historicity of Here-Being and World-History

The theme of this section is developed in a devious way, with an unusual jerkiness in important transitions of thought. This is due partly to the distracting rear-guard action Heidegger fights against the current theories of the "connection of life" and the subject-object relation, but partly to the number of preliminary steps through which the central point is reached. These are:

1. (a) To what extent is the world, as an essential constitutive moment of being-in-the-world, in itself historical?
   (b) To what extent are the beings we encounter in this world historical? Are they historical in themselves, or do they become so incidentally and in an extraneous way as objects for a historical subject?
2. (a) What constitutes the inauthentic historical character of an everyday being-in-the-world?
   (b) What is the meaning of history and of being in general that is implicitly understood in an inauthentic being-in-the-world?
   (c) How does the understanding that belongs to an inauthentic historical-being open up the horizon in which a question of the "connection of life" originates?

Let us now briefly consider how Heidegger works out these preliminary steps of the argument.

1. (a) Heidegger's answer to the first question is a foregone conclusion. On the ground of the ecstatic-horizonal temporality of care, a world essentially belongs to its temporalization. "*The occurrence of his-*

tory is the occurrence of being-in-the-world" (SZ, 388). The world which belongs to a factically existing being-in-the-world is historical in an original and primary sense.

(b) On the ground of the happening of world, within-worldish beings are already discovered. "*With the existence of historical being-in-the-world, things at hand and objectively present have always already been included in the history of the world*" (SZ, 388). It is not a mere metaphor to speak of the "fates" of certain works, buildings, or institutions. Moreover, it is not only man-made things that are historical, but also nature as territory for settlement and exploitation, as battlefield and place of religious cults. These beings are *as such* historical, and are not merely external paraphernalia that somehow accompany the "'inner' history of the 'soul'." They are in themselves *world-historical*. Heidegger uses the term *world-history* in an ontological and deliberately ambivalent sense. It means in the first place "the occurrence of world in its essential existent unity with Da-sein" (SZ, 389). Insofar, however, as beings are already discovered within the factually existing world, the term means at the same time the "occurrence" or "happening" of handy things and substantial things. The within-worldish happenings of historical processes and events, to some extent even of natural catastrophies, as well as what happens to individual things, for instance a ring that is passed on and worn, have a "movedness" which, according to Heidegger, is an ontological mystery. Here, for the first time, Heidegger hints that the vulgar conception of a linear, one-dimensional time may be inadequate to define even the world-historical happenings to and with things, let alone the primary happening of here-being. The hint, however, is not positively developed. What, then, is the positive result of these first steps of Heidegger's interpretation?

The result may perhaps best be appreciated by comparing it with Count Yorck's concepts of the "historical" and the "ontic." While Count Yorck saw the "historical" and the "ontic" in a fundamental antithesis, Heidegger takes them back into a deeper unity. Not only the historical being-in-the-world, but also the "ontic" beings within the world are as such historical. In this deeper unity, however, they are differentiable as the primarily and the secondarily historical. This differentiation is analogous to the difference between the primary and the secondary way of "being true." "To be true," we remember, means primarily "to be disclosing and discovering." Secondarily, it means "to be discovered." Discoverability belongs to within-worldish beings themselves; it is their specific possibility of being brought into the truth appropriate to them. The being of here-being, on the other hand, brings itself into its own truth, that is, discloses itself. By virtue of it, here-being as a being-in-the-world can discover within-worldish beings *as beings*—that is, as things that are. On the ground of their belonging to the world of here-being—the primarily historical—these things are in themselves historical in a secondary sense. They do not merely become so because the "subject of history" takes up a relation to them, but because the world of here-being is in fact the world of things. The world is, so to speak, the "go between" between man and things. It makes any kind of "between" and "relation" between man and things ontologically possible.

2. (a) In his everyday being-in-the-world, the factical existence loses himself to the things of which he takes care. The self-explanations of inauthentic existence are primarily drawn from the commonsense horizon of a care-taking absorption in things. These, however, are not immutably fixed, but have their own "history." Not only the work and the utensil, but also what *happens* to them belong to everyday experience, even though their historical character is not explained in an objective and scientific way. "On the basis of the temporally founded transcendence of the world, what is world-historical is always already 'objectively' there in the occurrence of existing being-in-the-world, *without being grasped historiographically*" (SZ, 389). The "world" itself as the theater of the changing scene belongs to the daily commerce with things. The others meet one in those activities in which "one oneself" takes part. In a common lostness to things, the "fate" of the individual here-being is made by what he has done and what has happened to him in his care-taking being-in-the-world.

(b) In a self-forgetful waiting for the occurrences and opportunities that the day brings, the everyday here-being understands his own history world-historically. The being of the world-historical, in turn, "is experienced and interpreted in the sense of objective presence that comes along, is present, and disappears"; that is, it has the ontological-temporal meaning of a not-yet-present, actually present, and no-longer-present reality (*Vorhandenheit*). This undifferentiated meaning of being holds not only an unquestioned predominance, but appears to be so self-evident that even where the concepts drawn from it are *negatively* rejected as inappropriate to the "historical subject," a *positive* interpretation is not forthcoming, or is thought to be superfluous.

(c) The inauthentic existence is so scattered into his manifold businesses and undertakings that, if he wants to *come to himself* at all, he must first of all "*pull himself together* from the *dispersion* and the *disconnectedness* of what has just 'happened' . . ." (SZ, 390). It is the inconstancy or instability (*Un-ständigkeit*) of the irresolute—that is, inauthentically historical—self which gives rise to the *question* how the successive experiences of the subject are to be retrospectively linked up into a coherent unity. The operative word, we must note, is *retrospectively*, for, as Heidegger rightly maintains, the *whole* of historical here-being must in itself and in advance be constituted as a coherent unity; otherwise no amount of subsequent putting-together could make up the whole. The question to be asked, therefore, is this: In which mode of existing does here-being lose himself in such a way that he must subsequently bring himself together from scatteredness and must think out an embracing unity which holds him together? The fundamental reason for losing "oneself" among "them" and in the world-historical lies in a flight from death, which "flight *from* . . ." reveals, inauthentically, the being-*unto*-death. The anticipatory forward-running resoluteness, on the other hand, brings the being-into-death into the authentic existence. The happening of resoluteness—the specific movedness of an anticipatory forward-running recollecting of inherited possibilities—constitutes the authentic historicity in which, according to Heidegger, there lies already the original, unlost stretchedness of the whole existence, which does not need a restrospective coherence.

> The resoluteness of the self against the inconstancy of dispersion is in itself a *steadiness that has been stretched along*–the steadfastness in which Da-sein as fate "incorporates" into its existence birth and and their "between" in such a way that in such constancy it is in the Moment for what is world-historical in its actual situation. In the fateful retrieve of possibilities that have-been, Da-sein brings itself back "immediately," that is, temporally and ecstatically, to what has already been before it. But when its heritage is thus handed down to itself, "birth" is taken into existence in coming back from the possibility of death (the possibility not-to-be-surpassed) so that existence may accept the thrownness of its own There more free from illusion. (SZ, 390–91)

The predominant temporal characteristic of a falling being-in-the-world was earlier shown to be an "unheld making present" of within-worldish things that "runs away" from the original temporality of care. In an authentic historicity, on the contrary, not only the instant presenting of the world-historical, but the whole of here-being and its continuity with what has been before it is brought into and held in a resolutely owned existence. In forward-running resoluteness the factical existence "stands fast"—is "faithful" or "loyal" or "true" to his own self—where the truth here is *Treue* (SZ, 391). This steadfastness, however, must not be mistaken for an obstinate insistence on a particular resolution once made. On the contrary, it is free and open to what our situation may "instantly" demand from us because, in running forward to the ultimate possibility, it has in advance anticipated all factical possibilities among which we may have to decide. The constancy of the self is not composed of a linking-up of successive "instants" or "Moments," but "these arise from the temporality *already stretched along*, of that retrieve which is futurally in the process of having-been" (SZ, 391).

The resoluteness in which an existence keeps faith with his own self is constantly "tuned" by a readiness to *dread*. Dread is the mood that most originally reveals our thrownness. It is not surprising, therefore, that the mood that tunes our recollection of earlier existences is akin to dread: it is the awe or reverence (*Ehrfucht*) "for the sole authority that a free existence can have, for the possibilities of existence that can be retrieved" (SZ, 391). This bare statement, which Heidegger does not explain further, raises a host of interesting problems. In one respect it shows an unexpected similarity to Kant's thought. Awe or reverence, according to Heidegger, is the mood that makes manifest an authority over us and in which we submit ourselves to it. Similarly, for Kant, respect (*Achtung*) is the pure moral feeling in which man submits himself to the moral law which he, as a free existence—as "practical reason" in Kant's thought—gives to himself. With this, however, the similarity between the two thinkers is at an end. For one thing, the "possibilities of existence that can be retrieved" are self-chosen, but not self-given. For another thing, their bindingness is not that of an unchangeable, absolute law; on the contrary, as we have heard, recollection *transforms* the inherited possibility. Its authority cannot therefore have the character of a sheer necessitation, but rather of a "guidance" which in advance guides the fate of here-being. And finally, why are the "possibilities of existence that can be retrieved" *authoritative*? Is it only because we have inherited them from former existences? Surely not, but rather because they are possibilities of *existence*, that is, of a way of being that *brings itself to light* in its essential possibilities. The self-disclosure of being, however, is essentially historical—hence the bindingness, authority, of its *retrievable* possibilities. Now, for Kant, too, reason belongs to the *essence* of man and can therefore no more be man-made than the existential way of being. But rationality is the essential structure of *subjectivity*, it belongs to an interpretation of man as the subject that is radically questioned and reinterpreted in *Being and Time*. As the present chapter has specifically attempted to show, the temporal-dialectical movement and stretchedness of here-being cannot be sufficiently explained with the help of the inherited interpretation of subjectivity.

The inappropriate question of how the successive experiences of a subject can be linked up into a coherent unity arises because the original stretchedness of here-being as fate remains hidden in an inauthentic way of being historical. The inconstant oneself-among-others loses itself in the presentation of the "today." In expecting the newest of the new, it has already forgotten the old. It cannot properly recollect what has-been, but retains and preserves the remains of the formerly world-historical and the present knowledge of it. Lost in the presenting of the today, it understands the past from the present.

> Inauthentic historical existence, on the other hand, is burdened with the legacy of a "past" that has become unrecognizable to it, looks for what is modern. Authentic historicity understands history as the "recurrence" of what is possible and knows that a possibility recurs only when existence is open for it fatefully, in the Moment, in resolute retrieve." (SZ, 391-92).

The twofold meaning that Heidegger assigns to "world-history" must, of course, always be kept in view. It means not only the happening of world, but at the same time the happening with and to the within-worldish things. With the thematization of the factual having-been-in-the-world of an existence, the things that belonged to his world are *ipso facto* drawn into the historical investigation. The things may, of course, outlast the world and may, as utensils, buildings, documents, be still discoverable in the present as historical material. But they can become historical material only because their own being has a world-historical character and they are in advance understood in their belonging to a world. The going-back into the "past" is not started off by the discovery and interpretation of the "material," but "rather already presupposes *historical being toward* the Da-sein that has-been-there, that is, the historicity of the historian's existence. His existence existentially grounds historiography as science, down to the most trivial, 'mechanical' procedures" (SZ, 394).

It is relevant to ask whether Heidegger's idea of history has so far shown any appreciable divergence from the actual practice of reputable historians. No great difference can be detected up to now, for the "fate" of man in his world has always been the main theme of historians, no matter how inadequately, according to Heidegger, the existential-temporal structure of historical-being may have been explained. But now Heidegger touches on a point that appears to give a jolt to generally accepted views. This point is introduced by him with the remark, "If historiography is rooted in historicity in this way, then we should also be able to determine from there what the *object* of historiography 'really' is" (SZ, 394).

The object of history, to be sure, has already been defined, but in such a general way that many different approaches to it and the selection of any one of its possible "aspects" may equally well claim to be essential. What Heidegger has in mind now is a stricter and narrower definition of the most "proper," most essential object of history and the perspective in which it can be disclosed. But from where can the proper theme of history be drawn in such a way that it is free from the arbitrary preference or the relative point of view of the individual historian? Only from an *authentic historicity*, to which a *retrieving* disclosure already belongs. The outstanding feature of Heidegger's interpretation of retrieval is that it understands the former here-being in his authentic possibility which has-been.

> The "birth" of historiography from authentic historicity then means that the primary thematization of the object of historiography projects Da-sein that has-been-there upon its ownmost potentiality-of-existence. Does not its whole "meaning" lie in "facts," in what has factually happened? (SZ, 394)

The gulf between Heidegger and the historians is not as unbridgeable as it looks, provided that facticity and possibility (existence) are understood from the existentiality of here-being and not from the reality of things. The "fact" with which history is essentially concerned, then, is the factical existence who has-been-in-the-world. If here-being is "really," "in fact" here only in his existence, in throwing himself forward into his possibilities, then the resolute forethrow of his chosen ability-to-be is just what constituted his facticity.

> What has "factually" really been there, however, is then the existentiell possibility in which fate, destiny, and world history are factically determined. Because existence always is only as factically thrown, historiography will disclose the silent power of the possible with greater penetration the more simply and concretely it understands having-been-in-the-world in terms of possibility, and "just" presents it. (SZ, 394)

The implications of Heidegger's idea of history are not at all easy to grasp. In the first place, Heidegger considers the question of whether the proper theme of history is only the series of single events that have happened once or also the "general" historical "law." Characteristically, Heidegger rejects this question as thoroughly misconceived, for neither the single, unrepeatable happening nor the universal law that somehow hovers over it is the theme of history, but "the possibility that has been factically existent." The authentic recollection of the former factical possibility has already made the "universal" manifest in the "singular." This may be understood in the following way: On the one hand, the finiteness that throws the factically existent possibility into its singleness prohibits its perversion "into the pallor of a supratemporal pattern." On the other hand, the *same finiteness* throws the factical existence back upon its *inherited* possibility. What has-been-here once is therefore not *repeatable* as a recurrent embodiment of an unchanging ideal that exists outside time, but it is *recollectable* or *retrievable*; that is, it can be brought back and forward again into the transforming forethrow of another existence. Hence the has-been is not irretrievably "past" and "gone" (*vergangen*), but is essentially "futural"; it remains in "coming" insofar as a factical here-being *comes-to-himself* in his *inherited* possibility. How, then, does the science of history originate in the authentically historical existence of the historian?

> Only factically authentic historicity, as resolute fate, can disclose the history that has-been-there in such a way that in retrieve the "power" of the possible breaks into factical existence, that is, comes toward it in its futurality. Historiography by no means takes its point of departure from the "present" and what is "real" only today, any more than does the historicity of unhistorical Da-sein, and then grope its way back from there to a past. Rather, even *historiographical* disclosure temporalizes itself *out of the future*. The "*selection*" of what is to become a possible object for historiography *has already been made* in the factical existentiell *choice* of the historicity of Da-sein, in which historiography first arises and *is* uniquely. (SZ, 395)

The existential origin of history, however, leaves us in considerable doubt about the concrete meaning of "retrieve" in *scientific practice*. In our factical existence, as we have heard, we recollect a former possibility by bringing it forward again into our own existence. In so coming-to-ourselves in an inherited possibility, we *transform* it according to our own historical situation in our own world. But can a "scientific" recollection aim at transforming the former possibility? Must it not rather present it precisely as it has-been in the world that belonged to it? Or, since the former possibility is essentially "futural" in the above-described sense, must the scientific presentation of how it has in fact been not illuminate just its "futural" character? No definite answer to these questions can be given from our present passage. All we can say is that the last suggestion seems to be in keeping with all that Heidegger has explicitly said.

On the other hand, Heidegger himself raises some questions about which misgivings may arise. In the first place, it may be asked whether the fatefully retrieving disclosure of the "past" does not condemn history to be wholly "subjective," and therefore not a science at all in the usually accepted sense. On the contrary, Heidegger replies, it alone guarantees the "objectivity" of history. The objectivity of a science means that it binds itself to the *beings* that have been thematized as the *objects* of its research. A science is the more objective the more undisguisedly it presents to our understanding the beings that are its theme in the primordiality of their being. These, as far as history is concerned, are the former existences in their historicity. Their disclosure and interpretation demand the authentically historical existence (understanding) of the historian, unlike, for instance, the scientific explanation of nature, for which it is irrelevant in what way the scientist is "historical." For reasons already indicated above, the validity of universal, unchanging laws sought by the sciences of nature is not the proper criterion for "objective" historical truth.

But if all this is admitted, can history be saved from a nebulous vagueness? Does it not need, like other sciences, the "hard facts" that give it a firm hold? These misgivings, according to Heidegger, are unfounded and do not follow from his interpretation. Just because the central theme of history is the possibility in which the former existence has-been-here, and has factually existed *world-historically*, the concrete research can

> demand of itself a relentless orientation toward "facts." For this reason factical research has many branches and makes the history of useful works, cultures, spirit, and ideas its object. At the same time history, handing itself down, is in itself always in an interpretedness that belongs to it, and that has a history of its own; so that for the most part it is only through traditional history that historiography penetrates into what-has-been-there itself. [. . .]
>
> Thus the dominance of a differentiated historiographical interest, even in the most remote and primitive cultures, is in itself no proof of the authentic historicity of an "age." Ultimately, the rise of the problem of "historicism" is the clearest indication that historiography strives to alienate Da-sein from its authentic historicity. Historicity does not necessarily need historiography. Unhistoriographical ages are as such not also automatically unhistorical. (SZ, 395–96)[7]

The "historicism" attacked by Heidegger means an uprooted and uprooting knowledge of all the world and a syncretizing comparison of all kinds of cultures, leading to a relativism and skepticism that was sharply criticized already by Nietzsche in his "On the Use and Disadvantage of History for Life" ("Vom Nutzen und Nachteil der Historie für das Leben," 1874). Heidegger must, in fact, have this work of Nietzsche's in mind, for its discussion occupies the whole of the succeed-

324   Part Three: Division Two of Being and Time

ing paragraph. Nietzsche has distinguished three kinds of history: the monumental, the antiquarian, and the critical, without demonstrating the ground of this threefold unity. Heidegger now proceeds to give his own demonstration, and at the same time to show that authentic history must be "the factical and concrete unity of these three possibilities" (SZ, 396). The "threefold unity" of history is grounded in the ecstatic-horizonal unity of temporality.

> Da-sein exists as futural authentically in the resolute disclosure of a chosen possibility. Resolutely coming-back to itself, it is open in retrieve for the "monumental" possibilities of human existence. The historiography arising from this history is "monumental." As having-been, Da-sein is delivered over to its thrownness. In appropriating the possible in retrieve, there is prefigured at the same time the possibility of reverently preserving the existence that has-been-there, in which the possibility grasped becomes manifest. As monumental, authentic historiography is thus "antiquarian." Da-sein temporalizes itself in the unity of future and the having-been as present. The present, as the Moment, discloses the today authentically. But since the today is interpreted in terms of understanding a possibility of existence grasped—an understanding that futurally retrieves—authentic historiography ceases to make the today present, that is, it suffers itself to become detached from the entangled publicness of the today. As authentic, monumental-antiquarian historiography is necessarily a critique of the "present." Authentic historicity is the foundation of the possible unity of the three kinds of historiography. But the ground on which authentic historiography is founded is temporality as the existential meaning of the being of care. (SZ, 396-97)

Even the most critical reader of Heidegger will hardly deny the brilliance of this exposition. It is, at the same time, an admirable example of a "transforming" interpretation of an earlier thinker. Furthermore, this passage is the only one where the meaning of "de-presenting" (*Entgegenwärtigung*) is explained at all. It is said to mean a suffering detachment (*das leidende Sichlösen*) from the publicness of a falling being-in-the-world that loses itself in the *presenting* of things within the world. Characteristically, it is in the mood of suffering and pain that Heidegger experiences the loosening of the bonds that keep us sheltered in familiar and unquestioned explanations. Nothing could be further removed from the half-baked enthusiasm or angry rebellion that is so often associated with an "existentialism" mistakenly ascribed to Heidegger.

In summing up the findings of the present section, Heidegger emphasizes that the principal task of historical thematization is to unfold the hermeneutical situation that is opened up—once historically existing Da-sein has made its resolution—to the disclosure in retrieve of what has-been-there. The possibility and the structure of *historiographical truth* are to be set forth in terms of the *authentic disclosedness* ("truth") *of historical existence*. (SZ, 397)

The basic concepts of all historical sciences are existential concepts. The "historical sciences" seem to be taken by Heidegger in such a wide sense that they include all studies concerned with "mind" or "spirit" (*Geist*) and their methods, in distinction from the sciences of nature, whose basic concepts are concepts of reality. A theory of nature is not dependent on an existential interpretation of historical here-being, but for a theory of the "sciences of mind" (*Geisteswissenschaften*) it is a necessary precondition. This was the aim approached by Dilthey. To conceive the same aim more fundamentally and to formulate it concretely as a problem has been the task of the present chapter.

Since the last thing Heidegger claims is that the problem has now been completely solved, it may be useful to look back on what has become clear and what remains obscure in Heidegger's interpretation. Perhaps its most outstanding feature is the decisive constitutive function of authentic "future," that is, the anticipatory forward-running resoluteness in which a factical here-being authentically comes-to-himself. This constitutes the forward-stretching movement in which the whole of here-being "stands" (endures) as fate, and at the same time originates the *rebounding movement* in which here-being comes-back to his own thrownness (having-been). Since, however, here-being is essentially a being-with-others-in-the-world, the coming-back to his own finite having-been opens up a wider dimension of temporality, in which the having-been-in-the-world of former existences becomes accessible. These are authentically understood in a resolutely forward-running recollection or retrieve, in which a factical here-being chooses his own factical possibility as *inherited*, that is, brings the possibility in which a former here-being existed forward into his own existence. The whole movement ("movedness") in which here-being stretches himself forward and back is the "happening" or "occurrence" (*Geschehen*) whose existential-temporal structure constitutes the historicity of here-being.

This short summary pinpoints the importance of authentic existence and its temporal structure for Heidegger's interpretation of historical-being. In the inauthentic happening ("history") of everydayness, it is just the decisive movement, stretchedness, and stability of historical here-being that remains hidden, or is distorted and misinterpreted from the reality of things. The chief difficulty in all this is not that Heidegger's explanations are obscure, but that in any concrete instance we find ourselves unable to distinguish between an authentic and inauthentic existence. And yet, as Heidegger insists, the distinction is not a mere phenomenological construction, but a concrete, factical possibility of each of us that makes itself known in the call of care. A further indication that these two different ways of existing can in fact be distinguished lies in the many distinguishing marks by which Heidegger describes them, and further, in the origin of history in the authentically historical existence of the historian. If we are to assume, then, that the distinction is not *in principle* impossible, we must conclude that the distinguishing marks that Heidegger gives us are insufficient to apply reliably as criteria to concrete examples. This was specifically brought to our notice with Heidegger's interpretation of authentic being-with-others and the authentic "happening" of the community as "common destiny." It remains obscure whether or not the "happening"of a community is *ipso facto* authentic, not to speak of our inability to point to this or that community, or this or that example of being-with-others as authentic.

A problem that remains not only obscure but is passed over without comment is the *mode of being* in which the things within the world would become manifest to a fatefully recollecting *instant presenting*, that is, to an authentically historical here-being. Both the *handy* presence of things discovered by the care-taking circumspection of everydayness, and its modification into the *substantial* presence of substances discovered by a theoretical only-looking-at things, are modes of being in which the within-worldish things are manifest to an inauthentically falling being-in-the-world. The position is not in the least altered by the new definition of things as "world-historical." This, it is true, brings into focus the dimension of time in which things can be handily or substantially "there," and raises the problem of the "movedness" of within-worldish happenings, but makes no difference to the ontological character of things which has been disclosed from an inauthentic making present. We are therefore faced with the anomalous situation that the world-historical things discovered by the "instant making present" of authentic here-being still retain the inauthentic ontological characters in which they meet a falling being-in-the-world. Worst of all, this anomaly is not even hinted at by Heidegger as a still-to-be-solved problem and may therefore be completely overlooked by the student of *Being and Time*.

XV

Temporality and Within-Timeness as the Origin of the Vulgar Concept of Time

1. THE INCOMPLETENESS OF THE FOREGOING ANALYSIS OF THE TEMPORALITY OF HERE-BEING

The previous chapter took no account of the fact that all "happening," both historical and natural, takes place "in time." It explained historical-being purely from the existential-temporal structure of care. The "vulgar" or popular understanding of history, on the other hand, explains it as an ontic-temporal happening in time. Similarly, the scientific explanations of nature define and measure its processes by time. A fundamental analysis of this time is one of the tasks of the present chapter, though not its first one. Its first consideration is the elemental fact that here-being, before any thematic-scientific investigation of nature and history, already "counts with time" and orientates himself from it. This way of relating himself to time is so original to here-being that it goes before all handling of time-measuring utensils—clocks and watches of any kind—and makes the use of clocks first of all possible.

What precisely does Heidegger mean by a "counting with time"? It is a mode of "taking care" of things within the world. Obviously, however, we cannot take care of time in the way of handling and using it as we do a hammer and nails, but in the way of taking account of it, counting upon it and reckoning with it. On the basis of this elemental taking-care of time, we say that we "have" time or have none, we "take" time or cannot "leave" ourselves time. But why and from where do we take the time which we can "have" or "lose"? In what relation does this time stand to the temporality of here-being? These questions must be answered before the present inquiry can turn to the time in which beings are and happenings take place. The emergence of these questions shows that the preceding analysis of temporality are not only incomplete "since we did not pay heed to all the dimensions of the phenomenon, but it has fundamental gaps in it because something like world-time belongs to temporality itself, in the strict sense of the existential and temporal concept of world " (SZ, 405). On the ground of the ecstatic-horizonal constitution of world, the beings within it must meet us "in time." The time-character of within-worldish beings is accordingly called by Heidegger "within-timeness."

The predominant way in which the everyday here-being exists in his world is in a care-taking being-near-to things. Hence he first discovers the time he "takes" for himself on the things which are handily or substantially there. The time thus discovered is understood in the horizon of the indifferent understanding of being as something that is also in some way "there" (*vorhanden*). How the popular concept of time grows from the taking care of time of the temporally constituted here-being will be explained. The popular concept of time will prove to have its origin in a levelling-down of original time.

The popular conception of time vacillates between the view that time is "objective" and the view that it is "subjective." In this popular conception time is something "really" there "in itself," that is, has an "objective" being, yet it is ascribed primarily to the "soul." Conversely, the time that is considered to be "in the soul" or "in consciousness" nevertheless functions objectively. In Hegel's time-interpretation both possibilities are in a certain way "elevated" (*aufgehoben*). It must be remembered, however, that *Aufhebung* in Hegel's thought has a threefold meaning. It is a suspending-preserving-reconciliation. Hegel's attempt to establish a connection between time and spirit (*Geist*) and to explain how spirit as history can "fall into time" will be discussed toward the end of this chapter and compared with Heidegger's own attempt to explain how world-time belongs to the temporality of here-being.

The fundamental-ontological question that *Being and Time* must ultimately attempt to answer is whether and in what way there *is* time. Does time belong in any way to the realm of *beings*, so that we can legitimately say of it that it *is*? If so, what meaning can the "is" have when it expresses the being of time? The peculiarity of this question becomes evident when we remember that time is the meaning of being, that time is the universal horizon from which being discloses itself in the whole range of its understandability. This question cannot yet be answered in the present chapter, for it must first of all be shown how temporality in the whole of its temporalization makes an understanding of being and an explanation of beings possible. This task is deferred to Division Three of *Being and Time*.

2. THE TEMPORALITY OF HERE-BEING AND THE TAKING CARE OF TIME

The first paragraph of this section leads into Heidegger's new theme via a short sketch of everyday being-in-the-world. Since the decisive transition to the interpretation of time is made in this paragraph, it will be quoted in full.

> Da-sein exists as a being that, in its being, is concerned *about* that being itself. Essentially ahead of itself, it has projected itself upon its potentiality-of-being *before* going on to any mere consideration of itself. In its project it is revealed as something thrown. Thrown and abandoned to the world, it falls prey to it in taking care of it. As care, that is, as existing in the unity of the entangled, thrown project, this being is disclosed as a There. Being-together-with others, it keeps itself in an average interpretedness that is articulated in discourse and expressed in language. Being-in-the-world has already expressed *itself*, and *as being-together-with* beings encountered within the world, it constantly expresses *itself* in addressing and talking over what is taken care of. The circumspect taking care of common sense is grounded in temporality, in the mode of making present that awaits and retains. As taking care in calculating, planning, preparing ahead, and preventing, it always already says, whether audibly or not: "then" ... that will happen, "*before*" ... that will get settled, "*now*" ... that will be made up for, that "*on that former occasion*" failed or eluded us. (SZ, 406)

The most striking feature of this paragraph is that, together with the *time* expressed in the "then," "on that former occasion," and so on, it brings *speech and language* itself to the forefront. The "speaking" (*Sprechen*), moreover, appears in three distinct forms: expressing *oneself* (Sich-*aussprechen*), addressing (*Ansprechen*) and discussing or talking over or about something (*Besprechen*). We are immediately compelled to ask what speaking has to do with the phenomenon of time. And why do just these three forms of speaking belong to time as it is understood in our everyday being-in-the-world?

Speech and language lie already in all explicit exposition, explanation, and interpretation (*Aus-legen*, literally: to ex-pose, to lay out or set out). That the temporally constituted everyday here-being *expresses himself* means that he articulates his own *temporality* as an awaiting-retaining making present, be it silently, be it audibly. The time, therefore, that is expressed in the "then," "on that former occasion," "now," is nothing but the *self*-expression in which existent temporality ex-poses itself, sets itself out into the open by articulatingly bringing itself to word. The everyday care-taking speaks *awaitingly* in the "then," *retainingly* in the "on that former occasion" and as *making present* in the "now." In the ecstatic unity of an awaiting-retaining making present, the making present is the dominant and leading ecstasis. This characteristic of a falling temporality determines its self-expression insofar as the "then" is implicitly understood as "not yet now," and the "on that former occasion" as "no longer now." In other words, these time-phenomena are understood primarily from the present, the "now." In the "now" the making present speaks in the horizon of the "today," in the "then" it speaks in the horizon of the "later on" ("coming"), and in the "on that former occasion" it speaks in the horizon of the "earlier."

In short, *the time* expressed in the "then," "on that former occasion," "now," has not merely a connection with speaking, but is nothing other than the articulating, interpretative *self-expression* of an awaitingly retaining making present.

> And that is again possible only because, in itself ecstatically open, it is always already disclosed to itself and can be articulated in the interpretation that understands and speaks. *Since temporality is ecstatically and horizontally constitutive of the clearedness of the There, it is already always interpreted primordially in the There and is thus familiar.* (SZ, 408)

Now we turn to the other two modes of speaking, the addressing and talking about things, which go hand-in-hand with the expressed now, then, and so forth. Since the concrete way in which we are-in-the-world is in a lost preoccupation with things, the self-expressing taking care essentially addresses itself to and discusses the things among which it loses itself. This "going out" *to* things is made possible by the ecstatic structure of temporality, all of whose modes are an ecstatic removal *to*. . . . The time expressed in the "now," "then," and "on that former occasion" *reflects* the ecstatic structure of temporality by referring itself to something. Each "then" is *as such* a "then, when . . ." (e.g., then, when the building will be finished); each "on that former occasion" is an "at that time, when . . ." (e.g., at that time when we met); each "now" a "now, that . . ." (e.g., now that it is raining). The essential reference-structure of the expressed time means that every "now," "then," or the like, can in principle be *dated* from something. At this

Temporality and Within-Timeness as the Origin of the Vulgar Concept of Time 331

stage, we must not yet think of the highly sophisticated "dating" of time from astronomically calculated dates in a calendar, but of its more original "dating" from within-worldish events by everyday care. The reference *to* something expressed in the "then, when . . . ," "at that time, when . . . ," "now, that . . . ," is called by Heidegger "datability" (*Datierbarkeit*). This reference-structure, whether expressly pronounced or not, essentially belongs to time, even where the "dating" from some definite event is vague or seemingly missing. The "then, when . . . ," "now, that . . . ," and the like, in which ecstatic temporality expresses itself already refer us to an addressing and discussing of things. And conversely, the most commonplace everyday pronouncements—for example, "it is cold"—tacitly imply the "now, that . . . ," because, in and with all speaking of something, everyday care expresses itself as a making present of within-worldish beings.

Heidegger himself ascribes a peculiar importance to datability, as is shown in the following passage.

> The fact that the structure of datability belongs essentially to what is interpreted with the "now," "then," and "on that former occasion," becomes the most elemental proof that what has been interpreted originates from temporality interpreting itself. [. . .] The *datability* of the "now," "then," and "on that former occasion" is the *reflex* of the *ecstatic* constitution of temporality, and is *thus* essential for time itself that has been expressed. The structure of the datability of the "now," "then," and "on that former occasion" is evidence for the fact that they *stem from temporality and are themselves time*. The interpretative expression of "now," "then," and "on that former occasion," is the most primordial way of *giving the time* [*Zeitigung*]. (SZ, 408)

According to our passage, datability "*proves*" that the "now," "then," and so on, *originate* in the ecstatic temporality of here-being, and in furnishing this proof, it verifies that these phenomena "*are themselves time.*" As to the first point, a proof is possible and necessary because the time expressed in the "now," "then," and so on, is already *derivative* and therefore demands a demonstration of its "origin." The proof itself, of course, is made possible only by Heidegger's own interpretation of here-being and temporality, but this is no real objection, because it is the nature of all similar philosophical proofs. What is surprising in the above passage is that Heidegger should consider it necessary to find a "proof" of the genuine *time*-character of the "now," "then," and "on that former occasion." Who, we feel inclined to ask, would question that these phenomena *are* indeed *time*? Heidegger may be thinking of certain attempts—perhaps Bergson's—to explain the externalized, measured time as space. Otherwise a "proof" would seem to be all the more superfluous because—as Heidegger himself stresses earlier in this section—we unquestioningly recognize the above phenomena as time, and take our familiarity with them far too much for granted. For where, Heidegger asks, have we found this "time"? Have we found it among the things that are simply "there" within the world? Obviously not, and yet we always know it and dispose of it without any further ado. What truly demands an explanation is not so much the remote mystery of time but its constantly familiar nearness.

Once these first decisive steps of Heidegger's analysis have been thoroughly grasped, its further steps are comparatively easy to follow. The character of time to which Heidegger next turns his attention is its "spannedness" or "duration." The explanation starts from the awaiting, which stands in an ecstatic unity with a retaining making present.

> If awaiting, understanding itself in the "then," interprets itself and in so doing, as a making present, understands what is awaiting in terms of its "now," the "and now not yet" already lies in the "giving" [*Angabe*] of the "then." The awaiting that makes present understands the "until then." (SZ, 409)

The cardinal point brought out by this passage lies in the "and now not yet," for it is from a primary view to the "now" that a predominantly presenting care-taking understands the spanned "until"— namely *until* the waited-for given *then*. The "until then" is articulatingly exposed in the "in-between," which can itself be "dated." Its datability is expressed in the "during which . . ." (e.g., between now and then, during which such and such can be expected). The "during" can, in turn, be articulated and divided up by awaitingly giving further "from then—till then," which, however, are in advance delimited by the primarily forethrown "then."

> The "lasting" ["*Währen*"] is articulated in the understanding of the "during" ["*während*"] that awaits and makes present. This duration is again the time revealed in the *self*-interpretation of temporality, a time that is thus actually, but unthematically, understood in taking care as a "span." The making present that awaits and retains interprets a "during" with a "span," only because in so doing it is disclosed to *itself* as being ecstatically *stretched along* in historical temporality, even though it does not know itself as this. (SZ, 409)

Heidegger's exposition of time-phenomena that are existentially well known to all of us throws an interesting light back onto his existential interpretation of temporality. While the datability of the "then," "now," and so forth, as we have seen, springs primarily from the *ecstatic* unity of temporality, the spannedness of the "during" springs primarily from its ecstatic *unity*, for only the unity of a making present that awaits can make the time *between* a "now" and a "then" disclosable and *expressible*. Since, however, temporality is an *ecstatic unity*, the datability and the spannedness that spring from it must mutually determine each other. Not only the "during" is datable, but conversely, every datable "now," "then," and so on, also has a span of variable width, for instance "now" during the intermission, at dinner, in the evening, in summer; "then": at breakfast, during the climb, and suchlike.

The enduringness articulated in the "until" and the "during" already indicates the possibility of a concept of time as an uninterrupted flow, as a pure "continuum." This concept, however, is a later development and is not yet characteristic of the stage at present under review. Everyday care-taking, as a making present that awaits and retains, "'allows itself' time in this or that way and gives this time to itself in taking care, even without determining the time by any specific reckoning, and before any such reckoning has been done" (SZ, 409). What does Heidegger mean by this obscure statement?

Let us start with that part of the statement which has already been unambiguously explained: everyday taking care gives itself time in the expressly exposed "then," "on that former occasion," "now." This "most primordial *time-giving*" is definable, that is, datable, from within-worldish happenings, without and before any *calculating* fixing of "dates" in a calendar. What is not so clear is how taking care is an allowing itself time (*Sich-Zeit-lassen*), and Heidegger's explanations on this point leave much to be desired. The preceding and subsequent passages, however, *imply* the following explanation. The time that care-taking allows itself to have is the *span between* the awaitingly given "then" and the presentingly given "now." This is what we unthinkingly express when we say "Between now and then *I have time*." Much the same thing is meant by "taking time," as when we say "Between now and then I shall take time to do such and such."

But how is it that everyday care-taking can *give itself* time and *let itself* have it? Because the care-taking-here-being is essentially *mine*, and so the time, which, as existent temporality, I give *myself* or let *myself* have, is essentially my time. And since, as existent temporality, I can exist as my own self or not my own self, I can let myself have time "in this or that way," that is, authentically or inauthentically.

The inauthentically existing here-being usually dates his time from what happens to occur and from what he pursues "during the day." It is just in this mode of existing, of "living unto the day," that the factical here-being does not understand himself as "running along in a continuously enduring succession of pure 'nows'" (SZ, 409). The reason is that when the inauthentic here-being becomes absorbed in the things he awaitingly takes care of, and,

> not awaiting itself, forgets itself, the more its time that it "allows" itself is *covered over* by this mode of "allowing." [. . .] By reason of this covering over, the time that Da-sein never understands itself has gaps in it, so to speak. We often cannot bring a "day" together again when we come back to the time that we have "used." Yet the time that has gaps in it does not go to pieces in this lack of togetherness, but is a mode of temporality that is always already disclosed and ecstatically *stretched out*. (SZ, 409–10)

All theoretical conceptions of a continous flow of nows must therefore be excluded from the explanation of how a care-takingly given and taken time "runs." The decisive consideration here is how a factical here-being "has time" according to his possible ways of existing.

The irresoluteness of an inauthentic existence, as was shown earlier, temporalizes itself in the mode of an unawaiting-forgetting making present. The "unawaiting-forgetting," it will be remembered, refers to here-being's own self. The more he loses *himself* to the "world," the more he constricts himself in a presenting of things, until even the inauthentic awaiting-retaining is modified. (See the temporal analysis of curiosity above, chap. 13, sec. 1, subsec. c.)

> The irresolute person understands himself in terms of the events and accidents nearest by that are encountered in such making present and urge themselves upon him in changing ways. Busily losing *himself* in what is taken care of, the irresolute person *loses his time* in them, too. Hence the characteristic way of talking: "I have no time." Just as the person who exists inauthentically constantly loses time and never "has" any, it is the distinction of the temporality of authentic existence that in resoluteness it never loses time and "always has time." For the temporality of resoluteness has, in regard to its present, the nature of the *Moment*. The Moment's authentic making present of the situation does not itself have the leadership, but is *held* in the future that has-been. The existence of the Moment temporalizes itself as fatefully whole, stretching along in the sense of the authentic, historical *constancy* of the self. This kind of temporal existence "constantly" has its time *for* what the situation requires of it. But resoluteness discloses the There in such a way only as situation. Thus the resolute person can never encounter what is disclosed in such a way that he could lose his time on it in an irresolute way. (SZ, 410).

At first reading this passage raises the hope that Heidegger is at last giving us some reliable characteristics by which we can distinguish between an authentic and inauthentic existence in a concrete instance. The phenomena he describes are certainly familiar to us from experience, especially the "losing our time" on trivialities. Unfortunately, these phenomena are neither unambiguously interpretable nor fully described. To take the last point first, the characteristic of a resolute here-being who never loses his time but always has it is felt by Heidegger himself to need further qualification. He always has time *for* what the situation demands from him, that is, *for* the factical possibility of his existence which he must choose for himself. But since all decison *for* one possibility must bear the *not*-choosing of others, it is just the authentic existence who will "have *no* time" for what he had to forego and reject. And, conversely, it is ridiculous to assume that all inauthentic existence must be a feeble drifting among what chances occur. There is no reason why he should not decisively "have time" for the possibilities he has chosen *within* the sphere of his lostness to things. And since the factical here-being can be equally decisively engaged in the world in *both* his ways of existing, how can we know whether a single-minded devotion to a chosen possibility springs from a resolutely owned self or from a flight from death into the complete self-forgetfulness of an absorbing activity? It seems, therefore, that no experience can enable us to distinguish between authenticity and inauthenticity in any concrete case, because the *same* experienced phenomena can belong to either, depending solely on how an existence faces his own finiteness, and this is just what we cannot judge, perhaps least of all in our own case. From where, then, does Heidegger draw the distinguishing marks of these two ways of existing? Are they not entirely drawn from a "phenomenological construction"? That a resolute here-being never, for instance, loses *his* time logically follows from the existential-temporal definition of "resoluteness." But this is a one-way street, for the concretely experienced "not losing *his* time" is too ambiguous to lead us back to its "origin," quite unlike, for instance, the unambiguously interpretable "datability" of experienced time.

In keeping with his usual method, Heidegger concludes the discussion of "taking" ("having") time and "losing" it by a statement of the existential-temporal conditions that make these existentiell-ontic phenomena possible: *"Factically thrown Da-sein can 'take' and lose time for itself only because a time is 'allotted' to it as temporaly ecstatically stretched along with the disclosedness of the There grounded in that temporality"* (SZ, 410).

What is "allotted" or "given" to each here-being is *a* time. This is the expressed and existentielly experienced time of a finite existence.

The original *self*-expression of its own temporality, as Heidegger said earlier, is not necessarily *audibly pronounced* and communicated with others. But since here-being is essentially disclosed to himself in his being-with-others, and usually understands his own hereness from the average explanations given by "them," the publicly pronounced "now, that . . . ," "then, when . . . ," and "on that former occasion" are in principle understandable, even when they are not unequivocally dated.

> The "now" expressed is spoken by each one in the publicness of being-with-one-another-in-the-world. The time interpreted and expressed by actual Da-sein is thus also always already *made public* as such on the basis of its ecstatic being-in-the-world. Since everyday taking care understands itself in terms of the "world" taken care of, it knows the "time" that it takes for itself *not as its own*, but rather heedfully exploits the time that "there is," the time with which the *they* reckons. The publicness of "time" is all the more compelling, the more factical Da-sein *explicitly takes care* of time by expressly taking it into account. (SZ, 411).

This concluding paragraph already forms the transition to the theme of the next section. Only one phrase in it requires comment here: ". . . but rather heedfully exploits the time that 'there is' ['*es gibt*'], the time with which the *they* reckons." "Es gibt" means literally "it gives," and we may legitimately wonder what Heidegger has in mind with the "it." In this specific context the "it" could well mean "das Man," the "they," the everyday "one-among-others" who gives the public time, in contrast to the time which each here-being gives to himself from what is *allotted* (given) to him by his *own* finite temporality. Our phrase could therefore be also read as: ". . . but rather heedfully exploits the time that '*one* gives,' with which *one* reckons." This interpretation of the "es gibt" is, of course, proper only in the present context. It does not cancel its first meaning, "there is," but compliments it.

3. Time Taken Care of and Within-Timeness

This section shows how the public time unfolds into a time-reckoning and how the measuring of time, as well as the utensils used for measuring (sundials, clocks, watches) are themselves made possible and necessary, by the temporality of here-being.

It has already been indicated that the publishing of time is not accidental, but springs from the understandingly interpretative way in which the temporally disclosed here-being factically exists. The dating of the public time can be accomplished from within-worldish occurrences, but even this elementary dating already happens in the horizon of a taking care of time that we know as astronomical and calendrical *time-reckoning*. This reckoning is not a matter of chance, but has its existential and ontological necessity in the fundamental constitution of Da-sein as care. Since Da-sein essentially exists entangled as thrown, it interprets [*auslegt*] its time heedfully by way of a reckoning with time. *In this reckoning* the "real" *making public* of time temporalizes itself so that we must say that *the thrownness of Da-sein is the reason why "there is" public time*. (SZ, 411–12).

It will be noticed that a new overtone in *auslegen*, to lay out, now makes itself felt. The explaining reckoning with time "lays it out," in a similar sense as we speak of "laying out capital," circumspectly distributing it to the best advantage. In his thrown being-with-others-in-the-world, the circumspect here-being does not "lay out" his time from his own finite temporality, but goes by the publicly reckoned time that must be more or less the same for every "one." Even for a public time-reckoning, however, the decisive thing is not that it "quantifies" time by numerically defining the "dating," but that it springs from the temporality of here-being who *counts with and on time*.

The temporal structure of a circumspectly care-taking being-in-the-world, as we have repeatedly heard, is a making present that awaits and retains. Even in his self-forgetful lostness to the "world," however, here-being still exists *for the sake of* himself, but understands himself primarily from his ability-to-be-in-the-world, taking care of the things relevant to his own existence. In his dependence on a "world,"

> Da-sein awaits its potentiality-of-being-in-the-world in such a way that it "reckons" *with* and *on* whatever is in eminent *relevance* for the sake of its potentiality-of-being. Everyday, circum*spect* being-in-the-world needs the *possibility of sight*, that is, brightness, if it is to take care of things at hand within what is objectively present. With the factual disclosedness of world, nature has been discovered for Da-sein. In its thrownness Da-sein is subject to the changes of day and night. Day with its brightness gives it the possibility of sight, night takes it away. (SZ, 412)

It is now clear what Heidegger meant earlier when he said that even the most elementary dating of time already takes place in the horizon of an "astronomical" time-reckoning. The "astronomy" of circumspect care-taking is altogether prescientific. It makes use of the "handiness" of the sun, which dates the carefully "laid-out" time of everyday here-being. This dating gives the "most natural" time-measure, the day. At the same time, the sun is the most natural time-measuring utensil ("time-piece") insofar as the division of the day into a number of care-takingly given "thens" also takes place with a view to the "wandering sun." The thrown here-being takes account of and counts on the regularly recurring occupation of distinctive "places" or "positions" in the sky by the wandering sun: sunrise, midday, sunset. On the around of this express dating of time, the "happening" of here-being is a *day-to-day* happening.

The enormously complex meaning of everydayness and its existential-temporal origin are only now beginning to come to light. It will be remembered that Heidegger has earlier identified everydayness with the inauthentic mode of historical-being. Now if historical-being is essentially a "happening" with others in the same world, then its inauthentic mode must in some prominent way be defined by the dating from the sun, which gives it its "day-to-day" character.

The sun, however, is not only exceptionally "handy" as the common measure of time in our everyday being-with-each-other. It is, as Heidegger said earlier, in eminent relevance for our ability-to-be-in-the-world. Its light gives the *possibility of seeing* to our circum*spect* care-taking. Hence the dating of the awaitingly exposed "then" comprehends in itself "then, when it dawns, it *is time for* the day's work" (SZ, 414). The carefully "laid out" time is essentially a "time for . . .": it is appropriate or inappropriate, the right or the wrong time *for* something. The reference structure of "for something" brings the *worldishness* of the published time into view. We remember that the *significance* that constitutes the worldishness of the everyday world is characterized by the "for," which, in turn, is ultimately fixed in the "for the sake of" here-being's own ability-to-be. Not only every utensil has the structure of "something *for* something," but the space discovered within the everyday world is also significantly defined by the "for"; so the places into which the within-worldish space is articulated are not merely indifferent points or locations, but the carefully allocated places for such and such utensils. The expressly explained time of everyday here-being shows the same world-character.[1]

> Thus we shall call the time making itself public in the temporalizing of temporality *world-time*. And we shall designate it thus not because it is *objectively present* (*vorhanden*) as an *innerworldly* being (that it can never be), but because it belongs *to the world* in the sense interpreted existentially and ontologically. [. . .] Only now can time taken care of be completely characterized as to its structure: It is datable, spanned, and public and, as having this structure, it belongs to the world itself. Each "now," for example, that is expressed in a natural, everyday way, has this structure and is understood as such when Da-sein allows itself time in taking care, although unthematically and preconceptually. (SZ, 414-15).

Temporality and Within-Timeness as the Origin of the Vulgar Concept of Time 339

Heidegger does *not* define the being of time in this passage, but only denies that *reality* is a mode of being that can be appropriate to it. The fact that time is not a within-worldish entity does not mean that it must be a total nothing, nor that it is "merely subjective," since the temporality of existent here-being is not identical with the subjectivity of a subject. Heidegger will recur to the highly problematic "being" of time later in this chapter. At the moment, having completed the structural analysis of interpreted time, he turns to the development of time-measuring and its foundation in one definite mode of the temporalization of temporality.

In comparing the "natural" time-reckoning with the more highly developed one Heidegger notes that a direct reference to the presence of the "natural clock," namely to the sun in the sky, grows less and less important. We can read the time off our manufactured clocks and watches, which, however, are ultimately regulated by the "natural clock." Just like the most primitive time-reckoning, so too the most sophisticated use of time-measuring utensils is grounded in the temporality of here-being, for it makes the dating of public time possible at all.

Already the "primitive" here-being to some extent makes himself independent from a direct observation of the sun by measuring, for instance, the shadow thrown by a conveniently available thing. A familiar example of this is the sundial, on which the shadow moves on a numbered path opposite to the course of the sun.

> But why do we find something like time at the position that the shadow occupies on the dial? Neither the shadow nor the graduated dial is time itself, nor is the spatial relation between them. Where, then, is the time that we read off directly not only on the "sundial" but also on every pocketwatch? (SZ, 416)

These seemingly childish questions—they are indeed just the questions a child might ask—serve to remind us that there is much more to "reading the time" than merely watching the changing positions of the clock hand (or shadow). In telling the time from a clock, the essential thing is that "*we say*, whether explicitly or not, *now* it is such an hour and so many minutes, *now* it is time to . . . , or there is still time . . . , namely *now* until. . . . Looking at the clock is grounded in and guided by a taking-time-for-oneself" (SZ, 416).

The time we "take" or "let-ourselves-have" is the span between now and then. Each "then" implies "and not yet now"; each "at that time" implies "and no longer now"—that is, they are understood from a primary view to the "now." This tendency becomes more pronounced in a "clock-watching" reckoning with time, which is essentially a *"now-saying."* That each "now" is already understood and exposed in its full structural content of datability, spannedness, publicity, and worldishness seems so obvious and natural that we take no explicit notice of it.

But why does the now-saying become so much more pronounced when we date our time from a clock or a watch than when we do it from a within-worldish occurrence? Because, Heidegger says, "The dating carried out in the use of the clock turns out to be the eminent making present of something objectively present. Dating does not simply take up a relation with something objectively present, but taking up a relation itself has the character of *measuring*" (SZ, 416–17).

This explanation is anything but clear. We can clarify it by remembering that *all* dating is accomplished by reference to "something there." So, for instance, when we say "now that the door is banging . . . ," we are dating the now by referring to the banging door. But this kind of referring does not *measure*, whereas, according to Heidegger, reference to a thing like a clock does. This is surprising, because we are not usually aware that by simply glancing at a clock (referring to it) we are in fact *measuring*. Why do we remain unaware of what we are doing? Because, as Heidegger says, "the number of the measurement (*Masszahl*) can be read off directly" (SZ, 417). When we see, for instance, that "it is four o'clock," we simply find the number four on the dial and so get the impression that it is the clock that does the measuring. What we forget are the preconditions that must be fulfilled in order that we can understand any number as a measure. Taking an ordinary twelve-hour clock as an example, it is evident that the "stretch to be measured" is that between two extreme positions of the sun, from midday to midnight and midnight to midday, and this is originally and "naturally" dated from two extreme positions of the sun relative to our position on the earth. This stretch is represented on the dial by the complete course the hand has to travel. The unit of measure, the hour or some other convenient fraction of the whole, is represented by the numbered lines or marks. In referring to the clock and seeing the hand pointing to four, we are presenting the unit of measure as being four times present in the present stretch to be measured. This complex presenting of a measure and something measured constitutes the dating of our time from the clock. Without it, there could be no clocks, but, at most, meaninglessly marked surfaces over which pointed things meaninglessly move.

Heidegger has now taken a decisive, "ground-laying" step toward explaining the "genesis" of the popular concept of time, which will be carried out in the next section. The problems that remain to be clarified in the present section still move on a more fundamental level. The first of these, the "coupling" of time and space, has already briefly appeared in Heidegger's remarks on the sundial, where it was noted that what we really find on the sundial—and of course on every kind of clock—is nothing but spatially extended things and spatial relations. Although none of these is "time itself," it cannot be an accident that they can be used for a measuring dating of time. As Heidegger has shown earlier (chap. 4, § 70), it is the temporality of a factical being-in-the-world that makes the disclosure of space possible and enables the "spatial" here-being to allocate to himself his "here" from the care-takingly discovered "there." Hence the *datability* of the time taken care of is bound to a definite place of the factical here-being.

According to Heidegger, then, untenable notions about the coupling of time and space arise from a confusion of the essential *datability* of time from a within-worldish occurrence—preeminently from the movement of the sun across the sky—with time itself as the express self-exposition of temporality. Just as space is an *irreducible* phenomenon that can never become time, so time can never be reduced to space through its dating from spatial relations that serve as a measure. For the time-*measuring* itself, as the preceding analyses have shown, it is not the numerical definition of spatial relations and movements that is ontologically decisive, but the preeminent making present of a thing in every now and for every one present. In our everyday now-saying we are so intent on reading off the number of measurement as such that we are apt to forget the measured as such, so what we "really" find on the clock is nothing but stretch and number.[2]

The world-time so pronouncedly made public in the measuring is the time *within which* within-worldish beings meet us. The time-character of their being is within-timeness (being-in-time). Here again the essentially dual role of world shows itself. Looking at the within-worldish beings, world-time is the time *within which* they are there, but looking at the factually existing being-in-the-world, world-time belongs to the ecstatic-horizonal constitution of temporality. It has, therefore, "the *same* transcendence as the world" (SZ, 419). But in what way *is* there world-time? What mode of being can be ascribed to it? This question, which was briefly touched upon before, is now more elaborately unfolded by Heidegger as follows.

> The time "in which" objectively present things move or are at rest is *not* "*objective*," if by this is meant the objective presence in itself of beings encountered in the world. But time is not "*subjective*" either, if we understand by that the objective presence and occurrence in a "subject." World-

> *time is more "objective" than any possible object because, with the disclosedness of the world, it always already becomes ecstatically and horizonally "objectified" as the condition of the possibility of innerworldly beings* (SZ, 419).[3]

The phrase "the condition of the possibility of innerworldly beings" can be misleading. It is well to remember that "the condition of the possibility" has a purely ontological sense, and not the ontic sense of a "cause" or a "condition" that allows something to come into being. What Heidegger means is that world-time is a necessary condition for within-worldish beings to be discovered *as beings*, that is, as things that *are*. The *being* of these beings can and must show itself as a being-in-time. That the world-time belongs to the temporality of existent here-being does not mean that he forces an alien "form" onto other beings, but means that his self-disclosing, self-exposing temporality first of all *enables* these beings to show *that and how they are in themselves*. Without the temporality of the factical being-in-the-world, these beings would not dissolve into nothing, but would remain beingless and nameless, neither hidden nor unhidden *as beings*, for the name "beings" already implies that they have come to light in their *being*.

Further, it may be asked whether and how far the "more objective" character that Heidegger ascribes to world-time is the same as the "objective reality" that Kant ascribes to the schematized, *temporally defined* categories. For Kant also does not mean by "objective reality" that these temporally defined categories occur in nature just like things, but means that they enable the things in nature to appear (show themselves) *as objects, as what they are*. The kinship between the two interpretations is unmistakable, but there are also essential differences. Quite apart from the fact that Kant's "nature in general" (*Natur überhaupt*) is not identical with Heidegger's "world"—they are two different attempts to explain the same thing—a decisive difference is that in Heidegger's interpretation the world-time is already expressly *exposed* with the disclosure of world, so that,

> contrary to Kant's opinion, world-time is found *just as directly* in what is physical as in what is psychical, and not just by way of a detour over the psychical. Initially "time" shows itself in the sky, that is, precisely where one finds it in the natural orientation toward it, so that "time" is even identified with the sky. (SZ, 419).

According to Heidegger, then, the natural, everyday understanding of time has it own rightness, even though it can give no explanation why it finds "the time" simply and *directly* on the things of nature. Heidegger concurs with this view, but gives a philosophically satisfying explanation of it; on the ground of the *self-exposition* of temporality, no *mediation* is required between the "psychical," the soul (*das Gemüt*), and the "physical," the things of the *phusis*.

> But world-time is also "more subjective" than any possible subject, since it first makes possible the being of the factical existing self, that being which, as is now well understood, is the meaning of care. "Time" is neither objectively present in the "subject" nor in the "object," neither "inside" nor "outside," and it "is" "*prior*" to every subjectivity and objectivity, because it presents the condition of the very possibility of this "prior." Does it then have any "being" at all? (SZ, 419)

We see that Heidegger only elaborates what and how time *is not*. The seemingly positive descriptions of "more objective" and "more subjective" do not, after all, tell us how time itself *is*. On the contrary, the disturbing question now comes explicitly to the forefront, "Has time any 'being' at all?"

If it has not, is it a mere nothing, "a phantom," or should we more truly say of it "it is" than of any concrete beings? These questions are not answered by Heidegger here, nor can they be answered until after the "question of being" (*Seinsfrage*) as it is posed and worked out in *Being and Time* has been solved. But although the answer is once more deferred to Division Three, these questions are not asked here merely to arouse idle curiosity; they have the positive aim of making us doubtful whether the distinction between the being of a self conceived as a subject and the being of objects is fundamental enough to allow a proper answer to these questions. It is clear that world-time can be neither "volatized 'subjectivistically' nor be 'reified' (*verdinglicht*) in a bad 'objectification'" (SZ, 420). No more satisfactory than these two unacceptable extremes is a "vacillating insecurely" between them. The next step toward a solution of this problem is to show how a theoretical concept of time grows out of the prescientic everyday understanding of time, and how it itself shuts out the possibility of understanding its intended meaning "in terms of primordial time, that is, as *temporality*. Everyday taking care that gives itself time finds 'time' in innerwordly beings that are encountered 'in time.' Thus our illumination of the genesis of the vulgar concept of time must take its point of departure from within-timeness" (SZ, 420).

4. Within-Timeness and the Genesis of the Vulgar Concept of Time

At the beginning of this section Heidegger asks how something like "time" first shows itself to a circumspect taking care. "In what mode of taking care and using tools does it become *explicitly* accessible?" (SZ, 420). The word Heidegger uses for "explicitly" is *ausdrücklich*, literally: *expressly*. But the word here no longer means the original "self-expressing" (*Sichaussprechen*) in which temporality ex-poses itself, lays itself out into the open. There are several stages or gradations of "expressness" until it comes to a fully fledged, theoretical conceptualization. The utensil in whose use time first becomes explicitly accessible is the clock; for here-being, in counting with and on *himself*, that is, with his own temporality, regulates himself *by the time* which publicly shows itself on the clock. What is decisive for the present stage of "explicitness" is a calculating *counting* of time, which grows from a *measuring* reference to the clock.

> The existential and temporal meaning of the clock turns out to be making present of the moving pointer. By *following* the positions of the pointer in a way that makes present, one *counts* them. This making present temporalizes itself in the ecstatic unity of a retaining that awaits. To *retain* the "on that former occasion" in *making present* means that in saying-now to be open for the horizon of the earlier, that is, the now-no-longer. To *await* the "then" in *making present* means: in saying-now to be open for the horizon of the later, that is, the now-not-yet. *What shows itself in this making present is time.* Then how are we to define the *time* manifest in the horizon of the use of the clock that is circumspect and takes time for itself in taking care? *This time is what is counted, showing itself in following, making present, and counting the moving pointer in such a way that making present temporalizes itself in ecstatic unity with retaining and awaiting horizonally open according to the earlier and later.* But that is nothing more than an existential and ontological interpretation of the definition that Aristotle gave of time: *touto gar estin ho chronos, arithmos kinêseôs kata to proteron kai hysteron.* "That, namely, is time, what is counted in the motion encountered in the horizon of the earlier and the later." (SZ, 421)[4]

It can hardly be denied that Heidegger's interpretation of the temporality of here-being and its self-exposure into world-time brings Aristotle's definition to clarity. Heidegger does not claim too much when he says that this seemingly strange definition becomes almost "obvious" when the existential-ontological horizon from which Aristotle drew it is defined. It is to be regretted that Heidegger gives here no interpretation of the whole passage in Aristotle's *Physics*, but this task first needed the completion of Division Three, and was therefore deferred to the unwritten second part of *Being and Time*.[5]

All subsequent time-interpretations, according to Heidegger, keep *in principle* to the Aristotelian definition. This means that the theoretical-scientific approach thematizes "the time" which prescientifically shows itself in a circumspect care-taking.

Time is the "what is counted," that is, it is what is expressed and what is meant, although unthematically, in the making present of the *moving* pointer (or shadow). In making present what is moved in its motion, one says "now here, now here, and so on." What is counted are the nows. And these show themselves "in every now" as "right-away-no-longer-now" and as "just-now-not-yet." The world-time "caught sight of" in this way in the use of clocks we shall call *now-time*. (SZ, 421)

A comparison with the essential structure of world-time shows that the datability of each "now, that . . . ," "then, when . . . ," and so on, as well as the significance-structure of the "time for . . . ," are *concealed* by the popular understanding of a pure succession of nows. This concealment "*levels down*" the articulated structure of the ecstatic-horizonal unity of temporality in which datability and worldishness are grounded. "The nows are cut off from these relations, so to speak, and, as thus cut off, they simply range themselves along after one another so as to constitute the succession" (SZ, 422).

We can now see why Heidegger has repeatedly emphasized that the care-taking reckoning with time *does not* attend to *time as such*: it was to show that the levelling-down concealment of the full structure of world-time is not accidental, but arises from the lostness of a falling care-taking in its makings and doings. The direct, unreflecting going-out-to things simply understands the counted nows *together with* the things in which it is absorbed. What happens when here-being begins to *reflect*, that is, come back to time itself from the things which are there? He finds that the nows are also in some way "there," and explains their "thereness" from the horizon of that undifferentiated, whether theoretical or pretheoretical, understanding of being by which he is constantly guided: being as "reality" (*Vorhandenheit*) in the widest sense. Even the commonsense view of time, of course, does not assert that the nows are "there" in the same way as the solid, tangible things, but, Heidegger maintains, it does "see" time in the horizon of the "idea of reality." As evidence for this, Heidegger cites the characteristic that everyday understanding ascribes to time. According to it, the nows "go away" or "pass away," and those which are gone make up the past; the nows which "come" and the coming make up the future. This characteristic implies that some kind of "independent existence" is tacitly ascribed to the nows, and "independent existence" is just an essential moment of being conceived as substantial reality. But even this misconception of the "being" of the now-time still reflects its origin in the ecstatic *unity* of temporality. This is necessarily so, because, as already Aristotle explained in the previously mentioned chapter of the *Physics*, the "now" could not show itself at all except in the horizon of the "before" and "after." What the commonsense view necessarily conceals is the datability and worldishness of world-time, for in the horizon of real "thereness," objective "presentness" (*Vorhandenheit*), these structures are not accessible at all.

This concealment grows more rigid and fixed in the *conceptualization* of the characteristics of time as popularly understood. Insofar as the now-succession is explicitly comprehended as in some way "there," it itself enters "into time":

> We say that *in* every now it is now, *in* every now it already disappears. The now is now in *every* now, thus constantly present as the *same*, even if in every now another may be disappearing as it arrives. Yet it does show at the same time the constant presense of itself as *this* changing thing. Thus even Plato, who had this perspective of time as a succession of nows that come into being and pass away, had to call time the image of eternity. (SZ, 423)[6]

Not surprisingly, however, Heidegger finds the most impressive evidence for the leveling-down concealment of world-time and of temporality as such in the thesis that time is *endless*. The endlessness of the now-time, as Heidegger rightly points out, is logically implied already in the conception and definition of the "now," for insofar as each now *as such* comingly goes-away, none can be the first or the last, the beginning or the end of the uninterrupted now-flow.

As in the preceding critical points made by Heidegger against the concept of now-time, the principal reason on which his argument is based is the misplaced ontological conception of the "being" of time as a being objectively there-in-itself—*Vorhandensein*. Similarly Kant argues in his First Antinomy of Pure Reason that the assumption of the "real existence" (*Wirklichkeit, Vorhandenheit*) of time constricts pure reason into insoluble contraditions with itself. But the supporting reasons adduced by the two thinkers are different, and above all, their starting points from the subjectivity of the subject and the temporality of here-being considerably diverge. This comes most clearly into view in Heidegger's elucidation of the reason why the above analyzed levelling-down of world-time takes place. The reason lies in the being of here-being as care, or more precisely, in its mode of a fallingly thrown lostness to the things it takes care of in making them present. What reveals itself in this lostness is *the concealing flight* of here-being from his ownmost existence, which accomplishes itself in a forward-running resoluteness. This flight *from* death looks away from the end of being-in-the-world and is the inauthentic mode of ecstatically *futural* being *to* an end. As we have already seen, the being-unto-death is grounded in the temporal structure of here-being's coming-to-himself in his utmost possibility; that is, coming-to-his-own-end. The falling everyday here-being looks away from the coming-to-his-own-end, and so conceals that his "futural" temporality essentially *ends itself.* In so disowning his own finite temporality, here-being forgets himself in being "one self among others," and conforms to the publicly explained "endlessness" of time. "One's" time may, in a certain sense, rightly be called "endless" because "one" *can* never die, insofar as death is singly *mine,* and authentically understood in *my* forward-running resoluteness. The disowned oneself, on the other hand, understands death as the end until when "one has always still time." This having time betrays the possibility of losing time, not in the sense of the finiteness of time itself, but in the sense of carefully snatching as much as possible of the time which still comes and goes on.

But just as in a fleeing being-unto-death death can never be wholly hidden, so the seemingly "harmless" passage of the endless "imposes itself 'on' Da-sein in a remarkably enigmatic way" (SZ, 425). Why should we speak so emphatically of the *passing* of time and not of its *coming* when, in view of the now-succession, both would be equally justified? Even in the commonsense view of time, the finite "*temporality,*" in which the world-time temporalizes itself, is *not completely closed off*" (SZ, 425). The seemingly commonplace experience of the "passing" of time is only the ground of a wanting-to-hold-time. In strictly existential terms, this means

> an inauthentic awaiting of "moments" that already *forgets* the moments as they slip by. The awaiting of inauthentic existence that makes present and forgets is the condition of the possibility of the common experience of time's passing away. Since Da-sein is futural in being ahead-of-himself, it must, in awaiting, understand the succession of nows as one that *slips away* and passes away. *Da-sein knows fleeting time from the "fleeting" knowledge of its death.* In the kind of talk that emphasizes time's passing away, the *finite futurality* of the temporality of Da-sein is publicly reflected. And since even in the talk about time's passing away death can remain covered over, time shows itself as a passing away "in itself."
>
> But even in this pure succession of nows passing away in itself, primordial time reveals itself in spite of all levelling down and covering over. The vulgar interpretation determines the flux of time as an irreversible succession. Why can time not be reversed? Especially when one looks exclusively at the flux of the nows, it is incomprehensible in itself why the sequence of nows should not accommodate itself to the reverse direction. The impossibility of this reversal has its basis in the provenance of public time in temporality, whose temporalizing, primarily futural, "goes" ecstatically toward its end in such a way that it "is" already towards its end. (SZ, 425–26)

In the last sentence Heidegger refers, of course, to the structure of care as a thrown being-to-an-end, or more strictly defined, as a thrown being-unto-death. The last paragraph completes the positive and new tasks of this section; what follows are comments on its findings. In the first place, Heidegger emphasizes once more that the common concept of time as an endless, passing, irreversible flow of nows springs from the temporality of a falling here-being. From this he draws the conclusion: "*The vulgar representation of time has its natural justification*" (SZ, 426). After a fundamental critique of this concept it may seem surprising that Heidegger should suddenly restore to it "its natural justification." Yet it is not altogether surprising, when we remember that the equally severely criticized inauthentic view of history as "an occurring 'in time'" was also said to "be justified within its limits" (SZ, 377). In this respect Heidegger stands entirely within our philosophical tradition, whose great exponents have again and again taken up the same ambivalent relation to "common opinion" or "natural consciousness." Its philosophical short-sightedness and one-sidedness have their own necessity and right, because the popular representation "belongs to the everyday kind of being of Da-sein and to the understanding of being initially prevalent" (SZ 426). The common view, however, *exceeds* its rightful limits when it claims to possess the "truth" and the right to prescribe the *only possible horizon* for the interpretation of time and history. The preceding analyses have demonstrated that the origin, the characteristics, and development of the "now-time" cannot be comprehended at all except in the horizon of the ecstatic-horizonal temporality of here-being. When, on the other hand, the start is taken from the common understanding of time, the primordial time—the temporality in which it originates—"remains *inaccessible*" (SZ, 426).

This is most clearly seen in that time-phenomenon which the two interpretations take to be most primary and basic. While ecstatic-horizonal temporality temporalizes itself *primarily* from the *future* (coming-to-itself), the basic phenomenon of the commonly understood time is the pure *now*, clipped of its full structure and called the "present." From *this now*, the ecstatic-horizonal *Moment* of authentic temporality can in no way be explained. Similarly, the common concept of the "future" as the still coming, levelled-down nows, is incapable of explaining the ecstatically understood future, the datable, significant "then," just as the "past" in the sense of the passed-away, pure nows cannot cover the ecstatic has-been, the datable, significant "on that former occasion." "The now is not pregnant with the not-yet-now, but rather the present arises from the future in the primordial, ecstatic unity of the temporalizing of temporality" (SZ, 427).[7]

Finally, Heidegger brings new evidence for what he has already repeatedly stressed: that through all the concealment that lies in the common experience of time, primordial time still shines through. Even where the world-time is thought to be somehow "there-in-itself," it is brought into a preeminent relation with the "soul" or the "spirit," and, moreover, this happens *before* philosophical questioning turns primarily to the "subject." Heidegger quotes two passages: "But if nothing other than soul or the soul's mind were naturally equipped for numbering, then if there were no soul, time would be impossible (Aristotle, *Physics*, 223a 25). The second quotation runs: "Hence it seemed to me that time is nothing else than an extendedness; but of what sort of thing it is an extendedness I do not know; and it would be surprising if it were not an extendedness of the soul itself" (St. Augustine, *Confessions*, bk. XI, chap. 26).

This is a question taken up by Hegel. However, before proceeding to the interpretation of Hegel given in the next section, it will be helpful to summarize the main steps taken so far in the present chapter.

Heidegger has tried to show that existent temporality expresses itself in speech. In the first place and for the most part, it is the inauthentic temporality of the falling being-in-the-world that expresses itself, so that its self-enunciation is in itself a care-taking turning-to and addressing of beings within the world. The time thus exposed *reflects* in its own structure the ecstatic-horizonal unity of temporality. The expressly exposed world-time essentially belongs to here-being. The worldishness of time makes possible the care-taking *measuring* of time by reference to the eminently relevant thing, the sun in its movement. The measuring dating develops into a *counting* of time in the use of clocks. This development goes hand in hand with the exclusive interpretation of world-time as in-timeness—as the time *in which* things and events occur. The growing explicitness and conceptualization of the counted time leads to a concealing levelling-down of world-time into an endless, passing, irreversible continuum of nows that is somehow "there-in-itself." Its origin in the finite temporality of the single here-being is unrecognized by common sense, but still shines through all concealment.

5. The Contrast of the Existential and Ontological Connection of Temporality, Here-Being, and World-Time with Hegel's Interpretation of the Relation between Time and Spirit

The present section confronts the expositor and commentator with particular difficulties of its own. Not only are the extracts quoted from

Hegel difficult in themselves, but Heidegger's interpretation of them can be challenged in some important respects.[8] The reason for that is not that Heidegger presents us with one of his "retrieving" interpretations, which are controversial simply as "retrieving." All he aims at there is a straightforward explanation that does not go beyond Hegel's own texts, but it is doubtful whether he does justice to what Hegel himself has said.

What is the central problem to be elucidated? It is Hegel's attempt to grasp how the spirit, as the self-comprehending concept, can "concretize" or "realize" itself in time, and so reveal itself in and as a historical process. "The development of history falls into time"—where history is essentially that of the spirit.[9] Hegel, however, as Heidegger points out, is not content with simply stating the "within-timeness" of the spirit as a fact, but

> seeks to understand how it is *possible* for spirit to fall into time, which is the "completely abstract, the sensuous." Time must be able to receive spirit, as it were. And spirit must in turn be related to time and its essence. Thus we must discuss two things: (1) How does Hegel define the essence of time? (2) What belongs to the essence of spirit that makes it possible for it to "fall into time"? (SZ, 428)

The way in which Heidegger formulates the problem already provokes thought. It is striking that the questioning goes entirely from the spirit to time, asking how it is possible for the spirit to fall into time, that is, to realize or externalize (ex-pose) itself, to become existent in time. But, we ask, is it not just as important to go the opposite way, from time to spirit? The question is all the more justified because Hegel's thought not only allows but demands this two-way traffic. Its very core is just the "return" of the spirit, through the historical process, to itself, in which "return" *aufhebt*—that is, reconcilingly preserves the "banished" or "annulled" (*aufheben* as *tollere*) differentiations, which are the only *seemingly* independent externalized moments of itself. Such a "one-sided" moment of the spirit is time in a preeminent way, for it is, as Hegel writes in the *Phenomenology of Spirit*, "the pure self, the merely intuited concept."[10] This is why, in the words of the *Encyclopaedia* that Heidegger himself quotes, "time has no power over the concept, but rather the concept is the power over time."[11] Unless this "power" were conceived as an external force imposed on an alien thing—an absurd notion—the subservience of time to the concept and the power of the concept over time can only mean that in their kinship the concept, that is, the spirit, has a precedence over time. The structural relation between spirit and time is that between the origin and the originated, that is, the same as that between the temporality of here-being and the ex-posed world-time. What makes Heidegger's own time-interpretation so impressive and convincing is just that he constantly goes back from the originated world-time to its origin in temporality. The moment a new characteristic of the world-time appears, he immediately refers it back to the original ecstatic-horizonal structure of temporality. If a fair comparison with Hegel is to be made, a going from spirit to time and back from time to spirit is essential, provided that Hegel's thought demands such a two-way traffic. But Heidegger's formulation of the problem, laying the whole stress on the *fall* of the spirit *into time*, already prohibits the making of such an attempt.

(a) Hegel's Concept of Time

Starting from a thus restricted problem, Heidegger perfectly consistently draws Hegel's concept of time from his *Philosophy of Nature*, for the time in *which* the spirit realizes itself as a historical process must be the same as that in which the events of nature happen. More questionable is Heidegger's thesis that the "systematic place" of a time-interpretation provides us with a "criterion" of the *basic views on time* held by a philosopher (SZ, 428). Whether this thesis holds in general, whether it applies to Hegel in particular, is not so clear as Heidegger suggests. Especially with regard to Hegel it can be reasonably questioned whether the natural-philosophical aspect of time is the most important and basic to his system.[12]

On the other hand, if we take Heidegger's explanation of the dialectical movement from space to time by itself, its excellence can hardly be denied, and it deserves to be followed up in detail.

In the first section of the "Mechanics," Hegel defines both space and time as "das abstrakte Aussereinander," the abstract outside-one-another.[13] But Hegel does not simply coordinate space and time. Space, according to him, "is" time, in the sense that time is the "truth" of space.[14] That is to say: "If space is *thought* dialectically *in what it is*, this being of space reveals itself . . . as time" (SZ, 428).

To follow up this dialectical movement Heidegger first turns to space. It is "the immediate (unmediated) indifference of the outside-itself-being of nature."[15] What this means is elucidated by Heidegger as follows:

> Space is the abstract multiplicity of the points distinguishable in it. Space is not interrupted by these points, but neither does it first arise from them by way of joining them together. Space remains in its turn

undifferentiated, differentiated by the differentiable points that are themselves space. The differentiations themselves have the nature of what they differentiate. But yet the point is a *negation* of space in that it differentiates something in space as something other than space, though in such a way that it remains in space as this negation (the point is, after all, space). The point does not lift itself out of space as something other than space. Space is the undifferentiated outside-one-another of the multiplicity of points. But space is not a point, but, as Hegel says, "punctuality" [*Punktualität*] (Enc., § 254, Supplement)]. On this Hegel bases his statement in which he thinks space in its truth, that is, as time.

"The negativity, which as point relates itself to space and develops in it its determinations as line and surface, is, however, in the sphere of being-outside-itself both *for itself* and its determinations therein, but at the same time as positing (itself) in the sphere of being-outside-itself, appearing as indifferent to the quiet beside-one-another. So posited for itself, it is time."[16] (SZ, 429–30)

Compare:

If space is represented, that is, directly looked at in the indifferent subsistence of its distinctions, the negations are, as it were, simply given. But this representation does not yet grasp space in its being. That is possible only in thought—as the synthesis that goes through thesis and antithesis and supersedes [*aufhebenden*] them. Space is *thought* and thus grasped in its being only if the negations do not simply subsist in their indifference, but are superseded, that is, themselves negated. In the negation of negation (that is, punctuality), the point posits itself *for itself* and thus emerges from the indifference of subsistence. Posited for itself, it distinguishes itself from this or that point; it is *no longer* this and *not yet* that one. In positing itself for itself, it posits the succession in which it stands, the sphere of being-outside-of-itself that is now the negated negation. The superseding of punctuality signifies that it can no longer lie quietly in the "paralyzed stillness of space." The point "rebels" against all other points. According to Hegel, this negation of negation as punctuality is time. If this discussion has any demonstrable meaning at all, it can mean nothing other than that the positing of itself for itself of each point is a now-here, now-here, and so on. Every point "is" posited for itself as a now-point. "Thus the point has actuality in time." *By what means* the point can posit itself for itself, always as this point, is always a now. The condition of the *possibility* of the point's positing itself for itself is the now. This condition of possibility constitutes the *being* of the point, and being is at the same time being-thought. Thus, since the pure thinking of punctuality, that is, of space, always "thinks" the now and the being-outside-itself of the nows, space "is" *time*. (SZ, 430)

The differences between Hegel's and Heidegger's approach to "space and time" could not be more striking, especially when we remember the concrete way in which, according to Heidegger, the "now-here, now-here" first shows itself in the care-taking, counting use of the clock. All the more important is it to perceive in what respects they are similar. In the first place, while Heidegger would never say that space "is" time, any more than that time "is" space, or that time is the dialectical "thoughtness" of space, he does say that the "truth" of space is *grounded* in time or, more originally, in temporality. It is the temporality of here-being that makes the disclosure (the "truth") of space possible; that is, it is the condition of the possibility of the "truth" of space. In the second place, Heidegger also holds fast to the "outside-itselfness" of "primordial time," defining it as the *ekstatikon* purely and simply, as "the 'outside-of-itself' in and for itself" (SZ, 329). But here again, the standing-out-of-itself of existent here-being is much more "concretely" conceived than is Hegel's abstract being-outside-of-itself. Even with regard to space, where the distance between the two thinkers seems greatest, a reflection of the earlier in the later can be found. Hegel's abstract, "indifferent" (*gleichgültig*) space is recognizably the "unworlded," universal space in which each point is "equally valid" (*gleich-gültig*), and into which the circumspectly discovered, *significantly* structured everyday world-space is levelled-down by a theoretical "only-looking-at-it (*Nur-hinsehen*).

The dialectical movement from space to time has now brought time itself into view. Hegel's definition of time is introduced by a passage taken from § 258 of the *Encyclopaedia*:

> "As the negative unity of being-outside-itself, time is similarly something absolutely abstract [*ideell*].[17] It is the being that, in being, is not, and, in not being, is: it is intuited becoming. This means that the absolutely momentary distinctions that directly supersede themselves are determined as external, but as external to themselves." Time reveals itself for this interpretation as "intuited becoming." According to Hegel, this signifies a transition from being to nothingness, or from nothingness to being.[18] Becoming is coming into being as well as passing away. Being, or nonbeing, "goes over." What does that mean with regard to time? The being of time is the now. But since every now either "now" is-no-longer, or now not-yet-is, it can also be grasped as nonbeing. Time is the "*intuited*" becoming, that is, the transition that is not thought, but simply presents itself in the succession of nows. If the essence of time [*das Wesen der Zeit*] is determined as the "intuited becoming," this reveals the fact that time is understood primarily in terms of the now, in the way that such a now can be found by pure intuition. (SZ, 430–31)

It is immediately evident that the definition discussed here is incomplete, for it considers only the "constant changing," the "becoming" purely "imaged" in the now-flow, whereas *what* changes, namely the constantly self-same now, is not yet mentioned here. If in Heidegger's comment on Hegel "das Wesen der Zeit" is translated by its admittedly more common meaning "the *essence* of time," the whole passage loses the very point it aims to make: that it considers solely the problem of *how* time *is*, the *existentia* of time, and not *what* time *is*, the *essentia* of time. The latter is rightly deferred by Heidegger to the problem to be discussed in the next subsection, namely, the kinship of the essence of the spirit as the *self-*comprehending concept with the essence of time as the pure *self-*identity, albeit the only looked-upon or intuited and not self-thinking identity of the "standing and staying" self-same now.

To come back to the theme of the present discussion, the *being* of time as a pure *becoming*, Heidegger's further comments only elaborate what has already appeared in the above passage: that Hegel's time-interpretation moves entirely in the direction of the common understanding of time, whose characterization from the pure now already presupposes "that the now remains covered over and levelled-down in its full structure, so that it can be intuited [*angeschaut*: looked at] as something objectively present, though objectively present only 'ideally'" (SZ, 431).

All Heidegger's subsequent citations from Hegel and his comments on them, as well as the exceptionally long footnote to pages 432 through 433 of *Being and Time* establishing the connection of Aristotle's and Hegel's time interpretations, concentrate primarily on the "now." For instance: "Moreover, in nature where time is now, no 'stable' [*bestehend*] difference between those dimensions (past and future) ever comes about."[19] "In the positive sense of time one can thus say that only the present is, the before and after are not; but the concrete present is the result of the past and pregnant with the future. Thus the true present is eternity."[20]

These and other citations aim at establishing that Hegel not only starts from the common experience and interpretation of time, but radicalizes it. Although Hegel speaks occasionally of time as the "abstraction of consuming," he is, Heidegger says, "consistent enough to grant no such priority to consuming and passing away as that to which the everyday experience of time rightly adheres; for Hegel can no more provide dialectical grounds for this priority than for the 'circumstance' (that he introduces as self-evident) that precisely when the point posits itself for itself, the now turns up" (SZ, 431–32).

Both arguments brought against Hegel are doubtful. As to the first point, speaking of time in its "positive sense," Hegel says that "only the present is, the before and after are not," and it is just the constant self-annulment of the now that constitutes the becoming. Hence the negativity, so vividly and concretely expressed in the "consuming," can be said on philosophically demonstrable grounds to predominate. Even more doubtful is Heidegger's contention that Hegel cannot prove (*begründen*) why the now should emerge just when the point posits itself for itself. One would have thought that the dialectical movement from space to time is *itself* the proof why this should be so. It is because the now is the *condition of the possibility* that the point can "rebel" and so step out of the "paralyzed stillness" of the indifferent sameness of space. Heidegger himself constantly advances this (though not dialectical) kind of proof for the groundedness of all structures of here-being in temporality. The latter is the *condition of their possibility*. It is through such questionable arguments that Heidegger establishes his conclusion:

> So even when he characterizes time as becoming, Hegel understands this becoming in an "abstract" sense that goes beyond the representation of the "flux" of time. The most appropriate expression for Hegel's interpretation of time thus lies in the determination of time as the *negation of the negation* (that is, of punctuality). Here the succession of nows is formalized in the most extreme sense and levelled down to an unprecedented degree. It is only in terms of this formal and dialectical concept of time that Hegel can produce a connection between time and spirit. (SZ, 432)

Even if the "abstractness" of Hegel's concept of time must be conceded, it does not necessarily follow that the "negation of the negation" is its "most appropriate expression." Indeed, it arouses immediate misgivings, because the "negation of the negation" is the formal structure of the dialectical movement itself, which lies already in every "concrete universal" reached through the synthesis of the thesis and antithesis, and is in no way specifically distinctive of time, whereas we would have thought that some quite unique relation is required to enable the spirit to "fall into time." On the other hand, this conclusion throws a sudden light upon a puzzling feature of this subsection. The attentive reader must already have asked himself why Heidegger starts from space. If the main theme is Hegel's conception of the being of time, then the whole discussion of space is really redundant. The start could have been made just as well, or much better, from the passage cited above which begins: "As the negative unity of being-outside-itself, time is similarly something absolutely abstract and ideal." But now the seeming redundancy turns out to be essential to Heidegger's purpose of establishing that the negation of the negation is the "most appropriate expression" of Hegel's concept of time. Whether this is truly the "sole" bridge that Hegel can throw across from spirit to time will be seen in the next subsection.

(b) Hegel's Interpretation of the Connection between Time and Spirit

To state the basic problem once more: How can spirit fall into time? What is the essence of spirit that enables it to realize itself, to become *existent* in time as a historical process? Heidegger's explanation starts as follows:

> The essence of spirit is the *concept*. By this Hegel understands not the universal that is intuited in a genus as the form of what is thought, but the form of the very thinking that thinks itself: Conceiving *itself—as grasping* the non-I. Since grasping the *non*-I presents a differentiation, there lies in the pure concept, as the grasping of the differentiation, a differentiation of the difference. (SZ, 433)

Before going on, let us clarify this difficult text. Concept usually means a *concipere*, a grasping together into one through a general characteristic that is common to many. The "intuited" common characteristic of the many, the genus, is thought in the form of the *concipere*, of a grasping together into one. Hence the concept in its usual meaning is the form of something thought. What Hegel means by concept, on the other hand, is the form of the self-thinking thinking itself.

In the not-I there lies already a distinction between the I, the self, and its "other," the not-I. The pure concept, in comprehending it*self* as the I, at the same time grasps the distinction between itself and the other, the not-I—that is, it distinguishes this distinction. In fully comprehending itself the I grasps and brings back into itself the not-I that has been distinguished from it by a negation (the "not"). This bringing-back-into-itself of its negated self, of the not-I, is accomplished by negating the negation whereby the self, the I, has been expelled into its other, the not-I. Hence, Heidegger says, "Hegel can define the essence of spirit formally and apophantically as the negation of a negation. This 'absolute negativity' gives a logically formalized interpretation of Descartes' *cogito me cogitare rem*, wherein he sees the essence of the *conscientia*" (SZ, 433).

If the kinship between the spirit and time is established solely by the sameness of their formal structure as the negation of negation, then it would seem that this goal has already been reached. Nonetheless, this is not nearly enough to show why the spirit necessarily, according to its own essence, concretizes and so reveals itself in time as history. The following citations from Hegel, and Heidegger's comments on them, serve to elucidate this necessity that lies in the nature of the spirit itself. In the first place, the concept has to be more concretely defined.

> The concept is the conceivedness of the self conceiving itself, the way the self is authentically as it can be, that is, *free*. "The *I* is the pure concept itself that has come to *existence* as the concept."[21] "But the I is the *first* pure unity relating itself to itself, not directly, but rather, in abstracting from all determinateness and content and going back to the freedom of the limitless identity with itself."[22] Thus the I is "*universality*," but it is "individuality" *just as* immediately" (SZ, 433-34)

What must be remarked here and for all that follows is that Hegel uses the word *Dasein* ("als Begriff zum *Dasein* gekommen") in the traditional sense of *existentia*, and not of course in the sense that Heidegger gives it in *Being and Time*. It is just for *Dasein* and existence in the traditional sense that Heidegger uses the interpretative term *Vorhandensein*, being-there, presence. He is therefore quite entitled, within the context of *Being and Time*, to interpret Hegel's *da-seind* with *vorhanden*, using the term, of course, in its widest sense and not in its narrow sense of the thereness of a thing. What remains to be seen, rather, is whether Heidegger makes enough of the concept that has come into existence (*Dasein*) and its relation to time. So far, what has come to light is the pure, limitlessly free self-identity of the concept as the I. Now Heidegger goes on to unfold the further implications of the concept as the negation of negation.

> This negating of negation is both the "absolute unrest" of spirit and also its *self-revelation*, which belongs to its essence. The "progression" of spirit actualizing itself in history contains a "principle of exclusion." However, in this exclusion what is excluded does not get detached from the spirit, it gets *surmounted*. Making itself free in overcoming, and at the same time supporting, characterizes the freedom of the spirit. Thus "progress" never means a quantitative more, but is essentially qualitative, and indeed has the quality of spirit. "Progression" is known and knowing itself in its goal. In every step of its "progress," spirit has to overcome "itself" as the truly inimical hindrance of its aim. The goal of the development of spirit is "to attain its own concept." The development of itself is "a hard, infinite struggle against itself." (SZ, 434)

Nothing could show more succinctly than this short paragraph that to regard the "negating of negation" simply and solely as a formal-logical abstraction is quite insufficient. It expresses—in a formal way, to be sure—the origin of movement, of *life* (the "absolute unrest"), in the very being of the spirit, which drives the spirit into its self-disclosing concretization, and drives it on through an endless fight against itself toward its return to a *self-conceiving* that "grasps," that is, embraces and elevates into itself its "externalized" moments (the not-I). The spirit has to overcome itself as its own most obstinate enemy because the seemingly fixed and true differentiations and determinations—for instance, the opposition between subject and object, in which each appears as an independent entity—are set by the *spirit itself* in its appearance as the "natural" or "naive consciousness" (roughly corresponding to the common understanding of everyday here-being in Heidegger). The in-itself-being of these seemingly fixed and independent entities like subject and object is just the "mere being," and therefore the negative and "untrue" being which has to be mediated—annulled—and preservingly elevated into the "true being" of the self-conceiving concept. This is the endless struggle of the historical development of the "concretized" spirit returning to itself. While these implications of the above-quoted texts are not elaborated by Heidegger, they have to be made explicit here in order to enable us to weigh up what Heidegger makes of them. His conclusions are summed up in the third paragraph following the above, but this is preceded by two important paragraphs consisting mainly of citations from Hegel. I shall quote these three paragraphs together and comment on them afterward.

> Since the restlessness of the development of *spirit* bringing itself to its concept is the *negation of a negation,* it is in accordance with its self-actualization to fall "into *time*" as the immediate *negation of a negation.* For "time is the *concept* itself that *is there* [*da ist*], and represents itself to consciousness as empty intuition. For this reason spirit necessarily appears in time, and it appears in time as long as it has not *grasped* its pure concept, that is, has not annulled time. Time is the pure self that is *externally* intuited [looked-upon] and *not grasped* by the pure self, the concept merely intuited."[23] Thus spirit appears in time necessarily in *accordance with its essence.* "Thus world-history in general is the interpretation [*Auslegung:* laying out] of spirit in time, just as the idea interprets itself in nature as space."[24] The "excluding" that belongs to the movement of development contains a relation to nonbeing. That is time, understood in terms of the revolt of the now [*aus dem sich aufspreizenden Jetzt*].
>
> Time is "abstract" negativity. As the "intuited becoming" it is the differentiated self-differentiation that is directly to be found, the concept that

"is there," that is, objectively present. As something objectively present and thus external to spirit, time has no power over the concept, but the concept is rather "the power of time" [*Encyclopaedia*, § 258].

Hegel shows the possibility of the historical actualization of spirit "in time" by going back to *the identity of the formal structure of spirit and time as negation of a negation*. The most empty, formal-ontological and formal-apophantical abstraction into which spirit and time are externalized makes possible the production of a kinship of the two. But since at the same time, time is yet conceived in the sense of world time that has been absolutely levelled down, so that its provenance thus remains completely covered over, it simply confronts spirit as something objectively present. For this reason spirit *must first* fall "into time." It remains obscure what indeed is signified ontologically by this "falling" and the "actualization" of spirit that has power over time and really "exists" outside of it. Just as Hegel throws little light on the origin of time that has been levelled down, he leaves totally unexamined the question of whether the essential constitution of spirit as the negating of negation is possible at all in any other way than on the basis of primordial temporality. (SZ, 434–35)

Let us now see whether these conclusions do not leave some essential points unexamined in the Hegelian texts quoted by Heidegger himself. First let us look back to Hegel's crucially important sentence: "Time is the *concept* itself that *is there [da ist]*, and represents itself to consciousness as empty intuition. For this reason spirit necessarily appears in time, and it appears in time as long as it has not *grasped* its pure concept, that is, has not annulled time." Time *is* simply there; its being is an unmediated "mere" being in contrast to the mediated "true" being of the *self-grasping or self-conceiving* concept; hence, although time is the concept itself, it has not come into its full truth. In its simple being-there, time presents itself to consciousness directly as an intuition, for time is the "nonsensible sensible," that is, the purely "viewable"—not to the bodily eye, but to subconsciousness. As this immediate intuition, time is "empty," and must be so if it is to be capable of taking up into itself all things that appear in time, that is, show themselves, become themselves "viewable" in time. Time is the pure, empty intuition as the form in which all existing things must appear and so reveal themselves to a looking-upon. Hence, if the spirit is to come into existence at all it must necessarily "appear in time," in which alone it can concretely reveal itself as a historical process. This explains from the point of view of time how it is in its own being capable of receiving the self-realizing spirit into itself and why it is *in time* that the spirit must necessarily appear in all stages of its concrete, historical "life." But now we must ask back from time to the spirit. How is the spirit itself such that it *necessitates itself* into its own concretization in time? The answer has already been given: *because* the spirit is the negating of the negation, and *because* this is not a mere formal abstraction, but the principle of life in the spirit itself, it necessitates the spirit into its endlessly self-overcoming (self-annulling) struggle, in which historical movement the spirit concretely lives. Time as the pure, "looked-upon becoming"—that is, the constant self-annulment of the now—mirrors and makes directly "viewable" the negativity of the spirit concretized in its historical movement, a negativity which constantly "excludes" moments of itself into a seemingly fixed and externalized "independent being," and constantly struggles to overcome itself by negating this negation.

Time most purely "images" the spirit; it is the pure "other" self of the self-comprehending concept. If the essence of the concept is its self-conception, then the essence of time, the "standing and staying" self-sameness of the now, images the concept's pure self-identity. The essence of time is to present itself "visibly" to the spirit as its own self, but as the unmediated, not-self-conceiviing self. This is clearly said by Hegel in the sentence "Time is the pure self that is *externally* intuited [looked-upon] and not grasped by the self, the concept merely intuited." The essence of time is *the same* as the essence of the concept, but time is the externalized, "visible," and not-self-comprehending identity in which the pure concept, come into existence as the "I," can look upon itself.

The affinity between spirit and time is therefore fundamental. Heidegger can quite correctly express it in the "negation of negation," but ignores the concrete content of this formal "sameness," brought out by his own quotations from Hegel. At the end, he still insists on treating the negation of negation as a purely formal abstraction.

But the most important point still remains to be clarified. Not only is the kinship between spirit and time far more fundamental than Heidegger admits, but the "relation" between them is not that between two partners of equal rank. This is indicated by Heidegger himself in the following way: "As something objectively present and thus external to spirit, time has no power over the concept, but the concept is rather 'the power of time' [*die Macht der Zeit*]" [*Encyclopaedia*, § 258]. Assuming that the preposition in this last phrase implies an idea of dominance like that explicitly expressed by the "over" used in the first part of the sentence, it has to be granted that as something external to spirit, time can have no power over it; but this in no way explains why the concept should be the power of time. To find out how and why the concept is the dominant "partner" in the relation, the questioning must be reversed and go back from time to the concept. How can the concept be the power either of or over time? Certainly not as the concretized spirit that appears and "is there" *in time*. This being-there-in-time of the spirit, however, as Heidegger hints in a single obscure phrase, is not the "true," the "authentic" being of the spirit; the spirit *truly is* itself only as the fully self-comprehending concept, and as such it is itself "true being." In its "true being," however, the concept is eternal and not "something" that is "there" in time. Hence Heidegger rightly speaks of the spirit "truly 'existing' outside time" (*ausser der Zeit "seiender" Geist*). Only this eternal, *truly* "existing," fully self-comprehending concept has the power to "banish time," because it *originates* the time that is "merely there" as its own externalized, self-excluded self. Fundamentally different as Hegel's "concept" and its "eternal temporality" is from Heidegger's finite temporality of existing here-being, the relation between the concept and time is the same as that between temporality and world-time. It is the relation between the origin and the originated. Moreover, it must be remembered that Heidegger's temporality is just as little an entity (*Seiendes*) existing "in time" as is Hegel's "eternal" concept. It is only because the origin disposes over the originated that the concept can be the power over time. And conversely, as Hegel beautifully says, "time appears as the very fate and necessity of spirit,"[25] for the spirit "is not in itself complete," but must seek to give "self-consciousness a richer share in consciousness" by concretizing itself in its historical movement.

Heidegger's interpretation fails to do justice not only to Hegel, but to himself. This comes perhaps most clearly into view in looking back to *Being and Time* from Heidegger's later works. In the closing subsection of this section, Heidegger compares Hegel's start from the spirit that must first of all "fall" into time with his own start from the "concretization" of the factually thrown existence, in order to lead back from it to its "original ground" in temporality. But as Heidegger's later works amply show, the start made in *Being and Time* is not the *only possible* one, nor one that Heidegger himself later thought to be the best, whatever his readers may think. In this later works Heidegger starts from the "self-destining" self-disclosure of being, the concrete understanding of which lies in a "dialogue" with earlier thinkers. In this, Heidegger is much nearer to Hegel than he would allow in the present interpretation.

The relation between spirit and time, and so the "origin" of time in the concept, does not remain as obscure as Heidegger contends, though it is not fully and systematically worked out. On the other hand, Heidegger rightly says that Hegel does not raise the problem of whether the essential constitution of the spirit is grounded in "original" temporality. If he had, there would have been no need perhaps for *Being and Time*.

XVI

Conclusion: An Attempt to Outline Heidegger's Answer to the Question Asked at the Beginning *of* Being and Time

The end of Division Two is designed to throw the reader's interest forward to the answer to be given to the question "Is there a way leading from primordial *time* to the meaning of *being*? Does *time* itself reveal itself as the horizon of *being*?" (SZ, 437). It is therefore pertinent to ask whether and, if so, how far it might be possible to discern the answer from what Heidegger has already written.

The solution of Heidegger's problem cannot be arbitrarily tacked on to the first two divisions of *Being and Time*. It must rise from them by inner necessity. If the ground has been well and truly laid, at least the main outlines of the answer must be discernible there, especially when some of Heidegger's later works, in which certain hints are made more explicit, are taken into consideration.

An attempt will, therefore, be made here to outline Heidegger's answer as far as possible. The short sketch to be given will at the same time serve as a concise summary of the most fundamental features of the way in which man exists, as far as they have been discussed in this guide.

For a start, we shall consider two questions: First, is there any problem left unsolved in Heidegger's interpretation of time? If so, it is reasonable to expect that the explicit working out of this problem will lead to the answer to Heidegger's central question. Second, does Heidegger give us any clue as to where the solution of this problem may be sought?

As to the first question, it may be observed that a problem is implied in the very first step Heidegger takes in his interpretation of time. A disclosure of being-toward-an-end, Heidegger says, is only possible because man exists in such a way that he can come toward himself in his possibilities. The whole problem lies in the "can." How is it possible that man can come toward himself at all? How and where does this "coming" originate? The answer to this question, we can reasonably assume, will explain the inner possibility of our understanding of being from time, and so the meaning of being as such.

As to the second question, in view of the central methodological importance of dread, it is not an idle guess to say that dread must provide the approach to Heidegger's answer. But if all the ways in which man can be are fundamentally timeish, then the basic mood of dread must have a peculiar and preeminent time-character. Does Heidegger give us any precise indication of this? He does so on page 344 of *Being and Time*: "In the peculiar temporality of *Angst*, in the fact that it is primordially grounded in having-been, and only out of this do future and present temporalize themselves, the possibility was shown of the powerfulness that distinguishes the mood of *Angst*."

Keeping in view the indications Heidegger gives in *Being and Time* as well as elsewhere, we shall now attempt to summarize what is most relevant to his answer.

We begin by considering once more the disclosing function of existential understanding. Its remarkable achievement is to forethrow possibilities. Since being is totally unlike any beings, "to understand being" means something like this: to forethrow a possibility in which this sheer "other" to any beings somehow reveals itself. This possibility evidently cannot be one among many others, but must be unique and incomparable. What is the unique possibility that reveals itself in Da-sein's, here-being's, existence? It is the extreme possibility of the sheer *im*possibility of being-in-the-world-anymore. In this "*im*possible" a *not* is revealed which in advance closes all other possibilities of existence. This *not* belongs to each Da-sein alone: it is solely his own being that is at stake, and not another's. The harshness of this *not* is so incomparable and in the strictest sense of the word abysmal that it can only rise from the abyss of Da-sein's being, from his thrownness into a world. It is the basic mood of dread that originally brings Da-sein face to face with the *not* that closes not only the end of his being, but dominates it from the beginning.

What is revealed by dread, however, is not a mere negation, such as we perform in a rational judgment. Dread does not reveal by negating all things, nor by announcing an impending annihilation of the world, but by bringing Da-sein's familiar, taken-for-granted being-at-home-in-the-world into the unfamiliar mood of an uncanny not-at-homeness. In the not-canny, not-at-home, the *not* is elementally revealed as a threat that does not come from outside, but rises from being-in-the-world itself.

The way in which dread gives Da-sein to understand the *not* is totally different from the way in which he acquires some information about a fact. "In fact," Da-sein may not know about death, its possibility may be kept covered over in the flight of disowned existence, dread may never be fully experienced in a lifetime; nonetheless, as soon as and as long as Da-sein is, the *not* is openly or covertly revealed as the extreme possibility in which he already is, and which is singly and uniquely his own.

It is the throw by and recoil from this *not* that throws Da-sein into the world and so originates the movement of his being. But what is the world itself into which Da-sein is carried by the impetus of the throw? It is revealed by dread as "nothing." The whereof of dread, the dreadsome, it was said, is nowhere and nothing. But it was made clear that the nowhere is not an absence and negation of all places; it is the original disclosure of place itself, of the pure *where* itself.

The world itself, as a fundamental character of Da-sein's being, is directly revealed in the nothing of dread. This nothing, however, is not the absence and negation of all things, but the totally "other" to things as such. The incomparable power of dread is to bring Da-sein directly before the nothing (world) itself. Face to face with nothing, Da-sein is in one leap beyond beings as a whole, among them first and foremost himself. The transcendence of Da-sein's being is only possible as this confrontation with the sheer "other" to any beings. What comes to light in this transcendence, however, is not something outside and beyond the world, but precisely beings as the beings they are, that is, in their being. It is the essence of the nothing to repel, to point away from itself, to direct and refer to beings, as totally other than itself. Only in coming to things from the disclosed nothing of world can Da-sein understand them in their strangeness: that they are something, and not nothing. And only in coming to himself from the utmost limit of his being-in-the-world can Da-sein understand himself fully as a self existing among other beings.

How is it then that Da-sein can come toward himself at all? The movement originates in the throw by and recoil from the *not* revealed by dread, which throws Da-sein into the world and whirls him away to the beings he meets within it. But at the same time, it throws him forward into the extreme possibility of death, in *rebounding* from which he can come toward himself in his ownmost possibility. The forethrow not only comes to a limit, but is thrown back by it: it is the rebound that enables Da-sein to come toward himself in his possibilities, and so exist primarily from the future.

But it would still remain inexplicable how and why this "coming-toward" should be the primary mode of time, or indeed any time at all, unless the *not* itself had a time-character. If, however, the movement of man's being is the original unity of time as future, past and present, the whole phenomenon of time seems to be accounted for, and it is hard to see what function remains for the *not* to fulfill. Heidegger leaves one possibility open: with the *not* is disclosed *time itself*. As the last sentence of *Being and Time* suggests, it is *time itself* that will reveal itself as the horizon of being. This is the problem with which Division Three would evidently have had to deal first, before the temporal interpretation of the idea of being could have been taken in hand.

In the absence of an explicit answer from Heidegger, do we have any hints from him where we might look for an answer? He gives us a hint in his analysis of conscience (SZ, 284). Conscience gives man to understand that he *owes* his being, that he can *never* go behind his thrownness and exist as the ground of his own being. In calling man back to the *not* revealed in his impotent thrownness, conscience makes manifest the *never*. According to the whole trend of Heidegger's thought, the never cannot be a mere negation of time: in it is disclosed the pure *when*, i.e. time itself. If, indeed, man constantly comes toward and back to himself from the *never*, then the whole movement of his being must necessarily have a time-character, or, as one might equally well say, a when-character. And if the *never* is the horizon into which man in advance looks out, it becomes immediately understandable why he must pro-ject all possibilities of being on to time, and why all articulations and modifications of being must have a temporal meaning.

The temporal interpretation of the idea of being as such, the final goal of Division Three, remains for the most part obscure. On the other hand, the way toward this goal is discernible both from the two divisions we have of *Being and Time*, and from Heidegger's later works. Above all, there can be no doubt of his answer to the most basic question: how is it at all possible for man to understand being? The significance-whole of world enables man to understand *that* beings are and *what* they are, i.e. their real existence and their essence. But the unity of the world is itself only possible on the ground of time; and time itself is revealed with the *not* that determines man's existence as a self.

Notness and nothingness (*Nichtigieit*) are the fundamental existential characters of a finite being. But it must be fully evident by now that when Heidegger speaks of the notness or nothingness of Da-sein, he cannot mean what is sometimes understood by these phrases: that Da-sein is a nullity in the world-all, that his being is of no account, or that he comes from nothing and dissolves into nothing and his existence is therefore meaningless and purposeless. Far from declaring Da-sein's being to be meaningless because it is finite, Heidegger shows for the first time that an understanding of being, and with it, an understanding of meaning and purpose, is possible only to a finite existence. Da-sein exists finitely, not because he does not in fact last forever, but because to him a *not* is in advance revealed, and this harsh, inexorable *not* alone has the revelatory power to enable him to understand being and so bring him into the dignity and uniqueness of a finitely free existence.

The disclosure of being calls Da-sein to the task of existing as the place of illumination in the world-all. This disclosure, however, cannot happen to some abstract Da-sein in general, but only to a single, factically existing Da-sein. The circularity of the problem of being has now come fully to light: the manifestness of the *not* makes it possible for Da-sein to understand being, but, on the other hand, his own factical self is needed to make manifest the *not*. This is the ground for Heidegger's thesis that ontology cannot be founded upon an "ideal subject," a "pure I," a "consciousness as such," but only upon the factically existing Da-sein, because he and he alone, in his own finite existence, is the place of the transcendental.

николNotes

Part One: What Is the Question?

1. The word *ontology* is used throughout this book in the sense defined by Heidegger. It is the inquiry into beings as beings. This inquiry considers beings purely in what and how they are, i.e., in respect of their being. Hence a second definition of ontology, namely as the inquiry into the being of beings, is often used by Heidegger as equivalent to the definition given first. Ontology, theology, logic, in their essential unity, constitute metaphysics as a whole. For a discussion of the threefold unity of metaphysics, see, e.g., Heidegger's lecture, "Die onto-theo-logische Verfassung der Metaphysik" (ID, 37–73, "The Onto-Theo-Logical Constitution of Metaphysics," ID(E), 42–76. A list of the abbreviations of titles used in references is given in the bibliography).

2. When the explanation of a key word has an essential bearing on Heidegger's thought, it will be given in the main text, unless it would interfere with the movement of an important passage. Purely technical remarks will be made in endnotes.

3. The fundamental changes within metaphysical thinking would naturally be given far more weight in a detailed discussion than can be done in this short sketch. For example, in the Latin word *substantia* there lies already a profound reinterpretation of the Greek idea of being as *ousia*. The term *substance*, according to Heidegger, is thoroughly inappropriate to Greek thought. At this stage, however, it is unavoidable to use a language that is familiar to the reader from the best-known translations of Greek thinkers.

4. Heidegger's interpretation of Descartes's *cogito sum* cannot be even approximately dealt with in this short sketch. It should be noted, however, that Heidegger is fully aware of the epochal change within metaphysical thinking that began with Descartes. The discussion of Descartes's "extended

world" in the first Division of *Being and Time* (chap. 3, B) is misleading because of its incompleteness. At the time of writing, Heidegger intended to publish a full treatise on the *cogito sum* as the second Division of Part II of *Being and Time*. Although Part II has not been and will not be published, Heidegger has repeatedly elucidated the meaning and importance of Descartes's principle in his later works (HO, 80ff., 91ff., G5, 86ff., 98ff., QCT ["The Age of the World Picture"], 126ff., 139ff.). One of the besetting difficulties for the student of Heidegger's philosophy is to grasp that his interpretation of the being of Da-sein accomplishes a radical break with the subjectivity of modern metaphysics, in spite of all appearances to the contrary. When Heidegger speaks of the "subject" in *Being and Time*, he postulates that the whole idea of "being-a-subject," and with it, of "being-an-object," must be fundamentally rethought and interpreted in the light of a new question of being.

5. The main outline of Heidegger's interpretation of traditional philosophy is clearly discernible already in *Being and Time*, and is amplified and expounded in many of his later works, for instance, in *Einführung in die Metaphysik, Was heisst Denken?, Identität und Differenz, Der Satz vom Grund*, etc.; also in numerous essays and lectures to be found in collections, e.g., *Holzwege* and *Vorträge und Aufsätze*.

6. The translation of Heidegger's word *Zeitlichkeit* by "time" in the early part of this guide is a temporary expedient that will be corrected at the first opportunity. Similarly, the meaning of *Da-sein* and the renderings adopted for it will be fully explained in the next part.

Part Two, Chapter I

1. The noun *Weltlichkeit* and the adjective *weltlich* would ordinarily be translated by "worldliness" and "worldly." These words, unfortunately, have so definite a meaning in English as to require supplementation by a warning or an alternative in the context of *Being and Time*. The expressions "worldishness" and "worldish" have the advantage of prohibiting the substitution of a familiar meaning for Heidegger's, as well as permitting parallel constructions with two other key concepts, *räumlich* and *zeitlich*. Their normal meaning, "spatial" and "timely," would be misleading, and they will therefore be rendered as "spaceish" and "timeish." As we shall see in due course, man is worldish, spaceish, timeish, i.e. world-forming, space-disclosing, time-originating.

2. Since the words "exist" and "existence" are indispensable in English, they will occasionally be used in this book for beings other than man. They will then stand in quotation marks and have the meaning of real existence. "Existent" and "nonexistent" will be used in a similar way.

3. This implies that all existentials answer the question *How?* It is evident that the *how* must have a very much wider application in Heidegger's thought

than it had traditionally. We cannot appropriately ask "What is man?" and even the question "Who is man?" applies to him only as a factical self. The primary and leading question concerning man's being is "*How* is man?"

PART TWO, CHAPTER II

1. For further light on the problem of world as it is posed by Heidegger in *Being and Time*, see especially his *Kant and the Problem of Metaphysics*. On Heidegger's interpretation of time § 35 of that work is especially illuminating.

PART TWO, CHAPTER IV

This chapter seeks to elucidate one of the most widely known themes of *Being and Time*, as it is presented in Div. One, chaps. 4 and 5 B. In view of the great interest of the theme itself and Heidegger's treatment of it, special care has been taken to follow his text as closely as possible, bringing to the reader, if only in a summarized form, as many passages from it as could be considered within the limits of this book.

1. Joan Stambaugh says "tolerance." [Ed.]

2. Joan Stambaugh translates *Gerede* by "idle talk" and uses "hearsay" for *Hörensagen*. [Ed.]

PART TWO, CHAPTER VII

1. The difficulties of Husserl's thought have already been pointed out. It is a study on its own, and no short description can make its basic principles genuinely understandable, let alone do justice to it. The reader who wishes to go thoroughly into the matter might perhaps best turn to the first volume of Husserl's *Ideen*.

2. The "as" is not expressed in speech but constitutes the interpretation given by what is said. For instance, the proposition "the hammer is heavy," by defining the hammer in respect of its weight, lets us see it *as* heavy. The *as* which constitutes the interpretation given in speaking is called by Heidegger the "apophantic 'as'." This is to be contrasted with the original *as*, whereby a particular thing comes to our understanding *as* a theater, *as* a bus, in one word, *as* a utensil of a specific character. This original *as* of interpretation is called by Heidegger the "hermeneutic 'as'" (SZ, § 7and § 32; the discussion of meaning [*Sinn*] above in Part One, sec. 2, is also relevant in this connection. Further, for the meaning of "hermeneutic," see US, 120 ff., G12, 114ff., OWL, 28ff.).

3. The extraordinary fusion of thought and language that distinguishes not only *Being and Time* but perhaps even more markedly Heidegger's later

works, opens up a topic of great importance and interest. Its discussion, however, would lead too far away from the main theme of this study, and must be passed over here.

PART THREE, CHAPTER IX

1. Joan Stambaugh uses "Temporality" for *Temporalität* and "temporality" for *Zeitlichkeit*. [Ed.]

PART THREE, CHAPTER X

1. The same thought was expressed by Heidegger already in Division One: "Da-sein *is* always its possibility" (SZ, 42). The not-yet indicates the time-structure of possibilities. Their peculiar *not*-character was commented upon in a preliminary way already in our discussion of Division One above in Part Two, chap. I, sec. 1.

2. This remark seems to be at variance with Heidegger's later thought (e.g., HU, 69ff., W, 157ff., G9, 325ff., P, 248ff., BW, 206ff.). There Heidegger explicitly says that living beings, plants, and animals, are not "set free" in a world: they "hang worldlessly in their surroundings." The reason is that being-in-the-world in the full sense is only possible when the differentiation between being and beings happens. Living beings, according to Heidegger, remain "on this side" of this all-important differentiation. It is indeed astonishing to think that even the higher animals, which stand in an extremely complex and purposeful relation to other beings in their environment, e.g., to their prey, are incapable of understanding them as beings in their own right, i.e., as beings that *are*.

This discrepancy between Heidegger's earlier and later thought turns out to be only apparent when the present short passage is more fully stated. What Heidegger says is that an ontology of life must be preceded by an ontology of man. His fundamental constitution of being-in-the-world must be taken as a guide for determining the constitution of purely living beings. Although a suitably reduced form of being-in-the-world is not defined by Heidegger, we may reasonably suppose it to be something like "being-in-an-environment." This structure would have to be analyzed by an appropriate phenomenological method. See GM, G29/30, FCM.

3. This passage is one of the few in *Being and Time* that have a direct bearing on practical decisions we may have to make. It might be well to examine it thoroughly. What is the concrete situation on which Heidegger bases his analysis? He speaks of the "dying" in quotation marks to emphasize that the word is not meant in the existential sense, according to whlch I *am dying* as soon as and as long as I am, i.e., death is constantly disclosed to me as my end. The dying one is a sick friend who may be nearing the "end" in the ontic-biological sense

that Heidegger calls "decease." To "persuade" the friend that he may "escape death," Heidegger argues, helps to hide both from him and from ourselves the ownmost possibility of existence.

The more carefully the argument is examined the less satisfactory it becomes. It turns on the ambiguity of "escaping death," which introduces the suggestion that we are trying to relieve our friend of the "being toward death," instead of expressing the hope that his decease may not be imminent. Such hopes, whether justified or unjustified, undoubtedly often help us to put off facing death to another day, but they need not necessarily do so. Heidegger's own concept of death in no way implies that the hope of recovery from an illness and the desire for a longer life are incompatible with a fully disclosed being toward death. If they were, we would be faced with the absurdity of rejecting all medicine as a thoroughly "disowned" business, for what could be more "reassuring" than good medical care? The reassurance is itself not the least part of medicine, since the outcome of a critical illness may well be decided by whether the sick man himself has hope of recovery or whether he has given himself up for hopeless.

Would a resolutely "owned" existence take it upon himself to assure his friend that his decease is imminent, and so perhaps rob him of his chance of recovery? It would seem so, considering that he is in every way the opposite of disowned existence. Yet this conclusion is not only insupportable, but goes fundamentally against Heidegger's own interpretation of dying. If death is always and only *my* dying, I alone am responsible for how I take it upon myself. It cannot be for anyone else to force me into facing it. No one would know this better than the man who has become transparent to himself in the finiteness of his own existence. He could indeed greatly help others to face their death, but solely by the courage and fortitude with which he faces his own, not by telling a sick friend that it is all up with him.

4. With a view to Heidegger's later time-analyses, it is useful to note the strange circumstance under which the basic when-character of time first comes emphatically into sight. It is evident that every "point" which we define in time is a "when." For example, we "fix" the date of a meeting for 4 p.m. on a certain day. In doing so, we so to speak freeze the "flow of time" at a selected point. Were time not definable by a "when," it obviously would not be of much practical or scientific use. What is so strange about Heidegger's inquiry is that it brings the "when" for the first time to our notice where it is completely indefinable. What significance this may have is impossible to see at the moment, but it may be illuminating to remember it later on.

5. This passage confirms the comment on illness and decease made in the first section. According to Heidegger's own interpretation, a proper being toward death has nothing to do with "hastening" of decease or with taking no steps to postpone it. It is also equally far removed from any romantic "death wish."

6. This passage is in itself a refutation of the frequent accusations that Heidegger's so-called existentialism provides the philosophical basis for and

necessarily leads to Nazism. The basic feature of Nazism is its total and ruthless disregard of the existence of others, culminating in the assumption of the right of one race to exterminate others. Heidegger's active support of the Nazi movement in its earlier days, and particularly his treatment of Husserl—it is reliably reported that he never greeted Husserl on the street after 1933—must be regarded as an almost incomprehensible fall below his own thinking. If it proves anything, it proves only that even the deepest ontological insight is no guarantee that one's practical-ethical decisions will be equally admirable. Whether this detracts from the thought itself is a disturbing and not easily answered question. In 1942, when the disillusionment with Nazism may already have set in, under threat of having the publication of *Being and Time* prohibited, Heidegger allowed the dedication to Husserl to be deleted (US, 269, G12, 259, OWL, 199–200). We may legitimately wonder whether *Being and Time* would not be an even greater work than it is, had Heidegger allowed it to be suppressed. Would it not have gained greatness in a different dimension from pure philosophy? And has this other dimension nothing to do with philosophy? However that may be, one thing is certain: Heidegger's thought neither justifies nor necessarily leads to Nazism any more than to any other political-historical ideology. What it does is to show that the greatest extremes of human conduct—utter ruthlessness as well as utmost self-sacrifice—are made possible by the existential constitution of man, from which alone they can be understood in a fundamental way.

Part Three, Chapter XI

1. Beda Allemann, *Hölderlin und Heidegger* (Zurich and Freiburg: Atlantis Verlag, 1954), p. 73.

Part Three, Chapter XII

1. This remark leads us to expect that Heidegger would at least complement his elucidations of the "I think" with that of the "I act." This expectation is all the more justified because for Kant the "practical person," the "moral agent," as the free, autonomous intelligence, is the "authentic self." But Heidegger, apart from the single reference quoted above, takes no further notice in *Being and Time* of the practical-moral self. How would he justify this omission? He would say that the ontological foundations of Kant's practical self are no more adequate than those of his "theoretical" or "logical" subject. Nor can the two put together make up the proper foundations, for unless man's being is in advance conceived ("projected") in sufficient depth and width to originate and carry both the "theoretical" and "practical" self, a subsequent merger between the two remains an ontologically bottomless undertaking. This thought is expressed in detail on page 320 (footnote), where Heidegger says that even if Kant's "theoretical reason is included in practical reason, the exis-

tential and ontological problematic of the self remains not only unsolved, but *unasked*. On what ontological basis is the 'working together' of theoretical and practical reason supposed to occur? Does theoretical behaviour determine the kind of being of the person, or is it the practical or neither of the two—and which one then? Do not the paralogisms, in spite of their fundamental significance, reveal the lack of ontological foundation of the problematic of the self from Descartes's *res cogitans* to Hegel's concept of the Spirit? One does not even need to think 'naturalistically' or 'rationalistically' and can yet be in subservience to an ontology of the 'substantial' that is only all the more fatal because it is seemingly self-evident." The soundness of Heidegger's position in this matter can hardly be denied. Nonetheless, it does not seem fully to justify his ignoring precisely that aspect of the self that is not only central to Kant, but is his nearest approach to the idea of an "authentic existence." The gulf between, say, Kant's "feeling of reverence" (*Achtung*), in which a free autonomous subject submits himself to a self-given moral law, and Heidegger's "resoluteness," whereby a free existence holds himself in readiness to be summoned to himself by the call of conscience, is not nearly so deep as that between the latter and the purely "logical subject." [For further reflections on Kant on 'I act' see Martin Heidegger, *Die Grundprobleme der Phänomenologie* (Frankfurt: Klostermann, 1975), G24, *The Basic Problems of Phenomenology*, trans. Albert Hofstadter (Bloomington: Indiana University Press, 1982), Part One, chapter 3. Ed.]

2. This interpretation, however, is open to serious objections. While it is perfectly true that Kant did not see the phenomenon of world in Heidegger's sense, he saw perfectly well that the coherent unity in which anything "empirical" can meet us must be a priori constituted. This coherent whole is conceived by Kant as "nature." The a priori laws, in distinction from empirical laws, which in advance constitute the unity of nature, are prescribed by the "synthetic judgements a priori," and *their* possibility is the whole problem of the transcendental aesthetic and logic.

Without minimizing in the least the fundamental ontological importance of Heidegger's being-in-the-world, we must maintain that Kant concretely tackled the same problem with his conception of the a priori constitution of a nature as such. The problem each thinker attempts to solve is this: How can a finite self have access to and knowledge of other beings, beings which he has not himself created and over which he has no control? Kant recognizes, no less than Heidegger, that beings can become knowable to us only if they are in advance made accessible to us in a *coherent wholeness*. The problem of the knowability of beings shifts therefore to the prior problem of how this coherent whole itself can be a priori constituted, i.e., the problem of world for Heidegger, of nature for Kant. It may be added that although the "I" of transcendental apperception must be kept free of all "empirical content," it has an a priori content in the categories, e.g., "I think causality," "I think substance," etc.

The difference and similarity between our two thinkers could be demonstrated by a comparative study of Kant's "highest principle of all synthetic judgments," and Heidegger's "definition" of the phenomenon of world. Kant's famous formulation of the "highest principle" runs as follows: "The conditions of the *possibility of experience* as such are at the same time the conditions of the possibility of the objects of experience" (*Critique of Pure Reason*, A 158, B 197). Heidegger's "definition," whose literal translation is almost incomprehensible in English, may be rendered in the following somewhat simplified paraphrase: *"As that for which one lets beings be encountered in the kind of being of relevance, the wherein of self-referential understanding is the phenomenon of world"* (SZ, 86). A far from accidental similarity lies already in the structure of the two pronouncements. As Heidegger points out, the decisive content of Kant's "highest principle" is expressed not so much in the italicized words, as in the "are at the same time" (KPM, 111, G3, 119, KPM(E), 81). A similar observation applies to Heidegger's definition: its operative word is the "As." A further illuminating comparison could be made by drawing into consideration the Parmenides Fragment V: *to gar auto noein estin te kai einai*, "the same namely are apprehending and being." As Heidegger says, the "at the same time" is Kant's interpretation of Parmenides' "to auto," "the same" (WHD, 149, WCT, 243).

Finally, it must be emphasized that the objections raised here apply only to the interpretation we have quoted from *Being and Time*; in his "Kant book" and in *Die Frage nach dem Ding*, Heidegger does far more justice to Kant than in the short passage above.

3. This sentence is typical of Heidegger's perhaps all-too caustic criticism of Bergson. What Bergson means by the "externalized," "spatialized" time is the time *measured* by spatial movements, e.g., of the shadow cast by the sun on a sundial—a phenomenon which, after all, Heidegger himself will have to deal with. This is contrasted by Bergson with the "qualitative time," the experienced time of "duration." The distinction corresponds to Heidegger's derivative, "measured," "counted," or "reckoned" time and original time. In spite of Bergson's insufficient ontological foundations, Heidegger's criticism seems of an uncalled-for severity.

Part Three, Chapter XIII

1. Heidegger translates Aristotle's words *lupê tis hê tarachê* as a *Gedrücktheit* or *Verwirrung*, depressedness or confusion. In W. Rhys Roberts's Oxford translation they are rendered by "pain or disturbance." Heidegger's "depression" seems to be chosen to emphasize his own interpretation of attunement, according to which all moods and feelings reveal in one way or another the "weight" or "heaviness" (*Last*) of thrownness. In being "depressed," we directly experience the weight of our being the *thrown ground* of our finite ability-to-be-here.

2. See William J. Richardson, *Heidegger: Through Phenomenology to Thought* (The Hague: Nijhoff, 1967), 54.

Notes to Part Three 377

3. The German text has an obvious error in the sentence "Des Wozu gewärtig, kann das Besorgen allein zugleich auf so etwas zurückkommen, wobei es die Bewandtnis hat." The *Wozu* is identical with the *Wobei* and the latter must be corrected in the text to *Womit*. The next sentence makes it clear beyond doubt that that is what Heidegger intended.

4. The preconcept of phenomenology is given in the introduction, chap. 2, § 7, C.

5. Although Heidegger makes no explicit statement on this subject, it is extremely doubtful whether he would think it possible to understand something in its bare *existentia* without any qualifications whatever. Even when he speaks of something that "only persists" (*nur besteht*), the only-persisting is precisely the mode of that something's being, its way of being-in-time. At the very least, being must necessarily be defined by time.

6. The interpretation given of Heidegger's extremely condensed text may be thought to go beyond what actually stands there. It is well warranted, however, by earlier discussions of "statement as a derivative mode of interpretation" (§ 33), and of "the traditional concept of truth" (§ 44, a and b).

7. Some interpreters might argue that in one of his late works Heidegger turns against his own early views, for there he *contrasts* Aristotle's *Physics* as a genuine philosophy with modern physics as a positive science that presupposes a philosophy (SG, 110-11, G10, 92-93, PR, 63-64. The date of SG is 1957, while FD dates from 1935-36). But this evidence is inconclusive, because it is quite possible, and indeed likely, that by "positive science" Heidegger means only the actual research-work and its results, which are of course irrelevant to the point in question.

8. See *Kants These über das Sein* (Frankfurt: Klostermann, 1962), 9ff., 12, 33, W, 276ff., 281, 304, G9, 448ff., 453, 476, P, 339ff., 453, 360.

9. It would take us too far afield to discuss how, for instance, the future is primarily constitutive of all identification. To identify something as the same with itself it is not enough to compare it as it presents itself *now* with what we remember of it in the past. For further detail see Heidegger's discussion of Kant's "synthesis of recognition in the concept" (*Critique of Pure Reason*, A 103-10; KPM, § 33).

Part Three, Chapter XIV

1. On pp. 129-30 of US (OWL, 35-36, G12, 122-23), published in 1959, Heidegger reminds us of the dominant ideas of the 1920s. A keyword in those days both inside and outside Husserl's phenomenological school was *Erlebnis*, which, in default of an expression like "a-living something," we are forced to translate by "experience." *Erlebnis*, like *experience*, means both the experiencing ("a-living") of something and the experienced ("a-lived") happening. As a the-

ory of the "connection of life," *Erlebnis* implies a reflexive movement, a bending back of life and of the "lived" experience to an I, a relating back of the objective to the subjective. In short, the concept of *Erlebnis* moves in advance in the dimension of the subject-object relation and is therefore in principle suspect to Heidegger. In the above paragraph, Heidegger touches on the fundamental reason why the current theories do not satisfactorily explain the "connectedness" of the whole of here-being.

2. In anticipation of the difficulties of the present chapter, an interpretation of the stretchedness of here-being has already been attempted at the place where it could be most appropriately explained. See chap. 13, sec. 4.

3. This section is not essential to an understanding of Heidegger's own thought and, except for the passage briefly discussed in our commentary, is therefore omitted from it.

4. This quite apart from the rightness or wrongness of "superman" as a rendering of Nietzsche's *Übermensch*. Cf. here Heidegger's "Wer ist Nietzsche's Zarathustra?" in VA, 101-26 ("Who Is Nietzsche's Zarathustra?" trans. Bernd Magnus, in David B Allison (ed.), *The New Nietzsche* (Cambridge: MIT Press, 1985), 64-79; also *The Review of Metaphysics*, vol. 20, no. 3, March 1967, 411-31). This important essay seems to be unduly neglected in favor of the much cited "Nietzsche's Wort 'Gott ist tot'" in HO, 193-247, G5, 209-67, QCT, 54-112. For Heidegger's interpretation of Nietzsche's philosophy see his *Nietzsche*, vols. 1 and 2 (Pfullingen: Neske, 1961), trans. David Farrell Krell (San Francisco: Harper and Row. 1979-1987), G43, G44, G46, G47, G48.

5. The philosophical break with Husserl came with the publication of *Being and Time* in 1927, at which time the personal relations between the two thinkers seem to have been close and not yet darkened by the Jewish persecutions of the Nazi period.

6. Heidegger's increasing preoccupation with language in his later works has often been remarked. This development goes hand in hand with his historical "dialogues" with other thinkers and poets. It may not be too fanciful to think that the present passage gives us a first, barely noticeable hint of the reason for this development.

7. *Historicism* (or perhaps better: *historism*) has had widely differing meanings in Germany. One came into use around the middle of the nineteenth century. It meant a way of thinking that seeks to understand achievements, actions, and values from the historical situation in which they arose, and believed that their material content and present significance can be sufficiently explained by a historical account. Historism also denotes a philosophical trend that sees in historicity the decisive and essential character of human existence, or indeed of being in general, and conceives the world as history. Dilthey, among others, represented this trend. Historism in this sense is not far removed from Heidegger's own position.

Part Three, Chapter XV

1. In discussing the transcendental (i.e. according to Heidegger, the transcendence-forming) function of pure space in the second edition of Kant's *Critique of Pure Reason*, Heidegger remarks that "time" understood as the pure succession of a now-sequence, which is formed in pure intuition, "stands in a certain sense always and necessarily on an equal footing with space" (KPM, 191, G3, 198–199, KPM(E), 135–36). The elucidation of a "world-time" makes it clear that Heidegger identifies Kant's purely intuited time and space with *that* modification of world-time and world-space in which they lose their *world*-character and are levelled down to the "indifferently" intuited time and space of a theoretically viewed nature. The same modification, it will be remembered, takes place when the "handiness" (handy reality) of within-worldish utensils is "unworlded" into the "objective presence" (substantial reality) of mere substances occurring in nature.

The passage in Kant discussed by Heidegger is B 291: "Even more remarkable is it that, in order to understand the possibility of things resulting from the categories, and so to prove the *objective reality* of the latter, we need not merely intuitions, but more than that, we need always *external intuitions*." This might easily lead to the conclusion that the primacy of time as the *universal* form of all appearing things, has fallen. Heidegger contests the validity of this conclusion on the ground that the purely intuited space, no less than the purely intuited time, in the sense described above, originates in the "transcendental imagination" which, more fundamentally penetrated and interpreted, is the *temporality* of here-being.

2. The above discussion of time and space has an evident bearing on the problem of time *measurement* in the theory of relativity to which Heidegger refers in a footnote (SZ, 417–18). His aim, of course, is not to enter into a scientific problem quite out of the range of a fundamental ontology, but to emphasize what far-reaching inquiries are needed to lay bare the foundations in which all scientific time-measuring is rooted. First of all, it is necessary to explain world-time and infinity from the temporality of here-being, secondly, to clarify the existential-temporal constitution of the discovery of nature and, thirdly, to demonstrate the temporal meaning of measuring in general.

3. *Ob-jicere*, we recall, is to throw forward, before or against.

4. Aristotle, *Physics*, 219bf. The translation given by R. P. Hardie and R. K. Gaye is: "For time is just this—number of motion in respect of 'before' and 'after'" (Richard McKeon [ed.], *The Basic Works of Aristotle* [New York: Random House, 1941], 292).

5. But see GP, BPP, G24, § 19. See also BZ, CT; PGZ, HCT. [Ed.]

6. Plato, *Timaeus* 37d.

7. Heidegger remarks in a footnote that the traditional concept of eternity in the sense of a "standing now" (*nunc stans*) is evidently drawn from the

common understanding of time and is delimited by the idea of a "standing" (constant) thereness, i.e., *Vorhandenheit*. This assertion could be contested only if "Vorhandenheit" were taken in the narrow sense of the bodily "thereness" of a thing, but not if it is taken in the ontologically widest sense in which Heidegger understands it. But the most intriguing part of Heidegger's footnote is the remark its author almost incidentally appends: "If the eternity of *God* could be philosophically 'constructed' it could be understood only as a more primordial and 'infinite' temporality. Whether or not the *via negationis et eminentiae* could offer a possible way remains an open question" (SZ, 427). What can Heidegger mean by "a more primordial temporality"? If our own temporality originates the time *in which* beings can come to light *in their being*, could a more original temporality originate these time-bound beings themselves? If that were Heidegger's meaning, it would come close to Kant's *intuitus originarius*, the infinite intuition that *creates* the concrete things and so knows them "in themselves," i.e., without any need for the anticipating preforming of their *being* (the *object*-being of the object) which our finite, uncreative intuition needs in order to receive the already given things in an intelligible way. And so an objection that might arise from Heidegger's own interpretation of being, the objection that only a *finite* temporality can disclose *being*, would be no objection at all, since an understanding of being must be alien and unnecessary to an infinite creator of beings. These notions, however, which arise from an analogy with Kant's *intuitus originarius*, are entirely speculative. Heidegger's suggestion is too problematic to allow any concrete interpretation. It seems likely, indeed, that *if* a philosophical "construction" of such a more original and "infinite" temporality were possible, it would move entirely in the sphere of negativity. For what could an "infinite" temporality mean? Certainly not the endlessness of a pure continuum of pure nows, but rather the measurelessness that reveals itself in the "negating of the nothing," in the inconceivable and not revealed nothing of beings (not-beings) and nothing of being (not-being). This negativity need not mean an absolute nothingness, but the repudiation of all possible measure and comparison with *finite* temporality. The reference to the *via negationis* seems to confirm this impression, but here again Heidegger deliberately leaves the matter open and so prevents the drawing of definite conclusions. In surveying Heidegger's thought as a whole, we may doubt whether he thinks that a genuinely philosophical construction of "the eternity of God" is possible.

8. For an excellent critical article on this section see Howard Trivers, "Heidegger's Misinterpretation of Hegel's Views on Spirit and Time," *Philosophy and Phenomenological Research*, vol. 3, 1942–1943, 162ff. With the most important conclusion of this article I am in complete agreement, though not with some of its minor points.

9. G. W. F. Hegel, *Die Vernunft in der Geschichte. Einleitung in die Philosophie*, ed. G. Lasson (Leipzig: Meiner Verlag, 1917), 133. [The Supplements referred to in this note and in note 24 are not included in *Reason in History: A General Introduction to the Philosophy of History*, trans. Robert S. Hartman (Indianapolis: Bobbs-Merrill, 1953). Ed.]

10. Hegel, *Phenomenology of Spirit*, trans. A. V. Miller (Oxford: Oxford University Press, 1979), 492.

11. Hegel, *Encyclopaedia of the Philosophical Sciences*, Part Two, *Philosophy of Nature*, trans. A. V. Miller (Oxford: Oxford University Press, 1970), § 258.

12. See Howard Trivers, op. cit., 162.

13. Hegel, *Encyclopaedia*, § 254ff.

14. Hegel, *Encyclopaedia*, § 257, Supplement.

15. Hegel, *Encyclopaedia*, § 254.

16. Hegel, *Encyclopaedia*, § 257.

17. *Ideell* is frequently used in German instead of the more ambiguous *ideal*, which can also mean an ethical pattern of perfection, a meaning to be excluded here. The opposite of *ideell* is *real* or *reell*, also *material* or *materiell*, i.e., that which pertains to or exists by way of the concrete reality of nature, in contrast to the *ideell*, which pertains to or exists by way of the idea, or spirit.

18. Hegel, *Science of Logic*, trans. A. V. Miller (London: Allen & Unwin, 1969), vol. 1, bk 1, chap. 1, C, 82–83.

19. Hegel, *Encyclopaedia*, § 259.

20. Ibid., Supplement.

21. Hegel, *Science of Logic*, vol. 2, 583.

22. Ibid.

23. Hegel, *Phenomenology*, 487.

24. Hegel, *Die Vernunft in der Geschichte*, 134.

25. Hegel, *Phenomenology*, 487.

Glossary of German Expressions

Ableben: decease
Abständigkeit: stand-offishness
Alltäglichkeit: everydayness
angänglich: approachable, touchable
Angst: dread
Ansprechen: addressing
Augenblick: Moment, instant, glance of the eye
Auslegung: interpretation, laying out
Ausrichtung: direction

bedeuten: to signify
Bedeutsamkeit: significance
Befindlichkeit: attunement, self-findsomeness
begegnenlassen: encounter
Behalten: retention, remembering
bei: near to, close to
benommen: enthralled, bemused, taken in
Beruhigung: tranquillizing
Besorgen: taking care, heedfulness
Besprechen: talking about
Bestand: persistence
Beständigkeit: standingness
bestehen: to persist
Bewandtnis: relevance
Bewegtheit: movedness

Bewendenlassen: letting things be relevant
Bewusstsein: consciousness
Bodennehmen: having gained ground

Da-sein: being-there, there-being, being-here, here-being, (man)
Durchsichtigkeit: transparency

eigen: own
eigenst: ownmost
eigentlich: owned, authentic
Einfühlung: empathy
Ekstase: ecstasis
Entdeckung: discovery
Ent-fernung: un-distancing, de-distancing
Entfremdung: alienation, estrangement
Entschlossenheit: resoluteness, resolution, dis-closedness
Entweltlichung: unworlding
Entwurf: fore-throw, project
Ermöglichung: enabling
Erscheinung: appearance
Erschlossenheit: disclosure
Erstreckung: stretching
Erwarten: expectancy
es geht um: it is at stake

es gibt: there is (it gives)
Existenz: existence
existenzial: existential
Existenzialien: existentials
existenziell: existentiell

faktisch: factical
Faktizität: facticity
Freigabe: setting free
freigeben: to set free
Fürsorge: care-for, concern, solicitude
Fürwahrhalten: being certain

Ganzseinkönnen: can-be-a-whole, potentiality of being a whole
Gegend: place, neighborhood, region
Gegenstand: object
Gegenwärtigung: making present
gehalten: held
Gerede: hear-saying idle talk
Geschehen: occurrence, happening
Geschichte: history
Geschichtlichkeit: historicity
Geschick: common destiny
Gewärtigen: awaiting
gewesen: having-been, has-been, "past"
Gewesenheit: having-been
Gewissen: conscience
Gewissen-haben-wollen: wanting (willing)-to-have-a-conscience
Geworfenheit: thrownness
grund-legend: ground-laying
Grund-sein: ground-being
Grundverfassung: fundamental constitution

in-der-Welt-sein: being-in-the-world
innerweltlich: innerworldly, within-worldish

Kategorien: categories
konstitutive Momente: fundamental constituents

Lebenszusammenhang: coherence or connection of life

Man (das): "they," "them," one, people
Man-selbst: "they-self"
Mitsein: being-with
Mitwelt: with-world

Nachsicht: (forbearing) looking-to (the other self), un-caring toleration
Neugier: curiosity
Nichtigkeit: notness, nothingness, nullity
Nichts: nothing(ness)

öffentlich: public, published
Öffentlichkeit: publicity, publicness, public disclosedness
ontisch: ontic

räumlich: spaceish, roomy, spatial
Realität: reality
Rede: discourse, speech
Rücksicht: considerate looking-back (on the other's thrownness), considerateness

Schicksal: fate
Schuld: owing, debt, guilt
Schwebe: swaying
Seiende (das): beings
Sein: being
Seinsarten: modes of being
Seinsverfassung: ontological constitution
Selbst-ständigkeit: standingness of the self, independence
Sich-aussprechen: self-expression
Sinn: meaning, sense
Sorge: care
Spanne: spannedness
ständige Anwesenheit: standing presentness
Ständigkeit: stability, standing

Überlegung: deliberation
Übersicht: overview

Überzeugung: conviction
um: for, around
Umgang: dealings with, going about (for something)
Umschlag: overturning
Umsicht: circumspect for-sight
Umwelt: surrounding world, for-world
umwillen: for the sake of (for the will of)
uneigentlich: disowned, inauthentic
unheimlich: uncanny, unhomely, not-at-home

Verendung: perishing
Verfallen: falling, falling prey or captive (to the world)
Verfängnis: entanglement
Vergangenheit: past, goneness
Vergegenwärtigung: bringing face to face
Verstehen, Verständtnis: understanding
verweisen: to refer
Verweisung: reference
Verweisungsganzheit: reference-whole
vorgängig: fore-going

Vorhandenheit: substantial, objective, reality or presence

Weisungen: directions, rule, law
weltbildend: world-forming, world-imaging
weltlich: worldish (worldly)
Weltlichkeit: worldishness (worldliness)
Wiederholung: repetition, retrieval
Wirbel: whirl
Wirklichkeit: actuality (reality)

Zeit: time
zeitigen (sich): to bring oneself to ripeness, to arise, temporalize
zeitlich: timeish
Zeitlichkeit: timeishness
Zerstreuung: scatteredness, dispersion
Zeug: utensil, useful thing
Zeugnis: witness
Zuhandenheit: handiness, handy reality
Zu-kunft: coming-toward, future
zunächst und zumeist: initially (in the first place) and for the most part
Zweideutigkeit: ambiguity

INDEX

a priori, 45–46, 53, 67, 104, 272; *see also* fore-going
actuality, reality (*Wirklichkeit*), 9, 33
addressing (*Ansprechen*), 329, 331, 349
affection, 237, 240
ahead-of-itself, 98, 145, 151–52, 157, 159, 210, 216, 220–21, 230; *see also* fore-throw
aisthêsis, 112
alienation (*Entfremdung*), 89
Allemann, Beda, 175
already, 56, 99, 151, 216, 220–21, 249
ambiguity, 87–88, 199, 243
analysis, static and genetic, 117
Anaximander, 78
animal, 13, 16, 20, 150, 372; rational, 40
anthropology, 14, 19, 150
anticipation, 159–61, 179, 201–7, 210, 218, 231, 242, 325; *see also* ahead *and* forward-running
anxiety (*Angst*), *see* dread
apophansis, 111
appearance (*Erscheinung*), 110–11; Kant, 111
approachable, touchable (*angänglich*), 57

arising (*Entspringen*), 229, 247, 274
Aristotle, *aesthêsis*, 112; analogy, 15–17; being, 3; fear, 238; Hegel and time, 354; *phusis*, 270; *Physics*, 377; time, 344–45; time and space, 43; truth, being and beings, 106
articulation, 57
as, 112, 116, 138, 264–68, 283, 376; apophantic and hermeneutic, 371; as such, 209, 211, 223, 316, 345; schema of presenting, 266
attunement (*Befindlichkeit*), 55–61, 83, 85, 93, 94–96, 161, 163, 221, 236–42, 289; dread, 121, 153, 178, 319; that I am, 182; timeishness, 125
Augustine of Hippo, Saint, soul and time, 349
authentic (*eigentlich*) and inauthentic, 40–41, 163–227, 232–34, 247–52, 278, 288–90, 291–92, 333–35, 349; historicity, 295, 298, 302–25; *see also* owned *and* disowned
average, 42, 79, 82, 84–85, 230, 290
awaiting (*Gewärtigen*), 231, 233, 237, 242, 247, 252, 258–61, 264, 267, 286–89, 330

being, to be (*Sein*), xix, 5, 7, 13,
  15–16, 22; analogy, 15–17, as
  such, 209, 211, 223; and beings,
  342; horizon of being, 126; how-
  being, 8, 15, 112, 140; humanity,
  49; I am, 13–15, 18, 20, 32, 47,
  97, 115, 117; is, are, 17, 21–23,
  30, 47, 61, 71, 115, 137, 223,
  254–55, 267–68, 276, 328; meaning, 126; nothing, 136; substantial, 10; temporality, 134–35; tenses, 135–36; that-being, 116; time,
  126, 328; *transcendens* pure and
  simple, 256, 275; truth, 262;
  unity, 15; what-being, 8, 15, 33,
  113, 140
being-here, *see* Da-sein
being-in-the-world (*in-der-Welt-sein*),
  25, 27, 45, 51–65, 74, 89, 92–97,
  187, 275–84, 289
being near (close) to (*bei*), 44, 64, 74,
  85, 99, 180, 216, 222, 244, 275,
  328
being-one's-self, 27, 75–90
being-with (*Mitsein*), 27, 56, 58,
  63–64, 74, 75–83, 180, 198, 222,
  304
beings (*das Seiende*), 9, 11–13, 16, 22,
  71–74; as beings, 106; being, 342;
  created, 15; in the whole, 138,
  176, 177–78; sinking away,
  176–77; *ta onta*, 11–12, 110; *see
  also* ontological difference
Bergson, Henri, 125, 226, 331, 376
bindingness, 180, 183, 319
birth, 120, 149, 295–96, 318
body, 20
boundary situation, 250

calculation, 15; death, 157, 158,
  160–61, 184, 333
care (*Sorge*), 25, 28, 35–36, 42, 64;
  the between, 297; conscience,
  122, 163–75, 193; everyday, 105;
  ground-being, 122; selfhood,
  212–17; structure, 119–20,
  122–23, 125, 150, 173, 210, 216,
  222; theory and practice, 199;
  time, 217–25; truth, 102, 104;
  unity, 123; whole, 37, 56, 97–100,
  120, 125, 241
care-for, concern, solicitude
  (*Fürsorge*), 76–78, 86, 192
categories (*Kategorien*), 33, 43–44, 99,
  116, 280; categorial structure, 46
causality, 266
certainty, 155–57, 160, 204
charity, 77
choice, 194–96, 198, 203, 306, 322
Christianity, 14, 309
circle, 23–24, 37–38, 95–96, 167,
  209–10, 234, 331, 367
circumspect for-sight (*Umsicht*),
  69–70, 78, 86, 243
coming-toward, future (*Zu-kunft*), 18,
  36, 124, 218–21, 230
common sense, 70, 168, 210, 329
communication, 308, 312
concealment, *see* covering over *and*
  hiddenness
concept, 135, 350, 356
connection, coherence of life
  (*Lebenszusammenhang*), 295, 315,
  319–20
conscience (*Gewissen*), 121–22,
  163–75, 190–95, 366; call, voice,
  163–75, 191, 193; care, 166, 167;
  existentiell and existential, 192;
  reprimanding, 191; wanting-to-
  have-a-conscience, 122–23,
  195–96; warning, 190–91
consciousness, 114–15, 117, 367
considerate looking-back (on the
  other's thrownness), considerateness (*Rücksicht*), 78, 243
constancy, 181, 183, 204, 216, 226,
  246, 281, 304; *see also* stability
conviction (*Überzeugung*), 156
correspondence, *see* truth
covering over, concealing, 112,
  155–56, 205, 272, 334; *see also* hiddenness

creation, 14–15
culture, 300
curiosity (*Neugier*), 86–87, 243, 252, 289; sight, 243–44

Da-sein, xix, 10, 12–14, 19–20, 23, 25–27, 94–95; care, 97; conscience, 164; day-by-day, 338; everydayness, 290–93; exists, 29, 51–65, 150; factically existing, 367; finitude, 62, 63, 120, 224–25; historicity, 323–24; individuation, 161, 177, 256; meaning, xiv–xv, 67–49; occurrence, happening (*Geschehen*), 296–97, 315–16; stretching (*Erstreckung*), 291, 295–97, 334; temporality, 327–43; that I am, 178, 204, 223, 249; transcendence, 175, 177–78, 180, 184–85, 275, 367; truth, 102, 104, 198, 204; understanding of being, 96, 328; unity, 120; untruth, 198; whole, 38, 120, 123, 128, 145–62, 206; world-forming, (*weltbildend*), 53–54, 67, 184–85; *see also* freedom
datability, 330–33, 335, 338–41
dealings with, going about (for something) (*Umgang*), 69
death, 120, 121, 123, 143, 157, 158, 160–61, 218, 295–96, 346–47; calculation, 157, 158, 160–61; certainty, 155–57, 160; death wish, 373; flight, 143, 153, 155, 157; impassability, 157, 160, 202; impossibility, 152, 159, 160, 161, 181, 364; indefiniteness, 157, 161, 206; individuation, 161, 177, 202; others, 146–47, 149–62; positive repulsion, 181, 250, 365–66; possibility, extremest, 121, 123, 124, 128, 152, 158, 162, 181; unrelational, 157, 159, 160, 202; when, 157, 158, 161, 206
debt (*Schuld*), *see* owing
decease (*Ableben*), 150, 156, 373

deliberation (*Überlegung*), 263–64; if-then schema, 263–66, 283
depression, 56
Descartes, René, 14, 45; *cogito ergo sum*, 205, 369–70; method, 116–17
destiny (*Geschick*), 292, 321; common, 308–9; self-destining self-disclosure of being, 361
dialectic, 174, 176
Dilthey, Wilhelm, 261, 299, 325
direction (*Ausrichtung*), 44, 55, 104, 185, 286
directions (*Weisungen*), rule, law, 188
disclosure (*Erschlossenheit*), 30, 58, 84, 91–97, 236, 272, 367; care, 120, 195; death, 121; resolute, 123; truth, 101–2, 105, 112, 306, 317–18
discourse, speech (*Rede*), 55, 83–86, 102, 111, 289; communication, expression, 312; conscience, 163; temporality, 252–55
discovery (*Entdeckung*), 102–3, 282, 316–17
disowned, inauthentic (*uneigentlich*), 37, 40–41, 60, 76, 78, 88, 92, 98, 120, 123–24, 141, 216, 252, 288–89, 290–92; attunement, 236–37, 242; death, 157, 159, 373; falling, 252; future, 230–32, 234, 237–38, 240, 245–47, 265, 278; past, 237, 240–41; present, 232; understanding, 235–36, 239, 258
distantiality (*Abständigkeit*), *see* standoffishness
dread (*Angst*), xv, 19, 23, 28, 91–97, 121, 152–54, 161, 166, 174, 178, 196, 206, 239–42, 289, 319, 364–65; indefiniteness, 206; whereof, 278
dwelling, 96, 200, 243, 293

ecstasis (*Ekstase*), 36, 124, 223–24, 230, 232, 249–50, 277, 289, 330; *ekstatikon*, 223, 353; unity, 288

eidos, 66
empathy (*Einfühlung*), 76
encounter (*begegnenlassen*), 233
end, 120, 121, 124, 127-28, 145-50, 181, 185, 295; endingly (finite), 248; endlessness of time, 347
entanglement (*Verfängnis*), 89, 245-47
enthralled, bemused, taken in (*benommen*), 59, 79
environment, *see* surrounding world
Erlebnis, 377-78
erring, 88, 105-7, 198
es gibt, 336
essence, 8, 13, 29-30, 33, 53, 114, 135, 272; existence, 33, 40, 114, 354; *existentia* and *essentia* of time, 354
eternity, 233, 346, 354, 361
ethics, 162, 168-70, 173, 189, 211
Europe, 13
everydayness (*Alltäglichkeit*), 21, 27, 41-42, 52, 68, 79-88, 105, 120, 128, 147; conscience, 164; Da-sein, 290-93; day-by-day, 338; death, 153; taking care, 125; time, 124, 328
evil, 151, 169, 191, 237, 240
existence, 9-10; Da-sein, 29, 32, 36-37, 43-48, 51-65, 83, 84, 95, 125, 159; essence, 33, 40, 114; *existentia*, 47, 134, 135, 183, 276, 354, 357, 377; finitely free, 367; light, 38; real, 12, 14, 19, 29; truth, 196, 202-3; *see also* self
existential (*existenzial*), 42, 43, 45-46, 52, 70, 84; conscience, 121; death, 151-53, 158-62; existential-onto-logical, 42-43, 44, 48-49, 52, 70, 80, 82, 122
existentialism, 19, 196, 249, 324, 373
existentials (*Existenzialien*), 43-46, 83
existentiell (*existenziell*), 46; existentiell-ontic, 120
expectancy (*Erwarten*), 231, 237, 240
extension, 15

face to face, bringing (*Vergegenwärtigung*), 263-64
facticity (*Faktizität*), 36-38, 43, 48, 52, 60, 84, 95, 105, 120, 125, 182, 249-50
falling, falling prey or captive (to the world) (*Verfallen*), 27, 36-38, 41, 43, 59, 74, 88-90, 125, 170, 193, 289; death, 154-55; temporality, 243-52; timeishness, 125
fate (*Schicksal*), 292, 305-7, 317, 321, 325, 334
fear, 57-58, 92, 93, 153, 237, 289; confusion, 238, 242
feeling, *see* attunement
finitude, 62, 63; closedness, 304; Da-sein, 97, 106, 120, 159, 160, 224, 367; endingly, 248; freedom, 27, 39-40, 120, 41; time, 18, 124, 225
fleeing, 143, 153, 155, 157, 169, 205, 215, 248, 318, 346-47
for the sake of (for the will of) (*umwillen*), *see* sake
forbearing looking-to (the other self), un-caring toleration (*Nachsicht*), 78, 86, 243
fore-going (*vorgängig*), 37, 38, 45-46, 53
fore-throw, project (*Entwurf*), 36, 170, 175, 179, 210, 218, 364; fore-structure, 59, 60-61, 70, 88-89, 97, 121
forgetting, 235, 237, 238, 242, 252, 258, 289
forward-running, 159, 160, 201-7, 234, 242, 298; resoluteness, 206, 208, 216, 218, 325; understanding, 121
freedom, 27, 39-40, 41, 58, 95, 104, 161, 172, 177, 194, 367; free play, 182; free will, 187; sake of (for the), 180; setting free, 160, 274, 372; transcendence, 181, 195
fundamental constitution (*Grundverfassung*), 44-45, 65, 68
future, 36, 136, 218-21, 230, 289; *see also* coming-toward

Index 391

Galileo, Galilei, 270
generation, 308
God, 14, 189; philosopher's, 14, 18
Goethe, Johann Wolfgang von, xv
good and bad, 187–88
Greek-Western thinking, 14–15, 18, 65, 66, 67, 74, 99, 101, 106
grim (*das Grimmige*), 188
ground-being (*Grund-sein*), 122, 143, 169–72, 175–87, 193, 215; founding (*Stiften*), 181–82; gaining or taking ground (*Bodennehmen*), 182, 304; grounding, proving (*Begründen*), 182
ground-laying (*Grund-legend*), 201, 212, 273, 340–41
guilt, 187–95; *see also* owing

handiness, handy reality (*Zuhandenheit*), 27, 65, 72–74, 77, 134, 262, 272; proposition, 103; sun, 337–38; utensils, 257–61, 266
having-been, has-been, (*gewesen*), *see* past
hearing, 84; conscience, 191, 199
hearsay, 85, 103
Hegel, Georg Wilhelm Friedrich, 125; Aristotle and time, 354; *Aufhebung*, 328, 350, 352, 358; becoming, 353–54; being and nothing, 137; concept, 356, 357, 359, 361; consuming, 354–55; history, 350; intuited becoming, 353–54, 358; life, 359–60; negation of negation, 355–56, 358–60; nothingness, 137; power of time, 360; punctuality, 352, 355; space, 351–53; space and time, dialectic, 353; spirit, 328; time and spirit, 328, 349–51, 356–61
held (*gehalten*), 246, 247
Heraclitus, 117, 189
here, 133, 161, 163, 166, 179, 199, 219, 230; there, 282
here-being, *see* Da-sein
hermeneutic phenomenology, 113

hermeneutical situation, 325
hero, 291, 311–14
hiddenness, 105–7, 113
historical situation, 182
historicism, 323; historism, 378
historicity (*Geschichtlichkeit*), 174, 175, 212, 226, 290, 291, 292, 295, 298, 298–326, 310; authentic, 295, 298, 302–25
historiography (*Historie*), 299, 314, 317, 320–21, 323; antiquarian, monumental, critical, 324
history (*Geschichte*), 10, 13, 105, 125, 150, 290–93; Hegel, 350; nature, 300; Nietzsche, 324; past, 301; vulgar understanding of, 300–2; world history, 301–2, 315–26
Hölderlin, Friedrich, 84
holy, wholesome, healing (*das Heile*), 188
hope, 242
horizon, 6–8, 94, 185–86, 286; being, 126, 180; meaning, 207; nothing, 232; possibilities, 182; schema, 267, 278–79, 283; time, 18, 125, 126, 267, 277; understanding, 24, 60, 66, 128
Housman, Alfred Edward, xv, 3
humanity, 49
Husserl, Edmund, xix, 26, 28, 42, 44, 45, 75–76, 107, 109, 310, 374, 378; intentionality, 114, 115, 116
hylê, stuff, material, 116

I, 76, 79, 210, 212–17, 367; *cogito ergo sum*, 205; Hegel, 357, 360
ideal, ideell, 381
idle talk, hear-saying idle talk (*Gerede*), 83–86, 103, 153, 243; tradition, 304
if-then, *see* deliberation
immortality, 151
impossibility, 121, death, 152, 159, 364
inauthentic (*uneigentlich*), 40–41, 76–77, 91, 232–40, 242, 288–89,

inauthentic (*uneigentlich*) (*continued*) 318, 320; attunement, 236–38, 242; falling, 252; future, 230–32, 234, 237, 240, 245–48, 265, 278; history, 290–91; past, 277, 240–41; present, 232; understanding, 233, 235, 238, 239; *see also* disowned
indifferent, 42, 77, 290; forbearance, toleration (*Nachsehen*), 78
infinity, time, 18, 124
inhabiting, 96
inheritance, 305–12, 319–25
initially (in the first place) and for the most part (*zunächst und zumeist*), 41, 290
instant, *see* Moment
intentionality, 114, 115, 116
interpretation (*Auslegung*), 84, 208, 211, 262, 273, 329–30; schema, 283; violence, 207; *see also* laying out

joy (*Freude*), 56, 58, 242

Kant, Immanuel, 2, 43, 111, 116, 117, 134, 141, 232; anticipations of perception, 185; awe, 319; being, 135; categories, 280, 283–84, 375; cause, 181; concept, 135; fortune, 307; morality, 169, 309, 374–75; nature, 375–76; practical reason, 274–75; pure reason, 279; respect, 319; schematism, 267, 283–84; self, 213–15; synthesis, 263, 280; time, 313, 342; time and space, 284–85, 379; totality, 280; transcendental object, 185; transcendental self-consciousness, 310; will, 195
Kierkegaard, Søren, 233
knowledge, 67, 104

lack, 145, 147–48, 151
language, 71, 83–86, 102, 141, 173, 252–55, 329, 378; speech, 329; *see also* addressing *and* discourse *and* self-expression *and* talking about
laying out (*Auslegung*), 337; *see also* interpretation
leaping ahead (*vorausspringen*), 77, 197
leaping in (*einspringen*), 77
letting, 58, 111, 112, 118; letting things be relevant, 258, 261, 376
life, 20, 42, 105, 150, 210; connection (*Lebenszusammenhang*), 295, 315, 319–20, 378; Hegel, 358; philosophy of, 299
logic, 10, 15–16, 100, 164
logos, 110, 111–12
lostness, 334–35, 337

man (*Da-sein*), xiv–xv, 7, 10, 12–14, 19–20, 23, 25, 29–30, 47, 97
manifestness, 142
mathematical physics, 270–72
mathematics, 10, 104–5, 273
meaning, sense (*Sinn*), 2, 6–7, 36, 42, 112, 257; being, 126; beings, 272; essence, 114; horizon, 207; ontological, 123, 217–25; *see also* signification *and* significance
meaninglessness, 367
means, by means of, 55, 61, 64, 69–70
measurement, 225, 379; astronomical, 292, 337, 339–41
medieval philosophy, 14, 16, 135; *see also* Schoolmen
metaphysics, 10, 13, 16, 20, 72, 118, 369; death, 151; beings, 138
method, 109, 112–13, 117, 142–44, 158, 175, 201, 212, 273; Descartes, 116–17; historical sciences, 325; violence, 207
mind, 19, 325
mine, 120, 147, 333, 373
Moment (*Augenblick*), 222, 233, 241, 248, 250, 289, 310, 313, 319, 334, 348
mood, *see* attunement

morality, 162, 169, 172, 173, 187–89, 198
movedness (*Bewegtheit*), 176, 234, 297, 316, 325; movement in space, 288

nature, 15, 19, 44, 45, 52, 53, 69, 269–71; history, 300; time, 342
Nazism, 373–74
necessity, 8; world, 139; historical, 10, 19, 29, 33
never, 171, 173, 174, 186–87, 304, 366
Newton, Isaac, 270
Nietzsche, Friedrich, 160; history, 323–24; *Übermensch*, 307, 378; will, 195
nihilism, 9
noein, 18–19, 66, 112
noema, 116
not, 8–9, 34–35, 39, 60, 63, 80, 96–97, 98, 174, 249, 251, 304, 365–67; debt, 122, 170–71
nothing(ness) (*Nichts*), 8–9, 93–94, 171, 175–87, 365; conscience, 164; horizon, 232; negates, 138–40, 170, 177, 206; notness, nullity (*Nichtigkeit*), 39, 122, 173, 224; shrinking back from, 176; time itself, 366; *see also* Hegel
now, 187, 233, 329–36, 339–40, 344–48; Hegel, 352–55
nowhere, 93–95, 365

object (*Gegenstand*), 15, 23, 68, 111, 282
obligation, 180, 188
occurrence, happening (*Geschehen*), 296–97, 305–6, 315–16, 325
on, to on, xv; *ta onta,* 11–12, 110
ontic (*ontisch*), 48, 68, 97, 150; ontic-existentiell, 46, 52
ontological constitution (*Seinsverfassung*), 44, 46, 272
ontological difference, 178, 273, 276
ontological structure (*Seinsstruktur*), 42, 84

ontology, 11, 22, 68, 369; essence, 272; fundamental, 11, 19, 25, 29, 46, 113, 173, 212; meaning of beings, 272; ontological-existential, existential-ontological, 42–43, 44, 48–49, 52, 70, 80, 82; regional, 19, 113, 270; traditional, 11–12, 19, 42, 71, 83, 99, 183
order, in order to, 55, 61, 69–70, 278
organism, 20, 42
otherness, 138, 178, 180, 186, 280, 365
others, 56, 64, 76, 99, 160; birth and death, 120, 146–47
ousia, 184, 369
overturning (*Umschlag*), 268
overview (*Übersicht*), 263–64
owing (*Schuld*), 122–23, 167–75, 186–200, 202, 216
own, 38, 47
owned, authentic (*eigentlich*), 38, 40–41, 76–78, 83, 91, 95, 102, 120, 123–24, 141, 143, 158, 163, 167, 201–27, 245, 246, 248–50, 288–89, 291–92; attunement, 242; death, 158–62, 373; existence, 187–200, 274; future, 232–34, 240, 252, 278; history, historicity, 298, 304–5, 315, 318–24; occurrence, 302, 314; past, 234, 238, 247; present, 233; science, 274–75; temporality, 310–11; understanding, 236
ownmost (*eigenst*), xviii, 32, 35, 154, 157, 159, 193

Parmenides, 106, 376
past, 18; having been, 36, 124, 136, 218–19, 234–35, 289
perception, 112, 115, 277, 282
perishing (*Verendung*), 150
phenomenology, 6, 26, 28, 75–76, 109–18; hermeneutic, 113
phenomenon, 18, 109–11
phusis, 270, 343
physics, 270–72

place, neighborhood, region (*Gegend*), 93-94, 128, 199, 223; indifferent, 269; place, places, 140
plants, 20, 150
Plato, 268
positivism, 173, 271, 273
possibility, 8, 31, 32-35, 38-40, 59-60, 63, 65, 70, 80, 88-90, 145, 152, 179, 203, 238, 364; dread, 95, 319; extremest, 121, 123, 124, 128, 152, 158, 162, 181, 193, 205, 234, 240, 318, 364; historical, 13; potentiality, 32-33, 166, 203-4; world, 139
practice, 65-66, 72; care, 200
preontological, 20, 207, 272
prephenomenological, 113, 213
present, make present (*gegenwärtigen*), 10, 37, 124, 205, 232, 236, 240, 242, 252, 253, 255, 258, 261, 263, 289, 330; presence, 12, 15, 73, 94, 232, 255, 281; schema of presenting, 266; vis-à-vis, 232, 281
presuppositions, 206-9
proposition, 102-3, 112, 164, 197
publicity, publicness, public disclosedness (*Öffentlichkeit*), xv, 41, 83, 85, 290-91; time, 124, 336-38, 340

real, reell, 381
reality (*Realität, Vorhandenheit*), 12, 18, 20, 26, 27, 29-30, 45, 53, 71-74, 115, 134, 276; real beings, 277; time, 345-46
reason, 12, 319; pure reason, Kant, 279
reduction, 115; phenomenological, 115-16
reference (*Verweisung*), 65; reference-structure, 134, 258; reference-whole, 67, 197
region, 286
relevance (*Bewandtnis*), 72, 257-58
repetition, retrieval, recollection, recapitulation (*Wiederholung*), 225-27, 234, 240-42, 310-11, 320, 322; explicitness (*Ausdrücklichkeit*), 311-12; Kant, 313; philosophical, 313-14
representation, 15, 206, 213-14, 263
resistance, 260-61
resoluteness (*Entschlossenheit*), 83, 163, 196-98, 201, 203-4, 252; fate, 306, 318; forward-running, 206, 208, 216, 218, 325
response, 313
responsibility, 82, 122, 173
retention (*Behalten*), remembering, 235-36, 258-59, 261, 264, 267, 275, 286-89, 330
ripeness, 37, 124, 148, 222
roominess, 284-89
running away, running after, 247, 252, 289, 318

sake of, for the (*Umwillen*), 31, 35, 39, 49, 51, 60-61, 65, 67, 68, 70, 73, 76, 78, 83, 170, 173, 179-81, 188, 221, 231, 258, 262, 263, 289; founding (*Stiften*), 182; freedom, 185; significance, 276-77
scatteredness, dispersion (*Zerstreuung*), 232, 247, 317-18
Scheler, Max, 261
schema, 267, 278, 283-84; *see also* as *and* deliberation *and* Kant
Schoolmen, 14, 16-17
science, 7, 10, 15, 67, 72, 104-5, 112, 150, 244, 261-62, 273, 322; conscience, 165; owned existence, 275; *see also* mathematical physics *and* physics
seduction, 88-89, 154, 248
seeing, sight (*Sicht*), 78, 86, 112, 113, 115, 337
self, 26, 40, 58, 76, 79, 83, 96, 123, 159, 172; care, 212-17
self-consciousness, 20
self-expression (*Sich-aussprechen*), 329-30
sense, meaning (*Sinn*), 2; *see also* meaning

significance (*Bedeutsamkeit*), 61, 65, 276–77
significance-structure, 69, 72–73, 197, 338
significance-whole, 83–84, 104, 197, 366–67
signification, 61, 69, 255
silence, 84, 163, 164, 166, 173, 196, 312
situation, 199–200, 219, 232, 241, 303, 334; boundary, 250; hermeneutical, 325; historical, 182
solicitude, *see* care-for
solipsism, 277
something, 8, 98, 138, 185–86, 281
soul, 13–14, 20, 213, 343; Aristotle and time, 349; Augustine and time, 349
space, 7, 44, 45, 63, 67, 104–5, 128, 132, 199–200, 223, 269–70, 284–89; irreducibility of space to time, 341; predominance of time over space, 293; truth of, 353
spaceish, spatial (*räumlich*), xv, 44, 199
spannedness (*Spanne*), duration, 332–33, 338, 339–40
spirit, 20, 44, 286, 300, 325; Hegel, 125, 328
stability, standing (*Ständigkeit*), 83, 183–84, 188, 215, 246; standingness of the self (*Selbstständigkeit*), 216–17, 296–97; *see also* constancy
stake, to be at (*es geht um*), 30–31, 35, 147, 152, 155, 160
stand-offishness (*Abständigkeit*), xv, 81, 82
standing presentness (*ständige Anwesenheit*), 183–84, 216
stones, 20, 30, 84
stretching (*Erstreckung*), 291, 295–96, 318, 332, 334
subject, 67, 68, 76, 213–17, 293; transcendental, 114–17

subjectivity and objectivity, 72, 141–42, 146, 282, 322, 328, 339, 341, 343
subject-object, 68, 282
substance, 10, 12, 15, 17, 67, 83
substantia, 369
substantial, objective, reality or presence (*Vorhandenheit*), 14, 73, 134, 165, 184, 272–73
surrounding world, for-world (*Umwelt*), 27, 60, 68–70
swaying (*Schwebe*), 86
synthesis, 111–12, 116, 263, 280

taking care, heedfulness (*Besorgen*), 64, 257–61, 289, 328, 349; deficient modes, 64–65; everyday, 125; timeishness, 125
talking about, discussing (*Besprechen*), 329, 331
tautologies, 136–41
technology, 15, 67, 184
temporality, 124, 134–35, 137, 220, 335, 343; attunement, 236–42; care, 217–25, 222, 225; circumspect taking care, 257–61; discourse, 252–55; everydayness, 290–93; falling, 243–52; horizon, 277–78, 282; roominess, 284–89; schema, 282; transcendence of the world, 276–84; understanding, 230–36
temptation, 88–89
thematization, 274
then, 329–36, 339–40, 344–48
theology, 14–15; conscience, 165
theory, 65–67, 72, 86, 243–45, 261–76; care, 200; of knowledge, 67, 275
there, 121, 133, 248, 281, 330; here, 282
there-being, *see* Da-sein
"they," "them," one, people (*das Man*), lostness in, 41, 80–82, 133, 153–54, 156, 166, 189, 197–99, 205; hero, 291

"they-self" (*Man-selbst*), 98, 122, 124, 133, 190
things, 8-9; real and ideal, 9, 20, 27, 44, 53, 71-74, 94; things themselves, to the (*zu den Sachen selbst*), 84, 109, 112
thinking, 14, 264; I think therefore I am, 14-15, 205; I act, 375
thither and hither, 289
thrownness (*Geworfenheit*), 20, 36-37, 42, 56, 58-59, 78, 88-90, 97, 99, 120, 122, 153, 170, 176, 179, 204, 216, 218, 246, 248-49, 251, 280, 283, 289
time, 7, 8, 9, 18, 104-5, 116, 117, 132, 139, 175; astronomical, 292, 337; calendars, 292, 333, 337; counting with, 327-28; datability, 330-33, 338-41; finitude, 124, 225; horizon of being, 126, 267, 328; infinite, 124; irreducibility of space to time, 341; measurement, 225, 292, 327; not, 366; origin of vulgar concept, 327-61; phantom, 343; predominance of time over space, 293; primordial, 141-42; published, 124, 336-37; reckoning, 336-37, 339-41; soul, Aristotle, 349, Augustine, 349; standing, 187; subjectivity, 341-42; timeishness (*Zeitlichkeit*), xv, 42, 124, 125, 134-35, 137; transcendence, 341; unity of care, 123, 216; within-timeness, 327-61, 336-43; world-time, 338, 341-42; *Zeitlichkeit*, 370
totality, *see* whole
tradition, 300, 304
tranquillizing (*Beruhigung*), 248
transcendence, transcendental, 44, 60; consciousness, 114, 117; Dasein, 175, 177-78, 180, 275, 367; freedom, 181, 195, 308; ground-giving, 183; philosophy, 310; subject, 114-17; time, 341; world, 181, 275-84, 280, 341

transparency (*Durchsichtigkeit*), 243
truth, 28, 66, 101-7, 198, 204, 254-55; being, 262; corespondence, 102-3, 266; existence, 196, 202-3; ontic, 101, 104, 211; ontological, 101, 104, 182-83, 211; phenomenological, 256; scientific, 104; *see also* disclosure
turn-round, from being and time to time and being, 128, 174, 187, 305

uncanny, unhomely, not-at-home (*unheimlich*), xv-xvi, 23, 86, 96-97, 166, 176, 193, 365
understanding (*Verstehen, Verständtnis*), 6-7, 22, 24, 25, 36, 54, 55, 58, 60, 70, 83, 96-97, 158, 163; average, 13, 85, 89; being, 161, 328, 364; existentiell-ontic and existential-ontological, 196; forward-running, 121; interpretation, 262; temporality, 230-36; timeishness, 125
undifferentiated, 42
un-distancing, de-distancing (*Ent-fernung*), 244, 281, 286, 289
untruth, 106, 198
unworlding (*Entweltlichung*), 269
utensil, useful thing (*Zeug*), 257-61, 266

values, 73-74, 172, 180, 188

wanting (willing)-to-have-a-conscience (*Gewissen-haben-wollen*): *see* conscience
when, 186-87; indefinite, 206; pure, 366
where, whereness, whereish, 93-94, 132, 365
whirl (*Wirbel*), 89-90, 106
whole, wholeness, totality, 37, 38, 43, 51-53, 94, 120, 123, 139, 145-62, 177-78, 204, 206, 280; *see also* Dasein

willing, 180, 195; *see also* sake of, for the
with-world (*Mitwelt*), 76
witness (*Zeugnis*), 156, 162, 163
world, 25, 51–70, 71–74, 93, 289; past, has been, 302; significance-whole, 367; transcendence, 181, 275; world history, 315–26; world worlds, 140, 180

world-forming, world-imaging (*weltbildend*), 53–54, 67, 184–85
worldishness, worldliness (*Weltlichkeit*), xv, 26, 27, 42, 51–70, 94, 124, 128, 338, 340
world-time, 338

Yorck, Paul, Graf von Wartenburg, 299–300; historical and ontic, 316